THE WORLD OF CULINARY SUPERVISION, TRAINING, AND MANAGEMENT

FOURTH EDITION

THE WORLD OF CULINARY SUPERVISION, TRAINING, AND MANAGEMENT

Jerald W. Chesser
Noel C. Cullen

PEARSON

Prentice
Hall

Upper Saddle River, New Jersey 07458

Library of Congress Cataloging-in-Publication Data

Chesser, Jerald W.
  The world of culinary supervision, training, and management / Jerald
W. Chesser, Noel C. Cullen. —4th ed.
      p. cm.
  Includes bibliographical references and index.
  ISBN-13: 978-0-13-158328-3
  ISBN-10:   0-13-158328-X
  1. Food service management. 2. Cooks. I. Cullen, Noel C. II. Title.
  TX911.3.M27C494 2009
  647.95068--dc22

                            2008015626

Vice President and Executive Publisher: Vernon Anthony
Acquisitions Editor: William Lawrensen
Editorial Assistant: Lara Dimmick
Project Manager: Alicia Ritchey
Production Manager: Wanda Rockwell
Production Coordination: Vishal Harshvardhan,
Aptara, Inc.
Creative Director: Jayne Conte
Cover Designer: Studio Indigo
Cover art: Getty Images, Inc.

Director of Marketing: David Gesell
Marketing Manager: Leigh Ann Sims
Director, Image Resource Center: Melinda Patelli
Manager, Rights and Permissions: Zina Arabia
Manager, Visual Research: Beth Brenzel
Manager, Cover Visual Research & Permissions: Karen
Sanatar
Cover Research: Rita Wenning
Image Permission Coordinator: Vickie Menanteaux

This book was set in 10/12, Times Ten Roman by Aptara, Inc. It was printed and bound by Hamilton Printing Co.
The cover was printed by Phoenix Color Corp.

Pearson Education Ltd., London
Pearson Education Singapore Pte. Ltd.
Pearson Education, Canada, Ltd.
Pearson Education–Japan
Pearson Education Australia Pty, Limited

Pearson Education North Asia Ltd.
Pearson Educación de Mexico, S.A. de C.V.
Pearson Education Malaysia, Pte. Ltd.
Pearson Education, Upper Saddle River, New Jersey

10 9 8 7 6 5
ISBN-13: 978-0-13-158328-3
ISBN-10:   0-13-158328-X

This Fourth Edition of The World of Culinary Supervision, Training, and Management *is dedicated to Marla, Justin, and Jondrea, who have supported me through the years. It is that support that has made it possible for me to complete many things, including this latest edition.*

CONTENTS

❧

CONTRIBUTORS

❧

Chef Talk

Contributor	Title
Kenneth G. Wade, CEC, AAC Chef/Owner PaddyMacs Palm Beach, Florida	Coaching, 14
Tom Peer, CMC, CCE, AAC Culinary Institute of America Hyde Park, New York	Building Morale, 52
Charles Carroll, CEC, AAC Executive Chef River Oaks Country Club Houston, Texas	Team Building, 72
Klaus Friedenreich, CMC, AAC Director The Culinary Art Institute of Fort Lauderdale Fort Lauderdale, Florida	Trusting Your Kitchen Team, 79 Chef Leadership, 143
Carol Kalkstein-Silkes, Ph.D., CEC Assistant Professor Department of Hospitality and Tourism Management Purdue University West Lafayette, Indiana	Permission to Succeed, 93
Clayton Sherrod, CEC, AAC President, Chef Clayton's Food Systems, Inc. Birmingham, Alabama	That Was Then, 95
Noel C. Cullen, Ed.D., CMC, AAC (deceased)	Pioneer Apprentice, 96 Teaching Old Dogs New Tricks, 187 My First Day, 272 Hostile Environment, 294 Using the Correct Language, 311
Jill K. Bosich, CEC, CCE, AAC (Regional Team Captain, Team USA 2007)	Leadership Is a Privilege, 130

Chef Talk

Contributor	Title
Executive Chef/Energy Programs Advisor, The Southern California Gas Company Downey, California	
Jerald Chesser, Ed.D., CEC, FMP, CCE, AAC Professor, The Collins School of Hospitality Management California State Polytechnic University Pomona Pomona, California	Leadership Axiom, 136
Reimund Pitz, CEC, CCE, AAC Executive Chef The Country Club of Orlando Orlando, Florida	Training: What's in It for You?, 157
Victor Gielisse, DBA., CMC, AAC Industry Solutions Group Culinary Institute of America Hyde Park, New York	Rethinking Your Most Valuable Asset, 168
Aidan P. Murphy, CMC, AAC Executive Chef Old Warson Country Club St. Louis, MO	My Way or the Highway, 214
Bert Cutino, CEC, AAC Co-owner, The Sardine Factory Restaurant on Cannery Row Monterey, California	Plan the Work and Work the Plan, 241
Michael Ty, CEC, AAC Las Vegas, Nevada	Team Players, 255
Keith Keogh, CEC, AAC Corporate Chef Levy Restaurants Chicago, Illinois	Induction by Fire, 274
John D. Folse, CEC, AAC Executive Chef/Owner Chef John Folse & Co. Donaldsonville, Louisiana	Finding Gilman, 325

What is This Business

Contributor	Title
Noble Masi, CMBC, CEPC, CEC, AAC	The Chef in America Yesterday — Today —

Certification levels of the American Culinary Federation are as follows:

CC: Certified Cook
CCC: Certified Chef de Cuisine
CCE: Certified Culinary Educator
CEC: Certified Executive Chef
CMC: Certifed Master Chef
CMPC: Certified Master Pastry Chef
CSC: Certified Sous Chef
CWC: Certified Working Chef
CWPC: Certified Working Pastry Chef
AAC: Member American Academy of Chefs

PREFACE

The Fourth Edition of this book continues to be an informational, educational, and training resource for all culinarians. The changes in this edition do not change the utility and functionality of the content; they enhance the content. The goal in this edition was to move the content solidly forward to meet the needs of the twenty-first-century student who will some day be a chef. The book continues to bring the matter of supervision in the kitchen to the fore. Since the First Edition of this book over a decade ago, the need for chef/supervisors in the kitchen to direct, mentor, and lead staff with the same high level of expertise and professionalism as they practice the art and science of culinary preparation has not diminished, it has continued to increase. The successful twenty-first-century chef will be both a master of the craft and an accomplished supervisor, manager, and leader.

The goal of this Fourth Edition is to make the content more "user-friendly" while enhancing the information being delivered. Part of this endeavor is a reorganization of the content to provide it to you, the reader, in a more connected manner. Additionally, although the text still uses "quality" as its touchstone, the theory of "total quality management" is given a more balanced place along with other theories of management.

Today's chef and the chef of the future must be well informed about the challenges facing both their kitchen team and their industry. This edition contains not only the "Chef Talks," those excellent insights from chefs, but also a new sidebar titled "What Is This Business?" These pieces provide insight from industry professionals who form and shape our industry every day, both in and out of the kitchen.

I believe that this book will provide you, the reader, with valuable information that will assist you in achieving your goals as a supervisor, as a manager, as a trainer, as a leader—as a Chef! I encourage you to remember that there is no single source of all knowledge on any subject. The more you read and the more you search for new information and insight, the greater will be the level of mastery you achieve in all of your endeavors. I wish you the best on your road to success.

We would also like to thank our reviewers for their contribution: Charies Caramihalis, University of New Hampshire: Amy Felder, Johnson & Wales University; John Maxwell, J. Sargeant Reynolds Community; David Schneider, Macomb Community College; and Mike Zemma, Elgin Community College.

Jerald W. Chesser
Ed.D., CEC, FMP, CCE, AAC

ABOUT THE AUTHORS

Jerald Chesser, Ed.D., CEC, CCE, FMP, AAC

Dr. Jerald Chesser, a Professor at The Collins School of Hospitality Management, California State Polytechnic University, Pomona where he teaches culinary, leadership and human resource courses. He has over 35 years experience in food service/hospitality industry including executive chef, restaurant owner, training consultant, university administrator and professor. Dr. Chesser is an internationally recognized speaker and expert in culinary education. He is one of the few individuals in the United States to hold the American Culinary Federation certification of executive chef and culinary educator, the National Restaurant Association certification of foodservice management professional and a doctorate in education. Dr. Chesser is a member of the Academy of Chefs. His previous publications include *The Art and Science of Culinary Preparation.*

Noel C. Cullen, Ed.D., CMC, AAC

Dr. Cullen was one of 58 American Culinary Federation Certified Master Chefs in the United States. He had over thirty years experience in food service/hospitality as an operator and educator including executive chef, manager, university professor and administrator. Dr. Cullen was the first chef in the United States to earn the prestigious level of CMC and a doctorate in education. Dr. Cullen was a member of the American Academy of Chefs and past president of the American Culinary Federation.

HOSPITALITY DEFINED

The world of hospitality places inordinate demands and expectations on the chef, as he/she engages in the daily task of supervising and training the culinary workforce. Today, chefs are expected to provide wholesome, safe, nutritious and great tasting meals to their customers each and every day. Furthermore, chefs need to be able to lead a motivated staff, meet the company's financial parameters, attend to certain PR activities, and be great communicators.

In short chefs need to be in command of many skills, however none more important than a fundamental appreciation and a sincere commitment to the general concept of HOSPITALITY.

Our industry is defined by one word, namely HOSPITALITY, a concept much talked and written about, however one that is rarely practiced in its true sense. Perhaps the most difficult task is to explain what true hospitality is really all about, as I have attempted to do with every incoming class at the Culinary Institute of America, yet it is based on very simple, but fundamental principles.

We should strive to extend our hospitality to members of our family, friends, and our co-workers and, of course to our customers, making sure that it becomes part of who we are and what we do. Hospitality cannot be turned on or off whenever one feels it is appropriate. In simple terms, hospitality requires mutual and reciprocal respect and extension of basic considerations and common courtesies. Once applied and practiced in a sincere and consistent manner, hospitality can be one powerful element that can overcome and compensate for flawed service and even for a less than perfect meal. Bringing this notion to an even more basic, yet comprehensive level, I would offer as the ultimate definition of hospitality, the following:

TREAT YOUR CUSTOMERS, CO-WORKERS, AND ASSOCIATES IN THE SAME MANNER AS YOUR FRIENDS THAT YOU HAVE INVITED INTO YOUR OWN HOME.

This practical, simple advice will allow you to practice and extend great hospitality, eliminating the snobbery and insincerity, which often gets in the way of extending true HOSPITALITY.

Ferdinand Metz
MBA, CMC, AAC
President, World Association of Chef's Societies

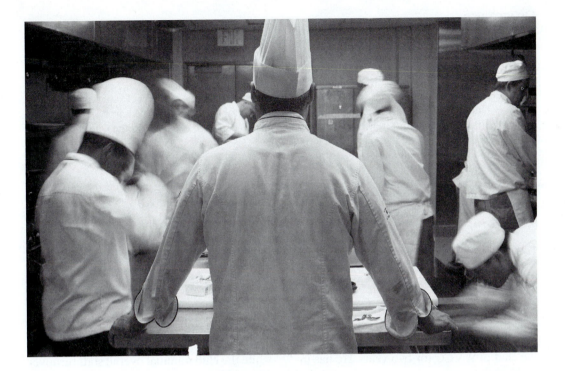

CHAPTER 1
SUPERVISION

OUTLINE

- ❖ Introduction
- ❖ Definition of supervision
- ❖ Attributes of the successful chef supervisor
- ❖ Chef supervisory role models
- ❖ Duties and functions of the chef supervisor
- ❖ Elements of kitchen supervision
- ❖ The concept of authority
- ❖ The evolution of supervisory chefs
- ❖ Conclusions
- ❖ Summary
- ❖ Discussion questions
- ❖ Notes

OBJECTIVES

When you complete this chapter, you should be able to:

1. Identify the central position the chef supervisor occupies in assisting management to reach goals and achieve quality throughout the operation
2. Identify and discuss the attributes, skills, duties, and functions of the chef supervisor
3. Outline the key elements and ingredients of a desirable kitchen work environment
4. Understand the difference between culinary skills and human skills and the role each plays in the supervisory and management process
5. Indicate trends and new dimensions associated with the development of the chef supervisor
6. Recognize the role that chef supervisors play with regard to management, customers, and team members

Case Study: WEST VILLAGE COUNTRY CLUB

The chef of the West Village Country Club (WVCC) is Jason Lightner. Jason has been the chef of WVCC for two years. He has increased the quality of the food served and the amount of food sales. Additionally, Jason has reduced the overall cost of food sold from 60 percent to 40 percent.

WVCC had had 250 members for five years before Jason became the chef. In the past twelve months there has been renewed interest in the community in joining the club. Membership has grown to 300 and is expected to reach 400 within the next two years.

The increase in membership, increase in food quality, and reduced food cost are related directly to Jason's close supervision of the preparation of every item served. Jason develops all menus and recipes used in the kitchen. He personally checks and adjusts the flavor of every food item prepared in the kitchen. Jason is fond of saying, "this is my food, and the quality of every item depends on me."

The club's general manager is very pleased with the improvements Jason has brought to the kitchen at WVCC, but he has just mentioned to Jason his continuing concern with the high labor cost for the kitchen

staff. In his latest discussion with Chef Lightner, the general manager pointed out that while the club's annual overall staff turnover rate of 50 percent was rather high because of the number of college students used in various service positions, the turnover rate for the kitchen staff had reached staggering levels, 150 percent for the past twelve months.

Chef Lightner reminded the general manager that he has dismissed only one kitchen staff member since his initial purge of the kitchen staff during his first six months as chef of WVCC. Although he does not conduct separation interviews, he is "certain that those who leave simply find the work too hard and the pace to fast." As Jason says, all new hires are told what to be prepared for, and that it is "my kitchen, my food, and my rules."

Before reading the rest of the chapter, answer the following questions about the case.

- What is the overall reason for the challenges in the West Village Country Club's kitchen?
- What are the major causes of the challenges in the West Village Country Club's kitchen?

- What role did supervision/management play in the decline in the West Village Country Club's kitchen?
- What specific steps could have been taken to avoid the current situation in the West Village Country Club's kitchen?
- What, specifically, can be done to overcome the challenges and generate motion in a positive direction for the West Village Country Club's kitchen?

After reading the rest of the chapter, complete the following exercises.

- Review your previous answers to the case study questions and note any changes you would make to your answers.
- Write a discussion of why you would make the changes that you noted in your review.

INTRODUCTION

The literal English translation of the term *chef* from French is "chief" or "director." All things change, and the role and duties of the chef are no exception. In the previous edition of this textbook the definition of *chef* was taken from *Webster's New World Dictionary 1988*. The word *chef* was defined as follows: "1. a cook in charge of a kitchen, as of a restaurant; lead cook, 2. any cook." This definition should be compared with the definition in the *Merriam-Webster Online Dictionary* in 2007 (www.m-w.com/cgi-bin/dictionary), which was as follows: "1. a skilled cook who manages the kitchen (as of a restaurant), 2. cook." The shift in the definition from "in charge of" to "manages" is a reflection of the evolutionary nature of the chef's role in the foodservice operation and also in the overall industry. The role of the chef as the chief cook in the kitchen, the person who is responsible for the food, continues to be at the core of the chef's role in the operation or company. This is no different from the fact that keeping the financial records of the operation or company is the core of the financial manager's role. The roles of both the chef and the financial manager, however, are larger and more complex. Today the chef is expected not only to be a first-class culinarian who can create gastronomic masterpieces, but also to be a supervisor who can motivate and lead the kitchen team toward the goals of the operation or company in a way that will maximize profits and please the customer. Of course, all of this must be accomplished in a compressed time period in a potentially stressful environment. It is therefore essential that chefs who supervise kitchen operations today be equipped with the finest culinary skills along with the highest-quality supervisory, training, and management skills. The following chapters will explore, outline, and develop the elements that contribute to making the modern chef supervisor. This book is not about cooking or food-cost control, but it does concern itself with the recipes and ingredients that make up the modern culinary supervisor, who is a combination of culinarian, leader, coach, trainer, and manager.

The qualifications for the chef supervisor's job are impressive. Chefs need to be technically competent and know the aspects that make up professional culinary practices: the processes, equipment, and quality standards. Technical competency also means knowing the foodservice organization's rules and the statutory regulations that govern the kitchen, from safety and sanitation standards to government regulations and labor laws. Chefs are selected to be supervisors because, among other things, they are good workers. Chef supervisors who fail do not do so because they lack technical culinary skills, but because they are unable to get others to work effectively. They lack

BOX 1-1

WHAT IS THIS BUSINESS?
THE CHEF IN AMERICA YESTERDAY—
TODAY—TOMORROW

In the early days of our country, cooking was a domestic chore; then, as the country expanded, inns were opened to accommodate travelers. As villages and towns expanded, community ovens were built; these ovens where tended to by the village baker. The first commercial bakery opened in Plymouth, Massachusetts, in 1640 and was operated by English and European bakers. Europe had established culinary and baking guilds as well as apprentice systems for training journeymen cooks and bakers. European-trained chefs immigrated to the United States and formed ethnic chefs' associations, which provided a steady stream of chefs, cooks, and bakers to hotels and restaurants in larger cities. Over time, these chefs left the hotels and restaurants to open their own family businesses.

In the American home in the eighteenth, nineteenth, and early twentieth centuries, cooking was still generally a domestic chore. Families dined together each evening, with special dinners on Sundays and holidays. There was a lack of mechanical equipment and no convenience foods. Cooking and baking were very physical, requiring strength and stamina, but the joy of these dinners inspired many young men and women to develop a passion for the hospitality industry. Unlike Europe, where there was an apprentice system, work was hard to find, and most had to start as dishwashers, prep persons, or servers. In the 1930s there were only three vocational high schools teaching culinary and baking; these schools were in New York City, Chicago, and Detroit. In 1929 the American Culinary Federation was formed in New York City The association's membership was once again mostly European-trained chefs, but unlike other chefs' associations, it embraced Americans who had not completed an apprenticeship. This was the first opportunity for most Americans to be mentored by European-trained chefs.

After two world wars the American household changed. During the wars many women went to work outside their homes, leaving less time for domestic chores. They purchased bread, pies, and already-cooked foods; they dined in luncheonettes and restaurants more often. The five years following World War ? created an expansion and opportunity for soldiers returning home; America experienced a new prosperity, with two incomes in many households. Two-income families doing fewer domestic chores led to the growth of the food-service industry; many domestic chores were replaced by purchases at restaurants, hotels, clubs, bakeries, and food markets. It is little wonder that up until 1972, cooks and bakers were listed as "domestic" workers in the federal register of occupational trades. The American Culinary Federation was a major force in getting the U.S. Department of Labor to change the listing to "professional" in 1972.

Recognizing that the apprentice and guild system was not working in America, Francis Roth, a New Haven, Connecticut, attorney, obtained a government grant to train returning World War ? veterans in foodservice trades. On May 22, 1946, the New Haven Restaurant School opened in New Haven, Connecticut. Three years later, Katherine Angel, the wife of James Roland Angel, president of Yale University, secured 5 acres on the Yale campus to become the Restaurant Institute of Connecticut. In 1951 it became the Culinary Institute of America.

In the 1950s and 1960s the U.S. population continued to grow and become more diverse. Vocational secondary schools provided strong fundamental education in the culinary arts and post-secondary schools trained many cooks and bakers. The 1970s to the year 2000 provided great opportunities for young culinarians. Throughout the United States, hundreds of high schools and colleges began offering a culinary education; this formal education replaced the European apprentice system. These schools taught culinary fundamentals and hospitality skills needed to keep pace with America's expanding market basket and menu diversity. The establishment of organized training programs gave professional recognition to cooks and bakers. In world competitions the U.S. teams finished consistently among the top three. Certification programs were developed to verify skill levels in cooking and baking. Colleges and universities offered advanced degrees in managerial skills, which helped to improve the work environment. Every American with a passion for cooking and baking could obtain the knowledge to become a professional chef.

The chef of the future will face many challenges. The chef will need to develop skills in managing the workforce, providing a more harmonious and productive environment, less demanding work schedules, and improved salaries for entry-level workers, and also to provide adequate benefit packages. The chef will face more competition and a demanding public. The key to profit will be utilization of food and resources, communications and marketing. Along with these challenges will come more opportunities. Future chefs should begin their education and work experience in grades 9–12 at a technical high school, followed by two to three years post-secondary schooling, five years work experience, and a baccalaureate degree in hospitality. During this training period they should travel as much as possible, studying local, regional, and international market baskets and menus, and developing their skills and knowledge by reading when travel is not possible. Grandiose opportunities may appear early in one's career, but caution is advised: Build your career with a strong foundation of culinary fundamentals and a strong work ethic. It is estimated that you will have to stay in the workforce longer and will change your job three or four times during your career, which is much different than it was for yesterday's chef, who may have spent thirty to forty years with one company. The twenty-first century will provide great opportunity for those chefs who are properly trained.

Chef Noble Masi,
CMB, CEPC, CCE, AAC, HOF
Culinary Institute of America
Hyde Park, New York

good people skills. Therefore, potentially all chefs are supervisors because of the necessity to work with others to satisfy guests.

Some foodservice organizations are content with a kitchen staff that functions traditionally. Other managers, using the same number of people doing similar tasks with the same equipment and technology, manage to improve productivity dramatically by establishing a climate in which people are willing to give their best and work in teams. When chefs acquire supervisory skills, they too can become outstanding supervisors who can build great culinary teams.

DEFINITION OF SUPERVISION

Simply put, a supervisor is anyone in the position of directing the work of others and who has the authority that goes with this responsibility. The legal status is defined by the federal Taft-Hartley Act (1947), which states that a supervisor is

> . . . any individual having authority, in the interest of the employer, to hire, transfer, suspend, lay off, recall, promote, discharge, assign, reward or discipline other employees, or responsibility to direct them, or to adjust their grievances, or effectively to recommend such action, if in connection with the foregoing the exercise of such authority is not merely routine or clerical in nature, but requires the use of independent judgement.

The knowledge and skills required to be a successful chef supervisor fall into four broad skill categories: personal, interpersonal, technical, and administrative.

Supervision in a kitchen requires not only a highly skilled chef but one who has the vision to know what to do, the necessary skills to know how to do it, and the ability to get it done by empowering other people to carry out quality standards of performance. Supervision, therefore, concerns those chefs who have the ability to communicate, plan, organize, train, lead, coach, and correct and at the same time stimulate the kitchen team to meet the establishment's goals and objectives. These objectives are achieved through supervising people in an effective and caring way and by creating a motivational environment in the kitchen and ensuring that necessary resources are available so that quality meals can be produced that meet and exceed customer expectations every time.

Philip Crosby states that "in the final equation, the supervisor is the person the employee sees as the company. The type of work accomplished and the attendance maintained by employees are very much indications of their relationship with the supervisor."[1] Crosby suggests that the good supervisor can overcome, at least to some extent, the poor management practices of a weak company. At the other extreme, the weak supervisor can offset the good management practices of a good company.

The role of supervision generally has changed. No longer can supervisors expect to control people. In the past, some chefs were viewed as autocratic. Today, this chef supervisory role has shifted to one of coach. The effectiveness of the chef as coach and supervisor is measured not just by customer satisfaction and customer retention but also through the ability of the kitchen staff to carry out the workload to meet and exceed set standards of quality. Poor chef supervisory skills affect not only the quality of the food produced but also the work climate and the kitchen team, the results of which are unhappy customers and high levels of employee turnover.

ATTRIBUTES OF THE SUCCESSFUL CHEF SUPERVISOR

Successful chef supervisors who see themselves as coaches undoubtedly have a greater impact in the foodservice industry. The business and management philosophies of today clearly advocate the supervisor as a coach. According to Bill Marvin, "When the foodservice staff starts to look at the person in charge more as a coach, their impression of their jobs change."[2] What, then, are the attributes of chef supervisors who see themselves as coaches? As in all good coaching, the coach tries to get the best possible performance from the team through motivation, training, leadership communication, and demonstrating respect for all the team players, with an acute awareness of their different strengths and weaknesses. Being sympathetic and approachable is clearly an asset. Unfortunately, in many instances these qualities are not traditionally associated with chefs. In the past, chefs were viewed as supervisors who ruled the kitchen with a rod of iron. Today's chef supervisor, in addition to being an excellent culinarian, must have developed a strong personal inventory of personal and professional qualities. An example of the chef supervisor's *mise en place* of personal inventories is shown in Figure 1-1.

Chef supervisors, perhaps more than any other category of supervisor, need to be able to bring all these qualities to the kitchen work environment and be able to coach and supervise under the pressures of busy meal service periods. Additionally, the chef supervisor should have the ability to understand the feelings, attitudes, and motives of others; communicate effectively; and establish good relations with the kitchen team and all other departments in the foodservice organization. These attributes apply

FIGURE 1-1 *Mise en place* for the chef supervisor.

- Positive personal attitude
- Innovativeness in dealing with problems
- Honesty and sincerity
- Awareness of employee problems
- Respect and courtesy in communicating with employees
- Impeccable personal hygiene and grooming
- Technical competence
- High motivation and the ability to motivate others
- Consistency
- Assertive and action-oriented
- Acceptance of diversity
- Ability to trust others
- Constantly searching for new ways to enhance skills
- Ability to praise others when deserved
- Leadership by example
- Team-building skills
- Loyalty to organizational goals and employees
- Ability to maintain control
- Good listening skills
- Desire to please customers
- Good persuasive skills and interest in imparting knowledge
- Love of cooking

whether the chef is employed in a restaurant, hotel, institution, club, the military, education, or any other foodservice organization.

CHEF SUPERVISORY ROLE MODELS

Professionalism and ethics are not only desirable in the chef supervisor but also essential. *Ethics* refers to the moral principles of individuals and society. Together with professional practice, ethics is concerned with the determination of right and wrong in human behavior. A code of ethics is particularly important in the foodservice industry. Employees and employers are affected by poor ethical and professional standards on the part of chef supervisors, but more important, the health and safety of the public is at stake.

An ethical code of professional practice is necessary for both employees and supervisor: "It serves as a framework in which various other standards can be evaluated".[3] Issues of professional practices include policies such as hiring/firing; confidentiality; stealing; lying; malicious gossip; harassment; racial, gender, or ethnic slurs; and any action that causes the loss of human dignity. Additionally, the chef supervisor should administer a code of professional practice fairly and without bias to all employees regardless of their position, gender, and ethnic or religious backgrounds.

History has provided us with examples of outstanding chef supervisors as role models. These chefs, renowned for their culinary prowess and advancement of culinary art through new gastronomic creations, new techniques of cooking, improvements in kitchen design, and contributions in nutrition, are an inspiration. Yet when we examine why these chefs are role models, it is not surprising to discover that they were also excellent managers, supervisors, trainers, and coaches with great legacies of passing onto others their knowledge, skills, and high personal and professional standards.

Antoine Carême, who came from humble beginnings in the postrevolution era of France, was probably the first role model for chefs. The sixteenth child of a workman, Carême had few advantages. He entered the kitchen as an apprentice chef at the age of 10. He taught himself how to read and write and wrote several books before his death at the age of 50. From his writings we get a sense of his professionalism. Describing a banquet, he provides a glimpse of the awful working conditions chefs had to endure at that time:

> Imagine yourself in a large kitchen such as that of the Foreign Minister at the moment of a great banquet [Talleyrand was Foreign Minister at the time]. There one sees twenty chefs at their urgent occupations, coming, going, moving with speed in this cauldron of heat. Look at the great mass of live charcoal, a cubic meter for the cooking of the soups, the sauces, the ragouts, the frying and the bain maries. Add to that the heap of burning coals in front of which bears a sirloin weighing 45–60 lbs, and another two for fowl and game. In this furnace everyone moves with tremendous speed; not a sound is heard; only the chef has the right to make himself heard, and at the sound of his voice everyone obeys. He concludes by saying, . . . "Honor commands, we must obey even though physical strength fails. But, it is the burning charcoal which kills us."[4]

Carême's power and influence is due not only to his writings and culinary creations, which still survive today, but also to his character and personality. His professionalism throughout his life asserted a new prestige for the chef. He was an innovator and simplifier who demonstrated all the elements of an outstanding chef leader and supervisor.

Alexis Soyer, born in 1809, lived almost exactly as long as the great Carême. Soyer's greatest days were as the chef at London's Reform Club. He also gained fame by being invited to go to the Crimea, where he did for military cooking what Florence Nightingale did for nursing. His dynamic contributions in the area of culinary arts and management included development of a luxury restaurant during the Great London Exhibition, a soup kitchen, and a cookbook priced for the poorer classes. He also invented a military cooking stove that was still in use during World War II. Soyer was an outstanding example of a chef leader. He could hold his own among the professional class of his time as much by his own personal qualities as by his culinary skills. He helped to further enhance the image of the chef through his writings and his superb organizational skills and leadership abilities.

Auguste Escoffier, known as the "King of Chefs" and the "Chef of Kings," dominated the first quarter of the twentieth century and continues to influence chefs and the culinary arts to this day. Escoffier is perhaps still the greatest role model for chefs as a culinarian and as one of the greatest chef supervisors and coaches of all time. He was a man whose talents dovetailed into the trends of his times and who was fortunate to be linked with a man who was perhaps the greatest hotelier of all time, Caesar Ritz. In the early part of the twentieth century, economic and social forces were changing, as were the dining and wining habits of society. Escoffier sensed perfectly the needs of these times and was prepared not only to go with trends but to anticipate them. He refined and simplified classic cuisine and created dishes that have become part of the classic cuisine repertoire. He was a supreme organizer. It was he who created the "partie system," a system that streamlined the work flows and processes of the foodservice industry.

FIGURE 1-2 Beliefs and innovations of Escoffier.

- Moved the kitchen out of its traditional location in the basement
- Created the "partie system"
- Demonstrated a high level of personal professionalism
- Insisted on the highest standards of personal hygiene from all staff
- Required that cooks wear the newly fashioned jacket and checked pants
- Discouraged staff from smoking and drinking
- Advocated education
- Strongly supported schooling for employees
- Proponent of life-long learning
- Began the standardization of recipes

Escoffier was a pioneer in the movement toward exquisite simplicity. He believed in the simple concept that food should look like food. Escoffier applied his beliefs to his kitchen and brought about change that helped to shape the modern kitchen. Some of his beliefs and innovations are shown in Figure 1-2.

Escoffier's obvious wisdom and professionalism explain why *Le Guide Culinaire* is still the most esteemed textbook for the professional chef in the world. Escoffier was not a prisoner of the classic traditions. Clearly a man of great foresight, his writing encouraged change so as to meet evolving culinary trends, a process that still continues today. Having started his career at the age of 12 (in 1859), Escoffier retired from active duty at the Carlton in London in 1921. He was then 74 years old and had practiced his art for over 62 years. Throughout the history of foodservice, there is no better example of professionalism. Escoffier remains today the supreme example of the professional chef with impeccable ethical standards—a leader who constantly sought to elevate and raise the image and prestige of the culinary profession. He achieved this through superb culinary art *and* brilliant supervisory, organizational, and coaching ability, all directed to the gastronomic satisfaction of his customers.

Ferdinand Metz is one of the people who has had and continues to have a lasting influence on how food is prepared around the globe today. As president of the Culinary Institute of America (CIA) from 1980 to 2001, Chef Metz initiated the development of extensive educational and training programs for aspiring culinarians in the United States and around the world. He was a leader in the establishment of apprenticeship and certification in the United States.

Chef Metz, through his work at the CIA and his activities in the American Culinary Federation, the National Restaurant Association Educational Foundation, the World Association of Cooks Societies, and other organizations, has been a major factor in the elevation of the culinary profession around the world. He was the manager of the American Culinary Olympic Team and led it to three consecutive world championships. In 1995 Chef Metz was named by *Nation's Restaurant News* as one of the fifty most influential people in the industry. He has, by example, established that the chef is a professional, an educator, and a business person.

Chef Metz has been recognized in many ways for his contributions to the profession. He is the recipient of both the James Beard and the American Culinary Federation Lifetime Achievement Awards. As an author and speaker, he continues to be a leader in the culinary profession.

Paul Bocuse is considered one of the finest chefs of the twentieth century and continues to influence cuisine and food preparation. He was one of the founders of the *nouvelle cuisine* movement in France in the 1970s. This cuisine is simpler and lower in calories than the traditional *haute cuisine*, and stresses the importance of fresh ingredients of the highest quality. Chef Bocuse has influenced the preparation of food through a chain of brasseries under his license.

Chef Bocuse was one of the first chefs to make public appearances away from his restaurant to promote the preparation of food. He has also authored numerous books. In 1987 he established the Bocuse d'Or. The Bocuse d'Or is considered one the most prestigious culinary awards in the world today. Through his extensive endeavors, Chef Bocuse has had a major impact on culinarians of today.

To be a leader, no matter what field of endeavor you are in, it is necessary to adopt a code of professional ethics to which others will aspire. It has been said that those

---

BOX 1-2

WHAT IS THIS BUSINESS?
CAN ANYONE EVER BE OVERQUALIFIED?

The obvious answer to this question is, of course, a resounding NO.

One may at times have more qualifications then a current responsibility may demand, but one can surely never be overqualified in anticipation of future career opportunities. Thus it seems prudent to take advantage of every opportunity whenever it presents itself, whether it is convenient at the time or not.

Easy to say, but this is exactly the path the author of this book, Dr. Jerald Chesser, and I took. Dr. Chesser realized early on that chefs of today need more credentials, both in the terms of experience as well as academic proficiency. I am sure that it was not easy for the author, a certified chef on several levels, to earn an EdD, which made him almost unique among his peers.

In my case, when I joined the H.J. Heinz Company's R&D department, I enjoyed, for the first time in my life, regular "office" hours. Rather than becoming spoiled by this new-found luxury, I enrolled at the University of Pittsburgh and earned, over a seven-year period, a baccalaureate and a master's degree in business administration. At the same time, I did not neglect my responsibility at Heinz and to the Pittsburgh Chefs Association, as we established the national models for today's certification, apprenticeship, and master chef certification programs. Add to this my responsibility for managing the U.S.

Culinary Olympic Team and my own gourmet cooking school, and one can easily understand that my plate was full.

As the result of all these activities, I was in the early 1980s the only person in the United States who was a Certified Master Chef and had also an earned MBA. These and others were some of the credentials that gave me the ability to lead the R&D department of a global company and later to assume the presidency of the Culinary Institute of America, a position I held for over twenty-two years. My motivation to earn additional credentials was never with the goal of heading the most prestigious culinary school in the country, but it was the uniqueness of my credentials that qualified me for the position.

Whenever people have the opportunity to combine a specialized craft with academic credentials, they make themselves more valuable in their chosen field and gain a broader and more inclusive perspective for themselves. It is not by accident that today many academic institutions have come to value the concept of a specialized liberal arts program that recognizes the need for specific skills combined with academic credentials.

Ferdinand Metz,
MBA, CMC, AAC, HOF,
Partner, Masters Chefs Institute
Hyde Park, New York

preparing food for consumption by the public require higher ethical standards than those in the manufacturing sector. Food workers who lack professional ethics are a threat not only to the image of the foodservice industry, but more important, to the health and safety of the public. True culinary professionalism will always embrace high ethical standards.

DUTIES AND FUNCTIONS OF THE CHEF SUPERVISOR

In the past, chef supervisors reported mainly to the food and beverage manager. In many foodservice establishments, the manager supervised food and beverage operations, of which kitchen operations were a major portion. The food and beverage manager, or some higher level of management, usually evaluated the chef supervisor on the limited criteria of the achievement of a 30 percent food cost, along with the smooth production of meals with a minimum level of customer complaints. If this was achieved, then the manner by which it was achieved was left up to the chef. All major decisions regarding menu positioning and the recruitment, orientation, training, and termination of employees were within the manager's domain. Today, that is not the case. The functions of the chef as a supervisor, trainer, coach, and manager have widened considerably.

As decision making is pushed downward, the modern chef, in addition to being a highly skilled culinarian, must also be many other things: a people developer, supervisor, coach, and team builder—in short, a front-line leader with a major role to play in the development of the foodservice establishment.

The traditional notion of the chef supervisor was that this person supervised the foodservice operation from the back door to the front door—responsible primarily for receiving food products at the back door and then their processing by a kitchen team into a customer meal at the front door. Issues of quality management of the product in this process were given only cursory attention. Quality human resources management involving the kitchen staff as a team was not a major concern. This system was authoritarian by nature; directives and orders were given with little or no input from employees and even less interest in what the customers had to say. The modern chef supervisor is a team leader who exhibits a different style than those who were content with simply supervising or managing the kitchen.

This historical portrayal of the chef supervisor as an unreasonable temperamental artist has no place in the modern foodservice industry. It never had a place there, and it would not, quite correctly, be tolerated by management or staff today. Foodservice workers, like other workers, need to be recognized as contributing team members and want to know what is expected of them by their chef supervisor. As in other areas of industry, kitchen employees need an open and communicative environment in which they can develop a sense of belonging and in which there is even-handed and fair treatment by the chef supervisor. They want to give their best, and it's up to the chef supervisor to ensure that this work climate is provided. This is vital because a chef supervisor's success depends on his or her staff.

Today's chef supervisor is a customer-driven professional skilled in all aspects of high-quality food production and supervisory skills. The principal driving force behind the modern chef is customer satisfaction—managing the culinary operation from the front door to the back door rather than the other way around. One of the main reasons customers stop patronizing a foodservice establishment is an attitude of indifference by the staff. It makes little sense to prepare food that customers don't want. The chef should be aware of customers' preferences and be trained in all the contributing elements of customer satisfaction.

There are many new and not so new elements of supervising the functions involved in food production. Many of these ideas have swung with the pendulum of different management fads over the years, such as rationalization, downsizing, risk management, yield management, management by objective, and so on. However, several will remain part of a chef supervisor's arsenal of skills. The discussion of management theory in Chapter 2 will provide greater insight into management and the chef.

ELEMENTS OF KITCHEN SUPERVISION

SUPERVISING

Supervision can be best described as the most effective and timely use of personnel and materials to achieve the goals of customer satisfaction and retention by maintaining a highly motivated, well-trained kitchen team. Within this process, the chef supervisor actively participates in the employment of chefs and other kitchen-support team members.

Part of this process is the recruitment and interviewing of potential kitchen team members. Procedures for recruitment may vary. Placing advertisements in newspapers, magazines, or trade journals is the preferred method, while others recruit employees directly from culinary schools and colleges or through professional headhunter organizations. Checking job applicants' résumés and references and interviewing these applicants fall within the chef supervisor's functions. Other elements of the chef supervisor's general duties are shown in Figure 1-3.

PLANNING

Following the successful invasion of Europe by Allied forces during World War II, it was suggested to the supreme commander of the successful invading forces, General

FIGURE 1-3   Elements of the chef supervisor's duties.

- Preparing new employee induction/orientation programs
- Assessing training needs
- Preparing training objectives
- Developing standards of performance
- Implementing standards of total quality
- Ongoing and continuous training and team building
- Coaching and correcting employees
- Setting high standards of personal hygiene and grooming
- Setting excellent standards of conduct and fairness
- Developing and encouraging teamwork
- Providing decisive leadership
- Building and fostering professional pride
- Providing timely employee feedback on performance
- Encouraging a desire to meet and exceed customer expectations
- Demonstrating a total quality respect for all kitchen team members

Dwight D. Eisenhower, that he must have had an outstanding plan to have carried out such a massive operation, moving thousands of men and equipment with all the ancillary support of materials and men. His response to this question was most enlightening: "The plan is nothing, but planning is everything."[5]

In addition to the obvious need to plan menus, considerable planning is required to run a smooth, efficient foodservice operation. The first step in all good planning is to plan time to plan. The major areas of planning for the chef supervisor include:

- Planning and forecasting workloads
- Preparing employee work schedules
- Ascertaining guest satisfaction levels
- Planning equipment repair and replacements
- Determining food and supply inventories
- Developing employee empowerment programs
- Planning future personnel levels
- Providing effective communication with team members and other departments
- Determining training needs
- Setting standards of performance
- Conducting employee performance appraisals

ORGANIZING

When plans have been made, it is necessary to organize people and materials to secure the successful fulfillment of these plans. This happens through good organizational ability on the part of the chef supervisor, using the available resources and being prepared to adapt as circumstances and conditions warrant. Typical organizational goals of a kitchen department include:

- Organizing the kitchen team to produce and serve meals in the most efficient, economical, and effective fashion, and utilizing each team member within a limited time period and within criteria of effort and productivity
- Organizing and determining the five W's of empowerment: who, what, where, when, and why
- Defining job tasks, analyses, and descriptions
- Preparing task lists to accomplish the planned goals
- Determining relationships with each member of the kitchen team together with management, other departments, and customers
- Organizing support areas of purchasing, receiving, storage, and stewarding
- Organizing training sessions
- Organizing and implementing employee empowerment and reward systems
- Organizing and implementing recycling programs

COACHING

Coaching means guiding and correcting kitchen staff to perform their jobs in a way that is compatible with the goals and objectives of the organization. It means creating an environment in which staff members feel comfortable enough to give their best. Good coaching requires excellent communication and leadership skills, but more important, it requires chef supervisors who trust people. Chef supervisors should be consistent and not subject to wild mood swings, fair at all times, firm when appropriate, approachable and friendly, and possess an overriding commitment to the "team" concept. Additionally, the chef supervisor is the link between two groups: management and players. A good coaching style involves:

- An interest in helping people attain personal goals
- Sincerity, honesty, fairness, and impartiality
- Sensitivity and respect for different cultures
- Strong ethical and moral values
- Respect for the dignity of every individual in the team
- An emphasis on the future rather than the past
- A positive people attitude
- Praise where praise is due
- Mistake correction without apportioning blame

The chef supervisor therefore must be an adept coach who is constantly improving and applying good coaching techniques toward the kitchen team so as to meet the needs of the situation and the customer's gastronomic satisfaction.

BOX 1-3

CHEF TALK: COACHING

Building a successful kitchen team requires a great deal of patience and a lot of time and effort. Ten years ago, when I took over at Harpoon Louie's ($6 million a year in sales), I found a kitchen staff without a single professional chef on board. My first step was to recruit four experienced people who had worked with me before and understood what had to be done.

With these four on board, a foundation was set. The professional chef's uniform was mandatory for all kitchen cooks. The fryer cooks, broiler cooks, and all other cooks were terminated, and those who were interested in becoming professional chefs were rehired as apprentices. No specialized positions were offered until such time as all the cooks had become competent in all areas of the kitchen.

Hiring procedures were developed and implemented. Crucial to these new procedures was the hiring of kitchen team members who had a real and genuine interest in cooking. We started our formal apprenticeship program soon after, under the auspices of the American Culinary Federation Educational Institute.

Constant coaching, in-house cooking classes, and encouragement of our apprentices to compete in professional chef competitions were key to bonding the team together. Once the team was in place and working, employee retention became a priority. As is common in other establishments, financial reward alone does not guarantee retention. It is vital to be sympathetic to the needs of the team, which can be very demanding, but with careful motivation, a team spirit can be maintained.

Respect is key. It has a tremendous bearing on what type of coach you are. Unskilled employees in the kitchen are a vital part of the foodservice operations. How these team members are treated is reflected dramatically in their performance level. The coach must be sure to communicate with these team members on a regular basis—coaching, correcting, and offering words of encouragement. Chefs who have to wash their own pots know how important their team members are and have a great deal of respect for them. I very clearly see myself as a coach rather than a manager. Today's kitchen staff should be led rather than managed or directed. Without a team approach at our restaurant, we would not be successful.

Kenneth Wade, CCE, AAC,
Chef/Owner, Paddy Macs,
Palm Beach, Florida

TEAM BUILDING

Kitchen employees can be developed into teams with the help of a committed chef supervisor. In an effective kitchen team, each member has an assigned role. When the members integrate their skills to build on strengths and minimize weaknesses, foodservice quality objectives are assured. On the other hand, when members of the kitchen staff are poorly led and work as individuals, they will often fail. Unfortunately, many chef supervisors fail to recognize their roles as team builders. In the past, many failed to understand how to transform their employees into productive teams.

Effective teamwork has no level. It is just as important among top executives as among kitchen employees. If the chef supervisor does not place high value on teamwork, it will not occur. Teamwork takes conscious effort to develop and continuous effort to maintain. (See Chapter 4, on building teamwork in the kitchen.) Part of that maintenance is recognition of team performance through celebration of positive performance and acknowledgment and assistance in correcting negative performance. If all the stated goals of supervision, planning, organization, coaching, and training have been accomplished, then a high level of controlling, or supervision—also called micromanagement—of employees, is not necessary. Chef supervisors should champion the kitchen team, make heroes out of them, sing out their praises, and turn "controlling" into a positive celebration of the kitchen staff's success and accomplishments. Central to team building is investment in the individual and the team. The chef supervisor who ensures that the team has the training, equipment, and guidance to succeed will know success.

COMMUNICATION

Communication is an integral and crucial element of the supervision process. Quality supervision often breaks down or fails because of poor communication. Communication is the lifeblood of supervision. All elements of supervision and management require effective communication. This process involves a sender and a receiver exchanging and understanding information so that the information can be received and understood.

Communication is the foundation for understanding, cooperation, and action. A good communication system maintains a two-way flow of ideas, opinions, information, and decisions. The first step in any effort to open communication is to establish and maintain a climate that encourages the free exchange of ideas. It is the umbrella under which all effective supervision lies.

DELEGATION

Delegation means granting to a kitchen team member the authority to oversee specific tasks and responsibilities and letting other team members know that these responsibilities have been delegated to this team member. Telling a team member to perform a task is not delegation; it is work allocation. Allocation may be sufficient for simple, short-term jobs, but more complex tasks that require a sustained effort should be delegated.

Before delegating, the chef supervisor should determine:

- Does the team member understand the purpose of the task?
- Is the value of the task recognized by the team member?
- Is the workload too much for just one person?
- Has the employee been provided with detailed, step-by-step instructions?
- How will satisfactory completion of the tasks be evaluated and measured?

Chef supervisors should not "delegate" those portions of their work they consider unpleasant, unimportant, or risky. Kitchen team members are seldom deceived by the chef supervisor's efforts to "dress up" the task. What usually results from such practice is resentment, demotivation, and a considerable amount of effort on the part of the team member to avoid or off-load the task.

In addition, before delegating, it is useful to consider:

- Is there acceptance and understanding of the task?
- Has a reason for delegation been given?
- Is the task being delegated a worthwhile and whole task?
- Can the team member be trusted and encouraged to do the job correctly?
- Have checkpoints been built in to check progress?
- Has knowledge been shared by pinpointing possible problems?
- Has information been withheld that could have simplified and speeded up the task?
- Have sufficient training, encouragement, coaching, and leadership been provided to make the team member look good and succeed?

Delegation by the chef supervisor encourages cooperation among kitchen team members, demonstrates trust in the team, and builds morale. The advantage of delegating is that the workload is spread in a planned, sequential way. It allows more time for creating and planning. The chef supervisor who tries to do everything will not succeed. Support of the kitchen team is essential; it is impossible for a chef supervisor to prepare, cook, and present every meal every day. The chef supervisor who fails to delegate to other team members will be frustrated, unproductive, and viewed as a weak leader by the entire kitchen team. (See Chapter 8, on leadership.)

EMPOWERMENT AND OWNERSHIP

Empowerment is the process of enabling people to do what they have been trained for and are qualified to do. Empowerment leads to a feeling of ownership. A team member who has a feeling of ownership—a personal stake in the operation—will work harder to make the operation a success. Empowering kitchen team members to take more initiative is an important part of team building and of quality supervision and management. There is no better way to create a shared vision and to generate commitment and loyalty than through empowerment and the feeling of ownership. A term that describes the concept of empowerment and ownership effectively is "buy-in." The belief that the chef supervisor and the company not only care about them but respect their contributions and ideas, combined with training, are critical to team member "buy-in." The "buy-in" will lead to continuous improvement and innovation.

In 1992 and in 1999, the Ritz-Carlton Hotel Company won the Malcolm Baldrige National Quality Award. The Ritz-Carlton is the first hotel company to win this award. Part of their winning strategy in 1992 was called "applied employee empowerment." According to Horst Shulze, the Ritz-Carlton's chief operating officer, "all our employees are empowered to do whatever it takes to provide instant pacification. No matter what their normal duties are, other employees must assist if aid is requested by a fellow worker responding to a guest's complaint or wish."[6] When the Ritz-Carlton won the award in 1999, as part of the company's employee empowerment program, every employee was empowered to spend up to $2000 to immediately correct a problem or handle a complaint.[7]

The biggest challenge to the concept of empowerment and ownership is its acceptance by chef supervisors. The position of chef has long been associated with power and control. This is changing now and will continue to change in the future. Team building and employee "buy-in" have become key components of supervision and management throughout the hospitality industry and in many kitchens.

SANITATION

Food safety is clearly an important issue for the chef supervisor. According to a Centers for Disease Control and Prevention study, over 6 million people become ill from contaminated food annually in the United States, and almost 80 percent of these illnesses occur at foodservice establishments.

One food safety and self-inspection system that the chef supervisor should be thoroughly familiar with is the *Hazard Analysis Critical Control Point,* more commonly known as HACCP. There are many chances in the food preparation and serving flow for food to become contaminated. The HACCP system targets these areas. By emphasizing high-risk foods and handling procedures, the chef supervisor can reduce the risk of food contamination. You can learn more about HACCP at the Food and Drug Administration website, www.cfsan.fda.gov/~lrd/haccp.html.

It is important, therefore, for the chef supervisor to adopt a proactive position relative to sanitation. All foodservice workers are potential disease spreaders. This fact requires the chef supervisor to analyze the procedures involved in food receiving, preparation, cooking, storage, use of food leftovers, and effective supervision of sanitation. The foodservice operation should be looked at through a customer's eyes: What sanitation messages are being sent? Is the kitchen team clean, well groomed, and trained in the prevention of food contamination? This important aspect of the duties of the chef supervisor requires constant supervision.

SAFETY

One goal of excellent foodservice operation is to reduce the possibility of accidents in the kitchen. Accident prevention works best when it involves the participation and cooperation of all kitchen team members. A safety program should have incentives to encourage the entire team to work safely. Rewards may be given to kitchen team members who remain accident-free. The issue of safety needs to be incorporated into induction and orientation training programs, and its importance needs to be stressed and emphasized thereafter on a continuous basis.

TECHNOLOGY

The chef supervisor must stay ahead of technological advances in equipment and machinery in order to be competitive and focused. New innovations in labor-saving devices and training devices become available each year, along with computer-managed information programs that allow the chef supervisor more time to concentrate on developing and coaching kitchen team members to become more efficient team players.

LEADERSHIP

Leadership styles and skills are vital to making all the factors and elements of supervision in the kitchen work. Because almost everything necessary for high-quality supervision requires effective communication and leadership skills, these topics are treated in depth in Chapters 5 and 6.

THE CONCEPT OF AUTHORITY

The chef supervisor is the formal leader of the group by virtue of the authority of the position. Supervisory success for the chef, however, depends on more than this source of authority. It depends on many skills. A high level of team-building skill is critical to the ability of the chef supervisor to increase the kitchen's team productivity and job satisfaction. When team-building skills are applied rather than solely authoritarian leadership, foodservice employees cooperate more with each other and other departments as well as developing better interpersonal relationships and a great team spirit. The requisites of authority are

- To require an obedience in which employees retain their freedom
- To strike a balance between authority and individual freedom
- To lead individuals toward growth
- To possess practical judgment skills
- To act as a uniting element of a group's common goals
- To enhance cooperative efforts
- To reserve the right and power to make decisions

For authority to be genuine, chef supervisors exercising that authority must know what they are requesting of team members and why they are making those requests. Authority for the sake of power is useless. It must seek to inspire desired outcomes from each person. Requests or demands made on employees without good reason often lead to anger and frustration on the part of both the employee and the chef supervisor. Remember, kitchen team members will respond more freely to a request than they will to an order.

THE EVOLUTION OF SUPERVISORY CHEFS

As has often been said, the primary difference between the United States and Japan in the area of human resource management is that in Japan people are managed as a true resource, whereas in the United States people are managed as a cost center. Although this statement is not entirely true, the concept of utilizing the collective human resources of an organization in a way that makes employees feel that they are participative members of a team is relatively new, certainly in the foodservice industry. Foodservice organizations often lagged behind manufacturing industries in providing a work environment in which employees are encouraged to contribute to decisions, which ultimately affects the single most important issue—customer satisfaction.

Chefs often complained that in many instances they were the last to be consulted on topics such as kitchen design, menu concepts, and supervision of kitchen employees. However, management often complained that chefs were difficult to deal with and did not want any part of issues that chefs considered to be the food and beverage manager's responsibilities. Competition has increased, and foodservice organizations must now pursue a more discerning and diverse customer, who has an acute awareness of first-class service, good food, and value for money. There is therefore a need for chef supervisors to be committed to a strong customer focus and, more important, to develop the kitchen team and the kitchen work environment to meet these new competitive challenges. In order to prepare the chef supervisor in modern approaches to the creation of a motivational kitchen environment, the following elements trace the evolution of two theories of people management. Additionally, this section of the chapter will examine the different trends, directions, and strategies that have evolved to meet the current foodservice business climate.

THE HAWTHORNE STUDIES

Begun in the 1920s, the Hawthorne studies represented an effort to determine what effect hours of work, periods of rest, and lighting might have on worker fatigue and productivity. These experiments were conducted by university professors Elton Mayo, Fritz Roethlisberger, and J. W. Dickson at the Western Electric Company's Hawthorne Works near Chicago, Illinois. These studies represented one of the first endeavors to evaluate employee productivity. The Hawthorne studies revealed that the attitudes employees had toward management, their work group, and the work itself significantly affected their productivity. Initially, the results of the research on the small study group baffled the researchers. Despite altering the work environment and measuring productivity against this changing environment (reducing rest periods and eliminating rest time), the productivity of the study group increased continuously, and this group had fewer sick days than other workers who were not in the research group.

The leaders of the research group concluded that productivity increased, not as a result of any of their contrived stimuli, but rather as a result of the absence of any authoritarian supervision and the interest shown in employees by the researchers. The fact that they were being studied was sufficient for the workers to improve their productivity. This phenomenon is still referred to by researchers as the *Hawthorne effect:* Change will occur simply because people know they are being studied, rather than as a result of some form of treatment. However, the most important result of the Hawthorne studies was that people respond better when they have a sense of belonging.

The findings of the Hawthorne studies produced a new direction for people management. As a result of these studies, greater emphasis was placed on managing employees, with concern for them as individuals. The studies also focused attention on the need for managers and supervisors to improve their communication skills and become more sensitive to employee needs and feelings. This new movement also emphasized the need to develop more participative, employee-centered supervision.

In the 1940s, Renis Likert conducted research into the creation of a productive and desirable work climate. He observed four approaches to supervision and leadership.[8] The first type was an authoritative approach that was potentially explosive. It involved high pressure on subordinates through work standards. It obtained compliance through fear techniques. This approach resulted in high productivity over short periods but low productivity and high absenteeism over longer periods. The second approach was authoritarian but benevolent in nature. The third approach was a consultative supervisor/employee approach. The fourth approach was group participation in which the supervisor was supportive and used group methods of supervision, including group decision making. The last three approaches yielded high productivity, low waste, and low costs, along with low absenteeism and low employee turnover.

Likert also developed the "linking pin" concept that focused on coordinating efforts through layers of middle management. It provided a formal, structured approach. Central to its philosophy was the idea that each level of management is a member of a multifunctional team that includes the next upward level.

We can only guess how long it will take for this new supervision focus to permeate the foodservice industry. Supervision in kitchens has a long history of being authoritarian, with a resulting high staff turnover. The rise of modern human resources management in the foodservice sector of the hospitality industry directly parallels the major demographic changes in U.S. society. Highly trained chefs, usually of European origin, were in high demand during the 1960s and 1970s. Most of these chef positions were in hotels. The foodservice industry grew during the 1970s and 1980s with the explosive growth of popular chain and fast-food restaurants. Trained chefs were in short supply. It was also during the 1970s and 1980s that the growth of culinary schools and programs was witnessed. In addition to the culinary education expansion, there was tremendous growth in the restaurant, hospital, institutional, and industrial foodservice sectors, which also became more customer-focused and -sensitive.

TRENDS

The end of the twentieth century was a very exciting time for the U.S. foodservice industry. The economy was strong, with rapid job growth. These good times brought about a change in American dining habits and a higher level of gastronomic sophistication. People were traveling more and consequently gained more exposure to different cuisines. The chef as a leader and supervisor, as a manager, became the norm rather than the exception.

This professional evolution was supported by the growth of culinary education programs in the United States from a handful to hundreds. Culinary education matured and encompassed all levels from K–12 to university. This growth was fueled by the glamour and prestige that began to be associated with the culinary profession and the chef. There was a corresponding increase in professional associations for chefs. These associations, such as the American Culinary Federation, Research Chefs Association, International Association of Culinary Professionals, American Personal and Private Chef Association, and others, encouraged the exchange of ideas and information, and promoted life-long learning and professional development through education and certification programs.

The successful chef had to possess additional skills, along with a new attitude to food production that had to be customer-driven and focused on quality. The chef became a supervisor and leader, someone who created a motivational kitchen environment with a team culture. The chef recognized the need for trained and educated team members and supported the growth of programs for culinary training and education in the United States.

The successful chef in the first decade of the twenty-first century is a supervisor and leader as well as a good culinarian. Today's chef values training, education, diversity, individual initiative, and team cohesiveness. The chef of today has evolved from a cook to a culinarian and from a chief to a manager. This evolution is not complete. As the food industry changes, the role of the chef will continue to evolve. Those who constantly pursue knowledge will help to shape the changes rather than just reacting to the changes that are always part of progress.

FIGURE 1-4 Attributes of the successful chef supervisor.

- Practice a code of ethics and administer this code fairly and without bias to all kitchen team members.
- Emulate the outstanding chef role models that history has provided, from Carême to Escoffier.
- Know, understand, and apply the elements of supervision and how these elements interrelate with the foodservice organization's goals, other departments, and the kitchen team.
- Know and understand the various steps in planning, organizing, coaching, team building, communicating, delegating, empowering, safety, sanitation, leadership, and technology.
- Separate and understand the concepts of authority, power, and leadership.

CONCLUSIONS

Quality permeates every aspect of what a chef does, from culinary art to supervision. It is the watchword for the modern chef. Quality must be driven by the need to meet and exceed customer satisfaction levels through quality food production and service. This will produce the consummate professional chef supervisor: Quality is a continuous process, not a destination.[9]

Chef supervisors have responsibilities to senior management, customers, and other team members. By understanding the different elements that are part of a chef supervisor's role, it will be easier to refocus efforts toward creating a motivational environment in the kitchen. Experience has shown that the establishment of a team culture in the kitchen that gives a feeling of ownership to the team members is the foundation of a quality conscious staff.

Summary

The modern chef supervisor's skill sets include the abilities to coach and lead the entire kitchen team by creating a motivational environment. Successful chef supervisors see themselves as facilitators and enablers whose job it is to develop the kitchen team. This means demonstrating attributes that include an understanding of feelings and attitudes that motivate the entire kitchen team. The attributes a successful chef supervisor demonstrates are shown in Figure 1-4.

The professional development of a culinarian, particularly a culinarian desiring to be a chef, has evolved from purely the skills of the craft to inclusion of the principles of supervision, training, and management. This evolution has occurred against the emerging development of the human resources management movement, from Hawthorne to Likert.

Discussion Questions

1. List and explain the functions of the chef supervisor's job.
2. What skills and attributes do you consider important for the chef supervisor's success?

3. How has the role of the chef supervisor's job changed? How do these changes affect the concepts of quality control and management?

4. Why is an ethical code of conduct critical to a chef supervisor's job?
5. What is meant by the concept of front-door to back-door management as it relates to the chef supervisor's job?
6. What are the elements of kitchen supervision? Describe them.
7. What are the benefits of team building and empowerment within the foodservice industry?

8. What is the concept of authority?
9. What is meant by the evolution of the chef with regard to supervisory positions?
10. How does the chef supervisor's role affect management, team members, and customer satisfaction?

Notes

1. Philip Crosby, *Quality Is Free* (New York: McGraw-Hill, 1978), 111.
2. Bill Marvin, *The Foolproof Foodservice Selection System* (New York: Wiley, 1993), 12.
3. Anna Katherine Jernigan, *The Effective Foodservice Supervisor* (Rockville, MD: Aspen, 1989), 213.
4. *Larousse Gastronomique* (London: Hamlyn, 1971), 303.
5. Peggy Anderson, ed., *Great Quotes from Great Leaders* (Lombard, IL: Carrier Press, 1989), 52.

6. Ritz Carlton publicity pamphlet, The Ritz Carlton Co., Boston, MA, 1993.
7. www.nist.gov/public_affairs/bald99/ritz.htm.
8. Arthur Sherman, George Bohlander, and Herbert Crudden, *Managing Human Resources,* 8th ed. (Cincinnati, OH: South-Western, 1988), 352.
9. James A. Belasco, *Teaching the Elephant to Dance* (New York: Crown, 1990), 28.

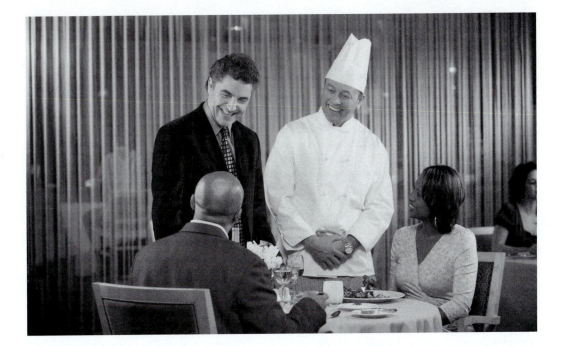

CHAPTER 2

THE CHEF SUPERVISOR AND MANAGEMENT THEORIES

OUTLINE

- ❖ Introduction
- ❖ The foodservice customer defined
- ❖ Philosophies, concepts, and theories of management
- ❖ Scientific management: a historical perspective
- ❖ Management by objectives
- ❖ The excellence movement
- ❖ Reengineering
- ❖ Total Quality Management
- ❖ Contemporary Management Theories
- ❖ Quality
- ❖ Change
- ❖ Conclusions
- ❖ Summary
- ❖ Discussion questions
- ❖ Notes

OBJECTIVES

When you complete this chapter, you should be able to:

1. Define the customer within the wider context of the foodservice industry
2. Identify the principles and philosophies of scientific management, management by objective, reengineering, the elements of the excellence movement, and total quality management
3. Discuss contingency, systems, and chaos management theories
4. Discuss the development, strengths, and weaknesses of the different concepts of management
5. Identify major trends and developments in the workplace that affect chef supervisors
6. Discuss quality in relation to the foodservice industry
7. Apply Deming's fourteen quality principles to the kitchen and the chef supervisor
8. Discuss the nature and importance of change and why people resist change
9. Indicate the guidelines for overcoming resistance to change

☙

Case Study: AMBER LIGHT STEAKHOUSE

The management of the Amber Light Steakhouse has received increasing numbers of guest complaints in the past twelve months. The restaurant has been in business for ten years in the same location. There has been very little change in the traditional chophouse-style menu offerings that have been the cornerstone of their success. The staff of the restaurant, both front- and back-of-the-house, has been relatively stable during that time. The customer base for the restaurant has not changed, and the steakhouse still seems to be drawing its regular crowd. The customers are complaining about both the quality of the food and the service. The management is concerned that if the level and severity of complaints continue, business will be affected.

Management has brought their concern to the attention of the chef and the dining room manager and has directed them to motivate the staff to reduce the number of complaints. The response of both department heads has been to increase supervision of production and service. Additionally, each has met privately with the general manager to explain that the poor performance in the other department head's area is undermining their individual efforts to reduce the number of complaints.

The kitchen and service staff are comprised primarily of individuals with five or more years with the restaurant in the same positions. They were well trained when originally hired and have been doing the same job for a number of years. They are generally unconcerned about the guest complaints because when a guest complains, they respond quickly to correct the problem.

Based on what you have learned from the previous chapter and the content of this chapter, answer the following questions.

• What is the overall reason for the challenges at in the Amber Light Steakhouse?
• What are the primary causal agents of the challenges at the Amber Light Steakhouse?
• What role did supervision/management play in the decline in the Amber Light Steakhouse?
• What specific steps could have been taken to avoid the current situation at the Amber Light Steakhouse?
• What, specifically, can be done to overcome the challenges and generate motion in a positive direction for the Amber Light Steakhouse?

INTRODUCTION

Traditionally, the foodservice industry has been a follower rather than a leader in the area of management theories. Most management models were developed with manufacturing industries in mind. The hospitality and foodservice industries are strongly people-oriented and sell services to and make a profit from people. It has been said that a restaurant is a manufacturing plant attached directly to a distribution center and retail outlet. Foodservice professionals must manage production at the same time as they are managing distribution and retail sale. There is an additional twist for the foodservice professional in a restaurant, quick-service, catering/banquet, club, or others setting in which the consumer is served food directly. In all of these settings, the consumer reacts immediately to the quality of the product, the service, and all other factors that may affect their experience. The consumer's reaction is communicated through the chain of production and delivery, requiring analysis and possibly changes. At each point in that chain, the human factor affects the analysis and change. Bearing this in mind, it is understandable that foodservice professionals—owners, operators, managers, and chefs—have been less inclined to embrace theories of management that focus on manufacturing (production) without consideration of distribution and interactions with the consumer.

According to the National Restaurant Association, in 2007 the restaurant industry employed approximately 12.8 million people and will employ 14.8 million people by 2017. The restaurant industry is the second largest employer in the United States, with the U.S. government being the largest.[1] The number of people employed in the hospitality and leisure industries in the United States increased by 16.2 percent from 1996 to 2006, according to the U.S. Department of Labor.[2] In 1955 the restaurant industry captured 25 percent of the consumer money spent on food. In 2007 that share was 47.9 percent. The restaurant industry had $322.6 billion in sales in 1997. It is projected that it would have $538 billion in sales in 2007.[3]

The growth of the foodservice industry shows no signs of slowing. As the foodservice industry grows, there will be a greater need for chefs with people skills along with great culinary talent and a strong customer focus. These elements will produce a formidable combination in any chef supervisor. Increased customer awareness and new supervisory and management skills all combine to mold the modern chef. It is therefore important that the chef supervisor be secure enough in his or her level of understanding of this refocused role to delegate and trust kitchen team members to carry out the workload to the required quality standards. There is no magic to being a good chef supervisor. It just takes some understanding of human behavior combined with the timely application of effective leadership. The successful company in the twenty-first century and beyond will require the highest-quality supervision and leadership from its managers, including the chef.

THE FOODSERVICE CUSTOMER DEFINED

A *foodservice customer* is any person of any demographic group who frequents any commercial hotel; restaurant; or institutional, industrial, or military dining establishment and who is prepared to pay for wholesome, nutritious meals prepared by professionals utilizing first-class quality food products and outstanding culinary skills in a safe and sanitary kitchen and served by friendly, caring, efficient dining room staff. The customer is more clearly defined in Figure 2-1.

FIGURE 2-1 Who is the customer?

Any of these at any age:
- Casual restaurant diner
- Hotel/motel restaurant guest
- Cafeteria diner
- Room-service guest
- Hospital patient
- Senior-living-home resident
- School or college diner
- Catered-party guest
- Airline, train, or cruise passenger
- Fast-food diner
- Theme and recreation park diner
- Banquet diner
- Office/factory diner
- Upscale white-tablecloth restaurant diner
- Delicatessen and supermarket customer

PHILOSOPHIES, CONCEPTS, AND THEORIES OF MANAGEMENT

In recent years many theories, philosophies, strategies, and concepts have been developed and put forward to assist business organizations, managers, and supervisors to restructure, refocus, and plan for change. All of these include within them the elements of change, customer focus, quality, and leadership. Many of these theories have their roots in manufacturing industries.

Foodservice organizations and chef supervisors are not immune to the actions and effects of these business strategies and philosophies. The main thrust of this book is toward supervisory management for chefs rather than business management; nevertheless, many of these philosophies, strategies, and theories contain elements that directly affect the chef supervisor's job. One way or another, as we look to the future, chefs will be required not only to cook, but also to know, understand, and apply these theories and philosophies.

The following section identifies some of these common principles associated with change and leadership. Many of them include slogans that have become synonymous with quality, customer focus, and leadership. They are not listed in order of importance, and they include only those relevant to the chef supervisor's role.

SCIENTIFIC MANAGEMENT: A HISTORICAL PERSPECTIVE

Discussion of the topic of scientific management revolves around time-and-motion studies. The principles of scientific management were first put forward by industrial engineer Frederick Winslow Taylor around the turn of the twentieth century. Taylor held that human performance could be defined and controlled through work standards and rules. He advocated the use of time-and-motion studies to reduce jobs to simple, separate steps to be performed over and over again.

Scientific management evolved during an era of mass immigration. The workplace was being flooded with unskilled, uneducated workers, and it was efficient to employ them in large numbers. This was also a period of labor strife, and Taylor believed that his system would reduce conflict and eliminate the arbitrary use of power because so little discretion would be left to either workers or supervisors. The methods used included careful selection of workers who were deemed to be competent, conforming, and obedient, and constant oversight of the work performed. This system caused much bitterness between unions and management. It is from Taylor's period that the phrase a "fair day's work" came.

Scientific management gave to employers a system that increased productivity and reduced the number of workers needed. It was also rule-bound, hierarchical, and top-heavy with corporate structure. This began the era of standardization that many today believe contributed to the slow recognition of the changing nature of employees and the methods of managing them.

MANAGEMENT BY OBJECTIVES

Management by objectives (MBO) is a philosophy of management first introduced by Peter Drucker in 1954. It seeks to judge the performance of employees on the basis of their success in achieving set objectives established through consultation with managers and supervisors. Performance improvement efforts under MBO focus on goals to be achieved by employees rather than on the activities performed or the methods by which employees achieve these goals.

Management by objectives is part of a system-wide set of organizational goals that begins with setting the organization's common goals and objectives and eventually returns to that point. The system acts as a goal-setting process whereby goals are set for the organization, individual departments, individual managers, supervisors, and employees. A feature of MBO is a broad statement of employee responsibilities prepared by the supervisor, reviewed, and jointly modified until both the employee and the supervisor are satisfied with them. The goals are accompanied by a detailed account of the actions the employee proposes to take in order to reach the goals. Periodic review assesses the progress the employee has made. At the end of the review period, the employee does a self-appraisal of whether the previously set goals have been achieved.

Management by objectives enables managers and supervisors to plan and measure their own performance as well as that of the employees. It shifts the emphasis from appraisal to self-analysis. The major criticisms of MBO include the methods by which individuals achieve their goals. Factors such as cooperation, adaptability, and concern are not included as part of MBO rationale. Additionally, under MBO, employee-rated success is tied to issues that ultimately are not directed toward customer satisfaction. Another problem with MBO is its link to employee evaluation and rewards, which causes conflict between the supervisor's roles as judge and leader.

W. Edwards Deming was particularly critical of MBO. He believed that MBO is management by fear,[4] and that it does not have a place in the quality movement because of its reliance on performance evaluations. He also believed that MBO discourages risk taking, builds fear, and undermines teamwork. In a team, it is difficult to tell who does what. Under MBO, people work for themselves, not the organization.

THE EXCELLENCE MOVEMENT

If it ain't broke, fix it anyway.[5] About the same time that Deming's quality principles were being rediscovered, the "excellence" movement began: by Peters and Waterman in 1982, with their book, *In Search of Excellence;* by Peters and Austin in 1985, in *Passion for Excellence;* and by Peters in 1988, in *Thriving on Chaos.*[6] These books and their strategies blended perfectly into what was happening in the world of business as the pace of change gathered momentum. The basic business and management philosophies put forward by these authors were to make excellence in the management of product, people, and service a first priority. These works proposed many innovative approaches to management. They focused attention on the customer revolution and the need to gain a competitive advantage, to become more effective: "We must end excuse making and look for new organizational models fit for the new world. New survivors will welcome change rather than resist it, and realize that people power, not robot power is our only choice."[7] Figure 2-2 shows the requirements for an organization's survival and growth as advocated by the excellence movement and Peter's "Thriving on Chaos" philosophy.

Organizations must also see people as a prime source of "value added" and realize that they can never be trained or involved too much. Additionally, in the excellence movement, the structure of organization is flattened, layers of middle management are reduced, and the functional barriers are broken. Peters believes that "front-line supervisors as we know them give way to self-managed teams. Middle managers become facilitators rather than turf guardians. Leaders become levers of change and preachers of vision."[8]

Peters also believes that strategies, ideas, and concepts come from the bottom up. Staff functions support the line rather than the other way around. Sales and service personnel become heroes with customer relationships. Success in the health care, food, or computer industry will go to those who add value by developing customized products or services that create new market niches.

Clearly, the foodservice world has changed and will continue to change. In order to meet this change, chefs will need to be more than just "cooks." Each team member has a part to play; the operational employee, whether in manufacturing or foodservice, is a thing of the past. Each person has a valuable role in this empowered, motivated, decision-making, innovative, and well-led kitchen team.

FIGURE 2-2 The Excellence Movement and Drucker's *Thriving on Chaos.*

Requirements for an Organization's Survival and Growth
- A bias toward action
- A simple form and a lean staff
- Continued contact with customers
- Productivity improvement via people
- Operational autonomy to encourage entrepreneurship
- One key business value
- Emphasis on doing what they know best
- Simultaneous loose and tight controls

In *management by walking around (MBWA),* chefs are active people, and food production is activity-oriented. Good chef supervisors walk around and visit each person's workstation.

Ed Carlson, upon taking over at United Airlines, realized that it was a service business that had lost sight of the customer. He introduced MBWA and instilled a hands-on customer focus. He said, "In a service business, you can't have a rigid set of rules. You can have some guidelines, but you must allow people the freedom to make a different interpretation."[9]

REENGINEERING

Reengineering, if it is adopted across the board by foodservice organizations, will probably have the greatest impact on executive chefs of large multiunit hotels, casinos, or similarly sized operations. Reengineering essentially calls for a radical rethinking of the ways in which organizations do business. Business reengineering means putting aside much of the received wisdom of two hundred years of industrial management.[10] It has been described as "an approach to planning and controlling change."[11]

In reengineering, work units change from functional departments to process teams, jobs change from simple tasks to multidimensional work, and people's roles change from controlled to empowered. The focus of performance measures and compensation shifts from activity to results. Values change from protective to productive. Organizational structures change from hierarchical to flat. The role of executives changes from scorekeepers to leaders.[12]

Part of the reengineering process is also about positioning within different markets. This planned positioning determines what should be reengineered.

Reengineering involves integrating tasks into processes and reorganizing the company around them. What results, in contrast to the old system of organization by different departments, is a collection of people united in their common purpose of effort, reducing the need for continuous checking and controls. Conceivably, in this scenario, chefs could become restaurant or unit managers responsible not only for supervisory functions but also for complete management of a foodservice operation. Additionally, titles and individual lines of demarcation would disappear.

TOTAL QUALITY MANAGEMENT

The theory of total quality control first espoused by Armand Feigeinbaum in his 1951 book, *Quality Control: Principles, Practice and Administration,* and which was released in 1961 as *Total Quality Control,*[13] is a management theory that can be effectively applied to the foodservice operator in the service setting. At the heart of total quality control is the conviction that it is possible to achieve error-free quality product most of the time. This assertion is phrased in various ways, including "getting it right the first time," "working smarter," and "zero defects." When total quality control was introduced in the United States in 1981 by the U.S. Navy, the word *control* had been changed to *management.*

Total quality management (TQM) is not only about external customers, it is also about internal customers. In his book, *The Essence of Total Quality Management,* John Bank discusses the internal customer.[14] He defines this person as the person in a company who receives the work of another and then adds his or her contribution to the product or service before passing it on to someone else. In a restaurant, the chef has levels of internal customers in the culinary brigade and the service staff, and the chef must meet their requirements if together they are to please the guest.

The overreliance in the past on the narrow technical skills of supervision produced a supervisor who was not overly endowed with leadership qualities. Control was more of an issue than coaching and team building; certainly, the old-style chefs were big on control and power. The theory of quality management that came to be called TQM is about team building and investing in the development of people. The TQM movement peaked in the mid-1990s, and the use of the terms total quality management and TQM have become largely marginal in discussions of management theory. However, the concept of commitment by a company to total quality as defined by zero errors in all aspects of the operation through team building and investment in the development of people has not diminished in importance to the foodservice industry as a management design. The concept of developing a workplace culture that focuses on quality in every aspect of the operation continues to be central to any foodservice operation's success. We will discuss the concept of quality further later in this chapter.

CONTEMPORARY MANAGEMENT THEORIES

Contemporary theories of management attempt to account for and help interpret the rapidly changing nature of the business organization and business environment in today's world.[15] *Contingency theory* might be called the "it depends" theory. Contingency theory calls on managers to take into account all aspects of the current situation and act on those aspects that are key to the situation at hand when making decisions. Managers using this theory of management make decisions that "depend" on the current circumstances.

Systems theory proposes that a system is a collection of parts joined to accomplish a goal. Any action taken with one part of a system ultimately affects the total system. For example, removing a spark plug from an engine changes how the engine runs. In an organization, a change that affects one part of the organization also affects the total organization. Systems theory requires supervisors and managers to have a broader perspective of the organization. Managers and supervisors are driven to address issues in relation to the total organization. This is an important change in management perspective. In the past, managers generally focused on only one part of an organization. The result was often actions that had a positive impact locally but a negative impact on the larger organization. Systems theory is particularly applicable to the foodservice industry. The actions of the kitchen directly affect the dining room, and the actions of the dining room directly affect the kitchen. The more changes in these areas take into account both areas, the greater is the potential for changes to be positive for both team members and customers.

Chaos theory is more of a scientific theory for the world and life in general. The concept of chaos theory may have some application to management as businesses continue to grow. Chaos theory says that events are rarely controlled. In fact, it says that as the complexity of the system grows, the more volatile it becomes and the greater the energy required to maintain a semblance of stability. As more energy is expended, the more structure is required to maintain the system. This pattern continues until the system splits, combines with another complex system, or falls apart entirely. Does this

BOX 2-1

WHAT IS THIS BUSINESS?
THE CHEF AND THE "HOW" AND "WHY"

The word *reengineering* was certainly not found in any of my cookbooks or apprenticeship texts, and in order for me to understand this word's concept, I had to look elsewhere. My training as a chef over the past twenty-five years has been purely classical. Along the way, I managed to learn not only new cooking methods but also how to manage and motivate people in the kitchen environment.

I now have a much clearer understanding of the vision of the future for our industry. Reengineering is a tool to make this vision come true, and in many cases we have no choice but to go forward, accepting the changes that come toward us no matter how big or small they may seem.

In my case, reengineering came as somewhat of a surprise when I found out that many of my colleagues in the company were without a job and that executive chefs were no longer needed. After looking at this situation a little more closely, I found out that this reengineering concept was really not as bad as it seemed.

Reengineering gave me the opportunity to look at my organization with a totally different set of eyes, and it made me realize that things can be done differently; and in the long run, these changes would be beneficial to the customer and the company.

Once I was able to let go of the past, I was willing to accept the challenges of the future. With this new attitude, I was able to move forward and develop the necessary plan to put reengineering to work in my culinary world. This meant dismantling the current organizational structures, putting new concepts into place such as individual business unit leaders, eliminating departments, and redesigning job descriptions. During each of these steps, new questions and answers came up, and I changed or adapted to them as they came along.

Many already well-defined systems had to be changed, eliminated, or even completely redesigned in order to move forward. Throughout this process, many roadblocks were removed, only to show up again around the corner. Many personal egos had to be eliminated, and in some cases the people had to go along with them.

We were told by our corporate leaders that only the best would survive, and this was a problem for some. Those who were not willing to change found themselves struggling more and more. They were either terminated or quit during the process. Those who stepped up to the plate and started swinging at the ball made more progress than they even imagined.

We as culinarians should understand that if we don't change the way we do business, we will lose sight of our primary goal, which is customer satisfaction. It is the customer who steers in the direction we must go, and that is into the future.

Robert Harrington, Ph.D., CEC, CCE,
Associate Professor
University of Arkansas,
Fayetteville, Arkansas

sound like a company that you are familiar with? Chaos theory may be used most frequently in reference to biological systems, but it appears that its application to management is not unreasonable.

QUALITY

It is not possible to have a meaningful discussion of supervision, management, or training in the foodservice industry, particularly in the kitchen, without a discussion of quality. Quality must be the focus of any foodservice business and every part of that business, both internally and externally. In the foodservice industry, a quality service or product may be defined as one that fully meets the expectations and requirements of those who produce or use it. Continuous improvement in quality food production is fundamental for any success in the foodservice industry. Continuous improvement in all areas, including supervision, contributes directly to improvement in food quality.

W. Edward Deming's fourteen "quality" principles, on which much of the quality movement is based, recommend that each company or organization work out its own interpretations and adapt them to the corporate culture. Although Deming's quality principles were directed primarily toward manufacturing industries, they have many applications to quality in the foodservice industry. The following list demonstrates how Deming's fourteen quality points may be adapted for application to a total quality kitchen operation.[16]

1. *Create constancy of purpose toward the improvement of product and service.* Commit the kitchen staff to continuous improvement. Create a common purpose; get the kitchen team to embrace continuous improvement.

2. *Management must take the leadership role in promoting change.* Together with management, create a climate for change in the kitchen. Embrace change; make it your friend. Change with purpose, not just for the sake of change. Chef supervisors who embrace change will need to be supportive and train the kitchen team—be proactive rather than reactive. Create and live a vision for the kitchen department that will become a beacon for team building and effective supervision. Remember, the one constant is change, and change can be a frightening concept for individuals who are accustomed to living in a comfort zone.

3. *Stop dependence on inspection to achieve quality. Build quality into the product in the beginning.* Chef supervisory management must be dedicated to preparing meals and providing service in a way that provides high standards from the outset. Chefs should abandon the notion that they know more about what the customer wants than the customer; they must not be gastronomic snobs. Without foodservice customers, there would be no need for chefs.

This refocused direction applies equally to all foodservice establishments, whether white-tablecloth, health care, student dining, or fast-food establishments. Quality is perceived by the customer: *They* define quality, *not* the chef who produces the meal. The customer is the boss. One dissatisfied customer leaving the restaurant will tell twelve friends, who will tell six others, who will tell three of their friends; eventually, hundreds of people may hear about the poor meal and dining experience.

Involve the kitchen staff team in menu development; let them vote on new dishes before they are introduced on the menu. Involve customers; have *them* taste-test the menu items. Allow customers a vote on which dishes should be included on the menu. Ask the customers what they want and then provide it. If the meal looks fine and tastes fine to the chef preparing it, that does not necessarily mean that customers will feel the same way about it. They may not always be right, but they are always the customer, the person we want to continuously satisfy and retain, so that the foodservice business can grow and prosper.

Building quality into food preparation through team members at all levels is perhaps the single most important task of the chef supervisor. This end can only be achieved through excellent coaching and team-building skills, and instilling in the kitchen team a sense of pride and a passion for quality food standards. It is on the promise of high quality at all levels, provided through a motivated and well-trained kitchen team, that the success or failure of the modern chef supervisor rests.

4. *Move to a single supplier for any one item. Create long-term relationships with suppliers.* Chef supervisors should view suppliers and vendors as a vital part of the total quality improvement process in the kitchen. This means trusting suppliers and asking for their input. It means closer contacts and relationships with farmers and growers. More and more foodservice operators and chefs are dealing directly with local farmers and fishermen. Buying locally can mean access to fresher and organically grown products. Suppliers can customize their products to meet the specific needs of a foodservice operation. Using single suppliers versus as opposed to using two or more challenges the old strategy of playing one supplier against the other, using price and delivery as leverage and bargaining chips. As Bill Eacho stated, "Foodservice operators can improve quality and consistency, while at the same time lower costs by forming strategic partnerships."[17] While issues of price, quality, delivery, units of purchase, and credit terms will remain important business issues, quality product and produce from suppliers based on your foodservice specifications are paramount. A quality end product begins with quality ingredients.

5. *Improve constantly the system of production and service and thus decrease costs.* Quality equals profit, and motivated kitchen team members can reduce costs. Communicate the importance of each person's role in the quest for high quality standards. Support and explain decisions to help each kitchen team member apply quality standards. On a weekly basis, brief the team on progress, policy, and points of action. As food quality improves through continuous quality review, waste is reduced and costs decrease. Food cost–reduction programs in and of themselves do not often lead to improved quality. On the other hand, effective quality applications by informed team members lead not only to improved quality but also to lasting reduction in food and production costs as well. Quality and costs are not opposites or trade-offs, with one being improved at the expense of the other. Instead, both can be constantly improved. Total quality improvement is a never-ending journey. It is therefore essential for the chef supervisor to provide an atmosphere in which total communication can exist in the kitchen and in which it is possible to tap constantly the collective brainpower of the team.

6. *Institute training on the job.* Train all kitchen team members, including the support team. Practice equal training opportunities and gain support from management for the concept of on-the-job training. Set an example; coach employees to reach their potential. Diversity and multiculturalism are common to foodservice operations; therefore, a good deal of on-the-job training is often necessary. This training should always be conducted in a sensitive and caring way. (See the chapters on training in Part Two.)

7. *Institute leadership. The aim of supervision should be to help people and machines do a better job.* Chef supervisors must become better leaders. This requires delegating authority, empowering kitchen team members to become independent decision makers, providing guidance, and creating a positive work environment. Chef supervisors as role models, leaders, and trainers should provide the tools and necessary coaching required for the rest of the team to operate a successful total quality kitchen. Use technology and machines to support the efforts of the kitchen team, not just to replace them. Learn from successes and mistakes. Walk regularly around each team member's place of work, observe, listen, and praise. (See Chapter 7 on leadership.)

8. *Drive out fear, so that everyone may work effectively.* The greatest fears of a kitchen team member are fear of the unknown and fear of rejection or failure. What am I expected to do? How do I know if I am doing a good job? Create an environment in which team members feel comfortable offering suggestions and ideas. Just because members of a group do not say anything does not necessarily mean they have nothing to say. They may be shy or simply afraid to advance their ideas. Give constant feedback on team member performance. Feedback should be given only on issues of performance, not on the type of person the team member is. (See Chapter 3 on motivation, morale, and strokes.)

9. *Break down barriers between departments. Promote team building as people from different departments work together to solve problems and improve quality.* Customers react holistically to quality and service. The dining experience involves other people besides the kitchen team. Quality food must be complemented by friendly, courteous service by staff dedicated to meeting and exceeding customer expectations. The service staff is the chef's internal customer and an integral part of the foodservice quality drive. Customers recall the negative aspects of the dining experience before they recall the more positive ones; therefore, negative and positive experiences don't go together. The animosity that has traditionally existed between dining room staff and kitchen staff has absolutely no place in a quality operation: Chefs must realize that the waiter is also a customer.

10. *Eliminate slogans, exhortations, and targets for the workforce, asking for zero defects and new levels of productivity.* Slogans containing production numbers only—numbers of meals served and degree of difficulty associated with the production of certain menu items—should be avoided as tools of measurement. Food cost percentage targets are important but should not be the major measurement tool for chefs in foodservice. Develop the kitchen team—emphasize people, not profit, and hire kitchen staff with hospitality attitudes: Technical skills are important, but good attitudes and a desire to please the customer by cooking the best meal possible are more important. Remember, the reputation of the chef supervisor is a product of the last meal served to a customer, not on any previous accolades or gold medals won at food shows.

11. *Eliminate work quotas; substitute leadership.* Practical experience has shown that during service time, quality in the kitchen is at its lowest. To improve the kitchen work environment, instead of labor-intensive, boring work sequences, rotate team members. Ensure that no one is a prisoner of a particular station, area, or job. Design jobs and arrange work to encourage the commitment of individuals to the team. Communicate clearly so as to ensure quality performance standards; be understood and understand; be a good listener. Serve the team; care for their well-being and safety; work alongside team members and deal with grievances promptly.

Leadership within the kitchen must replace the old heavy-handed style of chefs. There must be recognition that team members will have initiative and creativity and that they can and will make valuable contributions to quality if they are provided a motivated work environment. Chef supervisors more and more will be required to lead a culturally diverse kitchen team, which will necessitate skills in understanding

FIGURE 2-3 Demotivating barriers to quality performance.

- Erratic mood swings by the chef supervisor
- Poor physical kitchen facilities
- High temperatures in the work environment
- Poor equipment
- Insufficient small wares
- Inappropriate floor surfaces
- Inconsistent treatment of individuals and no communication or feedback on job performance

the special values of diversity so as to turn this diversity into a total quality strength. Deming continuously honed these principles. According to Mary Walton, Deming stated: "For years point seven was a mandate to institute supervision, of late I believe leadership is a better word."[18] (See Chapter 7 on leadership.)

12. *Remove barriers that rob managers, engineers, and the hourly paid worker of their right to pride of workmanship. Change the emphasis from numbers to quality.* Almost all kitchen team members want to give their best. Chef supervisors should remove barriers in order to create a motivational environment. However, removing barriers alone will not create motivation; motivation comes from within each individual. Without motivating conditions in the kitchen, team members will operate at minimal performance levels. Figure 2-3 shows the most common demotivating barriers to quality performance.

In kitchen operation, chef supervisors must realize that elements that motivate them will probably also motivate kitchen team members. The example that the chef supervisor sets greatly influences the productivity and motivation of the team. Most kitchen team members take considerable pride in their work performance and the meals they serve. Simply blaming kitchen team members for poor business numbers and lack of revenues makes no contribution to operational success. Quality equals profit in the promotion of pride, and a sense of self-worth will enhance profits. (See Chapter 3, on motivation, morale, and strokes.)

13. *Institute a vigorous program of education and self-improvement.* Training and instructor skills are just as important to the chef supervisor as culinary technical skills. Invest in training; it will prove to be the greatest impetus toward the goals of continuous improvement. Chef supervisors who arm themselves with instructor training skills and techniques and who use them in planned training situations will win big. Training is not something that is done once; it has to be ongoing, a way of life in the kitchen. At times learning can proceed irregularly. Expect periods with no perceptible progress in some individuals but with changes taking place in the culture of the kitchen team and in other individuals. The single most unifying force in developing people and creating conditions for a real and genuine total quality product and motivated kitchen team is the planned implementation of sequential and progressive training programs. (See Part Two on training.)

14. *Put everyone in the company to work to accomplish the transformation. Make it an all-pervasive common goal and support it.* The advantages of chef supervisors investing in and applying Deming's quality principles is that they will not only produce satisfied customers and the practical abolition of complaints, they will also transform the role of the

FIGURE 2-4   Areas for continuous improvement.

- Improving external customer satisfaction
- Improving and developing closer supplier partnerships
- Improving communications within the kitchen
- Reducing waste
- Preventing special causes of food preparation variation
- Quantifying quality costs
- Improving food production and service methods
- Improving internal systems
- Providing flexibility and adaptability

chef supervisor, the team, and the work environment in the kitchen. However, the results cannot be maintained unless the entire organization and the various supporting departments along with management adopt them universally.

Chef supervisors who are proactive will recognize that it is necessary in today's foodservice industry to be more than an excellent cook with first-class culinary skills; they also must be first-class supervisors with great team-building skills. Great culinarians cannot cook all the meals; they need help. It is the help and this disposition toward the organization and the chef supervisor that ultimately will determine the success or failure of the foodservice establishment. Continuous improvement must become the norm; supervising or managing the status quo is no longer an option in an increasingly competitive and uncertain foodservice industry.

Figure 2-4 shows some of the areas that should be the focus of continuous improvement in the kitchen. Quality is not a procedure; it is a process; as such, it is never finished. The culture of quality promotes and sustains change.

The main aim of the Deming philosophy is empowerment of the individual. The lesson is that we have to empower all our people with dignity, knowledge, and skills so that they may contribute. They have to feel secure, be trained so that they can do the work properly, and be encouraged so that the organization can develop and grow.[19]

CHANGE

Change is a key component of management for continuous improvement. Studies have shown that people do not actually resist change; they resist being changed, and participation empowers change.[20] A major factor to be considered by chef supervisors when changing the foodservice operation is the people affected by the change. Resistance to change within any organization is as common as the need for change. After supervisors decide on making changes, they typically meet with employee resistance, usually aimed at preventing the change from occurring. This resistance generally exists because kitchen team members fear some personal loss, such as a reduction in personal prestige, a disturbance of established social and working relationships, and personal failure due to an inability to carry out new job responsibilities as a result of the proposed change.

Because resistance accompanies proposed change, chef supervisors must be able to reduce the effects of this resistance so as to ensure the success of needed quality

FIGURE 2-5 Change: questions team members will ask.

Questions Team Members Will Ask
- Will I lose my job?
- Will my old skills become obsolete?
- Will I be capable of being effective under the new system?
- Will my power and prestige decline?
- Will I receive more responsibility than I want?
- Will I have to work longer hours?

improvements. People need time to evaluate the proposed change before it is implemented. Providing no time to evaluate how proposed changes may affect individual situations usually results in automatic opposition to the change. Those kitchen team members who will be affected by the change must be kept informed of the type of change being considered and the probability that the change will be adopted. When fear of personal loss related to a proposed change is reduced, opposition to the change will be reduced. Individuals should receive information that will help them answer the change-related questions shown in Figure 2-5.

If the chef supervisor follows some simple guidelines, then implementing change need not be too stressful. The following steps will assist in getting the kitchen team members to "buy into" the change.

- Inform those concerned in advance, so that they can think about the implications of the change and its effect on their position within the kitchen team.
- Explain the overall objectives of the change, the reasons for it, and the sequence in which it will occur.
- Show people how the change will benefit them. Be honest with the team. If they are not to be part of the future plans of the kitchen objectives, tell them and provide support and ample time for them to secure new positions.
- Invite those affected by the change to participate at all stages of the process.
- Allow time and demonstrate patience as the team adapts to new work or quality-driven changes.
- Provide for constant communication and feedback during the changes.
- Demonstrate constant commitment and loyalty to the change. Indicate confidence in the team and each individual's ability to implement the change.

The most powerful tool for reducing resistance to change is open display by the chef supervisor of a positive attitude toward the derived benefits of quality improvements for the organization as a whole and the individual kitchen team members. As with all change, time should be taken for evaluation, to examine what needs to be modified, and what can be added to increase the effectiveness of kitchen operations. Evaluation of change often involves watching for symptoms that further change is necessary, particularly if team members are more oriented toward the past than the future or if they are more concerned with their own "pecking order" than with meeting the challenges of quality. A challenge for the chef supervisor is the immediate and constant negative responders. These are the individuals who react negatively to change of any type. Some of the statements that "kill off" creative ideas and change are shown in Figure 2-6.

FIGURE 2-6   Statements that kill change.

- Don't be ridiculous.
- We tried that before.
- It costs too much.
- You must be crazy.
- That's beyond our responsibility.
- It's too radical a change.
- We don't have the time.
- We've never done it before.
- Let's get back to reality.
- We're not ready for that.
- We'd be laughed at.
- We did all right without it.
- Let's shelve it for the time being.
- Let's form a committee.
- It's not practical for an organization like ours.
- It's too hard to get accepted.
- It won't work in our kitchen.

Chef supervisors should listen carefully for these types of remarks and monitor the dissent within the group. This dissent should be met with a positive approach and the benefits of the new ideas pointed out.

CONCLUSIONS

This brief overview of some of the major historical issues of people management is intended only to give the chef supervisor a glimpse of what has shaped different directions in supervision and management. Each theory has had its own champions at various times. What has happened is the subtle yet vitally important shift of designation from "personnel managers" to "human resources managers" and the greater emphasis placed on developing people. This shift clearly underlines the philosophy that people must be led, not managed. This overview provides insight and understanding of change. It also shows that workers have changed; they *can* be more than mindless, uninterested employees who need constant control and supervision. Supervision in the kitchen is evolving and changing. Chef supervisors must shift from old traditional "autocratic" rulers to coaches. Chefs who come to realize that not all change is bad will succeed in the future foodservice industry.

Summary

To be successful supervisors, chefs must have an understanding and knowledge of the business and management forces that propel a quality management philosophy. Among these quality attributes is the need for chef supervisors with strong people, culinary, and customer focus skills.

The theories of management have evolved from scientific management, total quality management, and management by objective to the contemporary systems theory. W. Edwards Deming provided strategies and philosophies directed toward continuous improvements in all aspects of production. These strategies may be applied in the foodservice industry. Deming's fourteen quality principles can be applied in a culinary operation by trained and knowledgeable chef supervisors.

Change is a constant. Chef supervisors must reduce the effects of resistance to change within the kitchen. Understanding the elements of change and the fear with which people approach change is key to moving toward a customer quality focus.

Discussion Questions

1. Quality in terms of the kitchen operation may be considered in relation to what areas?
2. What are the various foodservice industry categories in which a chef supervisor operates?
3. What were the main contributions of Frederick Taylor's scientific management?
4. How can Deming's fourteen quality principles be applied to the kitchen and the chef supervisor?
5. Discuss the importance and role of continuous improvement in quality food and service.
6. What are the main differences between management by objective, the excellence movement, and reengineering?
7. Which of the contemporary theories of management has the greatest application to the kitchen, and why?
8. What are the elements that contribute to people's resistance to change?
9. Who sets the pace for most change in the foodservice industry?

Notes

1. National Restaurant Association, *2007 Restaurant Industry Forecast* (Washington, DC: National Restaurant Association, 2006), 2.
2. U.S. Department of Labor, 2007, www.bls.gov/iag/iag.services.htm.
3. National Restaurant Association, *2007 Restaurant Industry Forecast,* 2.
4. Rafael Aguayo, *Dr. Deming* (New York: Carol, 1991), 243.
5. Tom Peters, *Thriving on Chaos: Handbook for a Management Revolution* (New York: Harper & Row, 1988), 3.
6. Thomas J. Peters and Robert H. Waterman, Jr., *In Search of Excellence* (New York: Harper & Row, 1985); Tom Peters and Nancy Austin, *A Passion for Excellence— The Leadership Difference* (New York: HarperCollins, 1985); and Peters, *Thriving on Chaos.*
7. Peters, *Thriving on Chaos,* 357.
8. Ibid., p. 358.
9. Tom Peters, "Putting Excellence into Management," in *Managing Behavior in Organizations* (New York: McGraw-Hill, 1983), 603.
10. Michael Hammer and James Champy, *Reengineering the Corporation: A Manifesto for Business Revolution* (New York: HarperCollins, 1993), 2.
11. Daniel Morris and Joel Brandon, *Reengineering Your Business* (New York: McGraw-Hill, 1993), 13.
12. Hammer and Champy, *Reengineering the Corporation,* 79.
13. Armand Feigenbaum, *Quality Control: Principles, Practice and Administration* (New York: McGraw-Hill, 1951); Armand Feigenbaum, *Total Quality Control* (New York: McGraw-Hill, 1961).
14. John Bank, *The Essence of Total Quality Management* (Upper Saddle River, NJ: Prentice Hall, 2000).
15. Carter Mcnamara, "Brief Overview of Contemporary Theories in Management," www.managementhelp.org/mgmnt/cntmpory.htm, 2007.
16. W. Edwards Deming, *Out of Crisis* (Cambridge, MA: MIT Center for Advanced Engineering Study, 1989), 111.
17. Bill Eacho, "Quality Service Through Strategic Foodservice Partnerships," *Hosteur* 3, no. 1 (Spring 1993): 22.
18. Mary Walton, *The Deming Management Method* (New York: Putnam, 1986), 34.
19. Mary Walton, *The Deming Management Method* (New York: Putnam, 1986).
20. James A. Belasco, *Teaching the Elephant to Dance* (New York: Crown, 1990), 49.

CHAPTER 3
MOTIVATION, MORALE, AND STROKES

OUTLINE

- ❖ Introduction
- ❖ Defining motivation
- ❖ Theories and motivational philosophies
- ❖ Morale
- ❖ Strokes
- ❖ Feedback
- ❖ Conclusions
- ❖ Summary
- ❖ Discussion questions
- ❖ Notes

OBJECTIVES

When you complete this chapter, you should be able to:

1. Define motivation within the context of the chef supervisor's job
2. List the major theories and philosophies of motivation
3. Explain the elements that contribute to a motivated kitchen team

4. Describe factors that are the ingredients of morale within the kitchen
5. Understand the elements of positive stroking
6. Explain why feedback is an important element of morale
7. Describe the elements and effects of negative stroking

Case Study: APPLETON CAFETERIA

Perry had been the dishwasher for the Appleton Cafeteria since before it had been the Appleton Cafeteria. The Appleton had originally had been the "Mom and Dad's Café." Perry was the first dishwasher hired at the "Mom and Dad's Café." When the Appleton Company bought the property, he was asked to stay on.

No one seemed to know exactly how old Perry was, but he was thought to be about 60. (His original application was lost in the buyout, and his new one had never been completed because his payroll records were in good order.) If he had any family, the management or staff did not know them. Perry could barely read and write. He could, however, wash pots and pans at an amazing rate.

Perry had always been a minimum-wage hourly employee. The only raises that Perry had received in his long history with Appleton and Mom and Dad's were as a result of increases in the minimum wage. Perry's schedule had always been to work a split shift from 11:00 A.M. to 2:00 P.M. and from 6:00 to 9:00 P.M. Monday through Saturday, for 36 hours per week.

Part-time Appleton employees received no benefits. A full-time employee was someone that worked 38 or more hours per week. Appleton had no full-time employees other than managers. Only full-time employees were provided with a meal. All other employees paid half-price for all food. Water, coffee, and tea were free to all employees. Employees paid half-price for any other beverages. The level of pilferage and theft at the Appleton Cafeteria was a constant challenge for managers (there had

been four managers in the past twelve months).

When the district manager caught Perry eating a piece of fried chicken in the pot-and-pan room, he informed the general manager that Perry had stolen the food and that he was to be fired. The general manager stated that Perry had not stolen the chicken. He stated that he had given the piece of chicken, and a soft drink the district manager had not noticed, to Perry as a reward for his hard work. The district manager expressed concern about the precedent that would be set by giving free food to employees. He told the manager he would have to pay for the items himself. The general manager paid for the items as instructed.

The general manager submitted his notice the following week.

Based on what you have learned from previous chapters and the content of this chapter, answer the following questions.

- What is the overall reason for the challenges at the Appleton Cafeteria?
- What are the primary causal agents for the challenges at the Appleton Cafeteria?
- What role did supervision/management play in the decline at the Appleton Cafeteria?
- What specific steps could have been taken to avoid the current situation at the Appleton Cafeteria?
- What, specifically, can be done to overcome the challenges and generate motion in a positive direction for the Appleton Cafeteria?

INTRODUCTION

An important function performed by the chef supervisor is the creation of a positive motivational environment, one in which great kitchen team morale is present. This can be achieved by providing strokes—for example, praise wrapped in units of attention.

It is the chef supervisor's job not only to structure and arrange work but also to motivate and build morale of the kitchen team so as to achieve the quality objectives that have been established. Part of this process is to determine how well the objectives and goals are being achieved and whether there are motivational barriers to the accomplishment of these goals.

DEFINING MOTIVATION

Motivation, as distinct from morale and strokes, requires definition. Motivation contributes to morale, and stroking is part of morale. Without all three working together, it is almost impossible to create a kitchen work environment in which team building, productivity, and continuous quality improvements can take place.

Motivation is an individual's inner state that causes behavior in a way that ensures the successful accomplishment of goals and objectives. Motivation explains why people behave the way they do. The term *motivation* derives from the Latin word *movere,* which literally means "to move."[1] Although a number of definitions exist, no one definition describes motivation adequately. What is known is that motivation is concerned with three factors: what energizes behavior, what channels such behavior, and the conditions under which this behavior is maintained. The triggers and drivers of motivation are the same for all individuals. The characteristics of the job environment, in this instance the kitchen, and the characteristics of the chef supervisor (the particular disposition and leadership style) will affect the elements of motivation. The more the chef supervisor understands the kitchen team member's behavior, the better he or she should be able to influence that behavior and make it more consistent with the goals of the foodservice organization. Because quality and productivity are central to the success of the chef supervisor, creation of the appropriate motivational environment in the kitchen is key to this success.

Each person sees the world from an individual viewpoint. An individual's perception of the world is determined by his or her background and personal experiences, among other variables. The kitchen and the world generally are viewed through this personal and individual lens. Therefore, a chef supervisor should attempt to learn how each team member is likely to respond to different events and understand the diverse cultural issues that occur in the foodservice department. Each kitchen team member perceives and interprets instructions, actions, and communications in a unique way.

A team member's values and culture are a strong determinant of behavior. A *value* is any object, activity, or orientation that individuals consider very important to their way of life. *Culture,* on the other hand, refers to the team member's beliefs, practices, traditions, ideologies, and lifestyles. Values and culture have been shown to be related to decision making, motivation, communication, and supervisory success. Values are influenced largely by the culture in which we live and work.

As we move into the twenty-first century, the makeup of the workforce in the U.S. foodservice industry will change dramatically. In the late 1980s, 47 percent of the workforce were native white males. The U.S. Department of Labor estimates that in the early part of the twenty-first century, 85 percent of the individuals entering the workforce will be minorities and women, and many of these new workers will enter the foodservice industry through the kitchen.[2] According to the National Restaurant Association, in 2004, 56 percent of individuals in foodservice occupations were women.[3] Hispanics, a rapidly growing minority presence in foodservice, has grown by 5 percent since 1992, to 18 percent; and African Americans comprised 11 percent of the industry workforce in 2004.[4] The diverse nature of the industry workforce is changing the culture of the workplace in the foodservice industry. This diversity will continue to grow in the next decade.

Humans function in an integrated manner, not as individual parts. It is the total kitchen team member we are interacting with. Although it is sometimes useful to focus our attention on certain segments of personality in order to have a better understanding of the person, in the final analysis the team member should be viewed holistically, as a unified and integrated person.

Chef supervisors must come to recognize that they cannot know the nature of many of the forces influencing the behavior of individual team members, for team members often do not reveal what they are currently experiencing in their lives away from the job. What happens to team members at home or through other activities will affect how they feel about their work and other aspects of their lives. What happens away from work also influences how well they perform at work and the degree to which they want their feelings known to others.

Remember, it is impossible to have the highest-quality team without the presence of respect for people, their differences, and the strengths this diversity brings to the kitchen motivational environment.

BOX 3-1

CHEF TALK:
BUILDING MORALE

To build morale at our club, we initiated several strategies that worked in creating a sense of family. One of these was the creation of an in-club newsletter through which all of the kitchen team could share their knowledge and different training experiences. The newsletter also acknowledged special awards employees had received as a result of their culinary skills. Special events such as birthdays, new babies, and marriages were included to add a personal touch. This type of employee recognition worked wonders for morale and team spirit.

I began to cross train all employees for all positions in the kitchen. Rather than having one person on a station for years, cross training provided an opportunity for employees to learn new skills and develop a better understanding of problems in areas with which they had previously been unfamiliar. Switching positions exposed both sides of "the fence" and helped to develop problem-solving skills. These programs served as a catalyst for a strong com-mitment to excellence. It demonstrated a willingness to develop new traditions and not to simply blindly imitate the past.

By providing these opportunities, we were able to attract enthusiastic young culinarians with great potential. This provided the shot in the arm we needed, and it inspired others to seek professional development and certification and to improve performance. The combination of all these changes helped to create improved conditions and build a terrific team spirit in the kitchen. It proved to us that a chain is only as strong as its weakest link. This experience also taught me that without people behind you, bonded by a common thread, nothing can be accomplished. This type of morale results in a strong team spirit and a staff that is dedicated and committed to culinary excellence.

Tom Peer, CMC, CCE, AAC,
Culinary Institute of America,
Hyde Park, New York

FIGURE 3-1   Maslow's hierarchy of needs.

THEORIES AND MOTIVATIONAL PHILOSOPHIES

Probably the most widely accepted description of human needs is the hierarchy of needs concept put forward by Abraham Maslow. Maslow states that we as humans possess five basic needs, and these needs can be arranged in a hierarchy of importance or order in which individuals generally strive to satisfy them. The needs (see Figure 3-1), listed in Maslow's hierarchical order, are (1) physiological, (2) security, (3) social, (4) esteem, and (5) self-actualization needs.[5]

Physiological Needs   Physiological needs relate to the normal functioning of the body and include the need for food, water, air, rest, and sex. Until these needs are met, a significant portion of an individual's behavior is aimed at satisfying them. If these needs are satisfied, behavior is aimed at the next level, security needs.

Security or Safety Needs   Security or safety needs are the needs individuals require to keep themselves free from bodily and economic disaster. The foodservice organization can best help employees to satisfy their security needs through good and fair salaries, because it is with these salaries that employees can buy items such as food and housing. As security needs are satisfied, behavior tends to be aimed at satisfying social needs.

Social Needs   Social needs include individuals' desire for love, companionship, and friendship. Overall, these needs reflect people's desire to be accepted by others. As these needs are satisfied, behavior shifts to satisfying esteem needs.

Esteem Needs   Esteem needs are individuals' desire for respect and are generally divided into two categories: self-respect and respect for others. Once esteem needs are satisfied, individuals turn to satisfying self-actualization needs.

Self-Actualization Needs   Self-actualization needs are the desire to maximize whatever potential the individuals possess. For example, a motivated kitchen team member who seeks to satisfy self-actualization or

self-realization might strive to become the leader or supervisor of the
kitchen team. Self-actualization needs are at the highest level of
Maslow's hierarchy.

These needs are the same for everyone. They apply when team members are at
work, at which time there may be problems of *how well* they work. Maslow's need
hierarchy theory is consistent with the reasons people work. However, individuals
move from one level to another and are *not* at any one level in life. The motivational
and self-realization environment in the kitchen is present only when these basic
needs are met.

HERZBERG'S TWO-FACTOR THEORY

Frederick Herzberg put forward the *motivator–hygiene theory*. This theory emphasizes
the roles of motivator factors and hygiene factors (also known as maintenance factors). Proposed in 1959 by Herzberg, it is also known as the *two-factor theory* of work
motivation. The factors that produce job satisfaction are called motivator factors because they satisfy a team member's need for self-realization. According to the theory,
hygiene factors are important, but they are *not* motivators.

Herzberg's Hygiene Factors and Motivators
Dissatisfaction: Hygiene Factors

- Company policy and administration
- Supervision
- Relationship with supervisor
- Relationship with peers
- Working conditions
- Salary
- Relationship with subordinates

Satisfaction: Motivation Factors

- Opportunity for achievement
- Opportunity for recognition
- Work itself
- Responsibility
- Advancement
- Personal growth

When hygiene factors deteriorate to a level below what a team member considers
acceptable, then dissatisfaction is present. However, removing the causes of dissatisfaction does not create satisfaction and will not motivate performance. If kitchen
team members are required to work in an environment that is unpleasant, unsafe, and
hostile, then a motivational climate cannot be created until such time as the hygiene
or maintenance factors are of an acceptable level. When the hygiene factors of policy,
supervision, working conditions, relationships, and pay are good and adequate, the
stage is then set for the motivating factors.[6] These motivational factors help create
job satisfaction, which in and of itself is the primary motivating factor. In Herzberg's
theory, the opportunity for kitchen team members to advance will require them to

seek recognition, assume responsibility, and achieve success through the job. Recognition is the most important factor, more important than pay or any other element of the hygiene factors. If the job or position of a kitchen team member can be enriched to include more motivators, then the opportunity exists to have a motivated, participative member fully committed to the principles of success.

Herzberg's ideas are strongly associated with the notions of job enrichment. In 1968 he stressed that "the only way to motivate employees is through challenging work in which they can assume responsibility."[7] This he proposed as a reaction to what he called the KITA (kick-in-the-ass) methods used widely by most managers and supervisors. Central to these proposals is the idea that strategies that modify jobs can offer a more meaningful role for employees and can give them the opportunity for recognition and, ultimately, greater responsibility.

THEORY X–THEORY Y

Another motivational theory involves chef supervisors' assumptions about employees and the nature of people. Douglas McGregor, a Massachusetts Institute of Technology professor, identified two sets of these contradicting assumptions. Theory X involves assumptions that McGregor feels supervisors often use as the basis for dealing with people, whereas Theory Y represents the assumptions that McGregor feels supervisors should strive to use.[8]

Theory X

According to McGregor, Theory X assumes that the average person has an inherent dislike of work and will avoid it if possible. Because of this human characteristic of dislike of work, most people must be coerced, controlled, directed, and threatened with punishment to get them to put forth adequate effort toward the achievement of organizational objectives. The average person prefers to be directed, wishes to avoid responsibility, has relatively little ambition, and wants security above all.

This view clearly dictates that motivation will primarily be through fear and that supervisors will be required to keep tight observations and control over their subordinates. Under the Theory X assumption, supervisors must protect employees from their own shortcomings and use the heavy-handed control-and-coercion approach.

Theory Y

Theory Y assumes that the expenditure of physical and mental effort in work is as natural as play or rest. People will exercise self-direction and self-control in the service of objectives to which they are committed. Commitment to objectives is a function of the rewards associated with achievement.

Under proper conditions, the average person learns not only to accept but to seek responsibility. The capacity to exercise a relatively high degree of imagination, ingenuity, and creativity in the solution of organizational problems is widely and normally distributed in the population.[9]

In contrast to Theory X, Theory Y emphasizes supervisory leadership through participative management and permits subordinates to experience personal satisfaction as they contribute to the achievement of objectives.

On the other hand, Theory X has a part to play in situations that require a firm but necessary position of authority. It has no part to play in team building or the creation of a kitchen team in which each player is expected to contribute to the overall success of the team. The empowering of team members to take an active part in all aspects of the team is most certainly not a part of Theory X. The successful kitchen team will fall under McGregor's Theory Y, which relies on the assumption that people are naturally primed and ready to contribute; the only missing pieces are great leadership and a motivated environment.

VROOM'S EXPECTANCY MODEL

Victor Vroom's expectancy model is based on the premise that felt needs cause human behavior. The model addresses the issue of motivation strength. Motivation strength is an individual's degree of desire to perform a behavior. As this desire increases or decreases, motivation strength is said to fluctuate correspondingly:[10]

$$\text{Motivation strength} = \text{perceived value of result} \times \text{perceived probability of successful completion}$$

According to this model, motivation strength is determined by (1) the perceived value of the result of performing a behavior and (2) the perceived probability that the behavior performed will cause the result to materialize. As both of these factors increase, an individual's motivation strength and desire to perform also increase. In general, individuals tend to perform those behaviors that maximize personal rewards over the long run.

An illustration of expectancy theory applied to kitchen operations might be: A team member believes that if he or she produces meals that satisfy the foodservice establishment's standards and meet the needs of the customer consistently, then the perceived value of utilizing quality standards will produce for the individual a perceived probability of further reward and success.

THE PYGMALION EFFECT

The Pygmalion effect states that the expectations the kitchen team have of themselves will determine how well they perform. If you expect great things, great things will happen. If you expect mediocre performance, mediocre performance is what you will get. This is also known as the self-fulfilling prophecy. If you emphasize the positive and what your team can do, team members will begin to believe strongly in themselves. The more the chef supervisor tells the team how successful they can become, the more competent the team will be. When high performance and quality standards are set and team members are told they can rise to the occasion, the self-fulfilling prophecy determines that they will. Positive expectations equal positive results.[11]

MORALE

Morale is defined in Webster's dictionary as the "condition with respect to courage, discipline, confidence, enthusiasm, willingness to endure hardship within a group or individual." So far in this chapter we have examined the different motivational theories pertaining to motivating people in the workplace. These are important; they provide insight into what makes some individuals perform well and why some others do not. Motivation contributes to morale. We cannot have great kitchen morale without the application of motivational tools by the chef supervisor. The kitchen is often a pressure-filled place of work during busy meal periods. A team spirit with good morale can reduce this pressure and increase the confidence, ability, and harmony of the team, and help to deal with busy service periods.

The first and most important element of morale is the leadership style of the chef supervisor, a leadership style that continuously demonstrates respect and a caring attitude toward the team. The chef supervisor who will have the greatest impact on morale is the one who believes in people, is sensitive to their difficulties in achieving the kitchen team's goals, and is sympathetic and approachable. There are elements that contribute to morale within the kitchen team. These elements include leadership attributes and a chef supervisor who can:

Create

- A happy, relaxed atmosphere in which everyone is clear on *what* to do, *when* to do it, and *how* to do it
- A supervisory leadership style that challenges each team member to contribute the best, a healthy competition, a passion and a pride in being the best, and a team morale that provides a sense of belonging
- An atmosphere in which individuals are encouraged to share opinions and ideas

Show

- A caring awareness of individuals' problems
- A sensitivity and understanding of ethnic diversity and the special problems of integration that may exist within the team
- Respect for individual team members' dignity
- A sense of humor
- Consistency of behavior in dealing with each member of the team
- Fairness at all times
- Displeasure for poor performance when appropriate

Give

- Praise when it is merited
- Reasons for uncompromising high-quality standards

Be

- An active listener
- A coach
- A team builder

Morale is also about empowering and trusting team members to make the right decisions and gives a sense of real involvement to individuals. Figure 3-2 shows what the chef supervisor should do when empowerment and trust are in place in the kitchen.

The chef supervisor must scrupulously avoid the appearance of favoring one person over another. This may be the most difficult challenge, as no human being is totally objective in dealing with another. We all have biases. We cannot be totally objective, but we must recognize our subjectivities and compensate for them. To build morale, each individual team member must be treated fairly.

Empowerment contributes to the *esprit de corps* of the kitchen team. Trusting people is a great way to build morale.

FIGURE 3-2 Empowerment and trust.

Activators
- Give the team members important work to do.
- Allow individual team members to do their work in their own way.
- Give them the resources to do the work.
- Make them feel their decisions are part of the overall plan.
- Actively encourage teamwork.
- Are tolerant with failure.
- Celebrate successes.

Communication is also critical to morale. Team members need to know what is expected of them. Without good, constant dialogue, standards of quality, goals, and objectives for the team and the individual cannot be communicated. Be honest with the team; they want to have confidence in your leadership. They will be more inclined to feel confident when a participative involvement is demonstrated. Be available for discussion, walk around the kitchen, and be visible. Make each team member's job more interesting and challenging, get to know each individual, have a sense of his or her social needs, and set a good example.

Another important element of morale consistent with Maslow's needs hierarchy is team member's security. Therefore, a stable, nonthreatening environment must be created, one in which unpredictable supervisor mood swings are not present.

As we have observed from considering different approaches to motivation, employees generally perform at their best when they feel useful and needed, in an environment in which they are contributing and valuable team players, where they enjoy a sense of belonging, are involved in decision making, and are trusted and not oversupervised. These elements make up individual and team morale. Creating and maintaining this morale is part of the chef supervisor's job. It is very easy to determine when there is poor team morale or no morale at all in the kitchen; it is difficult to tell if morale is just average; but it is very obvious when good morale is present. It is reflected in low employee turnover and a kitchen that is well led and productive, in which team members show pride in producing high-quality, customer-focused meals.

STROKES

Strokes are units of attention; they contribute to motivation and morale. Stroking may exist in the form of positive strokes, which are strong motivating contributors to morale and come in the form of praise or rewards. Negative strokes may be reprimands or put-downs and are considered demotivators. Strokes can be physical, verbal, nonverbal, or combinations of all three. Most of the strokes we get as adults are verbal and nonverbal, as opposed to the physical ones we received as children. Routine stroking is used to describe different aspects and factors that when applied to individual kitchen team members are motivators and builders of morale. Negative stroking in the form of put-downs, insensitivity, insults, sarcasm, poor working conditions, and poor leadership are considered demotivators; they can damage relationships and destroy morale.

FIGURE 3-3 Nonverbal and verbal strokes.

Nonverbal Strokes

- Making eye contact
- Giving listening signals
- Shaking hands
- Waving

Verbal Strokes

- Using a person's name
- Checking for understanding
- Making reference to past experiences
- Praising
- Greeting
- Thanking
- Saying farewell

POSITIVE STROKES

Positive strokes are necessary in the kitchen to satisfy the esteem and ego needs of individuals. At its simplest, a positive stroke may be a smile from the chef supervisor or a nod of recognition. Figure 3-3 provides examples of nonverbal and verbal strokes.

Positive stroking is also about catching team members doing a good job. The greatest example and the highest level of stroking is to receive praise in front of the team and other department employees.

The highest performance—the highest overall quality—is achieved when there is buy-in by the team members. This is achieved by involving team members in determining team direction and goals. When the team members feel that the organization's vision is "their" vision, they will achieve. Creating buy-in is part of stroking.

When a climate of cooperation and communication is established through organized, sensible stroking, individuals become team-participative. This is a challenge for the chef supervisor and the kitchen team, but the potential rewards for the foodservice establishment are great.

BENEFITS

Strokes are very important motivators, but not the most important. The prospect of earning more money does not motivate as much as recognition, responsibility, and the prospect of advancement. However, incentives and benefits can be used as methods of positive stroking. Organizations that provide health care and insurance benefits usually are ones that invest in people, that care, and that have low employee turnover. The costs of being sick and staying healthy are high for most people, especially lower-paid employees. The benefits of group programs of health care, insurance, and wellness schemes include reduced stress and increased motivation and morale.

INCENTIVES AND AWARDS

Incentives and awards are positive strokes and team reinforcements. Small rewards may be more effective than large ones. The small rewards may become a cause for

FIGURE 3-4   Strokes: little things with big impact.

Keep a calendar of team members' birthdays and recognize them with a cake, flowers, or a card, or by simply wishing them a happy birthday.

- Celebrate happy family events with team members.
- Have a special meal with the kitchen team to celebrate achieving a particular goal.
- Create a player-of-the-week or -month program.
- Dine with team members on a regular basis.
- Send thank you notes regularly.
- Create incentives to address gaps or needs in quality and production.
- Provide opportunities for team members to attend food shows or culinary arts–related seminars.

positive celebration. Awards, prizes, and ceremonies are important to kitchen team members. What Tom Peters refers to as "little things with high impact"[12] are shown in Figure 3-4. Whatever programs, awards, or rewards are instituted, it must be ensured that all team members are included and are eligible to participate.

NEGATIVE STROKES

Examples of negative strokes are reprimanding or putting down of a team member. These are also known as demotivators. If these are in widespread use in the kitchen, then morale is nonexistent and the leader is probably operating in a Theory X mode—a supervisor who leads through fear. If there are no positive strokes available to team members, then they will work for negative strokes rather than suffer the least acceptable situation—no strokes at all. Examples of common negative strokes or demotivators that should be avoided are shown in Figure 3-5.

FIGURE 3-5   Negative strokes—to be avoided.

- Inconsistent behavior by the chef supervisor
- Abusive or abrasive behavior
- Poor working conditions
- Fear of supervisor, loss of job, or change
- No team atmosphere
- Lack of recognition
- Poor supervisory leadership
- Lack of incentives, ambitions, or goals for the kitchen team
- Use of ridicule or sarcasm
- Oversupervision and lack of trust
- Unfair job allocations
- Decisions for the team made without consultation
- Lack of communication
- Lack of respect for persons of different age, ethnicity, gender, physical abilities and qualities, and sexual preference

When people are unhappy at work, absenteeism increases, productivity goes down, the quality of the meals produced is lower, and employee turnover increases, which all adds up to a failing business. Negative strokes contribute to low morale.

Chef supervisors are required to supervise, which from time to time will require some negative stroking, but this can be equally balanced by pointing to positive stroking on good performance.

Strokes are part of morale building, which together make up the motivational climate. As has been pointed out, motivation comes from within each individual. Simply removing negative stroking and demotivators does not really motivate kitchen team members; it simply brings them to average satisfaction. Therefore, a chef supervisor's leadership qualities and supervisory style will exert a great influence over the team and will determine if individual team members motivate themselves.

FEEDBACK

Feedback is not only a useful method of providing information to the team member on performance, it is also an excellent method of giving reinforcement and positive strokes. Quality feedback is driven by a number of factors, of which the first and most important is that *feedback must be intended to help the person.* Additional characteristics of quality feedback are shown in Figure 3-6.

The purpose of giving feedback is to reinforce team members' commitment and abilities. It should be given when requested by a team member. Feedback should be given on two positive levels, "needs improvement" or "is doing well."

Excellent morale within the kitchen is instilled by a chef supervisor who believes that most team members want to do a good job and in most instances will do a good job. The achievement and success of the team are the results of each employee at all levels of the team.

As Daryl Hartley Leonard, CEO of Hyatt Hotel Corporation, states: "If there is anything I have learned in my 27 years in the service industry, it is this; 99 percent of all employees want to do a good job. How they perform is simply a reflection of the one for whom they work."[13]

FIGURE 3-6   Characteristics of quality feedback.

- It is intended to help the person.
- It is given directly to the person (face to face).
- It actually describes what the team member is doing and the effects the actions are having.
- It is a description of a person's actions, not a type of person.
- It is specific, rather than general, with good, clear, recent examples.
- It is given at a time when the team member appears ready to accept it and as soon after the event as possible.
- It is given in private, where other team members cannot overhear.
- It includes only those things that the team member can reasonably be expected to do something about.
- It does not cover more than the team member can handle at any one time.
- It is always given when asked for.

CONCLUSIONS

What motivates? As we have learned, each person requires different things. The expression, "Different strokes for different folks," is perhaps the best way of summing up motivation, morale, and strokes. In the kitchen, people want to join in a group or pursue quality objectives that will enable them to realize their value and potential. They need to see that what they are doing is not wasted effort but is making a contribution to the kitchen team's goals. They must see value in what they are doing. Motivation comes not only from activity but also from the desire to become participative members of the team.

As the positive work environment of the kitchen develops and gains momentum, the team will support what they create. Being part of the quality objective-setting process is motivating; it allows people to feel needed and that their contributions *are* making a difference. When kitchen employees are given the opportunity to have input, they have a stake in the issue. Seeing objectives reached and becoming a reality along with helping to shape the future is fulfilling. Participation in setting objectives and being empowered to make decisions builds team spirit; it enhances morale and allows each team member to feel important.

Stroking and recognizing kitchen employees for accomplishing particular tasks also contribute to team morale. Team members want credit for personal achievements and appreciation for their participation in the overall kitchen team objectives. Often, giving team members recognition is another way of saying thanks. Kitchen employees are motivated when they know exactly what is expected of them and will then have the confidence to do it successfully. No one wants to assume a task that is vague. Give clear instructions; make the unknown known.

Motivation rises in the kitchen when the objective goals and individual responsibilities are made clear by the chef supervisor. Don't discourage individual team members' growth. Encourage the team to stretch; give them opportunities to try new things and acquire new skills. Chef supervisors should not feel threatened by the achievements and successes of individuals but should be supportive of their success.

Allow the team members to fail as well as succeed. Build a team spirit and *esprit de corps,* which says to each member of the team, "If you grow, we all benefit." Chef supervisors can establish morale through trust, direction, high standards of conduct, encouraging innovation, providing adequate training, treating each member with dignity, and being a servant of the team.

Summary

Chef supervisors cannot motivate individuals, but they can create a kitchen environment in which individuals can motivate themselves. Each person sees the world from a different and individual viewpoint. Chef supervisors should therefore learn how each kitchen team member is likely to respond to different events.

Motivational theories have demonstrated that most individuals are highly motivated when they can see their value to the goals of the food-service organization. Among these theories are Maslow's needs hierarchy theory, Herzberg's two-factor theory, Douglas McGregor's Theory X and Theory Y, Vroom's expectancy theory, and the Pygmalion effect.

Morale within the kitchen is closely related to the leadership ability of the chef supervisor who can create a happy atmosphere, show respect for individuals, seek their opinions, and build a team environment.

Strokes are units of attention that contribute to motivation and morale. Negative strokes such as put-downs, insensitivity, insults, sarcasm, and poor working conditions are demotivators, which damage relationships and destroy morale in the kitchen. Positive strokes are necessary to satisfy the esteem needs of individual kitchen team members. Feedback is an important element of giving strokes.

Discussion Questions

1. What is the definition of motivation, and how can the chef supervisor create a motivating environment within the kitchen?
2. What are the elements of Maslow's hierarchy of needs theory?
3. What methods can a chef supervisor implement to motivate the kitchen team?
4. What are the elements of Herzberg's two-factor theory?
5. What are Theory X and Theory Y as motivational concepts?
6. What factors contribute to developing morale within the kitchen?
7. What are the effects of using positive stroking?
8. Why is feedback important to morale in the kitchen work environment?
9. What effects do negative strokes have on motivation and morale?

Notes

1. Arthur Sherman, George Bohlander, and Herbert Crudden, *Managing Human Resources,* 8th ed. (Cincinnati, OH: South-Western, 1988), 290.
2. Mary L. Tanke, *Human Resources Management for the Hospitality Industry* (Albany, NY: Delmar, 1990), 45.
3. National Restaurant Association, *State of the Restaurant Industry Workforce: An Overview* (Chicago: National Restaurant Association, June 2006), 9; www.restaurant.org/research/ind_glance.cfm.
4. Ibid., 10–11.
5. Abraham Maslow, *Motivation and Personality,* 2nd ed. (New York: Harper & Row, 1970).
6. Frederick Herzbreg, *Work and the Nature of Man* (Cleveland, OH: World, 1966).
7. Frederick Herzberg, "One More Time: How Do You Motivate Employees?" *Harvard Business Review* 46, no. 1 (1968): 55.
8. Douglas McGregor, *The Human Side of Enterprise* (New York: McGraw-Hill, 1960).
9. Ibid.
10. Victor H. Vroom, *Work and Motivation* (New York: John Wiley, 1964).
11. Tanke, *Human Resources Management for the Hospitality Industry,* 204.
12. Tom Peters, *Thriving on Chaos* (New York: Harper & Row, 1988), 371.
13. Daryl Hartley Leonard, "Perspectives," *Newsweek,* August 24, 1987, p. 19.

CHAPTER 4

BUILDING TEAMWORK
IN THE KITCHEN

- ❖ Conclusions
- ❖ Discussion questions
- ❖ Notes

OBJECTIVES

When you complete this chapter, you should be able to:

1. Identify and describe the rationale for a kitchen team approach
2. Know and understand the principles of building a kitchen team
3. Identify the crucial elements of developing a kitchen team commitment
4. Define the elements of establishing goals and objectives for kitchen team building
5. Describe the key aspects of facilitating kitchen teamwork
6. List the major criteria associated with effective kitchen teams
7. Define empowerment
8. Explain the requirements of understanding and trust in relation to team building
9. List the steps essential to improving kitchen teamwork
10. Explain the requirements of interteam dependence in the foodservice industry
11. Identify and describe the elements that contribute to the creation of an organizational "vision"

Case Study: SOUTHERTON COUNTRY CLUB

Bob Larson, general manager of the Southerton Country Club, was excited about the inauguration of the club's first annual Epicurean Experience. The Epicurean Experience was three days of food and fun for which club members paid a flat fee. The general manager consulted extensively with event-planning specialists and chefs specializing in the various types of foods to be served, such as the roasting of a whole steer over an open fire. When the planning was complete and the menus determined, the general manager met with the chef and provided him with all the details about what would be required of his kitchen staff. To assist the chef with the specialty items, he hired a consulting chef to oversee the preparation of the major items for each of the nine primary meals.

The quantity and complexity of the foods to be prepared required that the kitchen crew work overtime for five days before the event and every day during the three-day event. The event was a major success. The consulting chef received tremendous praise from Bob and the club members for the outstanding food, service, and overall experience. Bob personally thanked the chef for the hard work of his staff.

Immediately following the conclusion of the event, Bob contracted with the consulting chef for a repeat performance the following year and began working with the consulting chef to develop menus and the event planners to create the theme. When Bob mentioned the planning that was taking place to the chef and other staff members, they showed little enthusiasm for the next year's event. Bob actually felt that they did not support a repeat of the event. Many of the staff indicated that they probably would not be available to put in the overtime required and that Mr. Larson might need to consider arranging for an outside crew to handle the event.

Based on what you have learned from previous chapters and the content of this chapter, answer the following questions.

- What is the overall reason for the challenges at the Southerton Country Club?
- What are the primary causal agents for the challenges at the Southerton Country Club?
- What role did supervision/management play in the decline at the Southerton Country Club?
- What specific steps could have been taken to avoid the current situation at the Southerton Country Club?
- What, specifically, can be done to overcome the challenges and generate motion in a positive direction at the Southerton Country Club?

WHAT IS TEAMWORK?

No individual is more important than the others. People on the team share varying degrees of responsibility, but the success of the kitchen team is really determined by the performance of each individual and the contribution of the individual makes the team effort.

> Never tell people how to do things. Tell them what you want to achieve and they will surprise you with their ingenuity.
>
> General George S. Patton, 1944

Teamwork is the fuel that allows common people to produce uncommon results:

T *ogether*
E *veryone*
A *chieves*
M *ore*

More and more management theories are being influenced by people who advocate teamwork, vision, trust, openness, flexibility, and participation. These concepts, ideas, and values form the core of team building. An important reason why foodservice organizations seek to develop teams is because teams are more effective at improving work processes and providing high-quality food and service.

Part of the approach to quality management is to ensure that everyone has a clear understanding of what is required of them and how their processes relate to the foodservice business as a whole. The more people understand the total business and what is going on around them, the greater the role each kitchen team member can play in continuous improvement.

Teamwork, which is vital to successful management programs, has become the dominant form of organizational design. Critical to effective teamwork is the need to become an effective team player and, indeed, to become a team leader. In this new team design, chef supervisors have come to realize that they have better, more inclusive communication with all staff. This means that people skills have become extremely important, and even chef supervisors will have to learn how to follow. This new approach to culinary supervision is also about chefs becoming coaches, facilitators, and teachers, rather than administrators, inspectors, bureaucrats, directors, and control agents. Chef supervisors are moving to become builders of teams and developers of strategies of commitment from employees. They maximize the value of employees by improving the organizational resources, by fostering teamwork, and by rewarding contributions by individual team members.

According to Marshall J. Cook, writing in *Motivating People,*

You don't want compliant subordinates. You want committed co-workers who identify their self-interest with yours and want excellent job performance. They'll work just as hard and just as well when you're not watching— because they're not working for you, they're working with you.[1]

A mature, well-trained kitchen/foodservice team is capable of making better-quality decisions than individuals. The use of a team approach improves the overall quality of decision making, and the level of commitment becomes much higher. When kitchen team members share the process of problem solving, they are more likely to "buy in" to the property and the company's plans and to do everything possible to transform the plans into reality. Collective wisdom is virtually always superior to individual wisdom.

This team approach, therefore, offers to progressive forward-thinking chef supervisors a positive management philosophy that gets results while at the same time respects each kitchen team member—his or her needs and capabilities.

Today, in many successful foodservice organizations the most widespread form of employee involvement is through teamwork. Simply defined, *teamwork* is a group of people organized into teams, doing similar or related work, who meet regularly to identify, analyze, and solve product, to process quality and operational problems, and to improve general guest satisfaction. The modern-day parable "Lessons from Geese," shown in Figure 4-1, speaks directly to what a team is and its effectiveness.

FIGURE 4-1 Teams: lessons from geese.

When you see a flock of geese heading south for the winter and flying in a "V" formation, you might consider what science has discovered as to why they fly that way. As each bird flaps its wings, it creates an uplift for the bird immediately following. By flying in a "V" formation, the whole flock adds at least 71 percent more flying range than would be possible if each bird flew on its own.

> People who share a common direction and sense of purpose can get where they are going more quickly and easily because they are traveling on the thrust of one another.

Each member of the flock is responsible for getting itself to wherever the flock is going: Each member of the flock looks to itself—not the leader—to determine what to do.

Every member knows the direction of the flock. Sharing the common direction makes assuming the leadership role easier. Every member is willing to assume leadership when the flock needs it. When the lead goose gets tired, a fresher goose from the back of the flock assumes the leadership position. This allows the flock to maintain the fastest pace possible.

Followers encourage leaders. Flock members honk from the rear to encourage leaders to maintain a fast pace.

Members of the flock look after each other, helping all members to achieve the goal. If a wounded goose goes down, two geese follow to protect and feed it until it either recovers or dies.

> If we have the sense of a goose, we will stand by each other.

When the nature of the work changes, the geese reorganize themselves for best results. They fly in a "V," land in waves, and feed in fours.

Source: unknown.

GROUPS AND TEAMS

"What is it that most of us want from work? We would like to find the most effective, most rewarding, and most productive way of working together."[2] Team building involves getting each employee to feel a sense of belonging and ownership in what they are doing as a kitchen team. It has been said that there is no other business that requires more teamwork. With a team effort, and with everyone helping each other, the job is so remarkably easy that few could imagine how it could be done any other way.

Dealing with a group of individuals is not quite the same as dealing with one individual. More is required when a person has to lead a team.

"Teamwork can be seen and felt—it is a tangible thing. The real problem is very often people are organized into groups; they are called teams but don't act like a team."[3] The words *group* and *team* tend to be used interchangeably, but one expression is central to both concepts, and that is *common identity*.

When is a group a team? If it is either, does it need leadership? If so, are there any special reasons that make the role of the leader more crucial in some circumstances than others? This is the central core of leadership and kitchen teamwork. What is clear, however, is that managers should at least appreciate their role as leaders and be able to see when the label "team" might be appropriate.

It is quite easy to spot sets of individuals who are not yet a team. They meet, and someone says, "What do we do now"? or "Who is going to start first?" or "Who is going to do what?" "Teamwork is one of the key features of involvement; without it, difficulty will be found in gaining the commitment and participation of people throughout the organization."[4]

When the concept of kitchen team building is adopted, it becomes easier to apply quality philosophies. It also provides encouragement for each team member to work together to develop a kitchen team spirit. It helps people to get to know each other so that they in turn can learn to trust, respect, and appreciate individual talent and abilities.

ABOUT TEAMS

Many leading foodservice executives see the formation of teams as a solution to the problems of continual quality guest–foodservice interactions. This means facilitating people working together, instilling a sense of teamwork, and recognizing the interdependence of all departments (guests react holistically). Plain and simple, a kitchen team is a group of individuals working together to achieve a common goal. A group of individuals performing their jobs to the best of their ability while supporting each other is successful teamwork. Members of the kitchen team recognize their interdependence and understand both personal and kitchen team goals. "Teams bring together skills and experience that collectively exceed those of any individual. Consequently teams can respond to a variety of challenges, for example, process improvement, product development, or customer service, more readily and more effectively."[5]

When one person is unable to perform at 100 percent, the difference must be made up by the other team members. This places additional stress on those teammates because they will have to work harder to meet the same goal. When this happens, it is clearly noticeable. It is extremely gratifying at the end of a successful day to know that all kitchen team members have pulled together and reached the goals.

BOX 4-1

CHEF TALK: TEAM BUILDING

Sometimes I think I'm spoiled because I work in a very controlled atmosphere. The Balsams Grand Resort Hotel is the only structure of any significance in Dixville Notch in New Hampshire. One-third of my kitchen staff are chef apprentices. They work, eat, and live there, and many of them play there. It's not surprising, therefore, that there is a sense of family and what makes it so is a strong team spirit.

Teamwork is very important at the Balsams. For me, it's vital for professionalism in the foodservice industry. I coach our apprentices on the importance of team spirit and the value of helping and supporting one another within the kitchen team. Team building is part of developing our young chefs. In addition to cooking skills, they also learn how to interact with each other. They learn to respect each member of the hotel team and the contribution each makes toward ensuring that our guests have a wonderful experience at the Balsams. They appreciate the standards our team sets, particularly in the area of sanitation and professional courtesy, and most importantly, they learn to respect themselves.

The nature of our work at the Balsams is both physically and mentally demanding. We work most weekends and public holidays; we are here early in the morning and late at night. Therefore, constant ongoing coaching is necessary to keep our kitchen team inspired and motivated. Team building, I find, requires a conscious effort. I ask the team for their input every day. We have a five-minute meeting each night at which time we discuss and assess the events of the day. Our apprentices are inspired by the different distinguished visiting chefs who visit the Balsams as part of our visiting chefs lecture series. We also encourage our apprentices to enter food shows. This is a great tool for developing teamwork. All the apprentices support the competition entry which produces a great team spirit.

At the beginning of each "season," we come together as a group and brainstorm. We discuss ways to improve menus and production methods and we try to identify new food trends. I seek the opinions of our chefs on new dishes and have them critique these dishes. Together we establish goals for the forthcoming year. This involves the apprentices identifying what they see as priorities in their professional development.

Each day we sit down together and eat as a group. Building a team is not an easy task, but without teamwork we would not be successful. We have a warm caring environment at the Balsams; team building contributes to this success. Our kitchen employees are a team—they have a sense of pride in their profession with respect for firm, fair, and friendly leadership and have a strong loyalty to our hotel.

Charles Carroll, CEC, AAC,
Executive Chef,
River Oaks Country Club,
Houston, Texas
(Formerly Executive Chef, The Balsams
Grand Resort Hotel, Dixville Notch,
New Hampshire)

DEVELOPING A KITCHEN TEAM

The development of a kitchen team requires the chef supervisor to think about a number of factors. One of these factors is why people become committed to a team. Figure 4-2 lists the primary reasons an individual commits to a team. The level at which each team member feels affected by these primary reasons will ultimately determine the level of his or her commitment to the team. The more that team members feel it is in their best interest to be members of the team, the greater will be the commitment they will have to the team.

FIGURE 4-2   Primary reasons for team commitment.

- **Self-interest.** The person believes he or she will gain a personal advantage by being a member of the kitchen team.
- **Belief in a vision.** The person believes he or she is helping a greater vision come to fruition.
- **Belief in the leader.** The person feels loyalty to the leader of the team.
- **Common values.** The person shares the team's set of basic beliefs about what is said and what is not important.
- **Mutual support.** The person feels a sense of comradeship with his or her kitchen teammates.
- **Sense of duty.** The person is committed because he or she believes that this is part of the price to be paid for being on the team.
- **Demanding tasks.** The person is committed because he or she wants to achieve goals or a standard of accomplishment that requires the assistance of others.
- **Feeling of accomplishment.** The person is committed to the team because by working together, the members participate in a shared celebration of success.
- **Structured socialization.** New people are welcomed and are made to feel a part of the team.

In the late 1970s a "new" philosophy of service was introduced to the dinner-house segment of the restaurant industry. This philosophy of service, which is very common today, was a team service system. The server was no longer assigned a specific set of tables and held responsible for that set. The server was expected to work as part of a total property service team, with the common focus of providing the highest possible level of service to all guests. This service system required a commitment by all team members to the success of the whole rather than just the success of their portion. This service system was readily adopted. It was a good fit to the dinner house, where efficiency of service was considered as important by the guest as personalization of the service.

Although service of the table by multiple servers diminished the personal aspect of the service to some degree, it made up for that in the efficiency of the service. Food came to the table hotter, beverages were refilled with greater regularity, and in general, a higher degree of the guest's needs were met. This service system made the concepts of self-interest, mutual support, sense of duty, and common values real and very connected to the individual's and team's success.

The chef supervisor has the ability to build that same team model in the kitchen. Building the kitchen team begins with the chef supervisor communicating the connection between the team members self-interest and the vision, both that of the company and that of the chef supervisor.

ORGANIZATIONAL AND OPERATIONAL TEAM STANDARDS

Ensuring that action follows insight requires the chef supervisor to establish the organizational and operational standards of the team. The more the team is involved in this process, the greater the "buy-in." The standards include team composition, scope of team and individual responsibilities, performance expectations, performance appraisal, timelines, and resources. Determination of all of these characteristics will be based on the anticipated work to be assigned to the team.

- *Team composition* is the combination of skills, knowledge, and physical and mental capability of the individuals and the number of individuals needed to accomplish the work assigned to the team in an effective and efficient manner. For example, the composition of the scullery team will include individuals with the physical capacity to lift heavy items with a high degree of regularity. The team members will need to have been trained or be willing to be trained in the proper operation of the dishwashing and pot-washing equipment and the janitorial equipment. The members of the scullery team may not need to have the requesite level of knowledge to determine and maintain the china, flatware, and glassware inventory.
- *Scope of team and individual responsibility* is both the amount of work and the complexity of work assigned to the team and ultimately to the individual. For example, the banquet prep team may be responsible for the preparation of food for the catering in the hotel, but they have no responsibility for determining the supplies needed and making certain these supplies are available. The scope of responsibility of the scullery team will probably include but not be limited to the ongoing cleaning, sanitizing, and returning to stock all china, flatware, and glassware used in the operation. The determination of appropriate inventory levels of china, glassware, or flatware would probably not be part of their scope of responsibilities. The individual members' responsibilities will be based on their assigned work. The scullery team member assigned to dishwashing during a particular meal period will be responsible for the cleaning, sanitizing, and returning to stock all china, flatware, and glassware used during that time, as well as maintenance of the dishwashing area in orderly, safe, and sanitary condition.
- *Performance expectations* are the clear definition of what the expected outcomes are to be from the work assigned. For example, the banquet prep team is assigned the preparation of canapés for 500 guests. Performance expectations will include the quality (taste, appearance, accuracy of recipe duplication) of the finished canapés; finishing the canapés on time; completing the correct amount of canapés; providing the canapés ordered, presenting the canapés in an attractive and appetizing manner; and protecting the safety of the canapés during preparation and storage.
- *Performance appraisal* is the evaluation of the completed work, which must be based on clear communication of how the performance will be measured. For example, the measurement of the team's attainment of the performance expectations that were communicated may include the following actions by the chef supervisor: random product tasting; inspection of finished products; regular inspection of preparation and storage areas; and guest satisfaction surveys. The effectiveness of performance appraisal is directly tied to the immediacy of the feedback. Once the appraisal is complete, feedback should be provided to the team and individuals, with direction for correction and improvement.
- *Time* refers to both the time requirements that come with assigned work and the general time requirements for the team and individuals. For example, a general requirement is that team members report on time for work and that they will produce an acceptable amount of product during a shift. A time requirement tied to assigned work is an order for 500 canapés by 5:30 P.M. today.

- *Resources* are the number of team members, equipment, and facilities needed for the team to perform its assigned work, as well as the food cost and overall expense expectations for the team and its work. For example, the team has a limited number of members, equipment, and space to be used in the preparation of the 500 canapés that have been ordered, and that is not the only order the team has for the day. It will be necessary to prioritize and use the available resources in an efficient manner to deliver on all orders not only in a quality manner but within the food cost target set for the team's work.

ESTABLISHING GOALS AND OBJECTIVES

Goals give a kitchen team something at which to aim. They may be broad and can be achieved in a variety of ways. An example of a goal might be: "*To improve food quality levels substantially.*" Goals are short, general statements of purpose and direction. On the other hand, objectives are very clear statements of what output you need to achieve. "*To reduce complaints in the dining room by 75 percent by year's end.*" Effective objectives are more comprehensive and, as shown in Figure 4-3, should be, according to Steve Smith, "SMART".[6]

The "buy-in" of team members is critical to the achievement of the goals and objectives of the team. Shared kitchen team goals are present when all members have participated in a process that clarifies the kitchen team's collective goals. Effective kitchen team members know and understand the purpose, objectives, and performance measures of the team. All members need to believe that the kitchen team's goals are both achievable and important. If the team's expressed goals seem to be impossible to achieve, team members will become cynical and demotivated. Frustration and disillusionment are the consequences of a kitchen team's failing to ensure that action follows insight.

FIGURE 4-3 Team objectives should be *SMART.*

- **Specific.** Express objectives in terms of the specific results to be achieved, not in terms of the activities needed to achieve them—that is, outputs, not inputs. Avoid ambiguity.
- **Measurable.** Identify what measures will be used to judge success. Make them as quantifiable and specific as possible—for example, time/quantity/quality/cost. Use customer-related measures as well as internal measures.
- **Agreed.** The team should have the opportunity to discuss and "buy in" to the objective rather than simply have it imposed.
- **Realistic.** The objectives are to be neither too easy, so that talents are underused, nor too difficult, so that the team may burn out. Take past performance into account in assessing realism. Be sure the objective is achievable given the resources available and the demands of other priorities.
- **Timebound.** The objectives should include a date by which they should be achieved. Also include interim milestones and review points if the overall timescale is long. Choose an appropriate time frame relative to the complexity of the task.

Source: Steve Smith, *Build That Team* (London: Kogan Page, 1997), 45.

FACILITATING KITCHEN TEAMWORK

A team of foodservice individuals—kitchen team members, servers, stewards, storeroom workers, supervisors, management, etc.—requires a great deal more coordination and integration of its efforts than a "group."

Just because a group is called a team does not mean its members will automatically function as a team. Teams may appear to be easy to form and operate, but it takes hard work by everyone involved for a kitchen team to be successful.

The role of a "team facilitator" or "leader" consists of leading team discussions and group processes so that individuals learn, and kitchen team members feel that the experience is positive and worthwhile. "A team leader is the person responsible for assuring that people will want to work together to achieve a common goal or objective. The important idea here is to want to *work together*, so a leader does not need to coerce, but rather facilitates the elements necessary for the team to perform well."[7]

Typical activities for a chef supervisor include team activities in which quality improvements are assessed. In group discussions in which all team members feel committed to the quality improvement actions, an enhanced awareness of kitchen team efforts usually exists. Participation by all kitchen team members is facilitated, and they are invited to present their viewpoints, levels of expertise, and attitudes regarding topics of quality. Team activities stimulate thinking, create enthusiasm, and assist in analyzing different approaches to quality service.

DECISION MAKING AND THE KITCHEN TEAM

Often in the past, chef supervisors failed to invite comments or feedback on initiatives from kitchen team members. Our kitchen team members expect leaders to "take charge," but leadership is also about service; therefore, the constituency leadership represents must reflect the views of that constituency.

When people work closely together, what one person does usually affects the other. Yet the chef supervisor often makes decisions or takes actions that affect kitchen team members without consulting them or even notifying them in advance. Doing so, unfortunately, usually upsets the kitchen team members who are kept in the dark and destroys good working relationships.

Why does the chef supervisor sometimes neglect to consult those affected by his or her actions? Usually, it simply doesn't occur to the decision maker, or it is assumed there is no need. Perhaps the chef supervisor thinks he or she already knows what the kitchen team members will say, or are sure the right decision has been made. Because the supervisor believes he or she has the authority to do so, the supervisor just "tells" the other person what has been done and expects that person to accept it. People do not like being controlled by others, even if what is decided is in their own interest. Kitchen team members like to participate in the decision-making process, even if they would have made the same decision anyway. The chef supervisor should always consult anyone who would be affected by any new decision.

WORKING TOGETHER

As each of us knows, it is possible to win at one level and lose at another—in other words, to get what is wanted yet make an enemy; or not to obtain what is wanted but strengthen a working relationship. That means thinking, "I will treat this person well whether or not I like what he or she thinks or does."

"Many believe that we should deal with difficult people in the same way those people treat them, by reciprocating what they receive. This may be called an 'eye for an eye' policy. If the other person yells at them, they yell back. If the other person insults them, they insult that person right back."[8] The "eye for an eye" policy is based on a traditional approach to justice. Unfortunately, in a modern organization, it is largely ineffectual and even dangerous, because the "victim" is often harmed as much as the perpetrator. Reciprocation sets off a negative spiral and does not resolve anything.

Each of us sees the events in our own lives and other people's behavior from our own vantage point. Even though only "part" of the whole is seen, each of us tends to think that our personal perspective is accurate and is representative of what is occurring. Unfortunately, there are at least two sides to every story and many ways to view every incident.

Reason and emotion must be balanced. It is understood that in some instances too much emotion can diminish performance. On the other hand, an organization with little or no emotion is dull and lifeless. Some experts say that the most effective leaders are extremely emotional—and even act as cheerleaders—about the goals they are trying to achieve.

Responding impulsively and emotionally to a difficult person usually only worsens the relationship, especially if one person is making the other person angry. A good working relationship with a difficult person requires a reasonable approach.

Whenever a kitchen team member is blamed for something that goes wrong, rather than looking at how the whole kitchen team was working together, the individual kitchen team member is undermined along with his or her sense of belonging to the team. A message is also sent to the kitchen team that individual performance is more important than the entire kitchen team performance.

UNDERSTANDING AND TRUST

Chef supervisors cannot deal effectively with difficult team members or difficult situations unless they understand them. Most people assume that what other people say is absurd or untrue and try to imagine what could be wrong with them to make them say something so ridiculous.

Therefore, working relationships are better among trusting people. People who can be counted on to keep their word are trustworthy.

> *If I believe you will do what you say, then I perceive you as trustworthy.*
> *If I suspect you will not, your credibility with me is low.*

Faith in people is fragile. Once broken, it is difficult to restore. Being trustworthy most of the time does not earn trust. Every breach of trust diminishes one person's confidence in another. Even if someone keeps his word nine out of ten times, others will remember the one time he did not and wonder when he will disappoint them next.

In any foodservice organization, when people are being difficult and one person has more authority than another, it is tempting to force or coerce others to do as you wish. However, compliance through coercion (such as threatening harm) provides only short-term gains and long-term losses. All team members resent being coerced and eventually

BOX 4-2

CHEF TALK:
TRUSTING YOUR KITCHEN TEAM

I learned some valuable lessons with regard to my co-workers during my time with the U.S. Culinary Olympic Team. When someone is trying out for the team, it is initially an individual effort. Later, when the team is formed, it becomes necessary to retrain one's self for the team effort. What makes a good chef supervisor in this case is one who is able to balance the many commitments. The demands from the U.S. Culinary Team may easily take more time than any other item such as your job or personal life. In my case, when the time arrived for tryouts, I had to make sure that my employer was in agreement to get the time off and to help financially.

Fortunately, I was able to build a strong team of chefs at the club, and this assured consistency in the quality of the foodservice operation while I was away. This requires placing a great deal of trust in the kitchen team and also trust in the chef supervisor from the employer.

Later, when I started my own restaurant, I used the time away from the restaurant in a positive way. Each time I had to go to a team practice, I made sure my guests knew about it;

and when I returned, I cooked special Olympic meals and made them aware of what I was doing. I had my own local support group who were cheering me on every step of the way. My kitchen team also benefited from the experience by seeing the new items prepared and from the projects I was working on. Being involved with the U.S. Culinary Team provided me with sufficient publicity to assure me of being able to find many qualified professionals who wished to work with me at the restaurant.

The important lesson I learned was that I could trust my team and leave my sous chef in charge. While that was a hectic time professionally, it also proved to be a very rewarding time when I, as captain, led our team to a Gold Medal victory. I could not have had any of this success without my kitchen team behind me; it also proved that by treating people with respect and demonstrating trust, they will always rise to the occasion.

Klaus Friedenreich, CMC, AAC,
Director, The Culinary Art
Institute of Fort Lauderdale,
Fort Lauderdale, Florida

express that resentment in angry outbursts or acts of revenge. Coercion creates competition to see who will win, and methods to create win/win solutions are overlooked. Rather than solve difficulties, coercion usually just perpetuates or escalates them.

A difficulty should be seen as a problem that both parties wish to solve through cooperation. Both should be on the same side of the line, attacking the problem instead of each other. Managing difficult behavior is not a contest. It is a challenge to invent a solution that all team members support and feel committed to implementing.

It is tempting to scorn and reject people who do not fulfill our expectations. A disappointed person becomes critical and disdainful, slamming the door on communication and giving up on problem solving.

INTERTEAM DEPENDENCE

Often, foodservice kitchen teams regard one another as neutral but still fail to communicate or recognize their interdependence. In the foodservice industry, kitchen teams must constantly interact, because guests think holistically, whether in the foodservice

FIGURE 4-4 Elements of inter-kitchen team dependence.

- Foodservice organizations can be likened to living organisms.
- The whole organism or system consists of a series of parts. Each part plays an important and vital role in the provision of a complete and high-quality foodservice experience.
- If any part of the system is defective, it will damage the entire organization.
- If kitchen teams are not sympathetic to one another and do not work together in a complementary fashion, the foodservice product may break up; if the discord is serious, it could become irreparable.
- A key function in maintaining a healthy foodservice product is for the boundaries that exist among its parts to remain open, allowing for the exchange of ideas and information. If boundaries are closed, the organism itself (the foodservice product) will be seriously damaged and possibly disappear.

or hotel sector of the industry. They don't separate segments or portions of their foodservice experience; they react and evaluate the entire product or service. Elements of inter-kitchen team dependence are shown in Figure 4-4.

The process of improving interdependence among kitchen teams requires a conscious effort at cross-team communications. Also, if team members get to know one another on a more personal basis, they will be more inclined to work together and to consider one another when they are making decisions. The need for personal contact becomes greater when the possibility of conflict exists.

Kitchen teams that work well together strengthen the entire foodservice organization. Each kitchen team has both internal suppliers and internal customers. As kitchen teams learn to collaborate, they overcome insularity and narrow thinking. Developing interteam collaboration also serves to strengthen individual kitchen teams.

> Southwest Airlines has two customer types—external and internal.
> Passengers pay our way—they are our external customers. Employees are
> our internal customers. As CEO, I must endeavor to satisfy both. Dissatisfied
> internal customers generally care little if they provide satisfactory service.
> Therefore, all customers eventually become unhappy.
>
> Herb D. Kelleher, CEO, Southwest Airlines

VISION AND TEAM DEVELOPMENT

A *vision* is the ability to perceive something that is not actually visible, or to see the future, or what could be. A vision also describes the way things should be. If everything were just exactly as it ought to be, what would it look like? That's your vision. It is a product of the heart as well as the hand and head. Vision is values-based.

Mission statements are very often referred to as vision statements, but a vision is not a mission statement. Mission statements are usually short, simple statements outlining what is unique about your establishment, items that positively distinguish it in the minds of everybody—guests and kitchen team members. A vision, on the other hand, contains a clear, inspiring, and empowering criterion.

A vision describes not just where the chef supervisor wants to be and what he or she wants to be like, but why he or she wants to be there, making what contribution, and serving what purpose (beyond making a profit). The vision should inspire; if it doesn't, it is not much of a vision. If it doesn't, then the chef supervisor certainly can't expect it to excite, inspire, or motivate the kitchen team.

The single thread that runs through all success stories is the involvement of team members in drafting a vision statement and empowering people to support this vision. It has been reported that kitchen team members, managers, owners, and chef supervisors who communicate their organization's vision effectively noted significantly higher levels of job satisfaction, commitment, pride, loyalty, and a clarity about the organization's values.

Involving kitchen team members in developing a vision produces powerful results. Kitchen team members can only be empowered by a vision they have contributed to and understand. Understanding is enhanced by participation.

ATTRIBUTES OF EFFECTIVE KITCHEN TEAMS

Often, successful kitchen teams share several attributes and demonstrate achievement in many areas. Leadership is shown by the chef supervisor who has the skills and the desire to develop a team approach and allocates time to team-building activities. Management of the foodservice team is seen as a shared function as illustrated in Figure 4-5. Team members other than the leader are given the opportunity to exercise leadership when their skills are appropriate to the needs of the kitchen team.

Kitchen team members are committed to the aims and purposes of the team. They are willing to devote personal energy to building the team and supporting their fellow members. Even when they work outside the team boundaries (e.g., chefs may have worthwhile suggestions on elements of the dining experience that are outside their control), the members feel they belong and represent the kitchen team.

The kitchen team climate encourages people to feel relaxed; they feel they are able to be direct and open and are prepared to take risks. The kitchen team is clear about its objectives. It sets targets of performance that require members to "stretch" mentally.

Effective team structures allow for the lively and energetic solution to problems. Roles are clarified, communication is open, and administrative procedures support the team's approach. The kitchen team generates creative strength and new ideas from its members; innovative risk is rewarded and good ideas are put into action.

FIGURE 4-5 Management as a shared function.

> **FIGURE 4-6** Improving kitchen teamwork: the chef supervisor and organizational support.
>
> - Support the kitchen team effort through the corporate culture of the foodservice organization.
> - Sustain the kitchen team activities through the expected plateaus.
> - Provide retraining or bring in an outsider to observe and report the findings to the kitchen team.
> - Allow the kitchen team to work on problem solving—not just operational issues, but also sorting through interpersonal and technical skills issues.
> - Provide career paths and opportunities for some kitchen team members to transfer out of the kitchen team if necessary, so that unresolved personality clashes between key people do not persist and drag everyone else down with them.
> - Expand kitchen teams to all parts of the foodservice organization or work on removing external barriers that may be hampering team operations.
> - Provide members with the full picture by providing information to give them more context.
> - Make sure personal and kitchen team growth is an objective.
> - Refine and improve kitchen team development.
> - Recognize team successes and make sure that it receives a great deal of acclaim, approval, and visibility.
> - Have a job rotation program by which members learn all the jobs as well as a better appreciation of the interdependence of the job. This can help the nonperformer see the light and improve.

Team and individual errors and weaknesses are examined without personal rancor to enable the members to learn from experience. Latent individual potential is often fulfilled through team membership. These members grow and become more outgoing and capable, and their professional competence is enhanced as they meet new challenges with one another's support.

Relationships with other kitchen teams are developed systematically. It is obvious in the foodservice industry that effective and cohesive interrelationships are vital. The guest thinks holistically and evaluates the complete foodservice experience—not sections of it.

The effective team is one that is in improvement mode continuously, and that improvement effort is supported by the actions of the chef supervisor and the organization. The type of support that the chef supervisor and the organization must provide is shown in Figure 4-6.

BREAKING DOWN BARRIERS

Every organization has a certain climate or culture. "That climate can be one that is positive, warm, and supportive . . . believe it or not, it can even be a climate in which people have fun and a desire to come to work."[9] In order to create the best possible kitchen work environment, there are a number of barriers that need to be defined, addressed, and overcome. Many of the issues that create barriers are often not even noticed. Some chef supervisors fail to anticipate or recognize potential barriers because of a lack of training, perhaps even insensitivity, and the notion that their supervisory style is okay, because "I treat my team members in a much better way than I was treated." This type of thinking is irrelevant. The chef supervisor who adopts this type of thinking usually fails to recognize the changing nature of the workplace and kitchen employees. Ted Balestreri and Bert Cutino, founders of the award-winning Sardine Factory in Monterey, California, state:

> We thought we had to do everything ourselves in the beginning. We realize, however, that there are people who can do things as well, if not better than we can. . . . By bringing talent to the kitchen, giving them the tools, the authority, and the incentive, we found we have moved a lot quicker than we ever thought possible.[10]

According to Jan Carlzon, "Everyone wants to be treated as an individual; everyone needs to know and feel that they are needed."[11]

The main objective of a quality kitchen team is internal and external customer satisfaction; removing and overcoming barriers is the first step in that process. The next step is to identify what constitutes a positive team work environment in the kitchen and apply it equally and fairly. A number of the barriers to building a team are shown in Figure 4-7.

FIGURE 4-7 Barriers to team building.

- **Inappropriate leadership.** The chef supervisor is unable or unwilling to use a kitchen team approach and does not encourage the use of kitchen team-building activities. He or she often uses a "command" decision style rather than a "consensus" decision style. The leader does not share his or her power or leadership responsibilities.
- **Unqualified membership.** Kitchen team members are not qualified (professionally or socially) to contribute to the kitchen team and as a result are unable to contribute to the successful completion of its goals.
- **Insufficient kitchen team commitment.** Kitchen team members are not committed to the aims and purposes of the kitchen team and are reluctant to expend personal energy on meeting the kitchen team's goals.
- **A non–kitchen team-building climate.** The kitchen team's climate and culture discourage members from feeling comfortable, from being direct and open, and from taking risks.
- **Poor perception of possibility of achievement.** The kitchen team may not understand its objectives; if it does, it may not believe that they are worthwhile. It may set targets that are either uninspiring or unachievable.
- **Poor upper-management support.** The kitchen team may be excluded from corporate planning. It may not understand or envision its role in the wider context of the foodservice organization.
- **Ineffective work methods.** Problems are not solved in an efficient, timely, and effective manner.
- **Lack of role clarity—who does what, when, where, and how.** Members' roles are not clearly defined, efficient communication procedures have not been developed, and administration are not supportive of the kitchen team's efforts.
- **Weak critiquing program.** Kitchen team weaknesses are not addressed adequately, in order not to upset members.
- **Member maturity.** Members may not have developed the maturity and confidence needed to be assertive or to deal with other members' strong personalities.
- **A lack of creativity.** Members do not generate new ideas and are unwilling to take risks that may be discouraged by the organization's corporate culture.
- **Negative relations with other teams.** Kitchen teams should be interdependent, but they compete rather than collaborate. Because kitchen teams do not meet to compare their plans and agendas, priorities may conflict.

EMPOWERMENT AND KITCHEN TEAMS

Customer satisfaction means something different to every guest who walks into any of our 73 hotels and resorts worldwide. It's what a particular guest says it is on any given day. That's why it is so important that associates are truly empowered to meet our guests' expectations on the terms the guests use to define customer satisfaction. A guest satisfied with the accommodations and services we provide day in and day out is the one who will come back and contribute to our continued success.

Jim Treadway, President, Westin Hotel Company

A customer is usually defined in commercial terms—for example, as a person paying for services or products provided. On the other hand, the term *guest* means something of a higher and more personal nature: A guest is someone we entertain in our home, someone we desire to please. This has an entirely different framework than that of a customer. Therefore, pleasing a guest is a lot different than satisfying a customer. Probably the only way to do this in a foodservice establishment is through the concept of empowerment.

SO WHAT IS EMPOWERMENT?

According to Ken Blanchard, empowerment is the process of enabling people to do what they have been trained for and are qualified to do. People already have power through their knowledge and motivation—empowerment is letting this power out.[12] Therefore, empowerment means increasing the amount of control and discretion each kitchen team member has over his or her job. Empowerment provides involvement in decision making that supports the guests' level of quality and satisfaction. Empowering kitchen team members to take more initiative is viewed as essential to quality guest service.

Empowerment is also a key element in team building. There is no better way to have a vision shared and to generate commitment and loyalty than through empowerment. This comes from the combination of pushing down the decision-making process to give greater latitude to each employee and then providing training that facilitates its inception.

Empowerment also seeks to improve the foodservice organization's performance by successfully solving problems that cause dissatisfaction for internal or external customers. Daryl Hartley Leonard of Hyatt Hotels says:

We know we've got atriums and fancy-schmancy resorts, but if you ask people what makes them stay here, the answer always come back, the employees. A large portion of guest problems are not foreseen, so every employee has to feel empowered to correct a problem on the spot. Our guests should expect an-above-and-beyond effort to fix any detail that goes wrong. In a service business, you can't have a rigid set of rules. You can have some guidelines, but you must allow people the freedom to make different interpretations.[13]

Open and ongoing communication with and within the team are critical to creating and maintaining high-performing teams. Empowerment plays a critical part in those communications. Part of being empowered must be the freedom to comment on and discuss policies, procedures, and decisions affecting the team without fear of reprisal. Quality standards must be established and communicated, but their execution is ultimately in the hands of the team members. The chef supervisor cannot be everywhere at one time, so reliance on team members to perform is a must.

Empowerment does not occur in a micromanaged environment. The chef supervisor who recognizes the need for team members to have the freedom and responsibility to make decisions about the methods for accomplishing assignments creates an environment of trust that drives quality performance. Part of establishing empowerment in a team is communicating that freedom to fail also exists. Team members who fear failure, for whatever reason, will not take the chances that are often necessary to find solutions.

Empowerment means actively seeking ideas from kitchen team members on how to improve. Empowerment comes from teaching others ways they can become less dependent on you. Therefore, empowered kitchen teams can do more than empowered individuals. Empowerment means encouraging innovation and allowing kitchen team members to implement their ideas. If the entire kitchen team is empowered and comes to realize that their opinions, views, and ideas are important, they will quickly take ownership of an innovation they have contributed, and they will seek to continuously improve it. Empowerment is not a substitute for leadership or a reduction of authority. The more the kitchen team is empowered, the greater is the need for leaders who can set goals and define a vision.

The paradox of power: In order to gain power, you must give some of it away.

The outcome of empowerment linked with training includes operational improvements in areas such as problem solving, safety and sanitation, cost, production, guest satisfaction—in other words, improvement of overall quality. These improvements are accompanied by or generated by a positive work environment. The outcome of a positive work environment includes respect for the individual and the team, the satisfaction of an internal and external guest focus, and employees who feel empowered to make decisions for the success of their individual careers.

A GREAT PLACE TO WORK

Why would kitchen team members want to say they have a great place to work? Is it because the atmosphere is so relaxed, nobody bothers you, people come and go as they please, the chef supervisor is a "pushover," there is no harsh discipline, and the pay isn't too bad either? No, it has nothing in common with this scenario. Some reasons why kitchen team members believe a certain kitchen is a great place to work is that it is well led by a caring, sharing chef supervisor who believes in challenging the other team members to participate in the running of the kitchen, who delegates responsibility and empowers the team, and is sensitive to the team's attitudes and feelings. This chef supervisor believes in building morale and a team spirit, and the kitchen is a place where people are treated with dignity.

A great place to work is characterized by employees who are proud of their work and organization, who are loyal, produce high-quality meals that meet and satisfy customer needs, where *they* encourage the chef supervisor, where high ethical standards are practiced, and where a shared purpose and appreciation exists among all team members. These items come first—pay and working conditions are part of "a great place to work," but they are not the most important parts.

John Maxwell notes, "I know that no amount of money, attention, privileges, and promises will motivate a staff member who really does not want to be on the team.[14] If a positive work environment is created in the kitchen, where no intimidation or anxiety exists, then the motivational, training, and communication environment is also created.

CONCLUSIONS

The use of teams has become standard in the foodservice industry. The terminology is used constantly, such as the title "Banquet Team." The question that must be asked is whether this is a title or a description. Calling a group a team does not make it a team. When a team has been developed, its power is greater than the sum of its parts. In a team, individuals know that their personal power is amplified by that of the team. The chef supervisor who builds a successful team has created a major resource for customer satisfaction, both internally and externally.

Discussion Questions

1. When the concept of kitchen team building is adopted, it becomes easier to apply quality philosophies. Explain.
2. Discuss the principles of building a kitchen team.
3. List the elements of kitchen team commitment.
4. What are the attributes of successful kitchen teams?
5. Describe the elements of a kitchen team environment that is conducive to great guest service.
6. What are the main advantages of empowerment programs in the foodservice industry?
7. Why is empowerment so important relative to dealing with guest problems and complaints?
8. List and describe the barriers to kitchen team building.
9. Why is it so important for the "corporate culture" to support the kitchen team effort?
10. Explain why inter-kitchen team dependence is critical to guest satisfaction in the foodservice industry.

Notes

1. Marshall J. Cook, *Motivating People* (New York: Macmillan/Spectrum, 1997).
2. Ken Blanchard, John Carlos, and Alan Randolph, *Empowerment Takes More than a Minute* (San Francisco: Berrett-Koehler, 1996), 23.
3. John A. Woods, *Teams and Teamwork* (New York: Macmillian, 1998), 56.
4. Dale G. Barrie, Cary L. Cooper, and Adrian Wilkinson, *Managing Quality and Human Resources: A Guide to Continuous Improvement* (Oxford, England: Blackwell, 1997), 31.
5. Steve Smith, *Build That Team* (London: Kogan Page, 1997), 6.
6. Ibid., 45.
7. Woods, *Teams and Teamwork,* 123.
8. D. H. Stamatis, *Total Quality Service: Principles, Practices, and Implementation* (Delray Beach, FL: St. Lucie Press, 1996), 67.
9. Wolf J. Rinke, *The Winning Foodservice Manager: Strategies for Doing More with Less,* 2nd. ed. (Rockville, MD: Achievement, 1992), 206.
10. Ted Balestreri, *Nobody's Perfect: Lessons in Leadership* (New York: Van Nostrand Reinhold, 1991), 18.
11. Jan Carlzon, *Moments of Truth* (Cambridge, MA: Ballinger, 1987), 5.
12. Blanchard et al., *Empowerment Takes More than a Minute*, 78.
13. Daryl Hartley Leonard, Excerpt from unpublished speech given to Council on Hotel, Restaurant and Institutional Education Conference, July 1994.
14. John C. Maxwell, *Developing the Leader Within You* (Nashville, TN: Nelson, 1993), 165.

CHAPTER 5
RESPECT

OUTLINE

- ❖ Introduction
- ❖ Respect and criticism
- ❖ Diversity
- ❖ Discrimination
- ❖ Conclusions
- ❖ Discussion questions
- ❖ Notes

OBJECTIVES

When you complete this chapter, you should be able to:

1. Describe issues and elements that create fear within the kitchen work environment
2. List the steps that contribute to encouraging team members to give feedback
3. Describe the changing nature of the kitchen work environment relative to a diversified workforce
4. Define the elements of diversity and capitalize on diversity as an advantage
5. Reduce potential conflict among kitchen members resulting from cultural misunderstandings
6. State the elements that make up sexual harassment and describe the legal responsibilities of the chef supervisor in this area
7. State and describe the primary laws regarding equal opportunity in the workplace

Case Study: ALTA LINDA REGIONAL MEDICAL CENTER

John Kirby, the chef of the Alta Linda Regional Medical Center, was an excellent administrator. He had to be in order to ensure total quality for the patients in the 1000-bed hospital. John had started working in kitchens when he was 16 years old. He had risen to be executive chef of the largest hospital in the state. He was responsible for an extensive kitchen staff that included line cooks, prep cooks, bakers, purchasing staff, and stewards and scullery personnel.

John worked very hard to maintain a team atmosphere among his staff. He had seen many changes in the individuals who made up a kitchen staff in his forty years in the kitchen. He had learned to accept the changes in the racial mix, the use of languages other than English, the open acceptance of different sexual orientations. John considered himself to be open-minded and unbiased. He expected individuals to do their job and become part of the team. If they did that, then they got along with John. John's team members considered him to be good leader, manager, and supervisor.

John even tried to get along with the people who worked in the dietetics department, but he did not feel they knew anything about how to cook. In fact, he did not think they really had true food knowledge. They were, however, responsible for assisting in developing the menus and providing the guidelines for the individual patient meals. John respected the importance of meeting patients' dietary requirements. John generally met suggestions made by the dietitians that moved beyond just dietary require-

ments with lack of interest or derision. John often made derogatory comments about the dieticians to the kitchen staff. He was quick to point out when a dietician was large and appeared overweight. He always suggested that the individual pay more attention to his or her own diet rather than telling him how to do his job.

John suggested to the head dietitian that she should follow John's example in team building, because the dietitians were not good team players. The head dietitian submitted a report to the hospital administration charging John with sexual harassment, discrimination, and abusive behavior toward her staff.

Based on what you have learned from previous chapters and the content of this chapter, answer the following questions.

- What is the overall reason for the challenges at the Alta Linda Regional Medical Center?
- What are the primary causal agents for the challenges at the Alta Linda Regional Medical Center?
- What role did supervision/management play in the decline at the Alta Linda Regional Medical Center?
- What specific steps could have been taken to avoid the current situation at the Alta Linda Regional Medical Center?
- What, specifically, can be done to overcome the challenges and generate motion in a positive direction for the Alta Linda Regional Medical Center?

INTRODUCTION

Do unto others as you would have them do unto you. This is something that is often heard but also often forgotten when we deal with other people. Respect in the workplace encompasses many things, but first and foremost it must result in a comfortable work environment. A comfortable work environment is one in which team members feel they are evaluated and judged by their performance and not their race, gender, or personal beliefs. It is a work environment that develops all team members to their fullest potential. Team members in a *Golden Rule environment* will not do things because they fear the consequences. Rather, team members will do things because they want success for everyone, including themselves and the operation. Point 8 of Deming's fourteen points, which were discussed in Chapter 2, addressed driving out fear, so that everyone may work effectively. Chris Arnold, a spokesperson for the 540-unit Chipotle chain, stated in an interview that "A funny thing happens when you treat people like responsible, capable and highly performing individuals: That's exactly how they operate."[1] According to Dina Berta, "Restaurants that can successfully brand themselves as a desirable place to work stand to have an edge in attracting talent in an ever-shrinking labor pool, according to operators and personnel experts."[2] The *Golden Rule environment* is key in branding an operation as a desirable place to work.

In the foodservice industry, and the kitchen in particular, the use of fear as a tool of control was not uncommon. The myths and legends of chefs who berated, threatened, and verbally abused the kitchen staff contain all too much fact. Both the industry and the chef, however, have changed in the last five or six decades. Effective chefs, and management at al levels, recognize that fear is harmful to the foodservice organization and to the individual kitchen team member. The use of fear as a control device prevents people from thinking: "It robs them of pride and joy in their work and kills all forms of intrinsic motivation. The thinking and creative potential of the workers are stopped cold."[3] Most chef supervisors who rely on fear believe that those working under them are incapable of thinking, and this concept becomes a self-fulfilling prophesy.

Chef supervisors may not be able to eliminate all fear from the lives of all the kitchen team members, but they can eliminate the sources of fear that are built into the management structures. Figure 5-1 shows characteristics of the supervisor who generates a *Golden Rule environment,* an environment free of management-generated fear.

FIGURE 5-1 Characteristics of *Golden Rule* supervisors.

- Sensitive to issues and interests of team members
- Respectful of differences in people
- Open and participative in problem solving
- Anxious to use the power of their position to serve the team well
- Fair and equitable in the distribution of work
- Constant in their efforts to find solutions that are both technically and politically sound
- Constant in seeking individual team member input on decisions
- Willing to put the welfare of the team before private interests
- Never "better" than other team members
- Honest and willing to consider retaliation a sign of serious weakness

FIGURE 5-2 Elements of threatening or abusive action.

- Silence and glaring eye contact
- Snubbing or ignoring people
- Insults or put-downs
- Blaming, discrediting
- Aggressive, controlling manner
- Threats about the job
- Yelling and shouting
- Angry outburst or loss of control
- Physical threats
- Racial, ethnic, or gender slurs
- Blatant or discriminatory comments

According to Ryan and Oestreich in *Driving Fear out of the Workplace,* supervisors who use threatening and abusive behavior "immediately destroy trust and end communication. They create a thick wall of antagonism and resentment."[4] No one respects a supervisor who repeatedly puts down others or who loses control of his or her temper. Elements of threatening or abusive actions or behaviors that demean, humiliate, isolate, insult, and threaten team members are shown in Figure 5-2.

RESPECT AND CRITICISM

A primary responsibility of any supervisor is the quality of the team's work. Achieving quality outcomes requires evaluating team members' performance. Performance evaluation is only fully effective when the findings are reported to the individual being evaluated. The findings are not always positive, but the goal must be to use the knowledge of both positive and negative performance as a vehicle for improving performance. This can only be accomplished when *respect* is part of the workplace. Criticism is never easy for an individual to accept, but when it comes from someone an individual respects, and whom the individual knows respects him or her, it is easier to accept. It is the acceptance of and ultimately acting on the criticism that brings about improved performance.

A supervisor who gives a team member negative feedback in a positive manner is demonstrating respect for that individual. Following are some guidelines for giving negative feedback in a positive manner.

> *Limit the comments to the team member's behavior.* Don't label the person as always stubborn, difficult, or easy-going. Do not criticize the *person;* focus on the *activity,* not on the type of individual the person is. Be specific, and don't generalize about a particular behavior.
> *Criticize as quickly as possible following the problem.* The problem is fresh in the mind of the team member, so you will probably get a better response.
> *Listen carefully to what individual team members have to say.* Get their opinion: Let them tell you what went wrong. Ask what they think the problem is. Do not prejudge an answer. Keep an open mind about what you hear.

Be considerate. Get your point across without being loud, rude, or abrupt. Losing control will put the other person on the defensive and probably won't help you solve the problem or determine its cause.

Don't present criticism with praise. This sends a confusing message. Often there is a tendency to want to say something nice to soften the blow. This rarely works: It may blunt the criticism, but the praise means nothing. The team member hears only the bad news.

Don't trap or humiliate kitchen team members. If a complaint is received from a customer, the chef supervisor should be straightforward in talking with the person about the complaint.

Don't blame the entire kitchen department for a problem. Mistakes happen. It may be someone's fault, but as a supervisor, you should not generalize and accuse the entire kitchen team of acting poorly.

Verbal criticism is usually less severe than written criticism. Unintended results may occur as a consequence of written criticism. Written criticism can be far more severe than verbal criticism, and it becomes part of the individual's record, which could affect promotions and layoffs. The kitchen team member may not have had an opportunity to respond or explain what occurred. Written criticism remains an issue for an extended period of time, and comments made may lack clear meaning because the tone of voice or any further explanation is not available to the reader.

Criticism should also be communicated in private. Choose a time that will facilitate solving the problem. Generally, the best time to criticize is early in the day, so that the team member can get on with the job.

Encourage the kitchen team to give you feedback. Encouragement communicates trust, respect, and a belief in someone else. Discouragement results in lowered self-esteem and alienation from others. A discouraging chef supervisor is one who constantly criticizes and points out mistakes and who has unrealistic expectations of others and does not allow for mistakes. Examples of phrases used by an encouraging supervisor are shown in Figure 5-3.

The difference between the best kitchen team members and the average ones often depends on the leadership style and ability of the chef supervisor. A good chef supervisor can turn some average team members into outstanding performers. It is what the chef supervisor does that influences performance. Sincerity is of the utmost importance. If team members are treated with respect, then they are their own best source of motivation. Ferdinand Metz, president of the Culinary Institute of America, recommends: "Build a team that will work towards a common objective. Lead by example. Always be willing to do what you ask others to do. They will respect you for this."[5]

FIGURE 5-3 Phrases of encouragement.

"What did you learn from that mistake?"
"You did a good job."
"Keep trying; you will succeed."
"Great improvement."
"If you need any help, let me know."

BOX 5-1

CHEF TALK:
PERMISSION TO SUCCEED

When I went to culinary school my class makeup was 50% female. I remember thinking; this can't be so bad—there are a lot of people just like me who desire to cook. When I went to work in a hotel kitchen I was the only female. I never really gave it much thought, though. I just figured if you worked hard, showed up on time, and possessed a strong interest in your job and the company, you would get promoted.

I started as a prep cook and worked in banquets, graduated to a line cook but was placed in *garde manger* making salads and desserts. I wasn't allowed to move over to the hot line. I was never given a chance. Male cooks were hired in and moved to the hot line with less experience and no formal training.

One day, I asked the chef to move me to the hot line. I told him I was ready for a chance. His response was, "The hot line isn't what you were cut out to do. Let the guys handle the hot line. You do such a great job with the salads and desserts. We really need you there."

About a week later I got my big break on the hot line when a line cook called in sick. I stepped up to grill spot and just started prepping the station for service. When the replacement guy came up from the back to fill in for the no-show, I sent him to the salad and dessert station. He didn't question where he was working because he was a fill-in and I had been in the kitchen for a year. I was busy prepping the grill station and looked like I knew what I was doing.

I worked the grill for the first time, working 200 covers, and had no returns. It was one of my greatest days in the kitchen. I remember thinking I know what I want to do for the rest of my life now. I felt like I could do anything after that!

The next day the chef called me into his office. I remember thinking I was going to get fired for the stunt I pulled telling a guy to work my dessert station. The chef asked me who taught me to work a grill so effectively. I told him no one really, I had been watching the grill cook for months and just waiting for the day he called in sick. He laughed, and told me to get back to work at my new station on the hot line.

Looking back, that was probably a turning point for my career, a defining moment. I was waiting for an opportunity to prove myself, to say that I was just as good as the guy standing next to me. I figured out I wasn't just as good, I was better. I kept waiting for someone to give me permission to succeed. In the end, I just took it. I don't regret my time at that hotel. The lesson I learned was priceless, it changed me. It made me a better chef, really a better person. When I became executive chef and had to make the promotion decision, I watched and listened to my employees. I gave everyone permission to succeed.

Carol Kalkstein-Silkes, Ph.D., CEC, CCE,
Assistant Professor, Purdue University,
West Lafayette, Indiana

DIVERSITY

> According to the Census Bureau, the ethnic population of the United States will continue to rise. Projections show that by 2050, Hispanics will account for more than 24% of the population, Blacks will make up over 13% and Asians will account for almost 9%.[6]

The foodservice industry has always employed higher numbers of minorities and women than most other industries in the United States. The diversity in the restaurant workforce is not diminishing.

Results show a 3% increase in the number of corporate executives from an ethnic/racial minority group from 2004 to 2005. The most diverse groups of employees work at the hourly level, where 50% of workers represent an ethnic/racial minority group, a 2% increase from the previous year's findings. In addition, the ethnic diversity of unit level management increased 3% from 2005.[7]

According to the National Restaurant Association, in 2006, 72% of the restaurant industry workers were women and minorities.[8]

As we move further into the twenty-first century, the foodservice industry is faced with issues of supervising not only greater numbers of people, but also a more diverse workforce. Supervision within the kitchen requires a greater respect for the values and cultures of all kitchen team members. An establishment that values diversity is one in which kitchen team members learn to appreciate individuality and avoid prejudging people. Encouraging an awareness of diversity will facilitate the discussion of assumptions each team member may hold regarding certain groups of people. "Understanding and accepting diversity enables us to see that each of us is needed; recognizing diversity helps us to understand the need we have for opportunity, equity, and identity in the workplace."[9]

"Now, companies are embracing diversity as a business focus and corporate value. Embracing diversity isn't just the right thing to do; there's a strong business case for it."[10] Acceptance of diversity by chef supervisors can mean getting used to different accents or languages or people who dress differently. It means feeling comfortable with team members whose skin is a different color. Diversity in a team refers to the following physical and cultural dimensions that separate and distinguish us as individuals and groups: age, gender, physical abilities, ethnicity, race, and sexual preference. Miller, Porter, and Drummond note: "Failure to understand and to respect the diversity of your employees can result in misunderstandings, tension, poor performance, poor employee morale, and higher rates of absenteeism and turnover . . . when diversity is respected, the working environment is richer."[11]

The first step in improving respect for diversity is communication. Establish a climate that encourages a free exchange of ideas. Explore how all team members come to the kitchen with a unique combination of backgrounds and influences. Start with yourself and your own background. Get to know your team members. Don't make ethnic- or gender-oriented jokes, and don't tolerate even good-natured jokes in this area. Encourage diversity and an awareness of different cultures through events such as special days in the cafeteria devoted to ethnic foods.

If individuals are having difficulty with English, be patient and encouraging. Ask them for their input. The fact that some people may not say anything does not mean they have nothing to say. Persons changing from one culture to another may experience culture shock, which may manifest as fear. Encourage the rest of the team to understand and respect differences in people. As a chef supervisor, believing and showing that you respect team members who come from different backgrounds is very important. The self-esteem of diverse team members will remain intact if they believe their backgrounds are accepted and respected.

The following is abstracted from a job notice that appeared in the *Boston Globe,* October 7, 1990. It demonstrates a comprehensive understanding of "valuing differences."

> In every aspect of life there is diversity. Accept this and you open yourself to endless possibilities. Close your mind to diversity and you are confined in isolation. Where one may see a problem, two may find a solution.
>
> We value and encourage the contributions of all. We recognize that while each one of us sees our own level of achievement, acceptance, and recognition, together we can attain higher goals. We can contribute to the well-being of our community by building strong bonds and implementing new ideas. This is our team—a group of people working together for the common good, while accepting the views, support, and uniqueness of each individual.

A kitchen work environment filled with ethnic diversity has the potential for conflict arising from differences. This conflict may be based on misconceptions or stereotyping by chef supervisors and other kitchen team members about other ethnic groups, languages, or cultures. Each side can misinterpret or dismiss the viewpoint of the other by failing to understand the framework in which the other operates.

BOX 5-2

CHEF TALK:
THAT WAS THEN

The years 1958–1960 ushered into the U.S. mainstream a new respect for quite a few things. It was also around this time that I began my career in culinary arts. It was during this era that most restaurant kitchens were manned by a staff comprised of an executive chef, a sous chef, and a kitchen manager (all Caucasian); the "grunt" crew was composed mostly of African Americans. Respect was a word seldom used in kitchens at that time. Fear was the order of the day, and authoritarian rule produced an atmosphere of fear and resentment. I am African American, and despite these intimidating conditions, I learned to love cooking. I also developed a resolve to be successful.

Today, I am happy to say that I have been successful in spite of the awful conditions that existed for African Americans in those pre–equal rights times. I am a chef supervisor as well as Chief Executive Officer of my own company. My background has conditioned me to be more sensitive to those that I am called upon to supervise. I constantly check my performance to ensure that I am not subconsciously reenacting the role of my earlier supervisors.

It is crucial that chef supervisors prepare themselves for a changing work environment in the kitchen. Minorities have proved that they are as capable and as competent as any other workers in the foodservice industry. When a chef supervisor understands that there are no "big I's" and "little you's," only an engine and the rest of the train, he or she can celebrate total quality respect in the kitchen.

Clayton Sherrod, CEC, AAC,
President,
Chef Clayton's Food Systems, Inc.,
Birmingham, Alabama

DISCRIMINATION

HARASSMENT

In recent times harassment in the workplace has become mostly synonymous with sexual harassment. However, there are many forms of harassment in the foodservice industry of people who are different: of gay and lesbian people, minorities, and physically or mentally impaired people. Federal laws, executive orders, court cases, and state and local statutes provide a broad legal framework that protects these categories of employees.

The Equal Employment Opportunity Commission (EEOC) issued guidelines on sexual harassment in 1980, indicating that it is a form of discrimination under Title VII of the 1964 Civil Rights Act. The EEOC states that sexual harassment consists of "unwelcome advances, requests for sexual favors, and other verbal or physical conduct of a sexual nature." The conduct is illegal when it interferes with an employee's work performance or creates an "intimidating, hostile, or offensive working environment." The *Uniform Guidelines* hold employers strictly accountable for preventing the sexual harassment of female or male employees. The EEOC also considers an employer guilty of sexual harassment if the employer knew about or should have known about the unlawful conduct and failed to remedy it. Employers are also guilty of sexual harassment if they allow nonemployees (guests or salespersons) to sexually harass employees. When sexual complaints or charges have been proved, the EEOC has imposed severe penalties that include back pay, reinstatement, payment of lost benefits, interest charges, and attorney's fees. Sexual harassment can result in criminal charges if it involves physical contact. Damages are assessed against both the offender and the employer. The number of charges of sexual harassment received by the EEOC declined from 15,889 in 1997 to 12,025 in 2006.[12] The percentage of charges of sexual harassment received by the EEOC from males increased from 11.6 percent in 1997 to 15.4 percent in 2006.[13]

Increasingly, foodservice organizations are becoming more proactive in the area of sexual harassment. There is a fine line between harassment, teamwork, and camaraderie. While certain working conditions in the foodservice industry may contribute to sexual harassment, it is people who commit the offenses. The majority of sexual harassment situations involve harassing women, but the occurrence of women harassing men is also on the increase. In both instances, not acting to prevent sexual harassment is the same as condoning it.

Chef supervisors have a responsibility to recognize and prevent sexual harassment in the kitchen. Every organization must have a clearly defined policy on sexual harassment. It should be clearly communicated to every team member. The best cure for workplace sexual harassment is a policy and an educational program designed to prevent it. Policy statements should be in writing and stress that harassment will not be tolerated. Figure 5-4 shows the fundamental elements of an effective sexual harassment policy.

EQUAL OPPORTUNITY EMPLOYMENT

The federal *Equal Pay Act of 1963* is considered by many to be the starting point of the equal employment opportunity movement in the United States. This law was passed as an amendment to the 1938 Fair Labor Standards Act. The amendment requires that men and women in an organization performing basically equal work must receive

BOX 5-3

CHEF TALK:
PIONEER APPRENTICE

In 1978 Elizabeth Tobin became the first female apprentice in my kitchen. Up until that time options for female chefs were confined to working as "cooks," usually in hospitals or other institutions or as assistants in the pastry shop. The title "chef" was reserved for males only. From the first day, I insisted that Elizabeth break from the traditional mold set for women in the kitchen. At that time women did not even wear the traditional chef's uniform. It was difficult for Elizabeth; she was battling 100 years of male dominance in the culinary world of the Gresham Hotel. She encountered many difficulties, not least among them the idea that women could not handle the stress and tension of service time in a busy kitchen or the often "rich" language used in kitchens.

Elizabeth was a pioneer female apprentice back then. Not only was she an excellent chef, but she turned out to be a great role model for aspiring young female chefs. She rotated through all the departments and graduated with flying colors.

The purpose of this insight into the first female apprentice in my kitchen (which was also the first time the trade union recognized female chefs) is to outline the progression in thinking from 1978 to the present time. As I reflect back on that time, it seems almost inconceivable that culinary arts or the kitchen in general were male-only preserves.

Noel C. Cullen, Ed.D., CEC, AAC,
(1948–2002)

equal pay. Although this law was passed in 1963, equal pay is still the subject of numerous lawsuits today.

Title VII of the Civil Rights Act of 1964 continued to emphasize equality in personnel policies. The law applies to all employers with fifteen or more employees. Title VII prohibits employment discrimination based on race, color, sex, religion, or national origin. Employers who have fewer than fifteen employees may be subject to state regulations. There are two exemptions to Title VII. A business owner is exempt who can prove that the discriminatory qualification is a *bona-fide occupational qualification* (BFOQ). Common examples of a BFOQ are women working in a women's locker room and specific ethnic performers for ethnic performances. The other exemption is

FIGURE 5-4 Effective sexual harassment policy.

- A system-wide comprehensive policy on sexual harassment should be developed. Experts in the area of sexual harassment should be involved in its preparation. This policy should be part of all new employee induction and orientation training programs. Current employees should be made aware what the policy is, and a strong organizational statement condemning sexual harassment should be issued by management.
- Chef supervisors should receive training in how to prevent sexual harassment in the kitchen.
- Procedures for dealing with complaints in this area should be established.
- Action should be taken immediately to investigate complaints of harassment.
- Offenders should be disciplined and in serious cases dismissed instantly. The policy should be equally and fairly applied to all team members.

discrimination based on a *business necessity*. This is very narrowly defined, and the employer must show that the practice is essential to its business. An example of a business necessity exemption would be reassigning a pregnant female security guard to a desk position during her pregnancy. The role of the guard position is to provide protection, and the ability of a pregnant guard to carry out that duty is diminished. It is important to note that in the case of both a BFOQ and a business necessity justification for discrimination, the burden of proof rests with the employer.

Discrimination may be direct or indirect. The terms currently used are disparate treatment and disparate impact. *Disparate treatment* occurs when individuals being considered for employment or who are employed by a company are treated differently based on race, color, sex, religion, national origin, or other protected characteristic. *Disparate impact* occurs when a policy has greater impact on one group than another.

In the restaurant industry, policies that have the potential to create disparate impact include uniform requirements, education requirements, and grooming requirements. The question that must be asked whenever a policy is being considered is whether the action the policy requires is actually necessary for a team member to do the job. Does a head covering that is required by a woman's religion actually prevent her from doing her job or reduce the restaurant's business by ruining the perceived ambience? Today's chef supervisor, and all of management, must address this type of issue with very open minds.

The *Age Discrimination in Employment Act* was passed in 1967. This law prohibits employers from discriminating on the basis of age against persons 40 years old or older. This law affects all employers of twenty or more employees and all unions with twenty-five or more members. Common abuses of this law are firing older workers to hire younger replacements or promoting young workers over older workers.

The *Vocational Rehabilitation Act* was enacted in 1973 and bars discrimination against otherwise qualified people with disabilities. The *Pregnancy Discrimination Act* was enacted in 1978 and prohibits discrimination against pregnant women. The *Immigration Reform and Control Act* was enacted in 1983 and prohibits recruiting and hiring aliens who are not eligible to work in the United States.

The *Americans with Disabilities Act* (ADA) was enacted in 1990. Although this act is similar to the Vocational Rehabilitation Act of 1963, the terminology used is somewhat different. The ADA also has broader application. It applies to most employers, whereas the Vocational Rehabilitation Act applied only to federal contractors and subcontractors. Specifically, the ADA prohibits workplace discrimination against people with disabilities. The ADA also requires employers to make reasonable accommodation to create an accessible workplace for all qualified employees.

The *Family and Medical Leave Act* was passed in 1993. This act provides opportunity for employees to take up to twelve weeks unpaid leave for birth or adoption. Additionally, the act allows the use of the leave to care for an elderly or ill parent, spouse, or child, or to undergo treatment.

CONCLUSIONS

The supervisor is a critical element in any possesive operation's success in creating and maintaining an atmosphere of respect in the workplace. The chef supervisor that models respect and makes it clear that all employees are valued will achieve that atmosphere of respect. The result will be a culture that encourages growth, embraces risk taking and supports advancement. The outcome of that culture will be success for both the operation and the employees with pride in achievement spanning all.

Discussion Questions

1. Point 8 of Deming's fourteen principles concerns driving fear out of the work-place. How is this linked to what Chris Arnold, a spokesperson for the 540-unit Chipotle chain, stated in an interview, that "A funny thing happens when you treat people like responsible, capable and highly performing individuals: That's exactly how they operate"?

2. What are the steps that can contribute to creating fear within the kitchen work environment?

3. What factors contribute to alienating team members in the kitchen?

4. What phrases can a chef supervisor use to encourage the kitchen team?

5. Women and minorities are often lumped together as a single class. What do these two groups have in common? What are the major differences between them?

6. How could a foodservice operation use diversity as a competitive advantage?

7. Why is management of diversity vital? Is this a temporary or a long-term phenomenon?

8. When is sexual harassment illegal? What are the consequences of these illegal actions?

9. Why do chef supervisors have a responsibility to prevent sexual harassment?

10. List and describe the primary laws affecting equal opportunity in the workplace.

Notes

1. Dina Berta, "Building an Employment 'Brand,'" *Nations Restaurant News,* www.nrn.com/landingPage.aspx?coll_id=632&id.

2. Ibid.

3. Rafael Aruayo, *Dr. Deming* (New York: Carol, 1991), 184.

4. Kathleen Ryan and Daniel K. Oestreich, *Driving Fear out of the Workplace* (San Francisco: Jossey-Bass, 1991), 75.

5. Ferdinand Metz, "Success Has a Future Perspective," *Lessons in Leadership* (New York: Van Nostrand Reinhold, 1991), 36.

6. Paul Frumkin, "At Your Service: Dining and Diversity: Catering to a Multicultural Clientele: As the U.S. Population Becomes Increasingly Diverse, Training Servers to Be Sensitive to the Distinct Desires of Different Groups Becomes More Important than Ever," *Nations Restaurant News* 39, no. 38 (September 19, 2005): 110.

7. Shyam Patel, "Just Published People Report Survey of Unit Level Employment Practices Highlights Rapid Shifts in the Workforce," www.peoplereport.com. www.enewsbuilder.net/peoplereport/e_article000733019.cfm?x=b8Rr58S,b520tHgk. January 2007.

8. Dina Berta, "Diversity at the Top: Quick-Service Outshines Other Segments with the Highest Percentage of Women and Minorities in Management Positions: Segment Study: QSR & Diversity," *Nations Restaurant News* 40, no. 6 (February 6, 2006): 33.

9. Max De Pree, *Leadership Is an Art* (New York: Dell, 1989), 9.

10. Richard Koonce, "Redefining Diversity: It's Not Just the Right Thing to Do. It Also Makes Good Business Sense," *Training & Development,* www.findarticles.com/cf_ntrstnws/m4467/12_55'/83045836/print.jhtml, December 2001: 1.

11. Jack E. Miller, Mary Porter, and Karen E. Drummond, *Supervision in the Hospitality Industry,* 2nd ed. (New York: John Wiley, 1992): 92.

12. U.S. Equal Employment Opportunity Commission, *Sexual Harassment Charges EEOC & FEPAs Combined: FY 1997–FY 2006,* www.eeoc.gov/stats/harass.html.

13. Ibid.

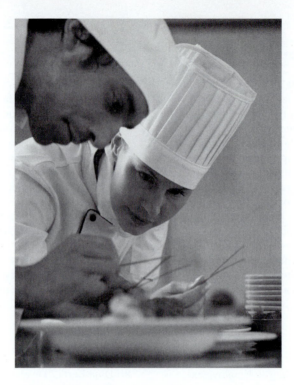

CHAPTER 6
THE CHEF AS COMMUNICATOR

❧

OUTLINE

- ❖ Introduction
- ❖ Elements of communication
- ❖ Barriers to communication
- ❖ Guidelines for effective communication
- ❖ Nonverbal communication
- ❖ Listening
- ❖ Giving directions
- ❖ Leading a meeting
- ❖ Written communication
- ❖ Communication via the grapevine
- ❖ Conclusions
- ❖ Summary
- ❖ Discussion questions
- ❖ Notes

OBJECTIVES

When you complete this chapter, you should be able to:

1. Describe the elements of effective communication
2. Identify barriers to good communication
3. Describe aspects of nonverbal communication
4. Define the elements of effective listening and describe ways to improve listening
5. Outline the steps for leading and managing kitchen team meetings
6. Identify methods of giving directions to kitchen team members so as to ensure satisfactory and timely completion of tasks
7. Communicate effectively in written form
8. Identify the positive and negative aspects of communication via the grapevine

Case Study: LA MAISON BLANC

Chef Herve is executive chef of La Maison Blanc, one of the city's finest restaurants and its premier banquet facility. Chef Herve has been with La Maison Blanc for two weeks, and he is extremely frustrated today because he does not understand why the food for the event in the second-floor ballroom is not ready. The function was scheduled to start at 5 P.M., and it is now 4:30 P.M. Additionally, the food that is ready was either improperly prepared or presented or, in many cases, both.

The function was assigned to Sous Chef Heinz, who has been with La Maison Blanc for three years and should know how to handle a function of this type and size. Chef Herve had discussed the event with Heinz for almost an hour the day before, to ensure that everything was going to be taken care of properly. Chef Herve has a clear recollection of the meeting.

At their meeting, Chef Herve read the work order to Heinz. This had taken longer than he anticipated because he had to answer the phone several times. He had then asked Heinz if Heinz had any questions. Heinz had asked some questions, and Chef Herve had answered his questions as

rapidly as possible between phone calls. Chef Herve did remember that he had not finished answering Heinz's last question because the phone range and Heinz had excused himself, returning to the kitchen.

Chef Herve does not understand why Heinz did not follow instructions. He has found Heinz to be a very conscientious worker and a skilled culinarian. Heinz has a reputation for being proud of his culinary team and the work they produce. When Chef Herve asked Heinz why the food was not ready, Heinz said that the function would not start until 7 P.M., the normal starting time for a function of this type. When he was asked why food was not prepared and presented as it was supposed to be, Heinz said that he and his team had done the best they could with the information they had.

Chef Herve instructed Sous Chef Heinz to complete the preparation of the food immediately and to get the guests taken care of. Chef Herve also told Heinz that they would discuss his failure to perform the next day when time allowed. Heinz responded that he would be there when Chef Herve found the time.

Based on what you have learned from previous chapters and the content of this chapter, answer the following questions.

- What is the overall reason for the challenges at La Maison Blanc?
- What are the primary causal agents for the challenges at La Maison Blanc?
- What role did supervision/management play in the decline at La Maison Blanc?

- What specific steps could have been taken to avoid the current situation at La Maison Blanc?
- What, specifically, can be done to overcome the challenges and generate motion in a positive direction for La Maison Blanc?

INTRODUCTION

A chef supervisor uses communication to gather, process, and transmit information essential to the well-being of the organization. Because this communication moves in many directions, the needs of peers, superiors, and fellow team members need to be given careful consideration. Communication is a crucial element of the supervisory process. Chef supervisors often run into problems because of their inability to communicate effectively. As much as 85 percent of a chef supervisor's day is spent in some form of communication, most of it speaking and listening to others.[1]

Communication involves a sender and a receiver, and the transfer of information from a source to a destination. Effective supervision—delegating, coaching, team building, and information transfer—depends on understanding all the elements of communication. It is the most exacting of all supervisory skills and the one the chef supervisor is most frequently called on to use. Communication is the basis for understanding, cooperation, and action in the kitchen. An open, well-developed communication system will result in a higher standard of quality food production and service through a two-way flow of ideas, opinions, and decisions.

Communication grows and develops in a positive kitchen work environment in which the elements of trust and understanding are adopted. The purpose of communication in the foodservice establishment, and particularly the kitchen, is to ensure that all individuals understand the vision, goals, objectives, policies, and procedures of the organization. Kitchen team members who are confused, unhappy, or *uninformed* may become discontented. Communication is much more than talking, speaking, and reading. If it is successful, the sender will direct or communicate a message that is clear and accurately understood by the receiver in a way that the sender intends. Most problems with effective communication lie in the middle portion of communication, which is known as the "noise" or the elements that cause misunderstanding.

Communication between sender and receiver passes through filters of culture, age, gender, education, and our different fields of past experiences, which cause noise in the understanding of messages.[2] This often leads to misperceptions, misinterpretations, and misevaluations. It is therefore necessary to recognize these differences and develop a communication style that helps each individual to understand. Words and gestures often mean different things to different people. Understanding these differences is an important skill for a chef supervisor.

Communication must flow in many directions—upward from supervisors to higher management, downward to subordinates, and laterally to team members. Effective upward communication can help team members contribute to the organization and can provide an opportunity for the chef supervisor to get to know and understand each team member better. The more avenues are created to facilitate communication within the kitchen, the better the work environment will be.

The chef supervisor should set an example of being open and honest. The more feedback and ideas are provided to the kitchen team, the more comfortable they will feel about sharing their ideas and feelings. To encourage open communication, the chef supervisor should reward rather than punish open expressions of feelings, opinions, or problems. Openness should be rewarded by showing appreciation for team members who share negative or sensitive messages.

Some chef supervisors may feel threatened by ideas from creative individuals in the kitchen. This need not be so. In some cases supervisors may talk down to individuals, thus causing feelings of anger and hurt. If messages are understood as intended, then effective coaching can become a reality. Misinterpretations can cause many problems in the kitchen, among the team and between different departments. For example, if a customer's meal order is misunderstood, not only is this costly in wasted food and time, it also contributes to customer annoyance and delays and exasperation on the part of the waitperson.

Because foodservice employees sometimes do not speak English well, it is important to understand the barriers to communication arising from different cultural attitudes, values, and beliefs. In some cultural groups, people say "yes" even when they do not mean "yes."[3] In addition to difficulty understanding English, nonnative speakers may have difficulty interpreting body language. These signals may have different meanings for different groups and thus cause communication problems. Good communication in the kitchen is essential for successful implementation of goals and objectives. It also ensures a safe work environment. Communication consists of many parts and has different elements that are discussed in the following sections.

ELEMENTS OF COMMUNICATION

The communication activities of a chef supervisor involve interpersonal communication. To be complete, the interpersonal communication process must contain the three basic elements shown in Figure 6-1.

- The **source/sender** is the person who originates and encodes the message he or she wishes to share with other members in the foodservice operation. *Encoding* is the process of putting information in some form that can be received, decoded, and understood by others. Using menus to convey ideas and thoughts is one such encoded message.
- The **signal/message** that the source (sender) intends to share is a message. A message that has been transferred from one team member to another is called a *signal*.
- The **destination/receiver** is the person who receives the message and with whom the sender is attempting to share information. The team member receives this information and decodes or interprets the message for its meaning. Communication, therefore, is an interpretive transaction between individuals. The sender of the message encodes it according to his or her knowledge (field of experience) and the receiver decodes it according to his or her field of experience.

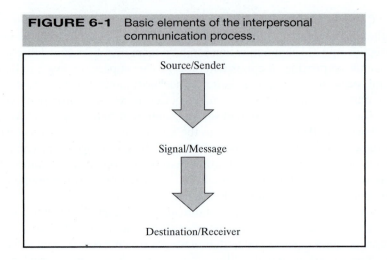

FIGURE 6-1   Basic elements of the interpersonal communication process.

What is important to effective, clear, and accurate understanding of information in the kitchen is the skill in encoding the message by the chef supervisor so that the message means the same thing to those receiving it. Team members in the kitchen come from many different backgrounds. Each will interpret a message differently based on his or her background (field of experience).

Often, jargon (for example, French culinary technical terms) is used to describe skills and culinary principles. Assuming that each individual has a clear understanding of these terms may cause communication gaps. It should not be assumed that information has been transferred and interpreted in the way intended, as is demonstrated in Figure 6-2.

Assuming that each team member understood what was communicated can cause confusion and frustration for both parties. Check for understanding; not doing so may cause operational problems. The aim of good communication is to ensure that the sender and the receiver both have the same picture of the message in their minds. To increase the probability that communication will be successful, the message must be encoded by the sender (chef supervisor) to ensure that the way in which the signal is decoded is equivalent to the receiver's experience of the way it should be decoded. Simply put, it should be phrased in such a way that the message is both clear and understood the same by both the sender and the receiver.

FIGURE 6-2   What went wrong?

This is the story of four people: Everybody, Somebody, Anybody, and Nobody.
There was an important job to be done and Everybody was sure that Somebody would do it.
Anybody could have done it but Nobody did it.
Somebody got angry because it was Everybody's job.
Everybody thought that Somebody would do it.
But Nobody asked Anybody.
It ended up that the job wasn't done, and Everybody blamed Somebody, when actually Nobody asked Anybody.

Anonymous

FIGURE 6-3 Subconscious barries to communication.

Age
Appearance
Eye contact
Facial expressions
Gender
Movement
Personal space
Skin color
Touch

BARRIERS TO COMMUNICATION

The interpretation of what is said by the chef supervisor is directly affected by each team member's knowledge, experience, and culture, just to name a few factors. The factors and issues that decrease effective communication in the foodservice operation, and in all communication, are called *communication barriers*. One of these barriers is language. A high proportion of foodservice workers do not speak English, and this can pose many problems that need to be overcome. When dealing with team members whose native tongue is not English, it becomes important to be familiar with not only their language but also their culture. There are also other factors that receivers subconsciously apply to messages they receive. These subconscious factors, shown in Figure 6-3, affect how the team members both interpret the message and assess the source of the message.

Barriers to effective communication become obvious during the first few minutes of interaction when attention span is at its highest, the eye and ear focus on the sender, and the brain receives what it sees and hears. People tend to focus on what they see first. It takes only two to four minutes to create a positive or negative impression.[4] Success as a communicator is measured by the impressions created in the kitchen. Four key questions need to be addressed to overcome perception barriers:

- How am I perceived by others?
- How do I "sound" to others?
- What do I say to others?
- How well do I listen to others?

Depending on the field of experience of the receiver, significance may be applied to a part of you that has little to do with your skills as the chef supervisor—for example, the nonverbal messages sent by body language, how quickly you speak, your handshake, and how well you maintain eye contact.

GUIDELINES FOR EFFECTIVE COMMUNICATION

The effectiveness of communication is the responsibility of both the sender and receiver. The sender can communicate more effectively with the receiver by doing all of the following.

- Keep the message focused on its original purpose. This makes communication clearer and easier for all team members to follow.
- Check for understanding by asking questions and requesting feedback.
- Demonstrate interest and encourage clarity of interpretation by using open-ended questions that begin with *who, what, when, where,* and *how.*
- Communicate your ideas at the proper time and place. Try to catch team members at a time when their frame of mind is receptive to information. Use nonverbal signals. This shows you are interested in what is being said.
- Enhance the receiver's (team member's) self-confidence and encourage communication by complimenting the receiver.
- Use the receiver's name whenever possible. This demonstrates respect and acknowledgment.
- Communicate by your tone of voice, facial expressions, words, body language, and appearance that you care about the receiver and the message. All of these factors affect the reception of the message.
- Have the message clear in your mind before communicating. The more systematically the chef supervisor analyzes the problem or idea to be communicated, the clearer it becomes. Planning is essential to good communication. Consideration of the attitudes and emotions of the receiver who will be affected must be factored into the communication plan.

The receiver can be a more effective receiver by doing the following.

- Summarize by paraphrasing or restating the core of the message.
- Ask questions when unsure. A lot of confusion can be avoided by asking the sender to repeat or rephrase the message.
- Respond to nonverbal cues. This clarifies the meaning of a bodily reaction. It will ensure that behaviors and words convey the same message and also demonstrates understanding.
- Sincerity—and insincerity—in communicating will become apparent if careful thought is not part of the reception of ideas and opinions. In any communication there must be feedback from the receiver to the sender. The receiver should be made to feel free to respond fully.
- Seek not only to be understood, but also to understand.
- Be a good listener. When we are talking, we are often not listening. Listen for the full meaning of the sender's message.
- Analyzing body language, eye contact, and the verbal message assists in reaching meaningful conclusions about the information.

Trust and success are built on consistency and balance of interpersonal communications. What you sound like tells a lot about your personality, attitude, and anxiety level. Being aware of how you sound can help to correct and improve your communication skills. It is possible to learn to recognize signs of tension and stress in your voice and the voices of others. What you say is reflected by how you say it. Balance between language and delivery is critical in removing barriers. Verbal skills should support and balance the nonverbal and verbal messages sent.

Because the kitchen team will be diversified, agreement on meanings will vary. There will be variations on what is a "pinch" of salt, a "dash" of pepper, a "big" steak, or what "seasoned to taste" means. Assumptions and expectations distort the intended

BOX 6-1

WHAT IS THIS BUSINESS?
THIS IS NOT ROCKET SCIENCE

What we do in the restaurant business is not rocket science. The recipe for success is basic: hire the right person, train them to do the job, and follow-up on their performance, praising often and correcting as needed. As simple as the recipe may seem, I was in this business for many years before I discovered this critical truth. I would describe my early management style as grounded in the 1950s and 60s. If I did not like what a staff member was doing, I asked them to leave. I did not discuss what they were doing wrong or try to correct their actions. I was afraid that I would lose the opportunity to get rid of them if I tried to discuss the situation or correct their actions. I believed even then that it is all a team effort. I believe that we all work together. The individuals that make-up Grill Concepts and its restaurants do not work for me, we work together. Yet in those early years I fired in a summary fashion. "Here is your check, leave because you do not work here anymore."

In the early days of The Grill on the Alley, Chef Fausto was part of the team. The operation was running at an unanticipated pace with a minimum of 200 and often as many as 300 covers per night. I was not satisfied with Chef Fausto's performance so I had his final check prepared and I called him in to my office and told him that he was fired and gave him his final check. When I did this, the look on his face was one of complete surprise. As he left, I realized that he had no idea that he was not doing exactly what I wanted him to do. That was a critical turning point for me as a manager: the realization and acknowledgment to myself that the problem was not "Chef Fausto." The problem was my failure to communicate.

The philosophy of Grill Concepts and its restaurants is the acronym PEOPLE: Pride–Excellence–Opportunity–Profit–Leadership–Enjoyment. PEOPLE is a philosophy that must be applied internally and externally. It must be imbedded in the Grill's culture. This philosophy must be constantly communicated through the actions of those in a position to lead.

When I was in my 20's, my father closed his restaurant and I was unemployed with a family to support. I took a job at a paint store. It was a temporary position because the store was closing and going out of business, but it helped me stay afloat until I could get another job. The first thing that we did when I went to work at the paint store was organize the inventory and the store for the sale. In a very short period of time everyone was coming to me to find out how to organize and where stock was located. I began to realize that people trusted me and would listen to me.

When I went to work later for a company called FEDCO, Mr. George Cohn told me that "Follow me" was one of the most effective management styles. Today this is called modeling. One of the keys to my success has been my "Follow me" style. I did not just lead or manage; I worked to literally take everyone forward with me. I let them know that this is a company founded by someone who used to wash dishes and has experienced setbacks and loses.

Communication is critical to the success of any operation and any company. Hiring the right person must be followed by training. Training is the communication of expectations for performance. In the training process the values and the culture are also communicated. Training must be followed by positive action. What is being done correctly must be praised, and what is not correct must be recognized and assistance provided to bring about change.

The goal of Grill Concepts is to hire, train, and follow through in a manner that makes becoming part of the Grill the last restaurant job the individual needs to find. The communication of a path to a career is critical to retaining high performers. I am particularly proud of the number of team members that have been with the Grill for 15, 20, and 25 years. These individuals

(continued)

<table>
<tr><td colspan="2" align="center">〈 **BOX 6-1** **CONTINUED** 〉</td></tr>
</table>

take pride in their work and that pride is critical. These team members do not produce outstanding food because they are told to, they do it because that gives them a feeling of satisfaction and fulfillment; a feeling of a job well done.

What we do in the restaurant industry is feed people. Follow me and we will execute this basic task with excellence. We give the customer pleasure and enjoyment. We help them understand that you eat to survive, but that does not mean it cannot be enjoyable.

Bob Spivak,
Founder, Grill Concepts
Los Angles, California

communication. Clarify and explain each piece of the message. Clearly, a skillful chef supervisor does more than just relay the message. The problem is that many barriers muddle the process and hinder clear communication.

It should not be assumed that just because the chef supervisor "gave the message," the receivers "got it." One of the biggest problems of communicating in a tension-laden kitchen environment is the emotions of people who are sending and receiving messages. If something is said in anger, then it is the anger that comes across and not the message. Tempers flare, the receiver is likely to hear things that were not said, and the sender is likely to say things that were not intended. When we are criticized, we often become emotional and excited. Defensive reactions to feedback on job performances are common.

The fundamental communication barrier between people stems from differences in backgrounds, personalities, beliefs, education, religion, life experiences, and professional outlook. Our ability to receive messages is limited by our tendency to hear only what we want or expect to hear. It is a normal human phenomenon that the mind resists what it does not expect or want to perceive. We have a natural tendency to judge or evaluate statements and to reach hasty conclusions. We evaluate messages from our own frame of reference instead of understanding the sender's point of view. This does not add up to effective communication. Instead, two ideas are being advanced without an exchange of information. A closed mind hinders communication.

Limits on time impede communication. Chef supervisors are busy people and tend to give hurried instructions and then move on to the next task. The receiver can be confused or frustrated by these incomplete messages. Additionally, chef supervisors should pay particular attention to the problem of stereotyping. *Stereotypes* are attitudes favoring or rejecting certain groups without examining individual circumstances or traits. The need to understand numerous tasks forces the mind to arrange things into easily identifiable groups. Another barrier that often surfaces in the kitchen is the tendency to see everything in black and white, which distorts reality and oversimplifies situations.

A great deal of jargon is used in the kitchen. This jargon is familiar to those in the chef profession but is usually unintelligible to outsiders. Care should be taken when using French culinary terms such as *mise en place, sauté, garde manger, sous chef, chinois, rechaud,* and *a la carte* and the names of various dishes in different languages. This use tends not only to alienate team members, it also adds to confusion. Because many words have several meanings, word meanings can easily become confused in conversation. They often convey meaning to a receiver quite different from the meaning intended by the sender. Nonverbal signals, such as tone of voice, gestures, and appearance, are the most important factors in determining how a message is received and understood.

NONVERBAL COMMUNICATION

In general, senders are consciously attentive only to the spoken word, but individuals often communicate without using words. This is referred to as *nonverbal communication* or *body language*. Elements of nonverbal communication include gestures such as nodding the head, use of the hands, and facial expressions. All of these actions send messages. Smiling and frowning convey emotion, as does voice intonation or loudness. Ideally, the right nonverbal cues accompany the verbal communication. Nonverbal communication may influence the impact of a message more than verbal communication alone.

The meanings of gestures and movements vary from culture to culture. Communication scholars agree that nonverbal communication is most successful between people of similar cultural characteristics. When these characteristics differ, communication barriers occur.[5] Nonverbal gestures that would not be considered offensive in some cultures may be insulting to team members from other cultures. Some common gestures and what they mean are shown in Figure 6-4.

The chef supervisor should be aware of the gestures and body language used as well as the signals sent with such gestures. Many cues may be picked up from nonverbal body language that will indicate when communication will be most effective. These aspects of nonverbal communication are expressed through facial gestures, posture, orientation, gestures, eye contact, and appearance.

FIGURE 6-4   Nonverbal gestures.

- Leaning forward is a positive gesture. The person is listening and wishes to hear what is said. This also suggests acceptance and willingness to take action.
- Direct eye contact is a positive gesture in Euro-American cultures. Lack of eye contact despite sincere words is interpreted as untrustworthiness. However, many Oriental societies find direct eye contact rude.
- Open hands may be a sign of agreement and careful listening, while crossed arms and legs or leaning backward may be considered defensive, resisting, and rejecting.
- Arms folded over the chest with fists clenched is usually a sign that the person is not listening. This is indicative of a person who is nervous, anxious, uptight, and holding in emotions.
- Leaning away from you in a chair may indicate disinterest in what you are saying.
- Leaning far forward with defiant expression, hands spread on table, is indicative of a person with a volatile personality who may be frustrated, angry, and explosive.
- Backing away or avoidance is generally a sign of disagreement with what you say.
- Shaking a closed fist is a threatening gesture.
- Shoulders hunched forward and down with arms extended and hands overlapped in front of the body will usually indicate shyness.

LISTENING

Communication is always a two-way process. One person says something and another person hears what was said. Because each person comes to the listening situation with a different field of experience, there is often a gap between the speaker's intention and the listener's interpretation. Listening is the complex and selective process of receiving, focusing, deciphering, accepting, and storing what we hear. Listening does not occur without these five interrelated, yet distinct, processes.[6] Hearing is the absorption of sound. Listening is something quite different. Ineffective listening can be a major communication problem. Chef supervisors who listen carefully to their team will have fewer problems and greater success in quality management.

Poor listening habits may result in conflicts, costly errors, and inefficiency. Becoming an active and effective listener in the kitchen has important benefits:

- The chef supervisor can gain information from sources that may have been previously missed through poor listening.
- Even though the supervisor may not always agree with team members, at least the supervisor wil be perceived as being open and fair-minded.

This is achieved by being open and listening to team members' work problems without jumping to conclusions. Maintaining eye contact, an interested facial expression, and a calm voice reflects a posture of good listening. If the chef supervisor is narrow-minded, then active listening is impossible. Understanding the active listening process allows supervisors to target deficiencies in their own listening skills and to better receive messages. In addition, active listening is one of the most powerful means of creating warmth and sensitivity, which contributes to the overall motivational environment in the kitchen.

TYPES OF LISTENING

- *Critical listening.* Critical listening involves analyzing a message and judging the message for facts, documentation, logic, relationships, inferences, and personal biases. We use this form of listening whenever people try to persuade us to their point of view.
- *Discriminative listening.* Discriminative listening involves comprehension and recall. It requires listening for details, sequences, and then developing questions and answers, summarizing main points, evaluating ideas, and giving feedback. This is an essential listening skill for a chef supervisor.
- *Therapeutic listening.* Therapeutic listening involves listening with an understanding of another person's feelings, beliefs, and values. It requires supportive and sympathetic verbal and nonverbal feedback. It is appropriate when kitchen team members have work-related or personal problems they want to talk out. Nonverbal feedback includes sympathetic gestures—smiling, nodding, and leaning toward the speaker. This type of listening creates an atmosphere that lowers the speaker's defenses, allowing him or her to verbalize the problem.
- *Appreciative listening.* Appreciative listening is generally reserved for relaxation, satisfaction, or gratification. It is for personal enjoyment and can range from listening to music or enjoying the sound of the speaker's accent—the tone, rhythm, or brogue.

- *Courteous listening.* Courteous listening is conversational and social listening. We use courteous listening to keep interpersonal relationships intact. Courteous listening is used mainly to keep lines of communication open.

WAYS TO IMPROVE LISTENING SKILLS

- *Avoid distractions.* When communicating with someone, avoid distractions. Focus; concentrate your attention. Don't let your mind wander. Most people think at a rate of 500 words per minute. People talk at a rate of 150 words per minute. Stay focused on what is being said, or you will risk missing key points.
- *Listen for main ideas.* People sometimes formulate ideas as the conversation develops. These ideas and comments may be vague. Individuals may have trouble coming to the point, particularly if it concerns sensitive issues. Restate the other person's main ideas in your own words and ask if you have understood correctly.
- *Ask questions.* Ask questions during the discussion or conversation. If something is unclear or seems to contradict your personal sense of logic, seek clarity. This encourages the talker and shows that you are listening and are interested in what he or she has to say.
- *Suppress your biases.* We all have biases, opinions, and prejudices. While listening, we often allow certain words, ideas, or statements to trigger emotional responses. Give the speaker a chance to make the point. We may not like what is being said, but we should listen.
- *Indicate to the sender your feelings about the communication.* This shows empathy and clarifies the sender's position. However, refrain from interrupting the person speaking until he or she has had a chance to complete the sentence or thought.
- *Give your full attention.* Refrain from fidgeting, squirming, scribbling, twiddling your thumbs, sorting papers, or writing menus. Give the speaker your undivided attention. Most of us can do only one thing well at a time. Looking away during conversation communicates indifference to what the other person is saying. Show the other person the interest and attention that you yourself would like to receive.
- *Be sensitive and seek understanding.* Listen for the rationale behind what the other person is saying. This is important if what he or she is saying does not make sense to you. A kitchen team member may be making a request on the basis of erroneous information about the organization. Be sensitive and make sure you understand why people say what they do.
- *Respond to nonverbal cues.* This clarifies the meaning of a reaction. It ensures that behavior and words convey the same message and shows understanding.
- *Don't stop the flow.* Listen to all messages, not just the interesting ones. If we are poor listeners, our inclination is to stop listening. Too often we allow external or internal distractions to divert us from the speaker's message. Active listening skills are key. Seldom is a message so boring that we can't find reasons to listen.
- *Listen to the other person's point of view.* Consider the other person's emotions and background. Some people's background and motivations are so different from ours that we tend to ignore their perceptions. You may learn something new.

Listening will help the chef supervisor to get in touch with the feelings of the kitchen team. Chef supervisors who actively listen demonstrate respect, sensitivity, and patience toward the kitchen team. In addition, team members may have suggestions

FIGURE 6-5 Ten commandments for good listening.

1. Stop talking! You cannot listen if you are talking.
2. Put the talker at ease. Help the talker feel free to talk. This is often called a permissive environment.
3. Show the talker that you want to listen. Look and act interested. Do not read your mail while he or she talks. Listen to understand rather than to oppose.
4. Remove distractions. Don't doodle, tap, or shuffle papers. Wouldn't it be quieter if you shut the door?
5. Empathize with the talker. Try to put yourself in the talker's place so that you can see his or her point of view.
6. Be patient. Allow plenty of time. Do not interrupt the talker. Don't start for the door or walk away.
7. Hold your temper. An angry person gets the wrong meaning from words.
8. Go easy on argument and criticism. This puts the talker on the defensive. He or she may "clam up" or get angry. Do not argue: Even if you win, you lose.
9. Ask questions. This encourages the talker and shows you are listening. It helps to develop points further.
10. Stop talking! This is the first and last commandment, because all others depend on it. You can't listen well while you are talking. Nature gave us two ears but only one tongue, which is a gentle hint that we should listen more than talk.

that might provide ways of speeding up production, and they may suggest new menu items and recipes. But unless the chef supervisor is willing to listen, the ideas are lost, and so are additional team-building opportunities. The "Ten Commandments" for good listening shown in Figure 6-5 give solid suggestions for being an effective listener.

People generally like to hear what is consistent with their own belief structures; they usually resist contrary ideas.[7] It takes an open mind to be able to listen to criticism. Feedback as an element of communication is closely linked with good listening abilities. Unfortunately, most people do not learn feedback skills and therefore give critical feedback poorly.

GIVING DIRECTIONS

Giving directions to other team members in the kitchen is what gets every task started. The communication flow for effective directions is illustrated in the model in Figure 6-6. The manner used to give directions is as important as the information given. The clarity of directions given, along with tone of voice and facial expressions, will determine how well the direction will be received.[8]

Timing is very important. Try to catch team members in a frame of mind to listen. Present one idea at a time. For example, if you are training team members in the preparation of a new dish, break the process into its most basic steps. Present each step separately and ensure that each step is understood before proceeding. Keep to the topic. Try to speak clearly. Avoid ambiguities. Moderate the volume and speed of your speech. Maintain eye contact and leave time for questions and answers. Give team members any background information they may need to fully understand the direction. Keep it simple by using basic language with commonly understood words. Explain

FIGURE 6-6   Effective directions.

any technical terms and take special care to explain culinary terms. Make it brief. Don't use more words or time than needed. Too much information is as bad as too little. Without making it too obvious, repeat anything that is important for the listener to remember.

Personalize what you are saying and present it to the team member. Avoid generalizing or sounding vague. Eye contact is important. It will enable you to gauge reactions. We cannot respond to one another without it. Sounding bored or looking disinterested tells the team member that what you are saying is unimportant. Speak clearly and loudly enough to be heard. Do not mumble or talk fast; a short, sharp growl will ensure that the team member will not accept the direction. Explain carefully; do not assume that the team member knows what you are thinking. Make sure you are understood. If team members look confused or don't question your ideas, chances are they have not understood. Encourage team members to give thoughtful answers. Ask questions about what you have said. This will allow you to check for understanding.

An atmosphere that is conducive to open communication, cooperation, and trust will help create a collaborative team that will accept directions as a natural extension of coaching.[9] Bringing team members together on issues of mutual interest to generate suggestions is one way to do this. When kitchen team members recognize the benefits of helping one another and realize it is expected, they will work together to achieve common goals. The effectiveness of the chef supervisor's ability to give direction to the kitchen team is related directly to the ability of the team to carry out the workload to the required total quality standard.

LEADING A MEETING

Effective supervision and management requires meetings on an ongoing basis. The chef supervisor who can manage these meetings skillfully will provide the basis for improvement by getting the entire kitchen team involved. These meetings should proceed on the basis of what is known rather than on the unknown information. Meetings can be time-consuming. Leading a successful meeting requires quality *operation, facilitation, and management* of the meeting. The following are some guidelines for each of these facets of leading a productive meeting.

Meeting Operation

- Keep the meeting to a maximum of twelve people.
- Start the meeting on time.
- Be informal. Put the team at ease.
- Respect the contribution of every team member. Never belittle or ignore any statement made; all individuals have the desire to be recognized. In their minds, whatever they say is worthwhile.
- Avoid arguments.
- Avoid disagreeing personally with a team member in the group. Instead, call on others for their opinions and convey your thinking through their answers.
- Be tactful when correcting statements or opinions.
- Avoid giving too many personal opinions and experiences.

Meeting Facilitation

- Help each person in the team share in the discussion. Ask people in the team to speak up. Be sure that any question an individual asks is heard by the entire group. If the question asked is still inaudible, repeat the question before giving the answer. It can be most annoying to the team when an answer is given to a question that most of the group has not heard.
- Help all team members to formulate a statement or to express themselves. If anyone is finding it difficult to put across his or her point or if the statement is being misunderstood, rephrase the comments briefly before any discussion begins.
- Recognize those in the group who are bored or fail to show sufficient interest in the meeting. Direct "opinion" questions to them. Disinterested team members invariably become interested when their opinions are asked.
- Be alert to guide and encourage the nervous or timid members of the team. Avoid asking them fact questions. Draw them into the discussion by asking their opinions, directing "do you agree" questions to them, and complimenting them when they volunteer correct answers, saying, "That's exactly right" or "That's a good point."

Meeting Management

- Direct a question to a specific person in the team or interrupt and summarize the key points under discussion when the meeting gets out of control. Conclude with the correct information and begin discussion on another topic.
- Direct rapid-fire questions as a review, calling on specific individuals to arouse discussion if the team appears disinterested or is slow to offer opinions. Make a negative remark to arouse a defensive response from the team, or ask debatable questions (such as "Which is a better method . . ." or "Which is more practical . . .").
- Compliment the team before you close the meeting if you have had a particularly good session.
- Develop interest in the next meeting before closing a meeting. Briefly give highlights of the next session.

Meetings with productive outcomes are greatly influenced by how well the chef supervisor manages the meeting. Keep the discussion focused, and don't let the team go off on tangents or other issues. Save other issues for future meetings. The goals of a good meeting are action and results. Summarize the meeting and assign key result areas to individual team members with agreed benchmarks for future areas of improvement.

WRITTEN COMMUNICATION

PRINCIPLES OF WRITTEN COMMUNICATION

Audiences

The first thing to do is to establish exactly who the audience is with regard to the written communication. When this is known, it will help in communicating to that audience in a more unambiguous and effective way. It will also help limit the task of getting the message across. Decisions regarding the interpretation of the message will become clearer. How much time is available to your audience to determine their attitude toward the topic and writer? What do they know already? How much do they need to know? How will they use the information?

Use of Language

Generally, simplicity is preferred in written communication. Avoid ambiguity, long words, and above all, culinary jargon. Simplify the subject for the reader and be brief. It is best to use action verbs rather than passive verbs.

Be direct and to the point at all times. This is essential, particularly when giving written instructions. Sentences should contain one idea and should normally average no more than twenty words. The correct use of punctuation in sentences is important in order to highlight certain items and avoid confusing the reader.

Paragraphs are used to signal the reader and contain a theme. They should be six to seven lines in length. The first sentence of the first paragraph sets the tone of the communication.

Short words are easier to read. Shorter words such as "so" (or phrases) are easier to understand than longer ones meaning the same thing, such as "accordingly" and "consequently." Some examples of suggested word usage are shown in Figure 6-7.

GENERAL GUIDELINES

In today's business world, between letters, memos, email, and phone communication, individuals can be overwhelmed. Before sending any communication, ask yourself, "Is the content worthwhile?" Figure 6-8 provides some baseline standards for worthwhile communication.

FIGURE 6-7   Examples of word choice.

Don't Write	Instead, Write
activate	start, begin
approximately	about
demonstrate	show
dispatch	send
discontinue	stop
endeavor	try
facilitate	make easier
implement	carry out
optimum	best
requirement	need
terminate	end

FIGURE 6-8 Worthwhile communication is. . .

- Relevant
- Informative
- Of significance
- Credible
- Complete
- Of interest
- Clearly beneficial
- At appropriate knowledge level
- Clear and understandable
- Easy to read

Effective business communication must be well organized. The writer must answer the question, "Is the documents organization sensible?

- Have you stated the major point or idea in the first sentence?
- Have you considered a plan for an audience that could be angered, resentful, or disappointed about the content? (explanation given before refusal)
- When presenting bad news, have you opened with a neutral statement that your reader will find agreeable?
- Have you provided enough transitions and connectors to signal relationships?
- Is the material organized for best emphasis?
- Have you used a topic (orienting) sentence to begin each supporting paragraph?
- Are your paragraphs short enough to be readable?
- Does the document have a distinct introduction, body, and conclusion?
- Have you closed positively?

The writer must also answer the question, "Is the style readable and appropriate?'

- Is each sentence clear? (understandable on first reading)
- Is your message concise? (the most information expressed in the fewest words)
- Are your sentences fluent? (sentences varied in construction and length)
- Is the document written in plain English? (words that the audience will understand)
- Is the language precise? (conveys your exact meaning)
- Have you replaced abstractions and generalizations with concrete, specific, exact language?
- Is the tone unbiased and appropriate for your purpose and audience?
- Have you focused on the audience's needs and interests? (their perspective)
- Have you addressed your readers directly?
- Have you eliminated sexist language?
- Is your tone informal and conversational?[10]

MENUS AND RECIPES

In a kitchen, many instructions are transmitted to the team via written menus. How these menus are written by the chef supervisor determines how well individual team members perform the skills required for high-quality culinary art. Menus that are "posted" may be forthcoming banquets, special functions, or seasonal offerings. Although the menu is designed primarily to convey descriptive meaning to customers, it can also be the basis for a more technical, annotated written document through which the team receives instructions.

An annotated, expanded menu will convey not only all the essential dish ingredients but also other information such as portion size and various accompaniments. A menu used as a written form of communication and job instruction to kitchen team members should contain the following:

- Full descriptions and recipes for each dish
- How the dish should be prepared: breaded, cutlet, etc.
- Method of cooking: roasted, braised, sautéed, etc.
- Cut of meat: shoulder, loin, rib steak
- Quality of grade: USDA choice, prime, etc.
- Method of serving: casserole, skewer, etc.
- Explanation of culinary terms
- Cooking-time instructions
- Garnishing information
- Number of portions to be cooked
- Who is to perform tasks

Providing complete information, including the where, when, what, and how, that is easily understood will allow your culinary team to achieve consistently high quality. They will be better able to make efficient use of resources and team member skills to save time and simplify their tasks. Effective written communication to the teams makes the unknown known, allowing them to plan and better integrate team member knowledge to improve efficiency and quality.

A critical part of effective culinary communication is the recipe. A common fault in recipe writing is the assumption that those both writing and preparing the recipe understand culinary terms. The following lists the essentials of writing a clear recipe (include a photograph of the finished dish).

- Menu classification: dinner, lunch, breakfast, brunch, banquet, room service, or take-out
- Name of dish
- Yield, number of servings, portions
- Equipment and smallware needed
- Ingredients in order of use
- Quantity of ingredients (allow for cooking shrinkage)
- Complete detailed instructions
- Timing and temperatures to be used and other information for each phase of the preparation, and an outline of any special instructions
- Descriptive passages (avoid long ones; use simple instructions)
- Equipment needed for service
- Setting times and temperature for reconstituting prepared items
- Template to assist layout

BUSINESS WRITING

In addition to menu writing, the chef supervisor is involved in other types of business writing, such as memos to team members, superiors, and other department heads; the preparation of job descriptions, policies, and procedures; and notices to and general

FIGURE 6-9   Before writing, ask yourself:

- Why am I writing this? Is there a better way of getting my message across?
- What do I want the reader to do?
- How will I approach my subject?
- Who are my readers?
- Why will they be reading what I write?
- What does the reader already know about the subject?
- How will the reader use this document?
- What should I include?
- What should I leave out?
- What should I say first?
- How will I know when I've said enough?
- If the reader forgets everything else, what key point do I want remembered?
- Should I be writing this at this time?
- Should I send this at all? Am I too late?
- Is someone else communicating the same information? Should I check with that person?
- Should I include deadlines?
- Is my method of transmission the best? For example, should I be using email, traditional mail, or fax?

business communication with suppliers and vendors. Before writing a communication, a number of questions should be addressed, such as "What am I trying to say?" Figure 6-9 shows additional questions you should address in preparation for writing a memo, letter, or other business communication.

Memos

Memos are frequently used by chef supervisors to convey information to the kitchen team. These memos may vary in length, although they tend to be short notes. They often serve as permanent records of decisions and plans made during telephone conversations or meetings. The memo might be a reminder, a request, an acknowledgment, or a complaint. It might also convey good or bad news, information, or speculations. Memos may be sent to one team member or other individuals within the foodservice organization. With this broad range of purpose and audience, memos vary considerably in formality.

Letters

Like memos, business letters vary in length and formality. Some are actually brief notes and others extend over a number of pages. Because letters allow chef supervisors to present themselves to outsiders, they can serve as important public relations tools. The businesslike format of a letter is as important as its clear prose style and coherent organization. The purpose of most letters is to inform, request, or persuade. Unlike a telephone conversation or other oral communication, letters provide written records and often serve as contracts. As in all written communication, revision and rewriting are essential. Write simply; using concrete words and short sentences. Unify paragraphs on a single topic. The first sentence should set the tone and give the reason for the communication. Last, never sign a letter until you are sure it is perfect. Regardless of who processes the letter, if you sign it, you are responsible for its appearance and content.

FIGURE 6-10 Guidelines for email clarity.

- Be careful about assuming the reader has the background knowledge and experience necessary to understand the message.
- Remember that the reader cannot hear the inflection in your voice or see the expression on your face. This can be extremely important in the use of humor or when responding to an emotional issue.
- Use correct spelling and punctuation.
- Avoid slang and idioms.
- Proofread your message.

Email

The primary form of interoffice/interproperty communication today is email. Email provides an inexpensive, efficient means of communication within the business. However, people often view email as a less formal form of communication and therefore do not apply the same principles of written communication. This perspective is faulty. Although email can generate actual dialogue between parties through an email "stream," it should be remembered by all parties that the email is written communication.

Misunderstanding can be an outcome of email. Users often respond to email as if they were talking to the person in person or on the phone. The content of the email is not always interpreted by the reader as intended by the sender, because the reader does not have the benefit of voice inflection to help guide him or her to the correct interpretation. Remember the concepts of sender and receiver discussed earlier in this chapter. When communicating by email, it is extremely important to ensure that not only are the words correct, but that they will be interpreted when read without voice inflection or nonverbal communication clues in the manner intended.

To ensure effective email communications, you should apply the principles of communication as you would to a letter or memo. Although speed of communication is a benefit of email, application of some simple guidelines will assist in making your email communications effective. Some basic guidelines for email communication are shown in Figure 6-10.

It is also important to remember that what you put in an email is a written record. Do not write something in an email that you will regret if it is made part of a document later. The key to effective email communication in the workplace is to apply the same principles to it that you do to memos and letters.

COMMUNICATION VIA THE GRAPEVINE

The "grapevine" is informal communication, and it typically follows the pattern of personal relationships among kitchen team members. Informal communication networks generally exist because team members have a desire to know information that is not formally communicated. The informal communication, grapevine, or gossip element can be a useful way for the chef supervisor to test a new idea or some proposed change. The grapevine has several distinct characteristics. It springs up and is not controlled by the chef supervisor. It is used largely to serve the self-interests of the kitchen staff.

Chef supervisors should be aware of the potential advantages and disadvantages of information conveyed via the grapevine. It may be used to test team members' reactions prior to handing down the "official" information. Obtaining feedback from the team informally can be used to gauge acceptance or compliance with new ideas or change. It is important that the information carried through the grapevine will not harm or frighten team members. Rumors relating to change can cause team members to feel insecure and create fear. If rumors are based on false or damaging information, the grapevine can be harmful to the overall foodservice organization. The degree of harm inaccurate information causes depends largely on the work climate prevailing in the kitchen. If morale is low and there is poor chef supervision, harmful rumors can easily find acceptance.

Some rumors should be dispelled immediately. To do this, the source of the rumor needs to be established. Ask the team members about the rumor and offer to share the facts. Rumors flourish when there is limited communication. By supplying the facts and adequate information in an open, honest, and free atmosphere, rumors can be quashed and the uncertainty on which they grow removed. Gossip regarding team members' personal dispositions should not be tolerated.

CONCLUSIONS

Communication is a vital element of the chef supervisor's job. Without open, honest, and continuous communication, quality diminishes and can be lost. It is not unusual, however, to encounter chef supervisors who believe that if they are "removed" and aloof from the rest of the kitchen staff, they are effective leaders. In the past this type of chef supervisor was acceptable. This is no longer true. Team building, coaching, and continuous improvement of the foodservice operation require communication, which is fundamental to supervision. A good chef communicator will be rewarded with a motivated team prepared to give their best and go beyond the norms. Communication, of which listening is such an important element, will also convey sincerity and develop trust among the team. Communication is important. It is the bedrock of quality management. Information is power. When transferred to the team, it *empowers* them to develop, grow in confidence, and make valuable contributions to the growth of the business and the reputation of the foodservice organization.

Summary

As much as 85 percent of the chef supervisor's working day is spent in some form of communication. Effective supervision relies on the ability of the supervisor to transfer information in such a way that it is understood by the receiver in a way that the chef supervisor intended. Open and honest communication is critical to this process.

Interpersonal communication contains three basic elements: the source/sender, the message, and the destination/receiver. Understanding these elements ensures successful communication. Barriers may exist that prohibit effective communication. Communication barriers between people stem from differences in background, personalities, and life experiences.

Nonverbal communication is important. The chef supervisor should be aware of gestures and body language used. Many cues may be picked up from body language.

Listening is an important aspect of good communication. Supervisors who listen carefully to their team have fewer problems and greater success in implementing quality management. Poor listening skills often result in conflicts, errors, and inefficiency. Ways to improve listening skills should be understood and practiced.

Giving directions is what gets the job done. The manner and methods used to give these directions are as important as the directions given.

Managing meetings effectively requires skills. Carefully managed and controlled meetings can make major contributions to continuous improvement and quality management. Productive outcomes are greatly influenced by how well the chef supervisor manages meetings.

Written communications via email, memos, letters, and the menu are important methods of transferring information. The language used should be clear and free of jargon. The principles of written communication should be applied to all forms of written communication.

The "grapevine" is also a method of transferring information. Therefore the chef supervisor should have an awareness of the potential advantages and disadvantages of this informal communication method.

Discussion Questions

1. Communication between sender and receiver passes through filters of culture, age, gender, education, and fields of experience. What are the effects of this process?
2. How do overlapping fields of experience often lead to effective communication?
3. What are the elements of nonverbal communication? How do these differ within various ethnic groups?
4. What are the different types of listening? Give a brief explanation of each.
5. In what five ways can chef supervisors improve their listening skills?
6. Giving directions to other team members is what gets every job started. What are the five steps essential to getting the job done?
7. Meetings can be time-consuming! What steps can be taken to decrease meeting time consumption and increase meeting effectiveness?
8. What strategies should be adopted with regard to written communication?
9. What are the guidelines for writing emails that clearly communicate the intended message?
10. How can communication via the grapevine be used to serve the interests of those within it?
11. What is meant by the phrase "information is power" with reference to the kitchen team?

Notes

1. Donna Fantetti, *Career Directions* (Providence, RI: P.A.R., 1987), 34.
2. Robert Heinich, Michael Molenda, and James D. Russel, *Instructional Media and the New Technologies of Instruction,* 3rd ed. (New York: Macmillan, 1989), 6.
3. Anna Katherine Jernigan, *The Effective Foodservice Supervisor* (Rockville, MD: Aspen, 1989), 31.
4. Fantetti, *Career Directions,* 34.
5. Franklin B. Krohn and Zafur U. Ahmed, "Teaching International Cross-Cultural Diversity to Hospitality & Tourism Students," *Hospitality & Tourism Educator,* November 1991.
6. Raymond Dumont and John M. Lannon, *Business Communications,* 2nd ed. (Boston: Brown, 1987), 526.
7. Bruce B. Tepper, *The New Supervisor: Skills for Success* (New York: Irwin, 1994), 48.
8. Robert B. Maddux, *Team Building: An Exercise in Leadership* (London: Crisp, 1992), 48.
9. Ibid., p. 49.
10. Adapted from Dumont and Lannon, *Business Communications.*

CHAPTER 7
THE CHEF AS LEADER

OBJECTIVES

When you complete this chapter, you should be able to:

1. Distinguish between supervision and leadership
2. Describe the elements of directive behavior and supportive behavior
3. Describe desirable leadership behavioral qualities
4. Explain directing, coaching, supporting, and delegating as they pertain to situational leadership
5. Outline actions that contribute to leadership self-confidence
6. Apply steps that are particular to culinary leadership

Case Study: CROWN HOTEL

Chef Mark Macklin, after thirty-six years as executive chef of the Crown Hotel, has retired. Chef Macklin was affectionately known as "Chef Mac," and he was held in high esteem by the hotel staff. Chef Mac had hired the hotel's thirty-five chefs and cooks and twenty-nine kitchen support staff, and many of them have worked at the hotel for over twenty years. It was widely known by the hotel staff that Chef Mac's decision to retire was encouraged by the hotel owners.

The chef who was selected to replace Chef Mac as executive chef is Chef Wayne Bryson. Chef Bryson is twenty-six years old. He is the youngest chef ever to earn the prestigious certification of "Master Chef." Chef Bryson has won multiple gold medals in state, national, and international competition. He has even been mentioned in culinary circles as a possible future manager of the American Culinary Olympic Team. Chef Bryson had been executive sous chef of the renowned Windsor Hotel for three years before coming to the Crown Hotel as executive chef.

The owners of the Crown Hotel have widely publicized that Chef Bryson will be leading the culinary team at the "Crown." The owners have been quoted in newspapers as saying that "Chef Bryson is a tremendous addition to the Crown family, an addition we anticipate will bring the Crown to new levels of culinary excellence."

The hotel grapevine says that the owners have instructed Chef Bryson to bring the Crown's food into the twenty-first century.

Chef Bryson has been at the Crown for three months. He meets at least once a week with the kitchen management team to present new initiatives that they are to carry out. He regularly notifies the other kitchen staff by memo of the initiatives and their role in the initiatives. Chef Bryson has developed new menus, and all of the recipes and other information to support the menus, for all areas of the hotel. Development of the recipes for the menus has required that Chef Bryson spend a great deal of time in the small catering and banquet kitchen, working closely with the small team of cooks that he brought with him from the Windsor. He has also spent a great deal of time working with the office staff, technology consultant, and print designer to finalize the menus and support material. Chef Bryson introduced the new menu and recipes to the kitchen management two weeks before the rollout of the new menus, with instructions for them to train their teams.

The new menus have been in place for one month with extremely poor results. Food and labor cost have both increased, customer complaints have increased, and absenteeism is at an all-time high. The nonguest count in the hotel's restaurants has declined by 10 percent. The hotel's "white tablecloth" restaurant, the only two-star restaurant in the city, is due for review in two months, and currently the possibility is strong that it will be downrated to one star. The owners of the Crown had anticipated that it would become the only three-star restaurant in the city with Chef Bryson on the team.

Based on what you have learned from previous chapters and the content of this chapter, answer the following questions.

- What is the overall reason for the challenges in the Crown's foodservice department?

- What are the primary causal agents for the challenges in the Crown's foodservice department?
- What role did leadership and supervision/management play in the decline in the Crown's foodservice department?
- What specific steps could have been taken to avoid the current situation in the Crown's foodservice department?
- What, specifically, can be done to overcome the challenges and generate motion in a positive direction for the Crown's foodservice department?

DEFINING AUTHORITY, MANAGEMENT, AND LEADERSHIP

Authority, management, and leadership are generally interrelated, but they are not synonymous. Consider carefully the following definitions:

- *Authority* is the right and power to command.
- *Management* is both the act of controlling something, such as a business, and the group invested with the authority to control something.
- *Leadership* is influencing, guiding, and leading people to follow a course of action or line of thought.

Authority, the right and power to command—in business and in the kitchen—is linked to the various positions. Simply put, incumbent in the position of chef is the right and power to command the staff in the kitchen. The level and extent of authority incumbent in a position is linked to the hierarchy of the positions in the establishment. Generally, positions and therefore authority can be viewed as a pyramid. The greatest, broadest authority is at the top of the pyramid and resides in a very few positions, as shown in Figure 7-1. The chef is generally close to the top or at the top of the pyramid.

Authority and power can be derived in three ways:

- Authority is vested in the position.
- Delegation of authority occurs because specific activities in the kitchen require a manager. This manager is often the chef with the most skill or experience. Skill or experience is frequently a factor in promotion to the position of supervisor.
- Situations occur that require leadership in the kitchen. Through a general consensus, one individual in the group earns that recognition. The leader assumes control.

Authority of position exists by virtue of the position, not the individual. The chef uses the authority of the position to manage the kitchen. The power of the authority vested in the chef's position provides the means for controlling and directing the kitchen team. How the authority is used determines the working environment for the kitchen team and ultimately the success or failure of the team. If the chef's authority is

FIGURE 7-1 Hierarchy of positions and level of authority.

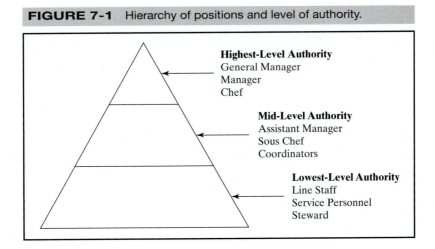

Highest-Level Authority
General Manager
Manager
Chef

Mid-Level Authority
Assistant Manager
Sous Chef
Coordinators

Lowest-Level Authority
Line Staff
Service Personnel
Steward

by virtue of the title alone, it is likely that there will be a lack of team commitment, poor morale, low productivity, and high turnover among the kitchen workforce.

Leadership does not rest with a position. Leadership is rooted in the individual and empowered by the group. Leadership is not the sole domain of those in positions of authority. Leaders are vested with power by the individuals they lead. People follow

BOX 7-1

WHAT IS THIS BUSINESS?
THE MANAGER IN THE CHEF AND
THE CHEF IN THE MANAGER

The foodservice industry is constantly growing and changing. This has been especially true in the past decade, with food television becoming so widely enjoyed as both entertainment and education. Chefs are more than creators of the masterpieces on the canvas of the plate; they are sensory rock stars of the palate and the maestros of the food industry!

So what does is take to be a chef in this evolving industry? There was once a day when the kitchen was off limits to front-of-the-house managers. Chefs ran the kitchen by different rules, their rules. The chef did not consider the rest of the operations their concern as long as the servers were there to pick up and run the food when it was hot, stacked their dished correctly, and listened up. Creations were king, purveyors

were the adversary, and the guests, well, depending on the chef, were not king, but unknowing and troublesome. Well, those days are long gone.

Today's professional chef, in many ways is more well rounded than any other member of the management team. Chefs have to be—they carry the biggest responsibility for costs: labor and food. They are the captain of the "engine," the conductor of the train; the chefs are the ones that can make or break the show. Sequence of service, food and beverage pairing, selection of the canvas of the food presentation, serviceware, and descriptions of creations, all these points and more are critical to chefs and their desired goal of menu mix, labor control, and food cost.

So, is the art lost? Is the art of creating the incredible dish that the guests will come

(continued)

BOX 7-1 *CONTINUED*

begging for, is that art lost? The leaders, the chefs who inspire through inspiration and intimidation, are they gone? The chef who knows it all and the guests who are left wondering "How did they do that?", is this gone? The answer to these questions is a resounding yes and no. What is for sure is that knowledge is power, and the knowledge is out there in buckets full! The availability of culinary education has exploded in the past few decades. The chef's knowledge of food and techniques must be solid, because guests aren't as easily impressed with dishes, methods, or tricks of the trade. The guests are also pursuing their food knowledge through books and food TV. They themselves are becoming great home chefs.

Food is not enough in today's market. Today's "new" chef must be able to do more than make a good *burre blanc* sauce. Today's chef must be a professional manager with a specialization in food. The quest for more knowledge must run through the chef's veins like a doctor studying medicine. This quest for knowledge must be the co-inspiration in the preparation and creation of delectable dishes. A passion for knowledge and a passion for food are the co-anchors for today's chef.

Computers and technology are a chef's best friends. Today's professional chef uses technology as a tool for managing the kitchen. Costing out recipes, studying menu mixes, order guides, training programs, product checklists, all these and many more are managed through technology.

With the "X" generation's desire for more, better, and faster, they are not as likely as in the past to study under a chef for three to five years to gain the experience. Training practices, evaluation methods, managing, leading, and inspiring need to be sharp. The team members are smart, and desire more explanation, which means that the teacher must be on top of the game. Concerns with team members used to be handled by Human Resources, but to keep the operation out of hot water, the chef needs to be very well versed in laws, regulations, and professional industry practices—the walls between the front of the house and the back of the house are disappearing.

The guests of the restaurant are expecting more. Food is being evaluated critically by much more educated consumers. They are aware of food-borne illness, of the difference between "select" and "choice," of heirloom vegetables and organics. They question the methods, temperatures, and pairings of food and beverage. Today's chef has to have knowledge of food and nutrition trends on a par with or ahead of that of the guests.

Purveyors are not to be viewed as pushy salesmen, but rather as allies in the quest to make great, profitable food. The products and services that they offer a chef is a support structure that can improve food cost and help control labor costs. The timeliness of deliveries, pack sizes of products, and product availability can keep an operation ahead of the curve and help make a chef and his operation successful.

The industry is alive and well and being developed by those who see the future of the professional chef. The manager is in the chef and the chef is a manager, one who utilizes the skills, talents, information, in other words, all the resources available.

Guy Fieri, Food Network Star
Owner, Johnny Garlic's and TexWasabi
Santa Rosa, California

a leader for a variety of reasons, including common beliefs, their belief in the leader's vision, respect for the leader, and their belief that through the leadership their goals will be achieved. There can be no leader without followers. Leaders exist at all levels of an organization. Appreciation of this fact will increase the chef supervisor's ability to manage the kitchen team.

Leadership in the kitchen does not depend on team member incentives or pleasant working conditions. The chef supervisor's ability to motivate people to perform is independent of these factors. Leaders are *made,* not born. Leadership can be learned the way chefs learn culinary skills. Myth associates leadership with superior position. It assumes that if you are on top, you are automatically a leader. But leadership is not a place; it is a process. It involves skills and abilities that are useful whether one is in the executive suite or on the front line.[1] The one who influences others to follow only is a leader with certain limitations. The one who influences others to lead is a leader without limitation.[2]

The chef can have the authority of the position and manage the kitchen without being a leader. Adding leadership to the mix of authority and management can bring another level of power. This power moves beyond directing and controlling to influencing, guiding, and leading the team. Leadership moves the chef from the authority to the leader of the team. The central theme of leadership is getting things accomplished through people. Leadership in the kitchen confers on the chef supervisor the privilege and responsibility to direct the actions of the kitchen team in carrying out the pursuits of the organization. As team leader, the chef can bring the team to a higher level of cooperation and teamwork. The successful chef supervisor will use the authority that comes with the position effectively and will earn the power that can be derived from leadership.

BOX 7-2

CHEF TALK:
LEADERSHIP IS A PRIVILEGE

Like a good recipe, there are many ingredients that make up a good leader; and like a good recipe, it takes quality components, just the right seasoning, and preparation to create a dish worthy to be called delicious. Leadership is tough but so rewarding! From my perspective as a female culinary professional, I've experienced the highs and lows of developing my own leadership style. When I get overwhelmed at times with my personal and professional responsibilities, I try to put it into perspective, think about preparing as I do a good recipe, choosing quality and continually working to polish myself into a well-seasoned individual.

Bottom line is this—Leadership is a privilege. Others put their faith, hope, and trust into you as an individual who can demonstrate competency from a technical as well as a conceptual perspective. As a leader, you have the dedicated responsibility of providing the right climate in which the goals of the organization can be met as well as those of whom you are

leading. What a challenge, and more than that, it's the most extraordinary juggling act!

In October of 2000, I was challenged with the opportunity to serve as captain for the Team 2000 US Culinary Olympic Team. My charge was to hone a team of chefs so tightly together that we could anticipate each other's needs, polish our skills, and achieve the goal of winning a gold medal at the 2000 Culinary Olympics in Erfurt, Germany. Not only did we win one of five gold medals in our category, we placed third in the overall championship out of forty-four teams worldwide. It was one of the greatest highlights of my professional career. But, as it is said, it's not the destination but it is the journey in getting there. It was not an easy path; we definitely had our share of obstacles. We experienced flurries of emotions, logistical challenges such as working in a foreign country, shipping food ingredients overseas and praying they got through customs! We had sleepless nights, we had laughs, and we had moments of

(continued)

BOX 7-2 *CONTINUED*

frustration. As the leader of this group, I had the duty to provide the atmosphere that would serve as the platform for us to realize our individual and team goals. When the officials placed that gold medal around my neck, and we shot our team photo, it was such a moment of accomplishment. As the one who was responsible for the team, even if we hadn't won, I can say with such confidence that we prevailed as we did because we were prepared.

As a leader, you must be prepared. It's a matter of taking the philosophies we instill in the kitchen as chefs and allowing those to trickle into other areas of our lives. *Mise en place* isn't just in the kitchen. It's important to have our professional and personal *mise en place* just as organized to be a successful leader! I believe it is paramount to choose to be a good example and demonstrate proper confidence. Almost anyone can manage a system if they are trained, but it takes extraordinary individuals to demonstrate themselves as a good example for others to follow as well as project themselves as dedicated leaders while managing what is going on around their environment. We desperately need better leaders in this field. There are too many crummy managers out there. We've all worked with them and had to tolerate them. It's a challenge to make a conscience choice to be the example, promote others through good management, and project ourselves as the outstanding leaders we can be. *Mise en place;* surround yourself in it, because it is the foundation to success.

Chef Jill K. Bosich, CEC, CCE, AAC,
Executive Chef/Program Advisor,
The Southern California Gas Company, Downey
(Regional Team Captain, Team USA 2007)

LEADERSHIP DEVELOPMENT

Leaders play a crucial role in quality. They have to be primary agents for improvement. They work to create an environment in which the kitchen team can experience pride. Their efforts are directed toward allowing all kitchen team members to perform their jobs to the utmost. Leaders take risks based on the self-knowledge that mistakes are opportunities, not failures. They have the ability to let go of concepts that block new ideas and learning. Leaders balance action against inaction and balance praise against correction. Competent leaders have sufficient expertise to make good judgments and get things done. President Dwight D. Eisenhower summarized leadership as follows: "The one quality that can be developed by studious reflection and practice is the leadership of men."[3]

Warren Bennus and Burt Nanus, in their book, *Leaders: The Strategies for Taking Charge,* observed the following myths:

Myth 1: "Leadership is a rare skill." Nothing could be further from the truth. Although great leaders may be as rare as great runners, great actors, or great painters, everyone has leadership potential. The truth is that leadership opportunities are plentiful and within the reach of most people.

Myth 2: "Leaders are born, not made." Biographies of great leaders sometimes read as if they entered the world with an extraordinary genetic endowment, that somehow their future leadership role was preordained. Don't believe it. Whatever natural endowments we bring to the role of leader can be enhanced.

Myth 3: "Leaders are charismatic." Some are, most aren't. Charisma is the result of effective leadership, not the other way around.

Myth 4: "Leadership exists only at the top of an organization." In fact, the larger the organization, the more leadership roles it is likely to have.

Myth 5: "The leader controls, directs, prods, and manipulates." This is perhaps the most damning myth of all. Leadership is not so much the exercise of power as the empowerment of others. Leaders are able to translate intentions into reality by aligning the energies of the organization behind an attractive goal. Once these myths are cleared away, the question becomes one not of how to become a leader, but rather of how to improve one's effectiveness at leadership.[4]

Traits that are the basic elements of leadership can be taught. If a chef supervisor wants to be a good leader, nothing can stop the process. Ninety percent of leadership traits can be taught and developed. The 10 percent who are gifted will succeed only if the development and growth of leadership are pursued.

As noted earlier the terms *management* and *leadership* are often used interchangeably. They can be synonymous, but they mean different things. In the past, terms such as *people management* were used to indicate authoritarian control. This people management philosophy has been shown to be folly. As H. Ross Perot stated, "People cannot be managed. Inventories can be managed, but people must be led."[5] The piece from the *Wall Street Journal* reproduced in Figure 7-2 subtly demonstrates the difference between management and leadership.

According to Patrick L. O'Malley, chairman emeritus of the Canteen Company, leadership in the foodservice industry is about:

> . . . doing the job at hand with the energy required with all your resources being used efficiently. It means getting the right people in the right place for the job they will be committed to do. It means motivating your colleagues and employees, directing them skillfully, providing adequate training, getting to understand them and communicating with them.[6]

FIGURE 7-2   Let's get rid of management.

> People don't want to be managed.
> They want to be led.
> Whoever heard of a world manager?
> World leader, yes.
> Educational leader.
> Political leader.
> Scout leader.
> Community leader.
> Business leader.
> They lead.
> They don't manage.
> If you want to manage somebody, manage yourself.
> Do that well and you'll be ready to stop managing and start leading.

Source: The Wall Street Journal.

FIGURE 7-3 Persistence.

Nothing in the world can take the place of persistence.
Talent will not; nothing is more common than unsuccessful men with great talent.
Genius will not; unrewarded genius is almost a proverb.
Education will not; the world is full of educated derelicts.
Persistence, determination alone are omnipotent.
The slogan "press on" has solved and always will solve the problems of the human race.

Calvin Coolidge

In order to lead the kitchen team skillfully, chef supervisors must master the skills of leadership and have a passion to succeed. They must show the way and lead by example. They must have a clear idea of what they want to do and the strength of purpose to persist in the face of setbacks, even failures. They know where they are going and why.

President Calvin Coolidge astutely pointed out that persistence in any endeavor will equal success, as shown in Figure 7-3. Developing leadership skills requires a great deal of persistence.

Leadership style is something that each chef supervisor develops individually. Essentially, style is based on two behaviors, known as directive behavior and supportive behavior.[7] *Directive behavior* is authoritarian behavior, which concentrates on control, structure, and strict supervision. *Supportive behavior* is about enabling, coaching, facilitating, and praising. Solid chef leadership is established using a combination of directive and supportive behavior. A true leader is a person that other people want to follow, because they trust and respect that leader.

BOX 7-3

WHAT IS THIS BUSINESS?
CO-WORKERS

My company, Lawry's Restaurants, Inc., is an "institution" nearly ninety-two years old. I use the word "institution" because, in so many ways, that is what we have become.

It was founded by, and is still owned and operated by, two families, the Franks and the Van de Kamps, by my father and uncle (my mother's brother) in 1915 as a tiny retail potato chip shop in downtown Los Angeles. This enterprise evolved over two years into a successful bakery chain (Van de Kamp's), later a food products manufacturer (Lawry's Foods), and the restaurant group we still control.

Very few family businesses spanning three generations of management have managed to survive and prosper. In our case, there were several good reasons for the accomplishment. For one, we had an entrepreneurial bent that led to the development of two famous brands; for another, we were in the right place (Southern California) at the right point in time. But, by far, the most important was the business culture that has engendered the continuous enthusiasm and loyalty of our employees. We call this our co-worker culture.

It began early on and was based on a set of business principles and ethics which the company founders embodied and believed in. My father never acknowledged that an "employee" worked for him. Instead, they were co-workers—beginning with him and including every other person on the payroll. The key to the culture is just that our co-workers have always considered themselves as just that, an important part of an important venture, regardless of the position they hold. Without that belief, the world falls flat, meaningless.

Remarkably, we have been able to instill this sense of self-importance in the co-workers of very different types of business, in many geographical locations, and over nine decades. It was done, in part, because the owners and executives have lived it, believed in it, and preached and promoted it. Co-workers follow suit and become ambassadors and salespeople to those newly employed, as well as to the other company constituents they meet, i.e., customers, purveyors, and its public at large. This engenders a sense that there is something unique and important about being a member of the organization. The co-worker "spirit" leads to a sense of pride and loyalty and a team attitude—all of which builds upon itself. If newcomers don't "get it" in a reasonable time, they don't fit in and they leave.

Some twenty-five years ago, I put the unwritten set of principles in writing. Called Lawry's Code of Business Principles and Ethics, a copy is given to every new co-worker as he or she joins the company, and plaques of the Code are prominently displayed in all places where our business is conducted. We want our customers, as well as our co-workers, to be aware of what we stand for. And often is the time when a question is asked—"Are we following our code of ethics if we do or say

that?" It actually forces a discipline of doing the right thing.

One very important positive that has endured from our company culture is the far lower co-worker turnover than is found in most competitive restaurant businesses and, in fact, in business firms in general. This phenomenon has occurred over the long period of family ownership, with the average of all co-worker tenure being five to ten years. And this is in kinds of businesses in which a large segment of the payroll is in low-wage categories. Twenty-five, thirty, forty, and even a few fifty years of service has not been unusual. We give out numerous long-term service awards each year and sponsor an annual Heritage Club luncheon for those who have given the company fifteen and more years of service. It's a looked-for and appreciated event.

This loyalty obviously is strongly identified in our company kitchens. Our executive chefs and their sous chefs, for the large part, have worked for us for years, and many started at very bottom jobs. They are very proud to be part of the team, and we are even more proud of them. These are the people and their fellow co-workers who made the business prosper and, while those of us in the "executive suite" may point the way, it's our co-workers who deserve the credit.

Richard N. Frank,
Chairman, Lawry's Restaurants, Inc.,
Pasadena, California

Leadership development is, first, a process of self-development. It is facilitated by education, training, mentoring, and experience. The success of a chef supervisor depends on more than the source of authority or having a title thrust upon him or her. The better the chef's leadership skills, the greater will be the satisfaction and productivity of the kitchen team. These kitchen leadership qualities and skill sets are shown in Figure 7-4.

These elements of leadership are necessary so that the team can have confidence in the chef as a supervisor and in the knowledge that there is direction and purpose to what they do. Trusting the chef supervisor is vital to leadership in order to have a productive kitchen team environment. Leadership includes open and honest communication and helps to promote loyalty and commitment of the team.[8]

FIGURE 7-4 Kitchen leadership qualities and skills.

- Creativity
- Confidence in one's abilities
- Good communication skills
- Ability to make decisions
- Trust in the kitchen team to do the job
- Desire to develop skills in others
- Comfort level in giving directions
- Ability to motivate the people
- Ability to take measured risks

TRAIT THEORIES

The *trait approach to leadership* is based on early research that seemed to assume that a good leader is born and not made. The reasoning was that if a complete profile of the characteristics (traits) of a successful leader could be summarized, it would be fairly easy to pinpoint those individuals who should (or should not) be placed in leadership positions. This was known as the "great man" theory.[9] The theory has been abandoned over the years because evaluation of a number of these trait studies proved to be inconclusive. Over eighty years of study have failed to produce one single personality trait or set of qualities that can be used consistently to separate those who are leaders from those who are not. Chefs of diverse backgrounds, ethnic origins, gender, and personality have been effective leaders. All they needed was the desire to lead. However, studies have also shown that there are some personal characteristics that distinguish effective leaders from ineffective ones.

Research has shown that there are two distinct dimensions of leadership, *employee-centered* and *production centered*. Therefore, a leader's personal characteristics and behavior do not in themselves guarantee leadership effectiveness. Perception of the kitchen team, the nature of the tasks, the relationship with the team members, and the organizational climate in the kitchen must all come together to provide effective supervisory leadership.

BEHAVIORAL THEORIES

Behavioral theories have been directed toward the study of leaders, supervisors, and work groups, rather than just focusing on the characteristics of successful leaders. In the past, emphasis was on studying the behaviors that provide effective interaction among workgroup members. Studies have shown that two independent characteristics are important elements of supervisory behavior. Elements of *consideration* include behaviors indicating mutual trust, respect, and a certain warmth and rapport between the supervisor and the group. *Structure* includes behavior in which supervisors organize and define group activities and their relations to the group.[10]

In their book, *The Leadership Challenge,* Kouzes and Posner similarly reported that behaviors followers expect from their leaders include honesty, competence, vision, and inspiration.[11] Another study, by Cichy, Sciarini, and Patton, discovered fourteen desirable leadership behaviors and qualities, which are shown in Figure 7-5.[12]

> **FIGURE 7-5**   Desirable leadership behaviors and qualities.
>
> - Provide a compelling message or vision.
> - Have a strong personal value or belief system.
> - Recognize that the ability to adjust is a necessity.
> - Make desired outcomes tangible.
> - Encourage and reward risk taking.
> - Listen as well as, if not better than, they speak.
> - Provide appropriate information, resources, and support to empower employees.
> - Be inquisitive.
> - Emphasize quality continuously.
> - Know personal strengths and nurture them.
> - Place a high value on learning.
> - Maintain precise desired outcomes.
> - Change your mind seldom.
> - Have strong family values.

Source: Ronald Cichy, Martin P. Sciarini, and Mark E. Patton, "Food-Service Leadership: Could Attila Run a Restaurant," *The Cornell Hotel and Restaurant Administration Quarterly,* February 1992.

Denis Kinlaw, in studies outlined in *Coaching for Commitment,* uncovered similar behaviors of superior leaders, which he summarizes under six sets of common practices:

1. *Establishing a vision.* Superior leaders create expectations for significant and lasting achievement. They give meaning to work by associating even menial tasks with valued goals.
2. *Stimulating people to gain new competencies.* Superior leaders stimulate people to stretch their minds and their wills. They freely share their own expertise and keep people in touch with new resources.
3. *Helping people to overcome obstacles.* Superior leaders help others to overcome obstacles. They help others to find the courage and strength to persevere in the face of even the greatest difficulties.
4. *Helping people to overcome failure.* Superior leaders help people to cope with failure and disappointment. They are quick to offer new opportunities to people who have failed at something.
5. *Leading by example.* Superior leaders are models of integrity and hard work. They set the highest expectations for themselves and others.
6. *Including others in their success.* Superior leaders are quick to share the limelight with others. People associated with superior leaders feel as successful as the leaders.[13]

LEADERSHIP STYLES

The emphasis of leadership study has shifted from the trait and behavioral approach to the situational approach. This modern situational approach to leadership is based on the assumption that all instances of successful leadership are different and require a unique combination of leaders, followers, and leadership situations. According to

Blanchard, Zigarni, and Zigarni, in *Leadership and the One Minute Manager,* the four basic styles of situational leadership are as follows

> *Style 1: Directing.* The leader provides specific instructions and closely supervises task accomplishment.
>
> *Style 2: Coaching.* The leader continues to direct and closely supervise task accomplishment but also explains decisions, solicits suggestions, and supports progress.
>
> *Style 3: Supporting.* The leader facilitates and supports subordinates' efforts at task accomplishment and shares responsibility for decision making with them.
>
> *Style 4: Delegating.* The leader turns over responsibility for decision making and problem solving to subordinates.[14]

These leadership styles have also been summarized as "Different strokes for different folks." There is no one best or appropriate style suited to all situations. A leadership style often described as being made up of the three F's—firm, fair, and friendly—is a combination of many elements, but at times this style does not work. The three F's presuppose that there is a homogeneous kitchen team that will readily react and perform favorably under this chef leadership style.

As a situational leader, the chef supervisor needs to analyze the team. Within the group there will be individuals who have high commitment to the team and its goals but without the necessary array of skills. In this situation the chef supervisor can use a detailed set of instructions to lead the team member—a directing style. Other team members may have some culinary skill competence but a low commitment to the team's vision and goals. Here, a coaching and correcting style that is highly supportive of the team members would be appropriate. A team member who is sometimes committed and has a lot of skills will require a supporting leadership style. Such a team member is capable of working alone with little direction, while team members with well-developed skills and a great deal of team commitment require that tasks be delegated to them in order for them to feel fulfilled.

Leadership ability is inextricably linked to motivation. As observed earlier, what motivates one person may not motivate another. Motivation comes from within the individual. The leadership style provides the basis for a motivational environment.

An extreme in leadership style is the strict authoritarian, aloof chef who rules the kitchen with a rod of iron. The advantage of this style is good control and discipline over the team. The disadvantages are resentment, lack of cooperation, and poor communication with subordinates. These are certainly not the ingredients of a coaching leadership style in a quality environment.

The other extreme is the chef who tries to be democratic—to be accepted by other team members as a complete equal. The democratic style promotes a good atmosphere, good communication, and cooperation. However, the disadvantages can outweigh the advantages, because the democrat is taken for granted, has no authority, and will eventually lose control of the team. Somewhere between these two extremes is the ideal leadership style.

The old-fashioned authoritarian, dictator-style chef has no place in the complex modern culinary world. Kitchen team members need to be led, not controlled or managed. The best leadership style in the kitchen is one that works for the individual chef

BOX 7-4

CHEF TALK:
LEADERSHIP AXIOM

When I was in college there was a group of us that gathered in the basement of the dorm to watch old movies on the TV on Saturday morning if we were not working or studying. One Saturday morning the movie was about young Thomas Edison, and it starred Mickey Rooney as the young Thomas Edison. At one point in the movie, young Thomas Edison's mother is extremely ill and will die before morning if the Doctor does not operate on her. The Doctor, however, cannot operate because this was before Thomas invented the electric light and there is no light bright enough for the Doctor to do the operation. Young Thomas proceeds to place a large number of kerosene lanterns in front of a large mirror on one side of a room, directing the mirror toward a mirror on the opposite of the room, reflecting the light of lanterns from mirror to mirror. (This procedure, I later learned, is called refraction.) The result was light far brighter than the lamplight that was not reflected from mirror to mirror. This concept of the increased intensity of the refracted light has stayed with me over the years and has become the basis for my own personal leadership axiom.

Many opportunities arise when an individual is in a position of authority to allow those working with them to showcase their expertise, abilities, and knowledge. Leaders who not only allow, but encourage, their co-workers, teammates, and subordinates to develop and showcase their capabilities and, when possible, to move into the spotlight and to advance themselves will find that the light refracted back on them by the success of those individuals is far greater than the spotlight itself.

My Leadership Axiom

Provide opportunities for the growth, development, and advancement of others. Be a role model and provide leadership directed toward the best interest of those you lead. Concentrate on the promotion of others and the promotion of you will take care of itself.

Jerald Chesser,
Ed.D., CEC, CCE, FMP AAC,
Professor, California State
Polytechnic University, Pomona,
Pomona, California

supervisor and is based on the makeup of the team, the personal characteristics of the chef supervisor, and the ever-changing daily situations facing the chef supervisor. Situational leadership provides the chef supervisor with a flexible approach to each situation as it arises.

THE NATURE OF CULINARY LEADERSHIP

Few concepts are as difficult to analyze as leadership. Why do some individuals seem to succeed effortlessly, and others fail so miserably? There are tremendous opportunities for leadership in the culinary world. As Jerry Hill, former chairman of the Michigan Restaurant Association, observed:

> If you are interested in developing leadership skills and tackling leadership responsibility, you'd be hard pressed to find another field that offers more opportunity than the foodservice industry. Not only are many leadership positions available, but those positions are likely to be true leadership roles. We fortunately have a wealth of culinary leaders to draw analysis from.[15]

But what is the nature of leadership? A good place to start is to look at the principles of leadership listed in the U.S. Army's leadership manual. The following ten principles have been adapted from this manual and can be applied to culinary leadership (16):

1. *Know yourself and seek self-improvement.* Identify your strengths and weaknesses. Set goals for each weakness or desired improvement. Develop plans to achieve goals. Evaluate progress toward goals.
2. *Be technically and tactfully proficient.* Be knowledgeable in all aspects of your job. Be able to pass this on to your fellow kitchen team members.
3. *Seek responsibility and take responsibility for your actions.* When you see a problem, initiate actions to solve it. Do not wait for others to tell you what to do, or say "it's not my job." If you have made a mistake, admit your error, accept your criticism, and promptly correct the matter.
4. *Make sound and timely decisions.* Use problem-solving, decision-making, and planning methods to come to a rapid assessment of the situation and make the most appropriate decision. Indecisiveness causes confusion and a lack of confidence.
5. *Set an example.* As a role model, this is the chef supervisor's most important leadership skill. You should not ask your fellow team members to do anything you would not do yourself. As a leader, you should earn the respect of the team, not demand it.
6. *Know your subordinates and look out for their well-being.* Take the time to learn about your team by listening to them. Know what it takes to motivate each member individually. It is important to recognize their need to be needed. If you take care of your kitchen team, they will take care of you.
7. *Keep your subordinates informed.* Don't just give orders; explain the rationale for the request. Informed persons consider themselves part of the team effort. Your kitchen team cannot grow and perform well if you keep them in the dark.
8. *Develop a sense of responsibility in your subordinates.* Delegation of responsibilities will enhance the development of the team. It will reflect your confidence in them and cause them to seek additional responsibilities. Acknowledging their accomplishments fosters their initiatives.
9. *Ensure that the task is understood, supervised, and accomplished.* Orders and directives should be clearly understood, and all team members should know what is expected of them. There is a fine line between undersupervision and oversupervision. Giving the order is 10 percent; the other 90 percent is ensuring that it is carried out.
10. *Train your personnel as a team.* Teamwork occurs when all members of the team are proficient in their individual assignments and have the mutual respect and trust of one another. A team must have its own spirit and confidence in its ability to accomplish the culinary and customer satisfaction objectives. Cohesion builds confidence and morale.[16]

These fundamental elements of leadership are all common sense. Each one has its own merits, and they complement each other. People leadership, unlike "thing management," has a connection with the heart. When chef supervisors resort to logic alone, not only do they risk treating their team members like machines, they also are often unable to motivate and inspire. In addition to being sensitive to the emotional needs of the team, the chef supervisor should encourage and reward risk taking to accomplish the organization's goals. Culinary leadership is demonstrated by the chef supervisor who:

- Can sacrifice personal glory for the good of the team, has strength of purpose to achieve the goals, cannot be easily discouraged, and does not compromise, but adapts
- Understands that working through hardship is an experience that builds courage, can deal with adversity and overcome mistakes, and can achieve anything for which he or she is willing to pay the price
- Does not allow team members' weaknesses to prevail over their strengths and will always set realistic goals for each team member based on his or her abilities
- Has an open style and believes in a win–win relationship with the team, and uses diplomacy based on respect of, trust in, and courtesy to the team
- Has a clear vision of the possibilities of the team's potential and inspires them through motivation and high aims, and who goes after things that will make a difference, rather than seeking the safe path of mediocrity
- Has stamina, a high energy level, tenacity, and a positive attitude; helps the team reach the foodservice organization's goals and objectives, communicates openly with the team, shares the risk taking, and leads by example
- Has a sense of humor, shuns publicity that may be at the expense of the team or the organization, and accepts failure in some things in order to excel in more important ones
- Focuses on problems as opportunities, is tolerant, and never confuses power with leadership
- Invests himself or herself in adequate training of the team, adopts a coaching and correcting style, and understands that training the team is the vital ingredient for quality supervision, and leadership

BUILDING LEADERSHIP SELF-CONFIDENCE

Confidence is a matter of style. Chef supervisors should be assertive, not overbearing. Leadership self-confidence can be developed in four action steps. All have to do with one facet—self-confidence—which will increase as leadership tasks are accomplished successfully. In his book, *The Art of the Leader,* William Cohen suggests the following action steps to increase leadership self-confidence:

- Become a leader by seeking out situations and volunteering to be a leader whenever you can.
- Be an unselfish teacher and helper to others. Others will come to you for leadership. Always treat those you lead with respect.
- Develop your expertise. Expertise is a source of leadership power.
- Use positive mental energy. Simulations in the mind are rehearsals for success. They are interpreted by the mind as real experiences. So they will boost leadership self-confidence just like the actual experience.[17]

The kitchen team will readily follow a chef supervisor who displays confidence. Confience demonstrates the right to authority. It also makes the team feel comfortable that there is direction and purpose to what they do.

The way the chef supervisor dresses is also part of developing leadership self-confidence. The chef's professional attire and grooming must always be outstanding. This obviously includes a clean, well-groomed white chef uniform with safe, polished shoes. Personal grooming should be immaculate and reflect the highest standards. The supervisor is the role model. Professional practices and high personal standards in the kitchen set the chef apart as a leader. Involved in this is the practice of a code of professional ethics for culinary art. Great leaders throughout the ages have understood that their number-one responsibility was their own discipline and personal growth. If chef supervisors cannot lead themselves and manage their lives, then they surely will be unable to lead others. Leaders can never take other people further than they have gone themselves. President Dwight Eisenhower once said, "In order to be a leader, a man must have followers, a man must have their confidence; hence, the supreme quality for a leader is unquestionably integrity."[18] Training and experience develop a personal assurance with which chefs can meet the challenges of leadership. Those who show a lack of self-confidence in their ability to carry out leadership assignments signal the team that these duties are beyond their capabilities. They therefore become weak leaders.

William Cohen stated, "The first way to develop self-confidence while you develop your leadership skills is to become an uncrowned leader."[19] There are many opportunities for individual chefs to become leaders. In the kitchen there may be team members who need help. Seizing the opportunity to lead can help these people build the confidence of the chef as a leader. Waiting for management to give direction on team building may stunt a chef's leadership potential. A thinking, proactive chef will not wait for direction from above. Instead, he or she will begin immediately to take charge and lead the rest of the team to greater culinary heights.

According to Bennus and Nanus, "Being a manager has to do with doing things right. Being a leader has to do with doing the right things."[20] It is therefore unnecessary to have an official-sounding title to be a leader. Leadership development is first and foremost a process of self-development.

DEVELOPING CULINARY LEADERSHIP

What is culinary leadership? Is it about winning gold medals at food shows? Is it about being a celebrated TV chef or being highly rated by some agency? Is it about being an executive chef in a large, prestigious hotel or restaurant? Well, the answer is, it could be all of these things, but not necessarily. The best rating you can have as a culinary leader is from the customers who come back to your restaurant and from a loyal kitchen team that follows the chef leader and is concerned for the success of the foodservice operation. Culinary leadership is all about high standards of culinary practices that satisfy restaurant guests and for which the kitchen team has been motivated and trained. Remember, quality is quality, no matter what size or type the foodservice operation is.

There are several areas in which leadership can be developed within the kitchen. The following are some suggestions that work and will assist in developing a great team atmosphere and contribute enormously to culinary leadership.

- Develop a particular food philosophy and style. Get each chef team member involved. Set up food tasting/critique sessions. Involve your customers and dining room staff in these sessions. Formulate your menu items based on the results of

these critiques. Aggressively put forward innovative culinary philosophies. Become known for a particular style of food.
- Educate yourself. Take development courses. Join a professional chefs' organization. Become certified in your profession. Read trade magazines. Study the latest culinary trends. Network with other chefs.
- Involve the team in entering food shows. This is an excellent method of building team morale and *esprit de corps*. Train your team. Invest continuously in training. Training a kitchen team is a never-ending task.
- Allocate days during the week for each chef team member to have his or her own signature menu item.
- Provide the team with distinctive uniforms.
- Insist on the highest culinary standards. At all levels, give the team the authority and responsibility to solve problems and prepare exceptional menu items.
- Build partnerships with your purveyors. Set specifications on quality with them.
- Seek out ways to constantly develop your team. Enroll them in development courses. Arrange for them to attend chef seminars and conferences.
- Involve the support team in all the chef and food philosophies.
- Maintain scrupulous standards of personal hygiene. Insist on high standards of safety and sanitation in the kitchen area.
- Show concern for the welfare of the kitchen team. Treat all members with respect, and trust them to carry out the assigned tasks. Be approachable and sympathetic in the kitchen.
- Visit the dining room. Meet your customers. Encourage feedback from them. Build a strong relationship with the dining room staff. They are vital to achieving culinary success.
- Recognize that empowerment is not a substitute for leadership or a reduction of authority. The more the kitchen team is empowered, the greater will be the need for culinary leaders who can set goals and define a vision. The paradox of empowerment is that in order to gain power, you must give some of it away.
- Implement solutions through the kitchen team. Solving a problem in the kitchen is not worth much unless you can do this.
- Celebrate your kitchen team and their successes, their promotions, awards, birthdays, marriages, reunions, anniversaries, and holidays, along with the organization's anniversary, the introduction of new menus, and the articulation of the foodservice organization's vision. Celebration in the kitchen can build individual self-esteem. Each team member will feel important and empowered. It enhances communication, promotes teamwork, and makes members feel bonded. It makes work fun and creates a positive outlook.

Developing culinary leadership involves encouraging the kitchen team to succeed. To encourage is to inspire others with courage and spirit. Encouragement will help kitchen team members change behaviors and attitudes. It will develop individuals' self-confidence and positive feelings about their own capabilities. Encouragement should be given during times of stress, particularly when failure is looming. It should be given equally and fairly to all team members, emphasizing the positive and not the negative. Encouragement will give the kitchen team a sense of belonging, provide positive self-image, and encourage positive attitudes toward the chef supervisor.

When the team is placed first, the highest possible productivity will result in the kitchen as well as total quality relative to culinary practices and customer satisfaction. Profits for the foodservice organization will follow.

HUMOR AS A LEADERSHIP TOOL

"Always leave them laughing." This old phrase is one of a chef leader's best guides. A kitchen that has a highly negative environment inhibits the development of a "Golden Rule" environment in the kitchen. As was stated in Chapter 5, "Team members in a *Golden Rule environment* will not do things because they fear the consequences. Rather, team members will do things because they want success for everyone, including themselves and the operation." A Golden Rule environment thrives on positivity. Positivity is the state of being positive. There is no better vehicle for achieving positivity in the kitchen than humor. Fun relieves tension and improves concentration. It counteracts boredom and reduces the potential for conflict in the kitchen. The bottom line: a kitchen team enjoying and supporting one another is more productive.

Clarification is called for here. Humor used inappropriately, such as at the expense of others or in a manner that demeans people, does not contribute to a positive environment; more important, it is wrong and should never be tolerated. Also, humor that distracts the team from its focus, its goals, is destructive and not constructive. The humor that is being talked about here is humorous to everyone and adds to a positive environment.

Although humor comes more easily to some than to others, we all have the ability to introduce humor into the mix. Remember, however, that humor works best when it is natural and not forced. Humor is a powerful tool for enhancing self-confidence and building empathy. Humor can promote positive attitudes within the team, making it easier to hear feedback and new information. Humor also distracts from worry; lightens stress, anxiety, depression, and pain; increases creativity; and offers perspective and balance. It can help express the truth when the truth is feared and repressed. The use of humor decreases discipline problems and pressure on team members to be perfect. It also improves listening and employee retention and creates a comfort level in the kitchen. Studies have shown that employees who have fun at work are less likely to be late or absent.[21] Figure 7-6 shows some suggestions to consider for using humor in the kitchen. As a team member, and eventually as a chef supervisor, work to cultivate a sense of humor and then use it to motivate and create a positive work environment.

FIGURE 7-6 Suggestions for using humor in the kitchen.

- Maintain a humor file.
- Include appropriate humor in your team meetings.
- Tailor your humor to the taste and preferences of the kitchen team.
- Look for humor in those little interruptions that occur during meetings or during the service period.
- Keep your humor brief.
- Recognize when humor is not appropriate.
- Don't joke about people's gender, ethnicity, and personal or physical characteristics.

BOX 7-5

CHEF TALK:
CHEF LEADERSHIP

During the thirty years of my career, I have experienced many forms of leadership, from the very simple and basic in the beginning to the complex and brilliant later. I had the privilege to learn from some of the best, not only in a working environment, but also during culinary team practices and association activities. In order to develop my own style, I was able to listen to good advice as well as experience some less desirable forms of leadership. For some reason it seems easier to recall the horrors than the positive situations. This may be due to the fact that good leaders seldom resort to extremes to get the job done.

During the early part of my apprenticeship, when I was very young, 15 in fact, a transformation of power was going on that I found interesting to reflect upon later. Being that young, my father was reluctant to give up his control over me. This was apparent by his overly protective interest in what I was doing. I spent most of the day working a split shift. I started at 8:00 A.M. and returned home at 10:00 P.M. with a three-hour break in the afternoon. My father wanted me to be at home to work during my break. My chef, on the other hand, wanted us to use this time to study and rest, because the workload from school was heavy and we worked six-day weeks. I was not doing well in school, and my chef realized that he needed to intervene. He suggested to my father that I should stay with other apprentices in the room at work and go home on my day off.

My father agreed reluctantly. My chef spent some time with me studying, and I made a remarkable turnaround in school.

Since my chef took an interest in me, I became more confidant in my work. Soon I was helping him with his work on shows, and during my last year, in 1960, he took me to Frankfurt to the IKA (Culinary Olympics) for my first exposure to this remarkable show. My chef's leadership style was not very polished. He could have been described as rough and abrasive. He would say, "Let them do hard and dirty work for one year and if they are still there I might remember their name." If you made it, however, it got better in the third year. The kitchen was run by the apprentices on Mondays, two from each year, when the chef and cooks were off. This was our turn to practice leadership by getting the job done. Since we had a daily menu, the third-year apprentices could write it and direct the kitchen. Looking back, I noticed that every Monday the crew elected me to be the chef. What made it happen was that I was willing to do the research necessary to write the menu, order the food, make the production charts, and most important, take the heat if something went wrong. Not much went wrong on my Mondays because I made sure everything was well planned.

Klaus Friedenreich, CMC, AAC,
Director, The Culinary Art
Institute of Fort Lauderdale,
Fort Lauderdale, Florida

CONCLUSIONS

There is no single best style of leadership. The best leadership pattern is the one that works best for *you*. Excellent personal qualities and characteristics help in being a good leader. However, leadership skill sets are learned and are not something you are born with. The team is the greatest resource the foodservice operation has. How they are led will ultimately determine the success or failure of the operation.

A very old leadership tenet states that you should be willing to do everything you ask those you lead to do. Therefore, personal example is very important. Most people do not like to follow leaders who cannot make up their minds or who have trouble coming to a decision. Therefore, be a decisive leader. The leader sets the tone. A large component of this tone is a leader's ego. If the leader sets a positive example—one of service, dedication, support, and concern—others will strive toward the same goal. The leader's role is one of service. His or her job is to create structures that allow each team member to achieve the desired quality result. Good chef leaders actively create structures and symbols that remind the team of their concern for the human side of the culinary operation. Items that support this effort include:

- Periodic social get-togethers
- Recognition of individual and team accomplishments; ensuring that everybody in the organization (not just the kitchen) knows what the kitchen team does
- Creating an internal kitchen team slogan
- Encouraging mild competitiveness among team members and between department groups
- On a rotating basis, putting up photos of various people in the team

Though such things may seem frivolous, they are important because they help maintain a human feeling in the kitchen.

There are only two ways to get others to do what you want. You can compel them to do it or you can persuade them. Persuading requires understanding what makes people tick and what motivates them—that is, knowledge of human nature. Great leaders possess this knowledge. Max DePree, in *Leadership Is an Art,* sums up what he feels are the traits and behaviors that most people resent in leaders:

- Superficiality
- Lack of dignity
- Injustice, the flaw that prevents equity
- Arrogance
- Betrayal of principles of quality
- Overuse of jargon, because it confuses rather than clarifies
- Viewing customers as interruptions
- Watching bottom lines without watching behavior
- Never saying thank you to others
- Failure to permit team members to do their best
- Dependence on policies and hierarchy rather than on trust and competence[22]

Many leaders note that the most efficient way to get good performance from others is to treat them like heroes. Giving public credit to someone who has earned it is a great leadership technique. Successful leaders often say that if you trust others to do well, they will. If, on the other hand, you believe your team will fail, they will. Good leaders learn to sound and look like winners. Competence will galvanize the team. They will look to you for guidance and direction. When they get excited about their work, all team energy is powered into the tasks. The best way for the chef supervisor to generate excitement is to be enthusiastic. Enthusiasm is contagious. Good leaders cannot do it alone. They should delegate. Make the team look good, and the team will make the chef supervisor look good.

Summary

Leadership in the kitchen confers on the chef supervisor the privilege and responsibility to direct the actions of the kitchen team in carrying out the goals and objectives of the foodservice organization.

Leadership can be learned in the same way chefs learn culinary skills. Leadership development is a process of self-development. It is facilitated by education, training, mentoring, and experience and depends on the chef supervisor's ability to lead people in such a way that team members will want to follow.

The trait approach to leadership was based on early research that assumed good leaders are born, not made. Behavioral theories are directed to the study of work groups, leaders, and supervisors, rather than focusing solely on the characteristics of successful leaders.

Situational leadership is based on the premise that different situations require different leadership styles. The four basic situational leadership styles are directing, supporting, coaching, and delegating.

Culinary leadership is as much about respecting and valuing kitchen team members as it is about great culinary creations.

Humor is a valuable leadership tool. Laugh with your kitchen team, not at them.

Discussion Questions

1. In what way is leadership different from supervision?
2. What are the more significant factors that affect chef supervisors' leadership styles?
3. What are the differences between autocratic and democratic leadership styles?
4. Is there one best leadership style? Explain.
5. What situations are appropriate for each of the four styles of situational leadership?
6. What are some of the myths associated with leadership?
7. What are the essential differences between directive and supportive leadership behaviors? When and why are they used?
8. The "great man" theory relied on profiling a certain set of characteristics. When these were summarized, it was believed that it would be easy to pinpoint leaders. Do you agree with this theory? Give reasons for your answer.
9. What are eight characteristics of chef supervisor leaders?
10. The paradox of empowerment states that in order to gain power, you must give some of it away. How does this affect the chef supervisor as a leader?
11. What are the benefits of using humor as a leadership tool?

Notes

1. Peggy Anderson, ed., *Great Quotes from Great Leaders* (Lombard, IL: Jossey-Bass, 1989), 53.
2. James M. Kouzes and Barry Z. Posner, *Credibility: How Leaders Gain and Lose It, Why People Demand It* (San Francisco: Jossey-Bass, 1993).
3. John C. Maxwell, *Developing the Leader Within You* (Nashville, TN: Nelson, 1993), 103.
4. Warren Bennus and Burt Nanus, *Leaders: The Strategies for Taking Charge* (New York: Harper-Collins, 1985), 222.
5. James M. Kouzes and Barry Z. Posner, *The Leadership Challenge* (San Francisco: Jossey-Bass, 1988), xv.
6. Patrick L. O'Malley, "Make Excellence a Habit," in William Fisher and Charles Bernstein, eds., *Lessons in Leadership* (New York: Van Nostrand Reinhold, 1991), 40.
7. Kenneth Blanchard, Patricia Zigarni, and Drea Zigarni, *Leadership and the One Minute Manager* (New York: Morrow, 1985), 31.
8. Delta Airlines, *Sky Magazine,* July 1993, 24–28.

9. Bennus and Nanus, *Leaders,* 5.

10. Arthur Sherman, George Bohlander, and Herbert Crudden, *Managing Human Resources,* 8th ed. (Cincinnati, OH: South-Western, 1988), 355.

11. Kouzes and Posner, *The Leadership Challenge,* 16.

12. Ronald Cichy, Martin P. Sciarini, and Mark E. Patton, "Food-Service Leadership: Could Attila Run a Restaurant," *The Cornell Hotel and Restaurant Administration Quarterly,* February 1992.

13. Denis C. Kinlaw, *Coaching for Commitment* (San Diego, CA: Pfeiffer, 1993), 122.

14. Blanchard et al., *Leadership and the One Minute Manager.*

15. Jerry L. Hill, "Steer Clear of the Minefields," in Fisher and Bernstein, eds., *Lessons in Leadership,* 135.

16. Delta Airlines, *Sky Magazine,* July 1993, 24–28.

17. William A. Cohen, *The Art of the Leader* (Englewood Cliffs, NJ: Prentice-Hall, 1990), 97.

18. Anderson, ed., *Great Quotes from Great Leaders,* 52.

19. Cohen, *The Art of the Leader,* 85.

20. Bennus and Nanus, *Leaders,* 23.

21. Joseph L. Picogna, *Total Quality Leadership: A Training Approach* (Morrisville, PA: International Information Associates, 1993), 348.

22. Max DePree, *Leadership Is an Art* (New York: Dell, 1989), 138.

CHAPTER 8

QUALITY AND TRAINING IN THE KITCHEN

OUTLINE

- ❖ Introduction
- ❖ Training is an investment
- ❖ A systems approach to training
- ❖ Types of training
- ❖ How people learn
- ❖ Adult learning
- ❖ Barriers to learning
- ❖ Starting right
- ❖ Preparation
- ❖ On-the-job training
- ❖ Conclusions

❖ Summary
❖ Discussion questions
❖ Notes

OBJECTIVES

When you complete this chapter, you should be able to:

1. Describe the contribution of training to long-term health and well-being and relate to the concept of training as an investment in people relative to the cost of quality
2. Describe a systems approach to training and explain how training interacts with the quality goals of the foodservice organization
3. Define the types of training models and their strengths and weaknesses, and describe situations that are appropriate for each method
4. List the major categories of learning, and explain how they influence the rate of learning
5. Understand the concept of androgogy, and outline the challenges in this area for the chef supervisor
6. Identify factors that inhibit learning
7. State the importance of starting a training session right
8. Identify the reasons for proper preparation for a training session
9. List guidelines for use of on-the-job training on a daily basis

☙

Case Study: JUNIPER CREST COUNTRY CLUB

Juniper Crest Country Club is located in a city of 35,000 people. Metro Oil, the city's largest employer, dominates the city's economy and the economic well-being of the club. Metro Oil is one of the largest oil companies in the world, and Juniper Crest is the home of Metro Oil's International headquarters. Metro Oil is generous in its support of the club, because the "Club" is the only place in the city where executives can "properly" entertain the individuals from around the world who visit the company's headquarters on a daily basis. The reason for the club's large membership is the number of members who hold memberships by virtue of their position with Metro Oil.

The executives of Metro Oil, many of who are on the club's executive board, and all of whom are club members, have begun expressing their dissatisfaction with the food

served at the club. These individuals, like most of the club's members, travel the nation and the world regularly on behalf of Metro Oil. Through their travels they are exposed to many cuisines and trends in cuisine. They have well-developed palates and enjoy the variety and change they experience when traveling. This has presented an ongoing challenge for the management of the club. The club has maintained for many years a reputation for high-quality food that is well prepared, with its long-standing menu of steaks, chops, local freshwater fish, and traditional local dishes. Management, including the chef, efforts over the years to change the menu has been frustrated by the lack of trained personnel in the local area and an inability to attract trained culinarians to Juniper Crest. The club has consistently offered above-average wages to attract individuals from outside the area, but the lack of a career path has still kept them from attracting trained, skilled culinarians.

After its last meeting, the executive board informed the general manager and the chef that they wanted changes made in the menu, and they wanted these changes accomplished within six months or they would look at finding a new management team for the club. The general manager and the chef immediately worked to develop a plan to make the changes that had been mandated. As a first step, with the approval and support of the board, the general manager and the chef made a whirlwind tour of the major culinary pacesetting cities in the United States. In a two-week period they traveled to San Francisco, New Orleans, Chicago, and New York. They spent two days visiting and eating at the top restaurants in each city. Additionally, they spent an extra day in Chicago, New York, and San Francisco consulting with faculty from the prestigious culinary schools in those areas.

The general manager and the chef utilized the information and experience from their trip to develop a new menu that incorporated different cuisines, new types of dishes and presentations, new ingredients, but that still included the most popular of the club's traditional items. The challenge was to train the existing staff to provide the new items to club members at the same quality level that had always been the hallmark of the club's food.

The training needed to familiarize the culinary team with the cuisines and products being introduced included their storage and handling as well as how to prepare the dishes. An aggressive timeline was developed for the training, and it was determined that the culinary team members would be paid for participating in the mandatory training.

The general manager and the chef knew that the integration of the training into the club's normal operation was a major challenge. The operation of the kitchen had to continue with no reduction in quality while the training was taking place. Additionally, although the extent of the changes that would take place had not been formally announced, the resistance of the culinary team to change was clearly evident. Many members of the team had already questioned the value of training that would not increase their wages or increase their opportunities for advancement.

Based on what you have learned from previous chapters and the content of this chapter, answer the following questions.

- What is the overall reason for the challenges at the Juniper Crest Country Club?
- What are the primary causal agents for the challenges at the Juniper Crest Country Club's culinary department?
- What role did leadership and supervision/management play in the challenges at the Juniper Crest Country Club's culinary department?
- What specific steps could have been taken to avoid the current situation at the Juniper Crest Country Club's culinary department?
- What, specifically, can be done to overcome the training challenges and generate motion in a positive direction for the Juniper Crest Country Club's culinary department?

INTRODUCTION

Quality is the key to success in any business. A critical factor in achieving success is training. How well team members do their job, the quality of the product and service received by the guests, the efficiency and effectiveness of communication internally and externally, the safety of the food served, the safety of the work environment—the impact that training has on the quality of every facet of the operation and therefore every facet of the kitchen is almost limitless. Quality management and quality team member performance cannot be achieved without training. Without a strong and committed investment in training, the kitchen team will not be successful. Part Two of this book is therefore directed toward training and how it affects the success of the food-service organization, in particular the culinary operation.

TRAINING IS AN INVESTMENT

Training is an investment. It is an infrastructure investment that leads to a tangible return on investment. Philip Crosby, in his book, *Quality Is Free*, argues that achieving quality costs nothing. He points out that the real cost of quality is doing things wrong—the cost of waste.[1] The ultimate aim of quality in the kitchen is to eliminate waste and not do things wrong at any stage in the culinary process. Therefore, if every stage is done correctly and conforms to the quality standard, then costs are not incurred and real value is accrued. Figure 8-1 shows the return on investment for training.

Commitment to quality and the training required to achieve it must emanate from the top levels of the organization. It should be communicated clearly and consistently and be reflected in all aspects of the organization's functions and systems, during recruitment, remuneration, recognition, promotion, and training. It involves the challenge of developing appropriate attitudes and values in the kitchen team and throughout the entire foodservice organization. Ultimately, quality will not be achieved unless there is a

FIGURE 8-1 ROI: Training is an investment.

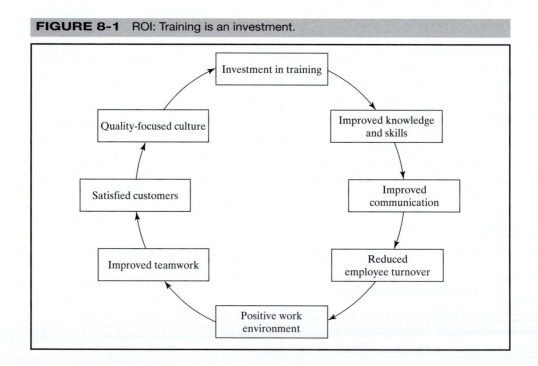

long-term strategy of continuous development and training of people in the kitchen. The real challenge is in making it all happen. The aim of training is to provide services and products both internally and externally that meet and hopefully exceed customer needs every time, and to deliver what was promised. We therefore need to be aware of what is acceptable and what is not from the customer's point of view.

Training is an investment in the long-term health and well-being of the organization.

A SYSTEMS APPROACH TO TRAINING

Training is a learning process that involves the acquisition of skills, concepts, rules, and attitudes so as to increase the performance of each team member. Training is not education. Training is the process of integrating personal and organizational goals. Training is used to close the gap between current and desired performance of individual kitchen team members. It is also about helping people learn and develop.

Training can be treated as a total systems approach, as a cycle with interrelated elements. These elements closely parallel the steps a person uses in solving a problem. Five steps, shown in Figure 8-2, are generally considered to be part of this closed-loop continuous process:

1. Analyze and determine training needs.
2. Develop training objectives.
3. Determine the appropriate training methods and materials.
4. Conduct the training.
5. Evaluate the training.

1. *Analysis of training needs.* This step is sometimes called *needs analysis*, and it has two main purposes: to determine what is needed in the first place, and to ensure that the training that does occur is based on sound requirements.[2] Therefore, the needs analysis process is the most important step in the development of a training program,

FIGURE 8-2   The training process.

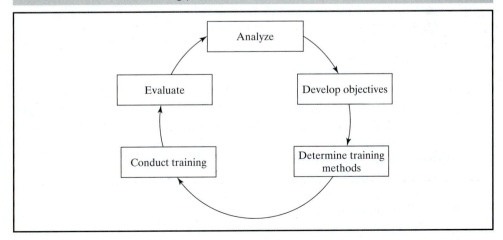

< **BOX 8-1** >

CHEF TALK:
TRAINING: WHAT'S IN IT FOR YOU?

In rough economic times, nothing comes under fire more than a training budget. It's an easy budgetary target. The alternative is just not to do any training.

Training is extremely important for the success of any foodservice operation. Without it the leader cannot motivate other members of the kitchen to achieve high-quality standards and cooking skills. Training is about setting quality objectives and then showing people how to perform these tasks to the required standard. More and more foodservice organizations are focusing on training the kitchen team.

Is it easy? No! There is often strong resistance from management because of a fear of giving up power and control. Where enlightened organizations have invested in training, their kitchen employees' success has followed. Training, in my view, is not only the path to success for the company but also sends a message to the individual being trained. Very often employees in training programs will remark, "If this company is investing in me, then they must value me as an employee." This sense of belonging engendered through training encourages greater effort by the individual.

There are all sorts of "buzz words" associated with training: empowerment, participative management, self-directed work teams, and others. What it all means is respecting the abilities of the individual kitchen employee and giving them the tools to do the job. Involve the employees in deciding what training is necessary. Ask for their input and then proceed slowly. It's really a win–win formula for success. You end up with a more productive team involved and participating in the successful accomplishment of the foodservice organization goals.

Reimund Pitz, CEC, CCE, AAC,
Executive Chef,
The Country Club of Orlando,
Orlando, Florida

because all other activities involved in the design, delivery, and evaluation stem from this process. A needs analysis typically contains the following steps:

a. Identify performance problems.
b. Identify knowledge, skills, and attitudes to perform the job.
c. Assess team member knowledge and skill.
d. Determine methods of gathering data.
e. Gather data.
f. Analyze data.
g. Prepare training plans based on data.

The needs analysis assists in determining the difference between present performance and desired performance, that is, the gap between what is and what ought to be. "Performance problems might be reflected in high employee turnover, a decline in productivity, grievances, poor teamwork, and/or customer complaints. If this is the case, the following questions should arise as part of the needs analysis."[3]

- What are the specific problems?
- What exactly is the desired outcome of training?
- What would the effect of *no* training be?
- Is training the best method of resolving the problems?

Once the problem or problems have been identified and it has been determined that it is training-related, the next step in the needs analysis process is to:

- Identify the knowledge, skills, and attitudes essential to performing the job.
- Assess individual team members. Analyze their strengths as well as their weaknesses. These strengths and weaknesses are measured against the specific job requirements identified in the needs analysis step.
- Design an instrument or methods of gathering information. The basic rule of thumb in a systematic approach is to collect only that information that is necessary to design the training program.

Principal methods of data collection in the kitchen are the following.

- *Observations.* The process of observation involves observing team members—their work routines and behaviors and how each person interacts within the team.
- *Interviews.* The face-to-face interview is also a useful method of gathering information on training gaps. The interview technique, like the observation process, can take the form of informal interviews to discuss problems or issues related to training.
- *Work samples.* Samples of work produced by the team member can be evaluated by having the individual prepare and cook a dish from the menu.

Once the data have been collected, it is necessary to analyze the information so that specific training plans and strategies may be formulated. The training plan should be prioritized on the basis of the needs analysis. In the needs analysis segment of a systematic approach to training, the basic purpose is to uncover the quality gaps—what it is that prevents a quality dining experience. It is also about utilizing scarce resources of time, money, and people so as to maximize the training effort in a planned, systematic, and sequential way.

2. *Training objectives.* Systematic and sequential planning of the training program is critical to its success. The development of precise and measurable training objectives is crucial in instructional delivery.[4] Good objectives ensure that learners are aware of what will occur during training. Objectives will also provide learners with information on what they will be able to do upon completion of the training session. In addition, objectives often serve as the basis for program and trainer evaluation.

3. *Determine training materials and determine instructional method.* Development of the training materials and determination of the instructional method are based on the training plan outline that resulted from the first two phases. Training materials must be matched to the desired learning outcomes and the instructional technique selected for the training. Instructional methods include job talk, demonstration, role-play, or lecture. Instruction can be trainer-driven, self-guided, or independent study. Instructional materials, whether written or technology-based, should include complete student materials such as reading materials, activity sheets, recipes, guide sheets, reference sheets, assignments, and practice quizzes and exercises. The materials should also include instructor lesson plans, tests and quizzes with answers, exercises and assignments with answers, equipment lists, recipes, and timelines. Technology used for instruction and instructional materials is rapidly expanding and changing and currently includes videos,

CD, DVD, online, and other computer-based instructional programs. Only the time spent on the training itself is greater than the amount of time spent on the development of training materials. The quality of the training materials contributes substantially to the overall quality of the training.

4. *Conduct the training.* This is where all the preparation pays off. The chef trainer's role here is to instruct, motivate, lead, enable, and facilitate learning. In addition to serving as a training instructor, the chef supervisor should facilitate the logistics involved in the training sessions.

The first few minutes of any training session are critical. The introduction should capture the interest of the entire kitchen team. The chef supervisor as a trainer has a considerable advantage in that he or she has an existing rapport with the group, which should facilitate getting the object of the training session across smoothly. However, different topics that are important to the success of the organization should be introduced to provide variety. This will help to generate additional interest. Successfully delivering the introduction will ensure that each team member is prepared to receive instruction.

5. *Evaluate the training.* Instruction is designed to bring about the learning of several kinds of skills. The outcomes of this planned training are learner performances that show that various types of additional knowledge, skills, and attitudes have been acquired. The chef trainer needs a system to determine how successful the training has been. There is a need to assess learner performance and to check learning to determine whether the designed instruction has met the training objectives. Evaluation is an essential component of training. It is often neglected because the chef trainer is not sufficiently adept at measuring learner performance. Materials that are used continuously need to be assessed so that improvements may be made. In simple terms, did the planned changes occur? Without evaluation, it is impossible to quantify the results of the training plan. Methods of evaluation include:

- Instructor evaluation of the training outcome when each segment is completed
- Learner evaluation of the course (What skills do I possess now that I did not have prior to training?)
- Third-party evaluation by guests or other work centers
- Field evaluation to determine if the learners are performing well in the roles for which the training was to have prepared them (Can they perform the skills at the level desired?)

Field evaluation is the most suitable method to determine training effectiveness in the kitchen. Learners may be assessed on the job by the chef supervisor. Coaching on the job is also facilitated through this method of evaluation. Evaluation is part of the continuous loop that feeds back into the cycle.[5]

TYPES OF TRAINING

There are many types of training. Each has its own relative strengths and weaknesses. The following training methods are appropriate to training in a culinary environment. The characteristics of each method and its strengths and weaknesses are shown so that each may be evaluated relative to the appropriateness of the training mission.

1. *Job talk* is a speech by the chef supervisor with limited opportunities for open discussion.

Strengths

- Clear and direct method of presentation.
- Good for large groups.
- Materials can be provided to each member in advance to help with preparation.
- Chef supervisor has control over time.
- Inexpensive training method.
- Little or no equipment is necessary.

Weaknesses

- Information not easily assimilated.
- Appeals to one sense only (hearing); therefore, overloading may occur.
- Group can become easily bored.
- Difficult to assess if your "message" has been understood and accepted by the team.
- Difficult to pace to the learning rate of each team member.

2. *Team meetings (group discussions)* generally include a speech by the chef supervisor with a lot of participation and interaction with the team. The meetings always require leadership. Team meetings are particularly useful for teams with mixed experience levels.

Strengths

- Good for a small number of people.
- All team members have the opportunity to present their ideas.
- More ideas can be generated.
- Good for total quality principles.
- Quality gaps can be identified.
- Effective for continuous improvements within the foodservice organization.

Weaknesses

- Team may get away from the subject matter.
- Chef supervisor may be inexperienced at guiding or leading the discussions.
- Possibility of one strong individual dominating the meeting.

3. *Role playing* is the creation of a realistic situation and having team members assume parts of specific personalities in the situation. Their actions are based on the roles assigned to them. Emphasis is not on problem solving. A role-play draws on the participants' experiences and knowledge and forces them to apply theory to practice.[6] It is effective for attitude awareness training.

Strengths

- Good if the situation is similar to the actual work situation.
- Team members receive feedback that gives them confidence.
- Good for interpersonal skills.
- Teaches team members how to act in real situations.
- Can be used to highlight sensitive topics such as personal hygiene and/or poor interpersonal habits.

Weaknesses

- Team members not actors.
- Role playing sometimes not taken seriously.
- Some situations cannot be implemented in role playing.
- Uncontrolled role plays may not lead to any results.
- Requires that incorrect and correct methods being role played both be described.

4. *Demonstration* is the use of actual equipment and ingredients to demonstrate an action. This is the most effective method for instructing culinary manipulative skills. Demonstrations make use of the learner's visual sense.

Strengths

- Has great visual impact.
- Instruction can be built step by step.
- Demonstration ensures that instruction is given in sequence.
- Difficult tasks may be shown in easy stages.
- Makes use of the natural inclination to imitate.
- Best if preceded by study assignment.

Weaknesses

- Suitable for relatively small groups.
- Requires a lot of preparation.
- Pace is often too fast.
- Learners often watch the demonstrator rather than the demonstration.
- Should be avoided unless adequate time has been allowed for preparation and practice beforehand.

5. A *case study* is a written narrative description of a real situation faced by chefs. Team members are required to propose one or more suitable solutions and/or make appropriate decisions.

Strengths

- Individual cases can be very interesting.
- Involves the team members in a lot of discussions and interactions, because there is no absolute solution.
- Develops kitchen team members' ability to communicate and encourages active participation.
- Develops the ability to analyze factors that influence decision making.

Weaknesses

- A slow method of training.
- Often difficult to select appropriate case studies for specific training problems.
- Requires a high level of skill by both chef supervisor and team members.
- Can sometimes be boring for some team participants.

6. *Apprenticeship training* is a culinary apprentice's work under the guidance of skilled chefs. The culinary apprentice rotates through all kitchen departments in a planned, sequential way. According to the American Culinary Federation, "the apprentice [chef] completes 6,000 hours of on-the-job training as well as the related theory courses, usually over a three year period."[7]

Strengths

- Develops culinary skills while working.
- Promotes understanding of the actual work skills required.
- Can involve extensive training over a period of years.

Weaknesses

- Takes a long time.
- Chef mentor changes may adversely impact continuity of learning, along with quality/quantity of skill development.

7. *On-the-job training (OJT)* is training conducted on the job using actual work situations with which the kitchen team member is involved.

Strengths

- Can be individualized to suit the learning pace of the individual.
- Provides immediate job application for the new team member.
- Integrates the new individual into the team.

Weaknesses

- Requires a good deal of preparation and application by the chef supervisor.
- Sequencing of on-the-job training must be planned and then recorded.
- Not all skills are addressed within one establishment.

HOW PEOPLE LEARN

No two people learn at the same rate. Some team members will pick up new skills very quickly, while others will require repeated instruction and supervised practice. There are several ways to classify types of learning, but all basically fall into what are called *domains*. These domains fall into the following four categories: cognitive, psychomotor, affective, and interpersonal skills.[8] (9).

- *Cognitive skills. Cognitive* refers to knowledge learning and includes the mental skills of classifying, identifying, detecting, and making decisions. This type of learning is experienced through self-paced individual interactive programs. The cognitive domain includes learner-controlled instruction, which is sometimes called self-instruction.
- *Psychomotor skills.* The psychomotor domain includes the manipulative, or physical, skills that require the learner to *do* something. In the kitchen, psychomotor skills are found everywhere. Culinary art requires a great deal of manipulative skill, from knife skills to whipping, chopping, and shredding.
- *Affective skills.* Affective skills reflect attitudes, values, and interests of the kitchen team. Personal leadership, such as the chef supervisor as coach of the kitchen team, is one way to facilitate attitudinal learning. Attitudes can be learned. The importance of good attitudes in the foodservice industry is vital. However, affective or attitudinal training is more difficult to do than any other method of training, because it is so difficult to measure.
- *Interpersonal skills.* Learning involves interaction among people. These types of skills are crucial to supporting total quality in the foodservice industry. Interpersonal skills are people-centered skills that involve the ability to relate effectively with others.

Examples include teamwork, counseling techniques, administrative skills, salesman-ship, discussion activities, and customer relations.[9]

Most learned capabilities actually contain elements of all four domains. They entail voluntary display (affective skill) of some observable action (motor skill) that indicates possession of some mental skill (cognitive skill) and working with other people and through people so as to meet customer needs (interpersonal skill).

We learn through our senses: seeing, hearing, touching, smelling, and tasting. The most important training sense is seeing, but when giving instruction, as many of the five senses as possible should be used to relay the message. Show things as often as possible. For example, if demonstrating sauce preparation, the method is ex-plained (learning), skills are demonstrated (seeing), what the texture should be is determined (touching), and finally, the sauce is sampled (tasting). A major advan-tage in culinary skills instruction is that it has the ability to make use of the learner's five senses.

Instructional techniques can be divided into two areas: passive and active tech-niques. Passive techniques require little or no activity from the learner. It is therefore difficult to assess what learning has taken place. Passive instructional techniques involve:

- *Telling:* The use of words to explain the subject matter.
- *Showing:* Trainers perform the activity.
- *Illustrating:* The use of visual materials to demonstrate the procedure.

Active techniques require the learner to participate by saying or doing something:

- *Question and answer:* Checking through communication to see whether information is understood.
- *Participation:* Involving the learner through actions.
- *Discussion:* Learners are involved through verbal communication.
- *Practical exercises:* Learners practice the techniques.

The best training techniques for culinary instruction are obviously "active." They allow the chef supervisor to check whether learning has taken place.

Most training in the kitchen involves hearing, seeing, saying, and doing, which indi-cates that this is the desired training method for all skills instruction. Figure 8-3 shows the retention level associated with these learning activities. These methods involve breaking down training into steps that are paced to the learner's ability so that he or she can assimilate this new information. Using this method, difficult tasks can be shown in easy stages. The unknown becomes known. Training is about helping people

FIGURE 8-3   Instructional techniques and retention.

Training experts generally agree that we retain:
- 20 percent of what we hear
- 50 percent of what we hear and see
- 70 percent of what we hear, see, and say
- 90 percent of what we hear, see, say, and do

learn and develop. It should be centered on the team member, and there are no reasons why it should not be enjoyable: "Individuals learn best when they choose what to learn—that is, when they learn things that interest them, which they find personally satisfying, and when the learning environment is in harmony with their own particular learning preference or style."[10]

ADULT LEARNING

Androgogy is the concept of adult education. At the heart of this concept is the assumption that adults *want* to learn. Adults prefer training sessions that will assist them in the successful completion of their daily work tasks. Therefore, instruction should be designed according to the needs of each participant.[11] If the need or relevance of the training topic is not evident to adult team members from the start, they may soon become disenchanted with the training process. To meet this adult need, the objectives of the training session should be stated and linked to job performance in the introduction stage of the training program or module. For the most part, adults enter training with a high degree of interest and motivation. Motivation can be improved and channeled by the chef supervisor who can provide clear instructional goals. Adults learn by doing. They want to get involved. Adults relate their learning to what they already know. This presents a challenge for the chef supervisor to incorporate participative activities into training, such as hands-on work, discussions, or projects. Variety of training topics and methods tends to stimulate and open all five of the team members' senses.

The need for positive feedback is characteristic of all learners. Adults, especially, prefer to know how their efforts measure up when compared with the objective of the training program. Additionally, adult learners may have certain reservations when it comes to training; among these are doubts about their ability to learn and a fear of failure.

Each training session should be opened with a good introductory activity that will put everyone at ease. Adults prefer to be treated as individuals who have unique and particular talents, and they prefer an informal environment.

Learning flourishes in a nonintimidating win–win setting without grades. Facilitators of the adult learning process can be described as *change agents*. The role of the chef supervisor as a change agent is to present information or skills in an environment that is conducive to learning, and the learner's role is to take that information (or skills) and apply it in the best way.

The establishment of a positive training environment hinges on understanding the characteristics of adult learners. The dynamics of the training process depend on the instructor having a clear understanding of these characteristics. For adults, training should be a highly motivating experience, after which they should be inspired and committed to trying out new ideas and approaches. Effective adult training should be relevant, practical, inspirational, dynamic, informative, and solution-centered.

BARRIERS TO LEARNING

Fatigue is a condition that prevents learning. It reduces physical and mental ability to accept and assimilate new information. It is therefore essential that training be planned and implemented at appropriate times. It should not be conducted at the end of work shifts.

Monotony can also be a problem. If the chef supervisor finds the training boring, it is highly probable that the team members will also find it boring. It is important for the chef supervisor to keep the sessions lively and interesting. The information may be routine for the chef supervisor, but it may not be so for the team members.

Distractions inhibit training. Plan time for training so as to avoid work-related distractions. People are usually tense when confronted with the unknown. It is up to the chef supervisor to create a positive training environment that is motivational and encourages quality performance.

Before the actual training begins, in addition to physical considerations of how, when, and where the training will take place, the team members should be analyzed to determine the following:

- What are their prior culinary work experiences, knowledge, and skills?
- What types of job duties must they perform?

A careful match must be made between what tasks each team member currently performs and what the training is preparing him or her for.

Before beginning the training session, review the training objectives. This review will serve to focus the chef instructor on the intended purposes of the training program and its desired outcomes. Development of the presentation is the next step. This includes the session topics and highlighting the learning activities designed to reinforce the learning. It is important at this stage to realize that excellent training session design does not guarantee excellent outcomes in terms of training.

Questions to consider with regard to creating the training environment include the smooth transition from a work-driven atmosphere in the kitchen to a training-driven atmosphere. Training sessions need not take up large chunks of the workday. Sessions can range from thirty minutes to two hours, but they must occur on an ongoing basis. What is vital is that the training period be totally uninterrupted by the requirements of work.

Plans should include arrangements for meals or coffee breaks during the session periods. Time allocation must be strictly adhered to when it is made part of the training plan. Where will the training take place? Even the most dynamic chef trainer can fail in poorly prepared facilities. Whether training is to be conducted on site or off-site, the facilities should be satisfactory:

- If the room is too warm or too small, a poor instructional climate will result.
- Is lighting adequate? Can the room be darkened to show visuals, yet still allow participants to take notes?
- Is the required audio/video and demonstration equipment in working order?
- Is there a writing board or flip chart available with marking pens or chalk?

STARTING RIGHT

Training sessions that begin correctly, in a positive environment, generally have a better chance of finishing well than those that start badly. If the first training session begins properly, the chef trainer will feel good about the session. Much more learning will probably take place. First impressions can be long-lasting ones, and the first training session sets the tone for the rest of the training program.

PREPARATION

There are several reasons why preparing well ahead of time is necessary:

1. It ensures that no essential detail is omitted.
2. Instruction can be arranged systematically.
3. Topics can be assessed to determine their relevance to overall objectives and organizational vision.
4. The chef supervisor's thinking can be directed to match the training needs of individual team members, and individual needs can be addressed to allow for different competency levels.
5. Unnecessary overlapping and repetition of topics can be avoided.
6. The amount and type of learner involvement is decided beforehand.
7. Good preparation ensures that maximum benefit is derived from the time allocated for instruction.
8. Most important, preparation helps to strengthen the chef supervisor's confidence in himself or herself as a trainer.

Adequate preparation often serves as a refresher and helps chef supervisors do their job more effectively.

ON-THE-JOB TRAINING

The unpredictable nature of the foodservice industry often makes it difficult to plan for training. In addition to structured training sessions, every possible advantage should be taken for quality training. The following are some guidelines for fitting training into the day-to-day routine:

- Take advantage of downtime to give short pieces of training instruction or review previous training topics. If downtime can be predicted, plan to use it for training.
- If possible, schedule team members with similar training needs to be in the kitchen at the same time, so that these needs can be addressed more effectively.
- Chef supervisors should use their own work as quality standard-setting demonstrations. Have team members watch while explaining critical elements during the demonstration.
- Take advantage of crises and problems to give on-the-spot correction and explanation of the correct way to perform tasks.
- Assign work that will allow each team member to practice new skills as soon as possible after instruction.
- Fit training in whenever possible. If only five or ten minutes is available, cover a portion of the task.
- Keep simple records to track the training you have given, to whom, and whether or not the training was successful.
- In addition, other experienced team members may be used as co-trainers. However, the chef supervisor is ultimately responsible for the culinary training.

By integrating training on the job, the chef supervisor is watching for gaps between the required quality and the way that each team member is performing, while giving praise and encouragement to the team.

CONCLUSIONS

Investment in training is investment in the health and well-being of the organization. It is an investment in the future. Success cannot be achieved without it. Therefore, the modern chef supervisor, in addition to the other necessary skills of supervision, must be a first-class trainer.

Training is a process, and it has various forms. It is the systematic application of:

- Analyzing training needs
- Developing training objectives
- Determining appropriate training methods
- Conducting and evaluating training

There are many types of training. Those training methods that have proved most suitable for culinary training are job talks, demonstration, role playing, case study, apprenticeship training, and on-the-job training. Each has strengths and weaknesses. Experienced chef supervisors can assess the training needs and determine the most appropriate training methods. The secret is to develop skill in using a variety of these training tools. The most critical roles of the chef supervisor as trainer are counseling team members through the learning process and being a subject-matter expert, teacher, and motivator of all team members as they rotate through the training process.

Understanding how people learn is key to effective training. No two people learn at the same rate or in the same way. There will be peaks and valleys in individual team members' progress.

Training sessions should be stimulating and inspiring and should be separate from the usual work schedule. The environment in which the training session is to be conducted should be one that is conducive to learning. The duration and timing of training are important. Training must be planned in a sequential and logical way and should not last too long. Dynamic presentations will always ward off monotony and fatigue.

Summary

- Training is the cornerstone of success for the organization at large and the kitchen team as a unit.
- Training should be viewed as a total systems approach; the steps are (1) determining training needs, (2) developing training objectives, (3) determining appropriate methods, (4) conducting the training, and (5) evaluating the training.
- Types of training used for foodservice training include job talks, team meetings, role playing, demonstrations, case studies, apprenticeship training, and on-the-job training.
- People learn at different rates and in different ways. Essentially, learning falls into the categories of cognitive, psychomotor, affective, and interpersonal skills; these are referred to as domains. Additionally, training is conducted through either active or passive training techniques.
- Androgogy is the concept of adult education. Adults learn by doing. They want to learn, are motivated, and relate training to what they already know. Positive feedback is a characteristic of adult learning. Learning for adults flourishes in a nonthreatening environment in which grading is absent.
- Training must be presented in an environment that is conducive to learning and at a time when the kitchen team member is ready to receive it.
- The modern chef supervisor must constantly invest in training the team to have success.

⟨ **BOX 8-2** ⟩

CHEF TALK: RETHINKING YOUR MOST VALUABLE ASSET

Today the hospitality industry is as dynamic as ever, full of rapid changes and opportunities to use newly learned skills. Therefore, productive training is more critical than ever.

Although the concept of training is straightforward and quite basic, the true challenge is applying it to the ever-changing issues that arise on a daily or weekly basis. Well-trained kitchen team members are crucial to the culinary operation. Part of this is understanding how team members relate to the product or services you provide and realizing that their values are not necessarily the same as yours. Remember, important elements that you may consider motivating factors could be regarded as simple satisfiers in a team member's eyes.

As an exercise, view your operation from an employee's perspective. Remember that you have the ability to control how your employees interpret your culinary operation. If their definition of what your business is all about does not concur with yours, you are likely to be vulnerable, because they are the main link with how your customer perceives your business. Chef leaders who are involved with their employees on a daily basis encourage spontaneous communication that creates an atmosphere that can increase their ability to think and respond to the needs of your customer.

Victor Gielisse, DBA, CMC, AAC,
Industry Solutions Group
Culinary Institute of America,
Hyde Park, New York

Discussion Questions

1. What is the difference between training and education?
2. What are the steps involved in a systems approach to training?
3. Before training can begin, a needs analysis is conducted. What is the purpose of this step?
4. What are the strengths and weaknesses of "job talk" as a training method? When should it be used?
5. Why is demonstration as a training technique appropriate for skills training in the kitchen?

6. What are the learning domains of cognitive and psychomotor skills? How can they be applied to training in the kitchen?
7. What are the advantages and disadvantages of passive and active training techniques?
8. Adults learn by doing. What training challenges does this present to the chef supervisor?
9. What are the important factors the chef supervisor should ensure in order to remove training barriers?
10. In planning training sessions, what physical factors should be considered?

Notes

1. Philip B. Crosby, *Quality Is Free: The Art of Making Quality Certain* (New York: John Wiley, 1989).
2. Richard L. Sullivan, Jerry R. Wircenski, Susan S. Arnold, and Michelle D. Sarkeess, *Practical Manual for the Design, Delivery, and Evaluation of Training* (Rockville, MD: Aspen, 1990), CD 1.
3. Ibid., CD 2.
4. Ibid., CD 37.

5. Tom W. Goad, *Delivering Effective Training* (San Diego, CA: Pfeiffer, 1982), 169.
6. Lois B. Hart, *Training Methods That Work* (London: Crisp, 1991), 65.
7. American Culinary Federation (ACF), *Apprenticeship Operations Manual* (St. Augustine, FL: ACF, 1985), 21.
8. Robert Heinich, Michael Molenda, and James D. Russell, *Instructional Media and the New Technologies of Instruction* (New York: Macmillan, 1989), 41.
9. Ibid., 42.
10. Brian Thomas, *Total Quality Training: The Quality Culture and Quality Trainer* (Berkshire, England: McGraw-Hill, 1992), 73.
11. Dugan Laird, *Approaches to Training and Development* (Reading, MA: Addison-Wesley, 1985), 25.

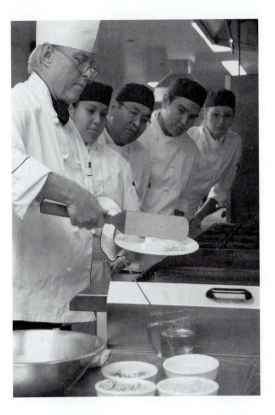

CHAPTER 9
PREPARING TRAINING OBJECTIVES

OUTLINE

- ❖ Introduction
- ❖ Definitions
- ❖ Hierarchy of objectives
- ❖ Training lesson plans
- ❖ Characteristics of a training session
- ❖ Steps in planning training sessions
- ❖ Conclusions
- ❖ Summary
- ❖ Discussion questions
- ❖ Notes

OBJECTIVES

When you complete this chapter, you should be able to:

1. Describe the components of good objectives and write a performance objective that contains each of these components
2. Identify the hierarchical elements that reflect how team members learn and the associated behaviors
3. List the rationale for preparing performance objectives
4. Identify and outline steps in preparing training plans and sessions
5. State the purpose and application of a lesson plan

Case Study: HAMILTON HOUSE RESTAURANT

The Hamilton family established the Hamilton House Restaurant in 1993. The time was right for the Hamilton family's entry into the restaurant marketplace. The country atmosphere and good country cooking offered by their restaurant was an instant hit. The restaurant became so popular that the family decided to build a second restaurant in 1996, a third in 1999, and a fourth in 2002. Each of the restaurants was within the same part of the state, and a member of the Hamilton family managed each. Each of the Hamilton House Restaurants was a success. The Hamiltons had succeeded in exporting the concept and product that made the original property a success to other properties with no loss of quality or consistency.

The Hamilton family held their weekly business meeting on Monday afternoon in the offices at the original restaurant. The purpose of the meetings was to report on restaurant activities, discuss challenges at the various restaurants, and plan for the future of the Hamilton House Restaurants. At the last meeting the decision was made to proceed with a plan to aggressively expand the Hamilton Restaurants as a chain. The goal was to keep the chain a family-held enterprise. The family decided to open three properties in the next twelve months and six properties per year for each of the

following three years. Months of discussion and site research had taken place in the months leading up to the final decision. The financing had been arranged, sites selected, and preliminary construction schedules developed for the first three properties. The discussion in every meeting, though, had returned to the one question that concerned the family the most: Who would run the new Hamilton House Restaurants? The family was out of family members to place in units as general managers. In fact, they knew that with the opening of the ninth property, only two years in the future, they would need all of the family members available for operations and development at the company level.

Based on what you have learned from previous chapters and the content of this chapter, answer the following questions.

- What are the overall challenges involved in providing management and staff for the new Hamilton House Restaurants?
- What type of information will the family need to begin addressing these challenges effectively?
- What specific steps do the Hamilton family need to take to develop effective training programs for the new restaurants?

- What specific steps would you take to develop a training program for future Hamilton House Restaurants culinary team members?
- Based on what you know about the management and organization of a Hamilton House Restaurant, what do you consider to be the greatest strength and the greatest weakness in the development of a training program?

INTRODUCTION

Learning often results in an activity that can be observed, measured, and recorded, a behavior modified by past and present experience. It is gaining knowledge, experience, and understanding.[1] Objectives in any of the learning domains discussed in the previous chapter may be adapted to the abilities of the individual learner. Objectives are intended not to limit what a team member learns, but to provide a minimum level of expected achievement.

Learning objectives are also called *performance objectives* or *behavioral objectives*. Whatever terminology is used, it is the concept that counts. The concept is that stating objectives for whatever type of training is undertaken in the kitchen will ensure that all efforts are directed to achieving only the desired results, and it will tell the chef supervisor whether or not the training objectives have been achieved. Knowing the objectives will force the creation of a training environment in which the objectives can be reached. Without explicit objectives, the kitchen team will not know what is expected of them. If objectives are clearly and specifically stated, learning and instructing become objectives.

A statement of objectives may be viewed as an agreement between the kitchen team and the chef supervisor, whose responsibility as an instructor is to provide training and coaching in a positive environment; as the learner, the team member's responsibility is to participate conscientiously in the training sessions.

Objectives are the instructional solutions to link what is and what is not desired through training. Problems of quality in the kitchen can be redefined as objectives that can be used to develop plans for training. Critical to all objective preparation is the statement of what the team member *will be able to do* after completion of a training session. Objectives should build the training needs of each team member in a logical and systematic way.[2]

DEFINITIONS

Three basic components make up performance objectives:

1. The performance of the task
2. The conditions under which the task is to be performed
3. The criteria or standards to which performance of the task will be compared

Expressed another way, objectives are an unambiguous statement of what the learner will be able to do as a result of some training. These can also be referred to as *enabling* objectives, which state what the team member is going to learn that will enable him or her to perform a task.

Whatever facilities, tools, equipment, and constraints under which the objective is performed should be included in the stated objectives. The level of performance in terms of time, accuracy, and completeness of the tasks should also be described. The statement of objectives must also have measurable attributes that should be observable in the team member upon completion of training. Otherwise it will be impossible to determine whether the training program is meeting the stated objectives.

The essence of a good objective is the description of a measurable performance. According to Robert Mager, author of *Preparing Instructional Objectives,* a complete objective will have three parts:

1. *Performance* —Use an action verb followed by the object of the action.
2. *Conditions* —Specify what the team member will be given to complete the task and under what conditions the task will be completed.
3. *Standards* —State the standard against which the performance will be evaluated and the level of mastery required.[3]

Examples of training objectives for the kitchen team are shown in Figure 9-1. These are precise statements of a future result. They make a promise to the team members indicating what they will be able to do when they complete a training session.

Tasks should consist of a single action verb and an object. The verb may represent the cognitive, affective, psychomotor, or interpersonal domain. A task should have a definite beginning point and should be independent of other tasks. For example, the task "Understand sauce making" is meaningless. What does *understand* mean? Where does it start? Similarly, the chef supervisor would have a difficult time observing the task "appreciate" in the importance of good sauce making.

Goals are statements of intent in the learning process. Goals are overall statements or general aims for a training program. They provide the chef supervisor with a general idea of what a given training session should achieve. Goals are different from objectives:

- Goals may be written to help select the area of knowledge and skills and may contain *immeasurable* verbs.
- Goals written as "knowing or understanding" do not provide specific actions that team members should perform to show that learning has occurred. This makes evaluation of the results of training difficult.

Because attitudes are difficult to measure, we write attitude "goals." Barbee and Bott state: "Training in the hospitality industry involves more than just the technical

---

FIGURE 9-1   Example objectives for the kitchen team.

- Upon completion of the training session on sauce making, the kitchen team member will be able to correctly prepare within 10 minutes 2 quarts of Hollandaise sauce from the recipe provided using the kitchen blender following all safety/sanitation procedures indicated within the lesson.
- After completion of the training session on quick breads, the kitchen team member will be able to properly prepare and bake 5 specified quick breads from the assigned list using the dough mixer and baking oven while observing correct timing and temperature.

⟨ **BOX 9-1** ⟩

WHAT IS THIS BUSINESS?
TREAT 'EM LIKE KINGS

Guest service counts . . . for far more than getting a good tip. It starts the moment a person steps *towards* our door and away from all else. That simple decision—to walk our way—sets in motion a relationship. The direction that relationship subsequently takes hinges on guest service. Swinging on the same hinge is the success or failure of the company. Guest service and corporate success are inseparable.

This bone-deep dedication to excellence in guest service must be taught to every crewmember. Good training yields good results . . . consistently. Consistency is critical. Regardless of the restaurant or the meal, we guarantee that every guest, on every visit, will enjoy his or her experience. We stand by this guarantee because we live by our crewmembers.

Great training begins with great hiring. The soul of guest service is hard to instill, but if it's there it's hard to miss. We look for this virtue when hiring entry-level staff, managers, and executives. We start with the best ingredients.

After being hired, everyone then receives training—indoctrination, actually. Our training creates and maintains our company culture, with its unique values, language, and expectations. The foundation of all our training is that every guest is, first and foremost, a guest in our own home.

Putting guests first only works when the whole team works together. We marry the value of our guests with valuing our colleagues through the "circle of responsibility" concept. This simple concept has powerful implications for the culture of our company: "If we're not there for each other, our guests won't be there for us."

The concepts of guest service and individual and team responsibility are interwoven throughout all aspects of our training and operations at every restaurant.

Our training is divided into two different tracks: crewmember training and management training. Each track is divided into two phases: classroom and practicum. Crewmembers are trained to become Ambassadors of Seafood: friendly in their demeanor, confident in their knowledge, secure in their advice, anticipatory in their service, and enthusiastic in their duties. Managers learn by doing the jobs of every person they will supervise. They come to see the restaurant through the eyes of the crewmembers by working shoulder-to-shoulder beside them, learning from them. Management training imparts empathy, team cohesion, open communication, and commitment to quality at every level. What is learned in both phases and in both tracks becomes the basis of our company-wide culture.

The teaching atmosphere is oriented toward adult learners. We utilize a "Tell, Show, Do, Review" approach to ensure that all learning styles are accommodated. It is safe, stress-free, hands-on, and fun. There are no uncomfortable surprises. Assessments are a combination of written quizzes, oral explanations, and live demonstrations. Classroom work is reinforced by four, real-life practicums conducted during actual shifts and observed by certified workgroup trainers. By investing early and heavily in the professional development of our crewmembers, our long-term objective is greater retention and better promotion within the company.

In purely monetary terms, it costs more to recruit good employees than to nurture good employees. Treat your staff well and they will do likewise. Treat them poorly and they will become someone else's asset. Service that is second to none starts with excellent employees.

What's our secret at King's Seafood Company? We treat 'em like a King.

Jeffrey King,
President, King's Seafood Company,
Los Angeles, California

skills common in other industries. Interpersonal skills are as important, if not more so."[4] At times, with attitude goals it is difficult to find precise words for the objective. However, objectives should always communicate the same intent to all people. One way of testing whether a written objective clearly defines a desired outcome is to answer the following two questions:

- How exactly do you intend the training to change the learner?
- How exactly will you know if the change has occurred?

A final criterion for a set of training objectives is to ask yourself if you would be fully satisfied if the team members achieved only the stated performance objectives and nothing else.

Objectives must be examined as a complete set of topics, levels, and skills of the overall training plan. Some of the more subtle quality objectives concerning attitudes or even the more complex kind of understanding may be missing. Whenever possible, these subtle objectives should be included.

Objectives must be attainable. This point may seem obvious, but objectives must be assessed carefully in relation to the knowledge, background, and expectations of the team as well as the resources available and the duration of the training session.

Performance objectives should fall into the category of learning the team member "needs to know" rather than what might be "nice to know." In searching for the neatness of fit between the culinary quality training plan and the team member's needs, performance objectives must contain the essentials that the person needs to know first and those that are desirable second.

HIERARCHY OF OBJECTIVES

Objectives should be prepared in a hierarchy that reflects how a person learns and associates behavior within each level of learning:

1. *Knowledge:* remembering previously learned material
2. *Comprehension:* grasping the meaning of the material
3. *Application:* being able to use the learned material in new and concrete situations
4. *Synthesis:* being able to separate the ideas into their component parts and examine relationships
5. *Evaluation:* judging by using self-produced criteria or established standards[5]

The flow of the hierarchy is shown in Figure 9-2.

Following are some action verbs that can be used in preparing performance objectives. The ones that concern most kitchen training objectives are the first three: knowledge, comprehension, and application.

Action Verbs

1. *Knowledge:* define, state, list, name, write, recall, recognize, label, underline, reflect, measure, reproduce
2. *Comprehension:* identify, justify, select, indicate, illustrate, represent, name, formulate, explain, judge, contrast, classify
3. *Application:* predict, select, assess, explain, choose, find, show, demonstrate, construct, compute, use, perform

FIGURE 9-2 Hierarchy of objectives.

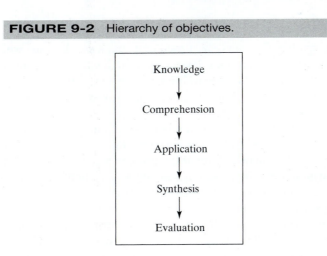

4. *Synthesis:* combine, restate, summarize, argue, discuss, organize, derive, select, relate, generalize, conclude
5. *Evaluation:* judge, evaluate, determine, recognize, support, defend, attack, criticize, identify, avoid, select, choose

Complete objectives state *standards* of performance and the conditions under which performance is to be evaluated. Objectives can be best described as:

- An intent about what the team members will be able to do when they have successfully completed a learning experience
- An intent communicated by describing a proposed change in a team member
- Precise statements of desired learning outcomes
- Worthwhile, nontrivial learning activity unambiguously stated that is necessary to both the team member and the culinary operation and is perceived as a benefit for the team member to progress in his or her job

Performance objectives are written in the compilation of training plans because they:

- Limit the scope of training tasks
- Remove ambiguities and difficulties of interpretation
- Ensure that measurement is possible
- Define the desired level of attainment and depth of treatment of each topic area
- Provide a basis for the selection of appropriate materials, content, and training methods
- Ensure that no essential details are left out
- Organize training instruction systematically
- Avoid unnecessary overlapping and repetition of training information
- Ensure maximum benefit from the often limited training time available in the kitchen
- Strengthen the chef supervisor's confidence in the instructional role

TRAINING LESSON PLANS

Just as training objectives serve as a road map and a check to see whether training has been accomplished, the training lesson plan guides the chef supervisor through the process of instruction that causes training to occur. A lesson plan may be thought of as a combination of speaker's notes, recipes, and scripts. It is an outline of everything that is to happen during the training event.

In the case of individual team member instruction, the lesson plan serves as the lesson specification from which text is derived. One of the requirements for being prepared is to have a lesson plan. Even if the training is a short thirty-minute presentation, a plan is essential. Learning is stimulated and aided when the chef supervisor can present a coherent and sequential series of training sessions, each of which has a clear training objective.

The four-step training method has been widely utilized in training in the kitchen. These four steps have been tried and found to be a successful pattern around which every training session can be planned and instructed. These four steps are

1. Preparation
2. Presentation
3. Application
4. Evaluation

CHARACTERISTICS OF A TRAINING SESSION

To be effective, a training session:

- Must be a complete unit of learning. What is to be learned should be made apparent to the team members in the title of the session.
- Should contain new material exclusive of review or some other training topic, previously instructed material for reinforcement, and new material for progression. Sullivan states: "Our primary duty is to teach our staff something new every day. Training is a philosophy, not a department."[6]
- Should be adapted to the needs of the team member. The material should be within the capabilities of the team member, and it should be consistent with the needs of the team in keeping with the purpose of the training and according to the progress of the entire kitchen operation.
- Should be reasonable in scope. It should be balanced, interesting, and neither too simple nor too complex.
- Have a clear beginning, a presentation, and an end. The language of the chef instructor should enable the team member to follow, comprehend the presentation, and finally absorb the material with a feeling of understanding and accomplishment.
- Should require a measurable standard of achievement in terms of high-quality standards of performance. High-quality standards of performance should start at the beginning and continue throughout each training session.

TYPES OF TRAINING LESSONS

The type of training session presented will depend on the type of lesson, and it is from these materials that the chef supervisor will develop training topics.

A *manual skills lesson* is a type of instruction in which the chef supervisor instructs team members in using physical skills in performing the manual phases of a culinary skill. The skill lesson is generally taught by demonstration. To further simplify and clarify the intent of any skill lesson, the question should be asked: "Am I going to teach the team member how to do something?" If the answer is yes, then the lesson will be a skill lesson.

An *informational lesson* is a type of instruction in which the team member is instructed in the theory and basic fundamentals of the area being taught. The area covered by a "theory" lesson appears to be broader than that covered by the skill lesson because so many subtopics can be included. This type of lesson is also referred to as "job talks."

STEPS IN PLANNING TRAINING SESSIONS

Careful and thorough preparation is essential to successful instruction. The effectiveness of the other stages of instruction will depend on how well the chef has selected training tasks and adapted this training material to the special needs, abilities, and interests of the kitchen team, arranged for equipment and materials needed, planned for activities, and anticipated problems. Many chef supervisors often feel there is never enough time for adequate planning. One solution to this problem is to use a systematic procedure in the preparation of training sessions. The following is a simple yet effective procedure, as you will see as we build a training session on the Frenching of a lamb rack.

Step 1: *The objectives.* This is the starting point for all planning of training activities. The chef instructor must realize from the start just what can be accomplished and the limits of time. (The objective, if well developed and written, will serve also as a tool to evaluate the training.)

The time for the Frenching demo will be limited to 15 minutes, with a 10–15 minute follow-up supervised practice. The objectives for the demo will be:

Upon completion of this demo the team member will be:

- Able to demonstrate the ability to French a 204A lamb rack
- Able to demonstrate the ability to cut the Frenched rack into chops
- Able to identify:
  - Fat cap
  - Lifter meat
- Aware of the use of trim from a lamb rack
- Aware of the characteristics of a lamb hotel rack

Step 2: *Analysis of the training topic.* This involves determining the specific objectives, skills, knowledge, or techniques the team member must learn for successful performance of the task. For example, the objective of a training session may be using the meat thermometer. An analysis of this subject, or breaking it down into instructional steps, would result in these teaching points: Describe a meat thermometer, show and explain the thermometer, demonstrate how to read the thermometer, and have team members measure internal temperature with the thermometer and sanitize after use. Each step would have subpoints in the presentation, but in the analysis only the major instructional steps required to accomplish the training are considered.

The steps in producing Frenched lamb chops are:

1. Remove fat cap.
2. Split membrane on rib (1.5 to 4 inches trim).
3. Push or cut rib free of membrane and surrounding muscle and fat.
4. Trim to eye.
5. French chop—cut chop.

Step 3: Equipment, facilities, and training aids. Requirements for and availability of training aids, equipment, training areas, and facilities need to be considered. Advance notice may be required to obtain training films, videos, or other media. Frequently, chef supervisors must improvise, and this often takes time. Last-minute arrangements for training aids or equipment usually result in slipshod instruction. The ingredients used for demonstrations must be selected and checked well in advance for quality and portion size.

The facility to be used for the Frenching demo is the prep table close to the protein cooler. The group of team members will be limited to four, so that each will be able to have a clear view of the procedure. The ingredients needed for the demo are limited to 5 prime, 204A hotel lamb racks. The lamb racks used for the demo and practice session will be part of the standard diner prep. The equipment list for the demo is: cutting board with anti-slip mat; boning knife; steel; sanitation bucket with sanitizing liquid; 4 side towels, 1 in the sanitation bucket, 3 dry; 21⁄2;-sheet pans with parchment paper liner, 1 for cut chops and 1 for trim; and a lamb chart if available. The equipment list for the practice session is 4 cutting boards with anti-slip mats; 4 boning knives; 1 steel; 2 sanitation buckets with sanitizing liquid; 6 side towels, 2 in the sanitation buckets, 4 dry. The practice chops and trim will go on the 1⁄2;-sheet pans used for the demo.

Step 4: *Availability of time.* If time is short, the training subject matter should be limited to the items essential for accomplishment of the training objectives. If time is available, more team participation can be used and more supporting material can be included.

Time for the demo is limited and cannot be allowed to interfere with dinner prep. Two members of the lunch protein prep team at the end of their shift and two members of the dinner protein prep team at the beginning will participate in the demo, and this will be repeated as needed to train all appropriate team members. The chops being prepared will assist in the dinner prep. The demo and practice are to be held to a maximum of 30 minutes.

Step 5: *Training condition.* Instruction must be flexible enough to remain effective even when obstacles to training arise. The basis of such flexibility is careful planning.

The schedule for the Frenching demo and practice session will be:

2:30 PM	Introduction: today's lesson and objectives
2:32 PM	Introduction to hotel rack (204A): description, placement in carcass, characteristics
2:35 PM	Fabrication of rack: Frenching technique; use of trim
2:40 PM	Fabrication of rack: cut rib chop
2:45–3:00 PM	Practice session / Q&A

Each team leader that has team members attending is to schedule work to allow for the absence of the team members. In case of interruption due to operational challenges, the lesson will be rescheduled to the earliest possible date.

Step 6: *Select and organize material.* Identify essential manipulative skills and related knowledge, then organize the materials for demonstration. Examples and stories can be used to make the lesson presentation or skill demonstration more interesting and meaningful. They should be related to the overall quality objectives of the foodservice organization and should be used whenever possible.

The purpose of this lesson is to insure consistency of the quality of one of the restaurant's to- selling menu item, Moroccan Grilled Lamb Chops. The follow-up to this demo will be a demo on the proper seasoning and cooking of the chops and pan grav . The use of a live demo will most effectively communicate the knowledge and skills to the team members. The team members will specifically learn and/or refine their ability to French a lamb rack and produce consistent Frenched chops. The team members will also be introduced to or review the use of the trim from the chops. A secondary benefit will be refinement of team members' use of the boning knife and steel. The information and skills presented in the demo will be immediately reinforced with supervised practice. The use of a lamb chart to indicate the location for the 204A hotel rack on the lamb carcass would be helpful, but is not mandatory. No other materials or teaching aides will be used, due to the confined space and short time available for the demo. If at a later date it is decided to make this a demo for a large group of team members, the use of closed-circuit video cameras and PowerPoint would be highly recommended additions to the demo.

The lesson plan ensures that the training session will be complete. It shows what material is to be instructed, in what order, and what procedures and training methods will be used. Each training lesson plan is an outline for one segment of the training plan. The purposes of a training plan are shown in Figure 9-3.

The lesson plan should be reviewed each time it is used. Few chef supervisors are gifted with such phenomenal memories that it is not necessary to refresh themselves on what is to be taught and how the training is to be conducted. This review will help to keep the training progression smooth and effective. The requirements of a good training lesson plan are shown in Figure 9-4.

Once a lesson plan has been completed, it should be thought of as a dynamic entity. Each time it is used, determine how it can be improved. Make notes each time the training lesson plan is used. It is a tool to help prepare for effective training.

FIGURE 9-3 Purposes of the lesson plan.

- Ensures a wiser selection of material and a more complete coverage of the topic and assists the chef supervisor in focusing on training objectives
- Assists in the presentation of training material in the proper sequence for effective learning
- Ensures that proper consideration is given to each part of the plan, that essential points are included, and that irrelevant material is omitted
- Provides time control
- Provides an outline of the training methods and procedures to be used in the instruction
- Assists in the proper use of presentation media technology
- Serves as a record of training provided to each team member
- Refreshes the chef supervisor's memory and keeps topics current

FIGURE 9-4 Requirements of a good training lesson plan.

- Must focus on one main thing to be learned.
- Must contain something new.
- Must not present too much material at one time.
- Must be suited to team members and their past experiences.
- Team members must derive satisfaction.
- Achievement should be measurable.

CONCLUSIONS

The training objective is the anchor for the training. Proper analysis determines the desired outcome of the training. Training objectives guide the training process to ensure that the desired outcome is achieved.

The effective use of each level of objective in the training process is critical to the kitchen team member gaining confidence and command of the training focus. It is through the training objective that the desired outcome is communicated to the team member. This can include what the team members will be able to do when they have successfully completed a learning experience, a proposed change in a team member, or a precise statement of desired learning outcomes.

It is through the development of the training objective that the focus on the desired outcome is finalized. The objective must be measurable and focused. It is the objective that drives the scope of the training, selection of materials, time required, and extent of resources required. It is the quality of the objective and the support given to the objective that will determine the success of the training.

Summary

Training objectives are the starting point in an overall plan for continuous improvements in the kitchen:

- They facilitate objective instruction and define the task performance.
- They are an unambiguous statement of what the team member will be able to do as a result of training.
- They provide criteria, standards, and conditions under which different tasks are to be accomplished.
- They allow for measurement of the training.
- They provide the basis for determining the *essential* and *desirable* training objectives.
- They separate tasks between knowing and doing.

- They provide time control, organize training systematically, and avoid unnecessary overlapping.
- Training plans are a road map to guide the chef supervisor through the process of training.
- Training plans require four steps: preparation, presentation, application, and evaluation.
- Each training session must be a complete unit of learning and should contain some old material for connection along with some new material.
- Training plans are classified as (1) manual skills and (2) the informational areas of the training topic.
- Training lesson plan outlines are prepared to ensure complete treatment of the training objectives.

- The needs and capabilities of the kitchen team should be important considerations of the training plan.

- Equipment and material needs for the training session must be planned for and secured before the training session is to begin.

Discussion Questions

1. Why is it necessary to prepare explicit objectives?
2. What are the three basic components that make up a performance objective?
3. Why is the essence of a good objective the description of a measurable performance?
4. What are the primary differences between goals and objectives as they relate to training?
5. Why are action verbs used in the preparation of performance objectives?
6. What are the four essential characteristics of a well-planned training session?
7. What method of instruction is generally considered appropriate for culinary skills?
8. What is the purpose of lesson plans as they pertain to training?
9. What are the requirements of well-developed training lesson plans?

Notes

1. Lois B. Hart, *Training Methods That Work* (London: Crisp, 1991), 15.
2. Robert F. Mager, *Preparing Instructional Objectives*, 2nd ed. (Belmont, CA: Fearon, 1971).
3. Ibid.
4. Cliff Barbee and Valerie Bott, "Customer Treatment as a Mirror of Employee Treat-ment," *Advanced Management Journal*, Spring 1991, 31.
5. Benjamin S. Bloom, *Taxonomy of Educational Objectives: Book 1* (New York: Longman, 1977).
6. Jim Sullivan, "Making It Stick: How to Eliminate Teflon Training," *Nation's Restaurant News*, April 1993, 22.

CHAPTER 10
UNDERSTANDING INSTRUCTIONAL DELIVERY

OUTLINE

- ❖ Introduction
- ❖ Getting started
- ❖ Your comfort level
- ❖ Effective interpersonal communication
- ❖ Training and diversity
- ❖ Getting the team involved
- ❖ Brainstorming
- ❖ Understanding group behaviors
- ❖ Summary
- ❖ Discussion questions
- ❖ Notes

OBJECTIVES

When you complete this chapter, you should be able to:

1. Describe the factors that contribute to an effective training presentation
2. Identify elements that are conducive to creating a professional training atmosphere

3. Describe methods used to achieve an effective presentation comfort level
4. Understand the appropriate communication style for effective training
5. Describe the steps appropriate to training a diverse kitchen team
6. Define training styles, trainer attributes and approaches, and attitudes toward training
7. Recognize the differences between open and closed questioning techniques
8. Define the dynamics of group behaviors and the activities associated with kitchen team training

Case Study: CYPRESS COVE RESORT

Cypress Cove Resort is an upscale resort that operates year-round but generates 70 percent of its annual revenue between Memorial Day and Labor Day. The resort operates with a skeletal year-round staff. Seasonal staff are hired to accommodate guests during the high season. The majority of the seasonal staff are college students, including interns from a number of college hospitality and culinary programs around the United States. The majority of the seasonal staff arrives for training one week before Memorial Day.

Don Hanson joined the Cypress Cove Resort in January as executive chef. The previous chef had been with Cypress for three years and left for a position with a larger resort. Before he left, the previous chef provided Don with the training schedule, manuals, and other materials that had been developed over the years to train the seasonal staff that would be part of the Cypress culinary team.

Don had previously been the sous chef in a hotel similar in size to the Cypress. As sous chef, Don had done some one-on-one specialized training for a few culinary team members. Don's executive chef, however, did any large-scale training that was required, while Don oversaw the day-to-day operation of the kitchens. The training that Don had done had involved very little formal preparation. He had just noticed that a team member needed assistance perfecting a particular skill and arranged a time to work with the team member on that skill.

Don admitted to himself that he enjoyed the one-on-one training that he had done, but the thought of conducting a full week of training for thirty people was intimidating. During the winter and spring, Don reviewed the materials and training schedules the previous chef had given him. He made very few changes because he was sure that they had been created by people who knew more about "that sort of thing" than he did. The training objectives sounded "alright," and he figured if they were not quit on target it would not really matter. He did slide in new recipes and remove old recipes to accommodate changes he had made to the Cypress menu. Don considered the timeline to be reasonable. If anything, he felt that there was too much time allowed for lecture, demonstration, and question-and-answer sessions. He thought trainees should just have the opportunity to "get in there and practice doing it."

When Labor Day arrived, all of the year-around culinary staff said that it had been one of the most difficult seasons they had ever had. "The seasonal folks just did not seem to be able to get the hang of it." Don had the same thought, which had been occurring to him throughout the season: "These college kids just do not get it! They will never make it in the industry!"

Based on what you have learned from previous chapters and the content of this chapter, answer the following questions.

- What is the overall reason for the challenges at the Cypress Cove Resort?

- What are the primary causal agents for the challenges at the Cypress Cove Resort?
- What role did leadership and supervision/management play in the challenges at the Cypress Cove Resort?

- What specific steps could have been taken to avoid the challenges at the Cypress Cove Resort?
- What, specifically, can be done to avoid a repeat of the challenges next year at the Cypress Cove Resort?

INTRODUCTION

Every time a chef supervisor enters the training room, what follows should be a dynamic and effective training session. An effective presentation can be the most exciting and rewarding aspect of the chef supervisor's job. The time invested in determining the needs analysis and preparing training objectives pays off as the chef supervisor becomes an instructor and learns to interact, discuss, question, and work with the kitchen team to reach the training objectives. Chef supervisors who are able to maintain team member interest with a dynamic delivery using a variety of instructional techniques are more likely to be successful in helping the kitchen team succeed.

The purpose of instruction is to communicate knowledge and skills from the chef supervisor to the team member. It is only successful if, at the end of the training, the individual team member can safely perform skilled activities to the required standard. Therefore, it is essential that the chef supervisor choose the instructional method most suited to the training topic and the needs of the team member. Do the following before proceeding with training:

- Specify to the team what needs to be learned.
- Decide on training priorities.
- Decide appropriate techniques of training.
- Specify when and how often training will take place.
- Decide on how much instruction can be given at one time.
- Decide over what period of time training will take place.

Every presentation should begin with an interesting introduction, to capture the kitchen team's interest and to prepare them for learning. Good introductions will prepare the team members, boost their confidence, and also set the stage for a positive learning environment. Dugan Laird says, "In professional instruction, learning processes are not blurred by an instructor's awkwardness or amateurism. Professionalism is often based on the mastery of a few teaching techniques."[1]

The training session introduction may be used to review the objectives, restate the culinary mission, and describe the activities that will be occurring during the training session. During the introduction step it is necessary to ensure that all of the team members participating in the training session are aware of what the chef supervisor is trying to achieve by the training and what is expected of them as a result of the training. The first five minutes of the training session can be the most important. Start off the session with an icebreaker, the purpose of which is to relax everybody.

BOX 10-1

CHEF TALK:
TEACHING OLD DOGS NEW TRICKS

A lesson I learned many years ago about improving the standard of cooking and food presentation involved a major personal commitment and investment in training my kitchen brigade.

The Shelbourne Hotel is a first-class hotel located on Dublin's famous St. Stephen's Green. It is one of the oldest, most celebrated hotels in Ireland. When I came to it as only its fourth executive chef in 100 years, I found a traditional kitchen designed on the old labor-intensive "partie system." Its cooking philosophy was deeply embedded in the traditions of classical cuisine. My arrival there coincided with the advent of the cuisine nouvelle period of the early 1980s.

One of the major goals set for me by management was to introduce a new style of cooking in line with the modern approach and style of cuisine that reflected the needs of the discerning, health-conscious customer of the 1980s. As a young enthusiastic chef, this was a challenge I was happy to accept. The a la carte menu that was in place when I arrived had not changed in many years. The repertoire of dishes included on this menu was rather limited, and my attempts to introduce new dishes and simpler methods of preparation and presentation were resisted by the older, more conservative chefs. Change was therefore necessary to bring the cuisine up to date.

Before any new dish was introduced, I had to develop an overall training plan for the traditional brigade, one that would meet with each person's schedule. Great consideration was given to the training methods to be used. The method I felt best suited my training goals was the demonstration training technique.

The problem I faced was how to convince the kitchen staff to attend my training sessions voluntarily. No budget was available to facilitate the training on company time. Because of trade union rules, I could not compel any of the chefs to attend these sessions. However, I decided to go full speed ahead with my plans. I selected Saturday mornings as the most appropriate training time and informed the kitchen brigade of my planned training sessions. For the first session, three apprentice chefs showed up, which, needless to say, was disappointing. Despite this initial disappointment, I continued with the training sessions each Saturday morning.

Key to my training philosophy and plan was my approach. I would demonstrate the preparation, cooking, and presentation of new dishes to be featured on our new menu, along with explaining the relevant techniques of preparation. I did the work, and then, with careful coaching and correcting on the job, the session participants grew in confidence and developed professionally. Demonstrating these new techniques showed the participants the benefits of the training sessions. Training made their jobs easier and provided them with additional culinary skills.

I believe a positive training atmosphere was set, one that was anxiety free, entertaining, and educational. What started out with three apprentices eventually grew to full participation by the kitchen brigade. When the older chefs learned of the training style adopted, they began to attend. They felt comfortable and unthreatened.

My training sessions did not happen accidentally. They were planned step by step. Careful planning made the training sessions work. The most worthwhile measurements of investing in culinary training are the increased skills and improved attitudes of those receiving the training, and that impacts on customer satisfaction. I am happy to say this happened at the Shelbourne. Within six months we had higher standards of professional practice from all our chefs, including the "old dogs." Training works, and the greatest compliment I received as a chef trainer was when the older chefs "bought into" my culinary philosophy and thanked me for sharing with them new skills that gave them a renewed pride in the culinary profession.

Noel Cullen,
Ed.D., CMC, AAC (1948–2002)

FIGURE 10-1   Suggestions for conducting a training session.

- Use effective facial expressions.
- Use and maintain eye contact.
- Move around the room and use gestures.
- Use gestures that are not distracting.
- Communicate with the team members in the training session on a personal level.
- Vary tone and pitch of voice.
- Emphasize key points and use relevant examples.
- Be certain to talk to, not at, the kitchen team.
- Select and use appropriate media technology.
- Make logical, smooth transitions between topics.
- Give clear directions for all subsequent activities.
- Greet all team members as they arrive for the training session.
- Be available during breaks to visit with each member to answer individual questions.
- Be available after the training session to answer any additional questions or to discuss concerns.
- Provide clear oral and written instructions for all assignments and activities.
- Maintain alertness.

GETTING STARTED

Appearance is very important. Choose your attire carefully. The best attire for the chef is, of course, a clean, crisp, smart chef coat. This helps the chef to bond with the kitchen team members. Overdressing can cause alienation from the group: "Be respectful. Right or wrong, some listeners will make judgments about your message based on their interpretation of the respect you are showing by your choice of dress."[2] The training environment is the same as the normal working environment of the kitchen team. A general rule to follow is, the more formal the training session, the more formal the attire.

Be conscious of body language. Good posture is important. Use body language that expresses confidence and that enhances the training presentation. Maintaining eye contact is essential. Put enthusiasm in your voice, speak clearly, and don't start with an apology for being there. Create a comfortable atmosphere. There is no reason why a warm, friendly atmosphere cannot be created and maintained throughout the training session. Try to establish this at the beginning. Other helpful suggestions for conducting a training session are shown in Figure 10-1.

YOUR COMFORT LEVEL

The key to success as a presenter is finding your comfort level. It is natural to be a little nervous just before beginning, but extreme nervousness generally has a source and that source is generally not being well prepared. The more familiar you are with the information being presented, the more comfortable you will be. To be fully prepared, you must practice. Practice your presentation and make sure you are very familiar with all of the material you will be presenting.

A chef is a busy person, so finding time to practice can be difficult, but it must be done. A common suggestion to executives is that they plan time into their day for planning. As a chef you must also plan into your day time for training development and preparation. The importance of training is tremendous, and your ability to achieve excellence as a trainer is equally important. Approach training team members with the same dedication that you approach the development of menu items. You would never put an item on the menu without testing it first. A training session should have no less attention.

Generally, if you take the time and do the preparation, your comfort level and nervousness will not be an issue. However, if you do begin to feel nervous, slow down and be more deliberate. This is a good way to avoid becoming tongue-tied. Also try not to worry about it. As Becker and Becker have stated: "Don't worry about it; this may actually be the best advice. Worry is like a rocking chair. It gives you something to do but it doesn't get you anywhere. Don't worry—do something about your fears."[3] In this case, rehearsing until you are confident that you are ready will help enormously. Mentally walk through the training session from beginning to end, picturing in your mind everything that you expect to happen.

EFFECTIVE INTERPERSONAL COMMUNICATION

Simplicity is the key to effective communication in the training setting. Simple, clear language usually is all that is required. Use of terminology and jargon causes problems. Use culinary terms with which the team members are familiar. This can build rapport within the group, but it must be handled carefully. The intention is to communicate, not to intimidate or impress. Therefore, the team will not be insulted if simple language is used.

Communicate on a personal level with each team member, and take action to ensure each one understands what is being said and demonstrated. When new terms are first introduced, work with the team members on the pronunciation and spelling of the terms. Deliver important concepts and points slowly, and cover less important material at a faster pace. Improve team member understanding by using appropriate gestures and visual aids to illustrate what you are saying.

When you are acting as a trainer, just as when you are acting as a supervisor, show that you believe in the potential of each team member and are sincerely interested in the success of each team member. This is done by taking an active interest in the learner's progress. Create an active rather than a passive learning environment by involving team members in the learning process. Ask the team members questions and for input pertaining to the demonstration or information session to reinforce what is being presented. This will also assist you in determining if team members are gaining an acceptable level of understanding of what is being presented.

As the training session progresses, watch for loss of attention. Be prepared to change direction or involve the team quickly in order to get back on track. Open communication throughout the workplace is important to having effective teams. This is includes training. As part of the training program, facilitate open communication by inviting the team to participate in identifying training that will provide continuous improvements.

As a trainer/presenter, there are also things that you should avoid because they can be barriers to effective communication. Examples of these actions are shown in Figure 10-2.

Imagery is an important part of the communication process. When speech is used to create a picture or scene, that image helps facilitate learning. Perception also plays an

FIGURE 10-2 Actions to avoid as a trainer/presenter/communicator.

- Eliminate "er," "ah," "ok," "you know what I mean," and similar nervous expressions from your vocabulary.
- Avoid long monologues. Make your presentation as natural as possible. Break up your speaking with other activities. Ask questions.
- Do not appear to be reading aloud. An outline is better than a complete script.
- Avoid all "-isms" (ageism, sexism, racism).
- Avoid using slang.
- Avoid "talking down" to the team.
- Avoid undesirable habits, such as fumbling with your hair, picking at your face, or cleaning your nails.

important part in interpersonal communication. It can either help or destroy the most sincere effort to communicate. People often hear only what they want to hear. Problems in perception can be created by team members with dissimilar attitudes, different cultural or educational backgrounds, and difficulty with the language being used.

The cultural backgrounds of kitchen team members has a strong influence on their receptiveness to new information. This includes verbal and nonverbal communication. A big consideration in nonverbal communication is distance.[4] The distance that people maintain when communicating has been determined as follows:

Intimate Distance

- Close phase: close physical contact
- Far phase: 6 to 18 inches; not considered proper in public by Euro-Americans

Personal Distance

- Close phase: 1 to 2 feet; comfortable if the people know one another
- Far phase: 2 to 4 feet; arm's length

Social Distance

- Close phase: 4 to 7 feet; impersonal business
- Far phase: 7 to 12 feet; more formal communication

Public Distance

- Close phase: 12 to 25 feet; can get away
- Far phase: 25 feet or more; set around important public figures

The distance that is accepted is based on the relationship between people involved and the circumstances. Depending on the physical nature of the training environment and the type of training to be given, the chef supervisor and the kitchen team's personalities can be categorized within the personal and social distance scales.

TRAINING AND DIVERSITY

According to the U.S. Bureau of Labor Statistics, women and minorities will make up the largest percentage growth in the workforce early in the twenty-first century. In a report in 1991, the U.S. Bureau of Labor Statistics predicted the number of white males in the workforce would drop to 39.4 percent, down from 48.9 percent in 1976.[5] According to Richard Koonce, writing in 2001, "only about 15 percent of new entrants into the American workforce are white males. The rest is a mix of Hispanics, African Americans, Vietnamese, Chinese, Russians, Europeans, and others."[6]

American culture is becoming increasingly diverse. It is no longer a melting pot in which new ethnic groups attempt to leave their original cultures behind them: "A more accurate image is a tossed salad, where various ingredients remain distinct even as they are mixed together."[7] Embracing cultural diversity in the kitchen requires the chef supervisor to adopt training skills and styles that are sensitive to valuing the differences within the kitchen team. Diversity in training is no longer just about correcting behavior in relation to racial discrimination and sexual harassment.[8] Training should embrace the diversity of the team and work to increase the capability of the team through that diversity.

Diversity includes everyone. It is not something that is defined by race or gender. It extends to age, education, lifestyle, sexual orientation, geographic origin, exempt and nonexempt status, physical abilities, religion, and where a person lives. There are also subcultures within any one of these categories. In practice, however, the word *diversity* has become synonymous with "people" who are other than white men.[9] According to Koonce, "Companies recognize the importance of creating workplaces that look like their marketplaces and that don't discriminate based on race, age, gender, ethnic background, religion, or sexual orientation."[10]

When viewed from a quality standpoint, cultural diversity in the foodservice industry is an advantage. Cultural diversity is an advantage that is a natural extension of the multinational nature of many kitchen teams. The naturally occurring diverse points of view can breathe life into a culinary operation. A diverse kitchen team can offer better customer service because the team reflects the differing needs and preferences of those who make up customers of the foodservice establishment. Key to developing this potential for better customer service is training. Diversity training and assisting cross-cultural communication can improve cooperation in multinational work teams.[11] What is required, according to R. Roosevelt Thomas, Jr., is "a new way of thinking about diversity, not as an us/them kind of problem to be solved but as a resource to be managed."[12]

The foundation for training and teamwork in a culturally diverse kitchen is valuing and appreciating *all* the differences within the team. This can be achieved by:

- Fostering awareness and acceptance of individual differences
- Helping team members understand their own feelings and attitudes about people who are different
- Exploring how differences might be tapped as assets in the kitchen
- Enhancing relations between people who are different
- Finding or inventing ways for each team member to collaborate

Thomas also stated: "You can manage diversity without valuing differences, but you can't manage diversity without understanding differences."[13] Tapping the team's full potential is about *empowerment,* and success depends on the ability to empower the entire workforce. However, acceptance, tolerance, and understanding are not by themselves enough to create an empowered team. To empower a diverse kitchen team to reach their full potential, training is needed. It is therefore important to understand the cultural values, attitudes, and beliefs of the team and the uniqueness this brings to the kitchen.

GETTING THE TEAM INVOLVED

Vital to the efforts of all quality improvement training sessions is getting each kitchen team member involved. The quality and the quantity of learning and continuous improvement are directly proportional to the degree of involvement by the kitchen team. Most people learn by doing. Key to the success of this method is to shift responsibility for learning to the team members. This technique is sometimes referred to as learner-controlled or self-paced instruction. Interacting with the team in this way requires the skills of a group facilitator. Team activities such as discussion, role playing, or case studies provide an opportunity for team members to explore topics, interact with each other, and share information by expressing their views and responding to each other's ideas and opinions. Although these group activities may be perceived by the team as informal, as an instruction method they need to be carefully planned. The role of a "group facilitator" consists of managing group discussions and group processes so that individuals learn and group members feel that the experience is positive.

Typical activities for a facilitator include group activities in which quality improvements are assessed. In group discussions in which all team members feel committed to the quality improvement actions, there exists an enhanced awareness of team efforts. Participation by all team members is facilitated. They are invited to present their viewpoints, levels of knowledge, and attitudes regarding various topics of culinary quality. Group activities stimulate thinking, create enthusiasm, and assist in analyzing different approaches to food preparation. The environment and characteristics of good team involvement are

- Informal, relaxed atmosphere
- Willingness to act as a group, communicate, and listen to each other
- Willingness to share new ideas
- Willingness to focus on differences about concepts, not about team members
- Readiness for action once a course of action has been arrived at through consensus

Questioning is a tried-and-true method for getting each team member involved. Questions arouse interest in the team member. They stimulate thinking, keep the team members on track, solicit information, and get individual team members involved. Questions can be classified in at least two ways. It is necessary to understand both types of questions in order to become successful using the technique. Questions are categorized as open/closed and direct/indirect questions. Other descriptions of these question types are overhead, direct, relay, and return.[14]

Open questions are the best suited to group discussions. They arouse interest, stimulate creative thinking, keep the chef supervisor and team on track, and provoke feedback. However, questioning, if overused, may send a message that the chef supervisor lacks confidence. Overuse of questioning can suggest to the team that constant reassurance is needed on matters being discussed. Open questions are questions asked of the entire training group. After each answer, the question is repeated to generate more answers. These types of questions are typically used to open discussions, introduce new topics, and give each team member a chance to comment. Open questions are recommended, because they arouse interest and encourage the team member to think creatively.

Closed questions, no matter how carefully they are asked, require only one answer. They don't contribute to advancing discussion or encourage the development of new ideas or concepts.

Direct questions are used to call on individuals for specific information and may be used to involve a team member who has not participated in the discussion. Directing

FIGURE 10-3   Examples of question types.

Examples of Open Questions

- What do you ask for in quality food presentation?
- How would you explain why this is so?
- Can anyone suggest a better method?
- What do you think would happen if?

Examples of Closed Questions

- Can anyone tell me who has ultimate responsibility in the kitchen?
- What are the ingredients for this recipe?
- How many methods of cooking fish are there?
- What is the order of preparation of this dish?

Examples of Direct Questions

- Jennifer, now that we have discussed our new menu composition, what other items should we include?
- Frank, how do you feel about the training program in the kitchen?
- Scott, tell me how you would prepare chili.
- Jude, what would you do to improve foodservice quality?

Examples of Indirect Questions

- The question that calls for an opinion—what are the team's views?
- How does the team view the new menu?
- Can anyone suggest new ways?
- What other methods might we try?

questions to specific team members also helps to even out the distribution. *Indirect or rhetorical questions* can be used to avoid giving an opinion on a topic but instead to encourage team members' opinions. Indirect questions are aimed at the entire team and can be useful for brainstorming.

Examples of each of the types of questions are shown in Figure 10-3.

Effective questioning means knowing how to seek information and stimulate insight. A *question* is defined as an inquiry designed to test, stimulate thought, or clarify. Questions can serve as an ongoing assessment of the learning taking place. As often as possible, use questions that allow the learner to respond.[15] When team members respond correctly, the chef supervisor can feel confident that the information or topic matter has been received. Questioning also provides the opportunity for dealing with any concerns individual members have before proceeding with training.

The primary purpose of questioning is to encourage team members to think about the training session topic, but involving the team through questioning also helps to maintain their interest and attention. Specific uses for questions in training include:

- Establish the learners' level of knowledge.
- Check learning and understanding.
- Reinforce information.
- Summarize information.
- Maintain learner engagement.
- Stimulate dialogue among team members.

In general the trainer/presenter should:

- Keep things simple.
- Maintain eye contact.
- Be aware of tone of voice and body language.
- Maintain awareness of team emotions.

BRAINSTORMING

Brainstorming is a great means of generating new ideas, but it can only work effectively within a formal structure that every participating kitchen team member knows and understands.

- A brainstorming session should be limited to a defined place and time. It is useful to precede it with a ten-minute warm-up session on a totally unrelated or even trivial subject. Plan thirty minutes for the real session objective. The session should stop on time even if it is in full flight.
- The session should be held in a relaxed atmosphere. The team must be encouraged and motivated to generate *their* ideas; evaluation of the ideas generated is strictly avoided during the sessions.
- The procedure requires each team member to come forth with new ideas no matter how extreme they seem. They should not "switch off" to other people's ideas and wait for a chance to have theirs included, but rather should develop the other members' ideas.

The functionaries during these sessions are the chairperson (who need not be the chef supervisor) and the note taker. The chairperson's functions are to:

- Define the objective or problem at the outset.
- Be independent of the issues that arise and resisting interference or domination.
- Direct the discussion and keep it on track.
- Act to control input from everyone at once, facilitating the less vociferous to be heard.
- Contribute to idea generation.
- Stop any form of evaluation during the session.
- Involve each team member and provide positive feedback to encourage more team member input.

The note taker's functions are to:

- Write down ideas as they are generated.
- Review written suggestions and stimulate additional ideas.

Using brainstorming in a structured way is an excellent method of resolving problems in the kitchen. It is also an excellent way of identifying training gaps. Getting the people involved is one of the best methods to facilitate training. It is the single most positive contributor to successful training.

UNDERSTANDING GROUP BEHAVIORS

People within groups often act out roles that are closely related to their individual personalities. Each person plays out a particular role or assumes a certain mental posture during training. Chef supervisors should be aware of these various roles. These roles can be divided into building and supportive roles, self-centered roles, and task roles. Team members in each category may be subdivided into more specific roles.

The *building and supportive role* can be subdivided into four roles: The Supporter is the one who praises and agrees with team members; the Supporter goes along with the team. The Harmonizer mediates differences between team members. The Tension Reliever cracks jokes and works to brings out humor in the team. The Facilitator works to opens channels for communication.

The *self-centered role* can also be subdivided. The Blocker is one who constantly raises objections and revisits topics when others have moved on. The Aggressor constantly expresses ill will and makes sarcastic remarks. The Recognition Seeker calls attention to himself or herself during the training session. The Dominator tries to run the session by giving orders, interrupting, and attempting to get his or her own way. The Apathetic member simply does not participate in team activities.

The *Task Role* is taken by the Problem Solver and Task Performer.

Other roles include the Initiator, who proposes new ideas, goals, and procedures; the Information Seeker, who seeks facts and additional information before making decisions; the Information Giver, who offers facts and information; the Opinion Seeker, who seeks clarification of the values involved; the Opinion Giver, who constantly states his or her own opinions; the Clarifier, who elaborates on ideas offered by other team members; the Coordinator, who brings together ideas offered by the team; and the Energizer, who prods the team to a greater level of activity.[16]

By listening carefully and watching the various verbal and nonverbal clues, each of the described roles may be observed. Recognizing these behaviors is the first step in developing a method of coping with them. Each team training session will take on a culture and personality of its own. The most serious lapse occurs when a chef supervisor appears to be taking over. This alienates the other team members, who may consequently lose sight of the objective of the training session. An inexperienced chef supervisor who is new to the training role often defers to a dominant type, which also has the effect of alienating the group, causing them to lose confidence in the chef supervisor. Another signal to watch for is the question that does not relate to the topic under discussion. This may be an indication of boredom or of a team member who is having difficulty.

Team building and maintenance relies greatly on team/group activities such as meetings, discussions, and training. Understanding the dynamics of the group enables the chef supervisor to recognize and deal with them. Each team training session will almost certainly include a selection of these various personality types. Expect to have them, but learn to cope with them. Continuous improvements in the kitchen cannot be made by one person. It takes the entire kitchen team. This is where the chef supervisor demonstrates leadership skills by overcoming these personality obstacles.

Summary

Vital to effective training is the understanding of all the elements that can lead to its success. Good introductions by the chef supervisor facilitate the training process. The first five minutes of the training session set the scene for the training that will follow. Attention to detail ensures success with training. Among the important elements of this process are

- Explaining the objectives of the training sessions
- Capturing the kitchen team's interest and preparing them for training

- Being cognizant of the message being sent through appearance and individual demeanor
- Creating a warm, friendly atmosphere, which facilitates training
- Being prepared and comfortable
- Using effective, clear interpersonal communication skills, avoiding the use of jargon
- Recognizing the nonverbal and distance aspects of communication
- Understanding the advantages of a diverse team in the kitchen and actively fostering training toward empowerment

- Recognizing the dynamics of group behavior and the role of the chef supervisor as team facilitator
- Using correct and appropriate questioning techniques
- Facilitating and planning the kitchen team's brainstorming sessions
- Understanding the dynamics of group behaviors, arranging meetings to elicit feedback, and identifying training gaps

Discussion Questions

1. Why is it important to outline to all team members what is expected of them as a result of training?
2. What methods can be employed to deal with nervousness?
3. What are the four levels of distance that team members often maintain when communicating?
4. What are the significant elements to be considered for training a diverse kitchen team?

5. What key points contribute to getting team involvement in training?
6. What are the closed, open, and directed questioning techniques?
7. What are the primary uses and benefits of brainstorming as a training technique?
8. Within groups, each member plays out a certain role. What are the three categories into which these roles fall?

Notes

1. Dugan Laird, *Approaches to Training and Development* (Reading, MA: Addison-Wesley, 1985), 76.
2. Dennis Becker and Paula Borkum Becker, *Powerful Presentation Skills* (Boston: Mirror Press, 1994), 65.
3. Ibid., 33.
4. Edward T. Hall, *The Hidden Dimension* (New York: Doubleday, 1966).
5. U.S. Department of Labor Bureau of Statistics, Washington, DC, 1991.
6. Richard Koonce, "Redefining Diversity: It's Not Just the Right Thing to Do. It Also Makes Good Business Sense," *Training & Development*, December 2001, www.findarticles.com/cf_ntrstnws/m4467/12_55/83045836/print.jhtml, 2.
7. Sally J. Walton, *Cultural Diversity in the Workplace* (New York: Irwin, 1994), v.
8. Koonce, "Redefining Diversity," 1.
9. Julia Christensen, "The Diversity Dynamic: Implications for Organizations in 2005," *Hospitality Research Journal* 17, no. 1 (1993), 70.
10. Koonce, "Redefining Diversity," p. 1.
11. Ibid., 4.
12. R. Roosevelt Thomas, *Beyond Race and Gender* (New York: AMACON, 1991), 10.
13. Ibid., 169.
14. David Wheelhouse, *Managing Human Resources in the Hospitality Industry* (East Lansing, MI: Educational Institute of the American Hotel and Motel Association, 1989), 170.
15. Bruce B. Tepper, *The New Supervisor Skills for Successs* (Boston: Mirror Press, 1994), 85.
16. Richard L. Sullivan, Jerry R. Wircenski, Susan S. Arnold, and Michelle D. Sarkeess, *Practical Manual for the Design, Delivery, and Evaluation of Training* (Rockville, MD: Aspen, 1990), 37.

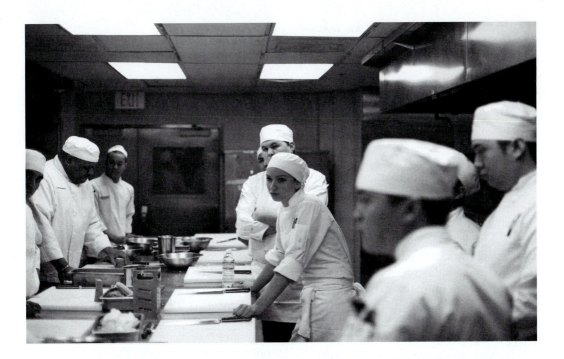

CHAPTER 11
TRAINING METHODS

OBJECTIVES

When you complete this chapter, you should be able to:

1. List the major techniques of training used for instructing in the kitchen
2. Explain which training techniques can be used to achieve specific learning objectives
3. Understand and describe the elements of training reinforcement
4. Identify negative training methods and state their effect
5. Identify characteristics of those team members with potential for development
6. Specify designs for evaluating training

Case Study: CHINA DELIGHT

The Hanon Restaurant Group began with the Select Seafood Restaurant in 1963. In January 1995 the company had 1191 restaurants around the world. These included 660 Select Seafood Restaurants, 480 Italian Palace Restaurants, and 51 China Delight Restaurants. They were the largest, most successful, and most stable restaurant company in the world. On March 1, 1995, Hannon Restaurant Group shocked Wall Street and the restaurant industry when, without any type of prior announcement, they simultaneously closed all 51 China Delight properties. On the afternoon of March 1, 1995, the company released the following statement:

> Hannon Restaurant Group has made the strategic decision to discontinue the China Delight Restaurant concept. The company has been unable to address recurring challenges in the area of food quality and consistency, service quality and workforce stability.

Hanon Group had determined during the initial conceptualization of the China Delight Restaurants that serving authentic Chinese cuisine would be one of the cornerstones of the concept. To achieve this goal, Chinese were hired as general managers, and the majority of the kitchen staff was Chinese. Managers, assistant managers, wait staff, and other personnel were not necessarily Chinese.

The management and operation of the China Delight Restaurants was built on the model that had been used so successfully for the Select Seafood and Italian Palace Restaurants. This model recognized the importance of the general manager and other members of the management team, but with close control from the corporate office. An operations manual was developed that effectively addressed every eventuality. Managers did not have to guess how to handle most issues; they simply had to refer to the manual. All sales, purchasing, and payroll information was forwarded to the corporate office on a daily basis. This information was analyzed, and guidance was provided to the management from the corporate office daily regarding the operation. All menu and recipe development was done at the corporate level and then distributed to the properties. Stringent guidelines were in place for the preparation of the food and sanitation in the facility. This tightly controlled model had been very successful for the company for many years. Their experience with 1000+ restaurants had yielded a wealth of knowledge and insight into the management and operation of restaurants. The model worked well in the first few units, which were created close to the corporate offices and initially opened by a team of Chinese and Chinese-speaking managers from other Hanon properties.

Based on the strength of the model and the initial success of the first few properties, the company rapidly expanded the China Delight Restaurants, building 51 in less than five years. The model did not continue to work. Expansion only compounded the problems that began to appear when the company had to hire individuals from outside the company to be general managers. The new general managers all had strong management backgrounds in the operation of similar-type restaurants. Because there had never been a chain of this type before, almost none had experience in operation of a chain restaurant. To assist them in the transition to the concept, they were put through a well-designed three-month training program to teach them the Hanon way and culture. This program was used as the starting point for all Hanon management personnel. Additionally, the managers were given one week of intensive training in the operation and systems specific to the China Delight Restaurants. The training program did not achieve the desired results.

The general managers did not submit their information in a timely fashion, and they did not pay attention to the input provided by the corporate office. Shoppers reported major differences in the menu items from one property to another. The sanitation levels in the properties were far below that of the other Hanon restaurants. Customer traffic at the properties began strongly but slowly crept downward. Guests complained of slow service, and the properties' food cost percentage were consistently out of line.

The regional managers consistently referred to the managers as too entrepreneurial when asked why they could not get control of the properties. One district manager stated, "They act like they own the business and can run it any way they want." The district managers also reported a disruptive level of friction between the front and back of the house. The district managers freely admitted that they had little ability to address problems in the back of the house directly, because the majority of the cooks did not have a good command of English and the district managers did not speak any Chinese dialect. All communication was through the general managers at the properties. The communications problem was compounded in the properties that had non-Chinese members in the management teams. These management team members, hired by the corporation and assigned to the property, complained of being excluded from the actual operation of the restaurant by the managers who spoke Chinese. They also reported that they were unable to communicate with the kitchen staff.

The president of China Delight characterized the speed-of-service issue as the application of Western restaurant management principles to an Oriental restaurant operation. He stated that speed of service in the restaurant was related directly to the number of woks in the kitchen. "One wok, one cook, one dish!" A Hanon Restaurant Group vice president stated that "going from three or four units to 50 was the kiss of death."

Based on what you have learned from previous chapters and the content of this chapter, answer the following questions.

- What is the overall reason for the failure of China Delight Restaurants?
- What are the primary causal agents for the failure of China Delight Restaurants?
- What role did leadership and supervision/management play in the failure of China Delight Restaurants?
- What specific steps could have been taken to avoid the failure of China Delight Restaurants?
- What, specifically, can be done by Hanon Restaurant Group to avoid a repetition of the China Delight Restaurant failure with their next concept rollout?

INTRODUCTION

All modern learning theories stress involvement by the learner. Learners should have a degree of ownership of the learning process. Training is therefore a learning process that involves the acquisition of skills, concepts, rules, or attitudes that serve to increase the performance of the kitchen team. These acquisitions are best gained through methods that actively involve the learner. Using individualized or group training techniques can accomplish training and retraining. This chapter will explore the instructional techniques and methods that best serve members of the kitchen team.

People grow to a point at which they are ready for new responsibilities beyond their initial assignments. When this happens, the foodservice organization can help them to develop and assimilate new roles and understanding of all the elements necessary to continuously improve themselves and the organization. Training is the critical factor. Training all employees, with special attention to hourly employees, will enable the kitchen to recruit and retain workers and keep a well-run foodservice establishment afloat and realizing its potential even in hard times.[1]

SPECIFIC TRAINING METHODS

JOB TALKS

Job talks are a method of instruction whereby the chef supervisor provides verbal information about a particular job. These are typically used in the kitchen when the chef supervisor is presenting information concepts and theories that are found in the cognitive learning domain. They are delivered by way of an illustrated lecture and may be supplemented with a variety of instructional materials such as slides, transparencies, projected computer displays, flip charts, instruction sheets, and/or videotapes. Job talks are, by definition, words spoken by the chef supervisor. It is a verbal medium, offering a passive, nonstimulating experience for the kitchen team member, unless the chef supervisor has unusual vocal talent. Interesting examples as well as colorful and persuasive language are needed to illustrate the job talk.[2] Job talks offer many advantages to the chef supervisor. They can be an effective method of reaching mixed groups of learners. Job talks can ensure that a large amount of information is delivered in a relatively short period of time. The strengths and weaknesses of the job talk are shown in Figure 11-1.

FIGURE 11-1 Job talk: strengths and weaknesses.

Strengths

- Gets the message across to a large group.
- Chef can communicate enthusiasm for subject matter.
- Covers material not otherwise available.
- Chef supervisor can serve as effective role model.
- Nonthreatening to the individual team member.
- Chef supervisor controls the material, time involved.
- Not necessary to plan group involvement.

Weaknesses

- Often does not allow for feedback from the team.
- Passive method of training.
- Difficult to maintain listeners' interest.
- Appeals to one sense only—hearing (unless illustrated).
- Overloading may occur.
- Difficult to assess if the "message" has been understood.
- Success dependent on public speaking ability of chef.
- Unsuitable for certain higher forms of learning such as analysis and evaluation.

The goal of the chef supervisor when conducting a job talk is to make the strongest possible connection with the team members and thereby achieve the highest possible level of understanding of the material presented. There are several keys to achieving this "maximum value" from job talks. The chef supervisor needs to make sure the team members see the relevancy of the subject matter to their current jobs or to professional development and advancement. Relevancy is a driver of the team member's interest in the subject matter. The team member's interest is key to the level of comprehension and mastery that will be achieved by the job talk.

Relevancy alone will not deliver success in a job talk. The chef supervisor must be an effective presenter/communicator. The chef supervisor must demonstrate enthusiasm for the subject matter. The chef supervisor can connect on a more personal level by calling team members by their names, displaying a sense of humor, moving around to achieve "eye contact" with each team member, engaging the team members with questions, and providing positive feedback. The chef supervisor should be a model in terms of dress, appearance, support for the quality objectives, and enthusiasm for the training program, and by facilitating each team member to grow and succeed.

There are three parts to the structure of a job talk. In the *introduction,* state what you are going to talk about and why. Start positively; go over previous information pertaining to the job talk.

In the *presentation,* avoid reading word for word. The presentation should be anchored with the key terms. Define the terms, and clarify them with examples that allow the team member to see their relevance and connect them to the focus of the talk. Develop the talk from the known to the unknown, from the simple to the more difficult. Build information in a logical way. Try to develop a picture in the team members' minds. Media technology may be used to emphasize and support the job talk. Vary your tone of voice, observe each person, and don't fix your gaze on a "challenging" individual. Avoid rushing the job talk, and try to pace it to the learning rate of the group. Do not allow too many long pauses.

In the *summary,* restate the key points of the job talk. Allow time for team members to ask questions. Use questions to determine what learning has taken place. Praise the team for their interest and link forward to the next job talk or training session.

Schedule job talks close to when the knowledge and skills will be used by each team member. Break the job talk down into fairly simple steps, then progress through each step until the entire job is learned. This provides an opportunity for the team member to experience success along the way, to remain interested, and to be motivated to learn the job. Team members can be overwhelmed if too much information is presented all at once, and this will cause frustration.

When a highly experienced person attempts to instruct the details of a job, significant points may be omitted, assumptions may be made that "everyone knows that," or some detail is so routine that it is overlooked. Do not assume anything. Concentration on the key points should help simplify the job talk. If the job talk preparation process is complete, then repetition and emphasizing of key points becomes easy to do. The tried-and-true method of preparing job talks, and all presentations, is "Tell them!" as shown in Figure 11-2.

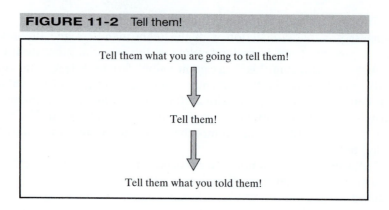

FIGURE 11-2 Tell them!

Tell them what you are going to tell them!

⬇

Tell them!

⬇

Tell them what you told them!

ROLE-PLAYS

In role-plays, team members simulate or act out a real or hypothetical situation in order to acquire the skills needed to manage the interpersonal dynamics of that situation. The strengths and weaknesses of role-plays are shown in Figure 11-3.

This training method can be used to build skill and confidence. It is usually followed by discussion and analysis among the kitchen team participants. Team members are asked to act out certain roles (such as a dissatisfied customer) in order for others to be able to practice how to handle such problems. The idea is for the team members to learn from playing out the assigned roles. In this way team members can be exposed to both sides of an issue. Role-plays are one of the training methods that offer participants the opportunity to be actively involved in the learning process. Videotaping role-plays allows for review and evaluation to improve their effectiveness. The following guidelines are recommended for role-plays.

FIGURE 11-3 Role-play: strengths and weaknesses.

Strengths

- Team members are involved directly in the training.
- Highlights key attitudinal issues.
- Develops awareness of other people's feelings.
- Similarity between role-play and work situations becomes clear to team members.
- Team members receive instant feedback that gives them confidence.
- Good for interpersonal skills.
- Allows team members to "see" problem areas as they exist.

Weaknesses

- Requires a lot of preparation.
- Suitable only for small groups.
- Sometimes not taken seriously by team members.
- Requires close monitoring and control by the chef supervisor.

- Allow plenty of time for each role-play.
- Introduce role-plays when team members' knowledge of the subject will assure success.
- Fully explain the purpose of the role-play (outline the training objective) as well as the expected results.
- Always demonstrate role-plays before team members try them.
- Keep the tone of the training session "serious."
- Invite the team member to choose a particular role; seek attitude changes during the role-play.
- Coach and correct team members during and following enactment of the role-play.
- Give positive reinforcement and praise and link forward to further training.

Total immersion in the learning process can be achieved by using a role-play. It is particularly useful for awareness training with regard to customer satisfaction and may also be used to demonstrate correct and appropriate interpersonal transactions. If done with enthusiasm by the chef supervisor, it can become a very effective method of training.

Role-plays may be highly structured, with the roles well defined, or they may allow the team members who are playing the roles a great deal of flexibility in acting them out.[3] Role-plays cast participants into real-life situations. Real-life situations in the kitchen take on special meaning when dealing with personal sanitation, grooming, and hygiene. Sensitive topics such as these are ideal subject matter for role-plays. Crucial to the success of these sessions are prior explanation of the training objective and follow-up discussions on the role-play content. In this way sensitive topics can be treated as part of a group role-play, with critical sensitive elements being highlighted. Remember, role-plays only work if the participants are able to let go of their inhibitions, feel empathy for the role they are asked to play, and really get into the situation. The chef supervisor's ability to understand team members' attitudes toward role-play training should enable him or her to improve personal awareness of individual shortcomings.

Training in the foodservice industry involves more than just technical skills. Interpersonal skills are as important, if not more so. Chef supervisors must not assume that team members know how to treat customers or other members in the foodservice organization in a polite and friendly manner. Instructing interpersonal skills by using role-plays is an efficient training method that results in increased motivation. Role-plays do not guarantee that the desired behavior will be used on the job, but they do provide examples of expected behavior. This method of training should be used with care and is most appropriate when the social competence of the team member is low.

DEMONSTRATIONS

Demonstration as a training method is very effective in skills training. By showing team members how to perform a task while explaining the procedure, the chef supervisor enables the kitchen team members to use more than one sense and one learning mode at the same time. They can listen to the chef supervisor while observing the proper performance steps of the task or skill being demonstrated. Follow-up activity

FIGURE 11-4 Demonstration: strengths and weaknesses.

Strengths

- Great visual impact.
- Instruction can be built step by step, given in sequence.
- Difficult steps or tasks can be broken down into easy stages.
- Makes use of the natural inclination to imitate.
- Most effective method of instructing a skill.
- Emphasis on safety/sanitation practices can be included.
- Food product quality and specifications can be observed.
- Required job skills or tasks may be repeated/reinforced.

Weaknesses

- Suitable only for relatively small groups.
- A great deal of preparation is required.
- Pace of demonstration is often too fast.
- Team members may watch the demonstrator rather than what is being done.

on the job then allows the team member to practice while being coached and corrected by the chef supervisor. The strengths and weaknesses of demonstrations are shown in Figure 11-4.

In a demonstration, actual kitchen equipment is used to illustrate the steps involved in the task. Demonstration alone makes use primarily of the team member's visual sense. He or she may hear and/or smell, which reinforces learning. Keys to an effective demonstration include:

- Ensure that all actions can be seen easily.
- Arrange all food ingredients, equipment, and tools needed for the demonstration in advance.
- Introduce the demonstration by reviewing previously instructed information and/or skills that are relevant to the demonstration.
- Introduce any technical/culinary terms that are relevant to the demonstration, particularly new terms.
- Demonstrate the manipulative skill or task in a way that closely resembles the actual kitchen environment and clarify why the skill is important.
- Stress food safety and sanitation.
- Check for understanding during the demonstration by asking team members questions.

The potential for a demonstration's success in bringing team members to the desired level of understanding or mastery can be improved by some simply actions. Use supporting materials such as a procedure sheet to reinforce the performance steps being demonstrated. Keep the demonstration focused and short, preferably fifteen to thirty minutes. Closely follow the demonstration with supervised practice and/or an assignment related to the demonstration, to reinforce the information presented. During, and after, the demonstration, show your interest in the team members' understanding and mastery by asking questions and providing positive feedback.

The chef supervisor should avoid demonstration as a training method unless it can be practiced beforehand and adequate time for preparation and checking of equipment and food materials has been allowed. The demonstration can be reinforced with an effective review and summary.[4]

A common mistake is to complete a demonstration and ask whether each team member feels he or she can perform the steps or understand the basic skills involved. The usual response in this situation is silence or affirmative nods. An excellent summary technique is to ask a team member to repeat the demonstration while the chef supervisor or another team member reads each of the steps. Following the second demonstration, the individual is ready to practice the steps.

Demonstrations are especially suitable for skills training (psychomotor objectives), but they can also be used as modeling to illustrate interpersonal, interviewing, or communication skills. Within the kitchen, demonstration is by far the single most effective method for instructing culinary art: the preparation, cooking, and presentation of menu items. As a method, it has the benefit of utilizing all five sense of the team member, and no other training method affords this total sensual integration.

Effective questioning and reinforcement techniques are employed during and following the demonstration to encourage team members to think about the training topic. In addition, questioning helps to maintain the individuals' interest. It provides the chef supervisor with feedback regarding team members' understanding of the topic and allows for feedback to strengthen the training climate in the kitchen.

CASE STUDY

The case study method of training presents to the kitchen team real or hypothetical situations for them to analyze. Ideally, the case study should force the team member to think through problems, propose solutions, choose among them, and analyze the consequences of the decision. Case studies are a popular way to get involvement by the team so that discussion and resolutions of problems may be brought down to the level of concreteness. The strengths and weaknesses of case studies are shown in Figure 11-5.

In traditional case studies, team members receive a printed description of a problem situation. The description contains sufficient detail so that the individual can make recommendations for appropriate corrective actions. Areas in which the use of case

FIGURE 11-5   Case study: strengths and weaknesses.

Strengths
- Emphasizes the analysis of a situation typical of a training need.
- May improve team members' communication skills.
- Exposes team members to true-to-life problems in the kitchen.
- May inspire interest in otherwise theoretical and abstract training materials.

Weaknesses
- Focuses on past and static considerations.
- Analysis often lacks emotional involvement on the part of the team member and therefore can become unrealistic in terms of what the team member would actually do in the situation.

studies as a training method is particularly appropriate in the kitchen include analysis of safety and sanitation procedures, teamwork, workflow, work organization, customer relations, and quality in all areas of organization.

Although many cases exist under these headings, it is possible for resourceful chef supervisors to create their own. Additionally, team members can be encouraged to write their own case studies from past real-life situations, and these may then be shared with the rest of the kitchen team. To increase total participation, team members may be split into small "buzz groups." When there are fewer people in each group, individuals are more inclined to participate at higher levels than if only one large discussion group is going on.

To facilitate and enable success with case study training methods, the technique of structured discussions is used. Structured discussions are conversations between team members aimed at specific learning objectives. These objectives distinguish them from more social conversation. The learning objective for the case study analysis should be announced in advance. Structure in the ensuing discussions can be facilitated by the use of an agenda with time controls. Agendas and timetables developed by the team afford ownership of the session to the kitchen team.

Attempting to conduct a structured discussion when team members have had limited exposure to the case study topic often will result in little or no interaction and an ineffective discussion. Creating an effective structured discussion begins with the environment. The chef supervisor must create an environment for the discussion that encourages not only engagement and interaction of the team members but that also ensures respect for all participants. This means ensuring that no team member will be ridiculed or rejected for expressing a thought on the subject under discussion. Provision of guidelines for the conduct of the discussion is critical to establishing an environment that will lead to truly open dialogue.

As with any training method, relevancy of the subject matter is a key to success. The chef supervisor must bring into focus for the team members the relevancy of the issue being discussed and provide positive reinforcement. The chef supervisor should act as a catalyst in the discussion, encouraging participation and stimulating discussion when lulls occur. The chef supervisor must not dominate the discussion.

Structured discussions are appropriate for use with case studies. They should have predetermined objectives. The chef supervisor must ensure that team members do not bring a negative viewpoint to these objectives. When used with case study analysis, structured discussions can be a motivating and useful training method in the kitchen.

ON-THE-JOB TRAINING

On-the-job training (OJT) is the most commonly used method to train kitchen team members. It is not necessarily the best training method for culinary standards of quality. The chef supervisor usually conducts it, and it has the advantage of providing "hands-on" experience under normal conditions. Although OJT is commonly used in the kitchen, it also is one of the most poorly implemented methods of training. Common drawbacks of OJT include:

- Lack of a well-structured training environment
- Poor chef supervisor training skills
- Omission of a well-defined high-quality job performance criterion

On-the-job training can be successful when the chef supervisor as trainer has an objective, a plan, and the knowledge that quality and continuous improvements can only be implemented on the job.

One benefit of OJT is that it provides immediate application and satisfaction for the new team member, who may often be anxious and fearful. The chef supervisor can determine which training method is most suitable for instructing different job duties. Additionally, for retraining or cross-training, different methods and techniques and/or combinations of these methods may be appropriate.

Steps and Structure of OJT

1. *Introduction*
   - Introduce what the team member *will be able to do* at the end of the session.
   - Indicate why the team member is to learn.
   - Discuss how this training relates to what the team member already knows.
   - Demonstrate equipment to be used during the training session.
   - Explain the steps involved in the task and the overall purpose.
2. *Presentation*
   - Highlight key points.
   - Demonstrate the procedure in sequential order.
   - Explain the what, why, who, when, how, and where.
   - Use training aids where appropriate.
   - Instruct at a pace that allows the team member to understand the task.
3. *Summary*
   - Demonstrate the task a second time, if necessary; repeat the key points and steps.
   - Encourage questions on points of clarification.
   - Give specific feedback.
   - Give praise when due.
   - When satisfied that learning has occurred, move to the next step.
4. *Practice*
   - Team members practice under supervision.
   - Ask questions to assess team members' understanding.
   - Coach and correct team members.
   - Praise when correct quality standards have been achieved.
5. *Follow-up*
   - The team member puts into practice what has been instructed under supervision.
   - Encourage further questions from the team member.
   - Decide on follow-up talk.
   - Show how every job relates to the importance of every other job and that failure of one affects the value of all of the others.
6. *Coaching*
   - Allow all team members to become involved with the procedures they will use.
   - Conduct correction interviews in private.
   - Permit team members to evaluate their own performance.
   - Allow ample time for skill development.
   - Use open questions to establish work problems.
   - Provide positive reinforcement.

The first step of coaching is to observe team members doing their job. If they are doing the job well, don't hesitate to tell them so. Everyone likes to be praised; try to catch team members doing good things.

Training is progressive, and it must be continuous. Repetition is the key to learning. Therefore it is important that the chef supervisor demonstrate a good deal of patience. If there appears to be a problem with some aspect of the team member's performance, check the following:

- Is the team member fully aware of what is supposed to be done?
- Does the team member have adequate equipment and materials to perform the task?
- Did the team member receive adequate feedback during the practice stage?

The next step is to confront, not criticize, the team member's poor performance. *Confronting* is a positive process used to correct job performance problems. Chef supervisors who confront are interested in helping team members feel confident about improving future performance, rather than making them feel inadequate and guilty about past performance. Praise in public, correct in private. Training means directing the growth of an individual. In the total quality kitchen environment, cross-training is becoming more important. Cross-training prepares individual team members to fill in as needed on jobs. This is also an excellent method of eliminating job monotony and fatigue. Another advantage of cross-training is that it makes flexibility possible; for example, when one team member is absent, another can perform that job.

APPRENTICESHIP TRAINING

Apprenticeship training is designed to provide young chefs entering the culinary profession with comprehensive training in the practical and theoretical aspects of work required in a highly skilled profession. Apprenticeship programs combine OJT and classroom training, with a skilled and experienced chef conducting the OJT during the apprenticeship period. The purpose of this training is to learn practical culinary skills on the job. Apprentices learn the theoretical side of the culinary profession in classes they attend outside the job. Subjects covered in classroom training are safety, sanitation, communication skills, mathematics, supervisory management, law, food cost control procedures, purchasing, and nutrition.

The culinary apprenticeship program in the United States is sponsored by the American Culinary Federation in cooperation with local chapters of that organization. It is the only national apprenticeship training program for chefs and operates in cooperation with the U.S. Department of Labor, Bureau of Apprenticeship and Training (BAT). The apprenticeship program also operates in conjunction with local postsecondary schools and colleges providing culinary theory courses.[5]

The culinary apprentice completes 6000 hours of OJT as well as theory-related courses, usually over a three-year period. Wages paid to apprentices usually begin at half those paid to fully trained chefs. However, wages are generally advanced rapidly at six-month intervals. The BAT has established the following minimum standards for apprenticeship programs:

1. Nondiscrimination in all phases of apprenticeship employment and training
2. Organized instruction designed to provide the apprentice with a knowledge in technical subjects related to the trade or skill

BOX 11-1

CHEF TALK:
MY WAY OR THE HIGHWAY

To train, to form by instruction, discipline, or drill. In the kitchen, chefs are involved primarily in training two types of culinarians: the apprentice chef (who is inexperienced in the area of culinary art) and the cook (who may have had many years of experience with other establishments). From personal experience, each culinarian should be handled differently when it comes to training.

In comparing the apprentice chef and the cook from a training standpoint, I feel most chefs would prefer to train apprentice chefs. The rationale is that the apprentice is new, has no preset ideas or bad habits, and is usually eager to learn. It doesn't take much for the chef to convince the apprentice of how things should be done. Let's face it, all of us chefs have different ideas on how things should be done. So with an apprentice, it basically boils down to what we as chefs are willing to commit to this person, and that should be everything we know about cooking and how to run a kitchen.

The experienced cook may have served an apprenticeship with another chef or be a graduate of a culinary school or of the "School of Hard Knocks." Either way, they are most assuredly going to do things differently from you.

How do we train such a cook? When I first became a supervisory chef, I thought it would be simple. My technique, in all honesty, was "my way or the highway." As I gained experience, I learned how to work with and train these individuals. In fact, sometimes I ended up as the trainee. Training becomes a watching process. I would watch new cooks in action, observing their skill levels, techniques, work methods, and the final product. When they prepared something that was different from our standards, I would compare both methods and discuss which method was better. If theirs made sense, we would change to that method and vice versa. If the end result was the same, and there was no difference in the cost or time factor, then either method could be used.

It is difficult to train persons if they are uncomfortable with the training method. I discovered that by utilizing an open training style and involving the cooks, they become more open to my suggestions because they realize their input is valued.

Adian P. Murphy, CMC, AAC,
Executive Chef, Old Warson
Country Club, St. Louis, Missouri

3. A schedule of work processes in which an apprentice is to receive training and experience on the job
4. A progressively increasing schedule of wages
5. Proper supervision of OJT, with adequate facilities to train apprentices
6. Periodic evaluation of the apprentice's progress, both on-the-job performance and related instruction
7. Recognition for successful completion

Upon graduation, the apprentice receives a Department of Labor certificate and/or a certificate of the American Culinary Federation and is admitted as a member of that organization.

WAY TRAINING REINFORCEMENT

People strive to achieve objectives they have set for themselves. The most frequently identified objectives of kitchen team members are job security, rewarding work, recognition, status, responsibility, and achievement. If training assists team members in achieving these objectives, then the learning process is greatly facilitated. When training provides greater opportunities for job advancement, team members will be highly motivated because they can see that greater rewards and job security will likely result. Knowledge of results (feedback) influences the training/learning process. Keeping team members informed of their progress as measured against a quality improvement standard helps in setting goals for what remains to be learned. The ongoing process of analyzing progress and setting new objectives greatly enhances learning.

Reinforcement theory states that behavior appearing to lead to a positive consequence tends to be repeated, whereas behavior appearing to lead to a negative consequence tends not to be repeated. A positive consequence is rewarded.[6] Praise and recognition are two of the most important rewards used in training. Each segment of training should be sequentially organized so that the individual can see not only its purpose, but also how it fits into the overall quality training program.

Perfect practice makes perfect, and bad practice will not make perfect. This is applicable to training in the kitchen. Repeating a job task several times develops facility in performing it. Practice and repetition almost always lead to effective training.

NEGATIVE TRAINING METHODS

It is impossible to effect standards of quality food production if chef supervisors do not actively engage in training their team. Yet it is not uncommon to observe poor or no training in some kitchens. Many chef supervisors assume that the experience in a previous job takes the place of training. They assume that new team members know how to do the job to the quality standards that they have set. There is also a misguided assumption that once a team member is hired, he or she will learn the job from other team members. Known as the "buddy system," this is rooted in the mistaken belief that other team members can train the new team member, often while still doing their jobs. Probably the most common negative training method is the one that allows the person leaving the job to train the person who will take over the job. Other negative training methods are:

- *Spectator method.* The new team member does not have the right to do anything and can only watch others. This is boring for the individual, produces nothing, and simply prolongs the training period.
- *Unskilled labor method.* The team member can perform only trivial jobs, for example, cleaning up or getting coffee. Nothing is learned and the team member feels useless and is not stimulated for the job.
- *Do-it-yourself method.* New team members are left on their own to "sink or swim." This method can be successful with individuals who catch on quickly and who like to show off their capabilities. The downside to this method is the risk that a new team member will develop bad habits, and this can harm team spirit. Later, these team members are usually unwilling to pass on to others what they know.

DEVELOPING THE TEAM MEMBER
WITH POTENTIAL

Training deals with the immediate concerns of the kitchen team; *development* deals with recognizing team members who possess obvious talent for leadership roles. Developing individual team members into capable chef supervisors of the future is

FIGURE 11-6 Characteristics of potential leaders.

- Are able to cope with problems and seek help when it is needed
- Are able to act without supervisory direction
- Are open-minded, calm, and tolerant
- Accept responsibility for their actions and don't try to blame others
- Maintain a level disposition
- Display high energy levels

the answer to continuous improvements necessary to provide better-quality food and service to customers. The team member with potential for growth needs nurturing and encouragement.

Human resources development is generally a combination of OJT and educational opportunities that will help a team member develop into a more productive and responsible member of the foodservice organization. Although there are no foolproof methods of determining who has the greatest potential for development, Figure 11-6 shows some of the observable characteristics that help identify potential leaders.

There are two important steps in developing a team member:

1. A series of jobs through which a team member can be promoted
2. Opportunities to receive training beyond each job for each team member who shows potential for leadership

Each job can be an opportunity for the team members to prepare for something better. Internal job mobility means that team members have a chance to grow and the foodservice organization has a reliable source of labor without the high cost of turnover and of training someone new.

TRAINING EVALUATION

Evaluation is necessary to determine whether training in the kitchen has had an impact on improving team members' knowledge, skills and attitudes, and job performance related to total quality. Evaluation of training is part of the cycle of the training process. Without it, the chef supervisor is unable to determine if he or she has been simply "spinning wheels."

Evaluating is the final step before reviewing and renewing training objectives and before starting the process again. Training is a very dynamic process. Its elements cannot be left for long without the possibility of their becoming stagnant, outdated, inaccurate, or even harmful to the total quality efforts of the organization. Additionally, team members do not always learn precisely what the training was intended to teach them. Evaluating the impact of training on kitchen team job performance revolves around finding the answers to the right questions. Examples of those questions are shown in Figure 11-7. The answers to these questions should be sought from the participants. Additionally, external input should be sought regarding the success of the training. If most of the feedback is positive, it can be assumed that the training was effective. If specific concerns were expressed, the data must then be compared to other methods of evaluation.

FIGURE 11-7 Questions for evaluating the impact of training.

- Did training make a difference?
- Is the team member able to perform the skills presented during the training session?
- What effect has training had on team attitudes?
- Were interpersonal skills improved?
- Were the resulting changes in team members worth the investment in training?
- Did team members provide suggestions for improving the training sessions?
- Did training correct identified problems?
- Were deficiencies related to method of training, content, format, and delivery identified?
- What recommendations are there for improvement?

The kitchen team members who received training are the most obvious source of data regarding the impact of training. Through the evaluation process, team members are asked to express their opinions and make observations about the effectiveness of the training. In addition to asking them to respond to specific questions related to tasks addressed during the training program, a number of general questions can be built into a survey instrument that will provide valuable information. Typically, participants are asked to complete a questionnaire with regard to the training they received. These questionnaires may be quite elaborate or simple. Figure 11-8 shows a simple example detailing elementary questions that can be asked.

This type of training participant evaluation is not too tedious to complete and is easy to follow. This "form type" of evaluation should be used at the end of the training session or segment of a teaching program. It is important that such forms not be overused. Evaluation tests can be administered at any appropriate time or when they will help. The reasons for testing are essentially the same as the reasons for asking questions.

When training is effective, team members completing a training program are able to perform the skills or apply the knowledge necessary to correct quality or implement correct standards. Evaluation also monitors the team members' performance on the job as well as the entire training process. Continuous monitoring and feedback ensure that the training process is successful and that the chef supervisor is able to fulfill the roles and responsibilities required in the design, delivery, and evaluation of training.

FIGURE 11-8 Example training participant questionnaire.

- Are job elements different than those taught during training?
- Was the benefit from training worth the effort spent?
- Were the course objectives explained clearly?
- Did the instructor demonstrate technical knowledge?
- Were the training topics sequenced logically?
- Were all your questions and concerns regarding training answered?
- Were facilities adequate and suitable for training?

Summary

Attaining maximum involvement of the kitchen team member in the training process is one of the greatest objectives of the chef supervisor. People learn best by doing.

Specific training methods suitable for the implementation of training in a culinary environment include the following.

- Job talks, which by definition are a one-way process by the chef supervisor, can be boring, and can be unproductive unless considerably enhanced and supported by stimulating visuals, good preparation, and interesting delivery.
- Role-play participants are asked to act out certain roles in order for other learners to be able to practice how to handle such problems. In this way, participants can be exposed to both sides of the role play issue. It offers full participation in the training process by the kitchen team member.
- Demonstration is a widely used training method in the kitchen. It offers the chef supervisor a method to carefully and slowly instruct skills. Team members can then practice under supervision while the chef supervisor coaches and corrects.
- Case study team members develop solutions and approaches to situations that are presented by means of written cases. Proposed and actual solutions and their results are discussed.
- On-the-job training is the most widely used method after demonstration. This is a combination of all methods of training and retraining. In this method the team member is placed into the real work situation and trained to do the different parts of the job by an experienced team member or the chef supervisor. OJT includes the following steps: introduction, presentation, summary, practice, follow-up, and coaching.
- Apprenticeship training in the kitchen is organized according to guidelines and structures set forth by the American Culinary Federation Educational Institute and the U.S. Department of Labor. Apprenticeship offers the foodservice establishment a long-term training program that can provide a long-term commitment from those in the program.

Reinforcement training theory is based on studies that show that behavior that leads to a positive consequence tends to be repeated, while behavior that leads to a negative consequence tends not to be repeated. Praise and recognition are two of the most positive elements of reinforcement training.

Negative training methods involve skills that the chef supervisor assumes team members either bring to the job or learn from others on the job. The results of negative training are that team members learn bad habits and are unaware of objectives or the quality vision of the kitchen team.

Developing the team member with potential is necessary to identify future leaders. Characteristics of these potential leaders manifest themselves in high energy levels. These people are problem solvers. Promotions and further training opportunities are ways to develop these potential leaders.

Evaluation of training is necessary to determine the success of the planned training. Evaluation is the final step in the training process. It provides the basis for a review of the objectives and applied methods.

Discussion Questions

1. What are the merits of using case study as a specific training technique in the kitchen?
2. What are the main disadvantages to apprenticeship training?
3. Why is on-the-job training sometimes considered to be one of the most poorly implemented training techniques in the kitchen?
4. Describe reinforcement theory. How can reinforcement facilitate quality improvements?
5. What are negative training methods? What is their impact on new team members?
6. What team member characteristics demonstrate potential for further development?
7. Why is evaluation of training programs necessary?
8. What are the links between training objectives and training evaluation?

Notes

1. Francine A. Herman and Martha E. Miller, "Training for Hospitality," *Training & Development,* September 1991.

2. Robert B. Maddux, *Team Building: An Exercise in Leadership* (Los Altos, CA: Crisp, 1992), 33.

3. Lois B. Hart, *Training Methods That Work* (London: Crisp, 1991), 70.

4. Herman Zaccarelli, *Training Managers to Train* (Los Altos, CA: Crisp, 1988), 48.

5. American Culinary Federation, *Apprenticeship Operations Manual* (St. Augustine, FL: 1985).

6. B. F. Skinner, *About Behaviorism* (New York: Alfred Knopf, 1974).

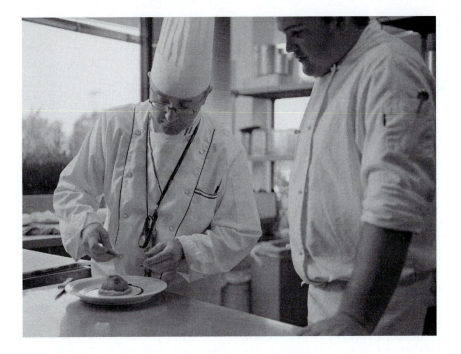

CHAPTER 12
TRAINING AND
TRANSACTIONAL ANALYSIS

OUTLINE

- ❖ Introduction
- ❖ Identifying ego states
- ❖ Crossed transactions
- ❖ Psychological games
- ❖ Summary
- ❖ Discussion questions
- ❖ Notes

OBJECTIVES

When you complete this chapter, you should be able to:

1. Understand the elements of transactional analysis and its benefits to the training process
2. State the physical and verbal aspects of the parent, adult, and child ego states
3. Indicate differences between crossed and uncrossed transactions
4. Recognize the benefits of using ego states to stimulate discussion relative to training sessions
5. Identify psychological games that are often used by team members to mask hidden agendas

Case Study: JOSHUA TREE RESTAURANT

Mother's Day is the Joshua Tree Restaurant's busiest day of the year. The restaurant has seating for 350 guests. On a normal Sunday the restaurant will serve a total of 1200 guests. Five years ago the owners of the Joshua Tree decided to try something different on Mother's Day. On Mother's Day the restaurant converted to all-buffet service. The Mother's Day buffets were an instant success and have been continued every year, with the number of guests served increasing every year. The Joshua Tree has become well known for its elaborate Mother's Day breakfast, brunch, and dinner buffets. Last year, between 8 A.M. and 8 P.M. the restaurant served 2800 guests, up from 2550 the previous year. The goal of the owners, managers, and senior staff (all of whom have been with the restaurant since the Mother's Day tradition began) is to increase the number of guests by another 10 percent this year, to a total of 3080.

The key to success on Mother's Day at the Joshua Tree is planning and execution of the plan grounded in a foundation of teamwork. Planning for this year's buffets began the week after Mother's Day last year. Ben and Martha, owners of the restaurant, lead a Mother's Day team (better known as the MDT) of managers and the chef in the planning process. Every aspect of the previous year's service, food, and logistics were analyzed to determine areas of strength and weakness. The MDT sought to improve and build on the strengths and remove weaknesses. This year, the MDT knew that in order to improve on the quality of food and service and serve an additional 280 guests, the guests' access to the food and the speed of clearing and resetting tables would have to

be increased. The MDT felt this required some investment in new equipment, but primarily it required increased teamwork. Every member of the Joshua Tree team had to be committed to the MDT's goals to achieve success.

The members of the MDT began the process of increasing teamwork in their various departments. Ben and Martha empowered each member of the MDT to address the need for increased teamwork in whatever manner they felt would work best in their department.

Chef Ian began the process with the kitchen staff by holding a series of job talks. In these talks he reminded the staff of how great a job they had done last Mother's Day, and that he felt they would do fine this coming Mother's Day but that team effort had to increase. Ian talked about what the MDT had determined from their analysis of last year's performance. He told them the goal for this Mother's Day. Ian shared with them the new menu and the *mise en place* schedule to be sure that they appreciated the effort that had been put into ensuring the success of this year's Mother's Day. Generally, if they pointed out a potential weakness, he told them, "Don't worry about it. I will take care of it. I want you to concentrate on becoming a more focused team." Common questions from the kitchen staff included how the increased product prep and product finishing would be accomplished, where the food would be stored, and how many more actual labor-hours the prep would take compared to the previous year. Ian told the staff, "Leave the details to me. I am taking it all into consideration and will figure it out. It really doesn't matter anyway, this team can do anything."

Based on what you have learned from previous chapters and the content of this chapter, answer the following questions.

- Do you believe that the Joshua Tree Restaurant will achieve the MDT's goals? Explain your answer, including the following:
  - Overall reason
  - Primary causal agents

- Role of leadership and supervision/management
- Specific steps that could have been taken
- Changes for the MDT next year

INTRODUCTION

Transactional analysis is a wide-ranging set of theories and techniques that can be used by individuals and groups to enable them to grow and develop to their full potential. The framework of transactional analysis is based on the theory of personality and communication founded by Eric Berne, a Canadian psychotherapist who wrote the founding work of transactional analysis, *Games People Play,* in 1964.[1] It captured the interest of millions worldwide and has been reprinted many times. The book was well written, easy to understand, and made use of ordinary language. Many people felt the theories detailed in the book made sense of their experiences; helped them to understand their feelings, thoughts, and actions; and offered them alternative behaviors to cope with the difficulties encountered in personal and working life.[2]

Essentially, transactional analysis is a tool that can help to improve interpersonal relations. It is a method of analysis by which one person can determine the basis from which another individual is communicating or interacting. Once this is established, it is then possible to decide how best to respond. It is a tool that can be used easily in the kitchen and in everyday work situations as well as in the training setting. As a trainer, anything the chef supervisor can do that helps to better understand where each individual team member is "coming from," and what his or her true feelings and disposition are, will contribute to successful training and supervision.

If an individual's behavior is observed over a period of time, it becomes clear that individual disposition changes. These changes manifest themselves in modes of speech, body language, interest, and attitudes. They do not remain constant; they fluctuate over time. According to transactional theory, there are three aspects or roles within each of us, the ego states of *parent, adult,* and *child.* These different ego states determine the way in which we communicate.

Berne based his theory on three obvious assertions:

1. Everyone has had parents (or substitute parents or caregivers), and everyone will have internalized—consciously or unconsciously—some of the views of these parents or parent figures.
2. Everyone is capable of behaving in a rational way, which means that each of us is capable of behaving according to the realities of the situation rather than reacting irrationally or purely in terms of emotions or prior conditioning.
3. Everyone sometimes reacts to situations the way they reacted to similar situations in the past.

IDENTIFYING EGO STATES

The following guide provides the basis for some of the verbal and physical aspects of the parent, adult, and child ego states.

Parent

Physical: Severe or stern expression, folded arms, furrowed brow, pointing finger, the "horrified" look, "eyes to heaven"; aggressive tone of voice, talking down to others; gestures of concern and helpfulness, patronizing others.

Verbal: "Never, do, don't, ought, should, must, if I were you, the best thing for you to do..., don't worry, I'll take care of it." Examples of automatic responses are "disgusting, shocking, ridiculous, not again, stupid, typical, will they ever learn, what can you expect from them." These words *may* identify the parent, but the adult can also decide on the basis of reasoning that certain things are shocking, disgusting, stupid, etc.

Adult

Physical: The adult face is open and expressive. It shows interest and listening when appropriate. Active listening is one of the recognizable behaviors of the adult.

Verbal: The adult vocabulary includes such words as "what, where, why, when, who, how." Other words are "how much? comparative, true, false, I think, in my opinion, probably, possibly, likely, apparently, it seems," showing reflection and evaluation.

Adult-to-adult interaction provides the basis for both groups to be productively engaged in training, planning, decision making, and organizing. Crossed transactions between unparallel ego states will usually be counterproductive. Therefore, recognition of the ego state will direct the course of the interaction and determine its possible outcome.

Child

Physical: Teasing, carefree excitement, laughter, curiosity, giggling, pouting, tears, temper tantrums, sulking, downcast eyes, anxiety.

Verbal: "I wish, I want, I don't care, big, better, best, hey that's fantastic, what am I going to do now." The tone of voice can be loud, energetic, compliant, whining, defiant, and demanding.

The three ego states are commonly represented as three circles arranged vertically as shown in Figure 12-1. The arrangement of these circles puts the parent on the top, the adult in the middle, and the child at the bottom. This does not, however, imply that a hierarchy exists. This is the basic structure of personality as described by Berne. It is the basis on which the chef as supervisor or trainer can attempt to determine in what ego state each kitchen team member is transacting.

In most cases the adult creates the most positive basis for communication by treating the receiver on an adult or an equal basis. However, the parent and child ego states also have their use, the child for humor and the parent for directive behavior.

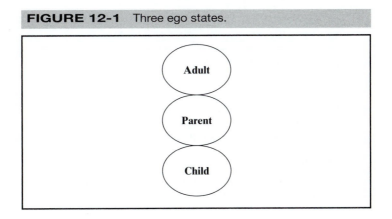

FIGURE 12-1 Three ego states.

The following examples of how transactional analysis (the ego states) is related to the chef supervisor's role as trainer demonstrate situations in which these ego states might be encountered in the kitchen:

- *Parent ego state:* "You have to learn this technique."
- *Adult ego state:* "You have been able to master all the other techniques up to now. I'm certain that with some coaching you will master this one too."
- *Child ego state:* "I'll never be able to do this."

In some cases it appears as though some team members are programmed to communicate in certain ways. Many times this is true. If chefs adopt the parent ego state, these team members will automatically respond just as their parents did. The adult mode is somewhat more difficult to achieve and maintain. The three ego states identified by Berne—parent, adult, and child—can be further divided into different styles. Subdivisions of the parent ego state are *controlling parent, nurturing parent, natural child,* and *adapted child.* These different ego states are also sometimes referred to as the "tape recorder in your head." People function from the point of view of these remembered ego states.

Generally, parent and child ego states are replays from the past. For example, in the parent ego state, attitudes, values, thoughts, and behaviors are copied from parents, mainly during the first eight years of a child's life. Similarly, Berne's theory states that the child ego states are replays of thoughts and feelings from childhood. The adult ego state includes the ability to deal with situations in the "here and now" and involves being objective, logical, and rational. The key contributing qualities and the potential problems of each ego state are shown in Figure 12-2.

The adult ego state is associated with the skills of problem solving and decision making: "Employing the concept of ego states gives us a method for checking our behavior and consciously selecting the most appropriate option for our current objective."[3]

CROSSED TRANSACTIONS

Communication is a two-way process, and in this process transactional analysis is most beneficial. An example of transactional analysis might be: If a team member speaking in the adult mode is responded to as an adult, the communication is likely to

FIGURE 12-2   Key contributing qualities and problems of ego states.

Key Contributing Factors

- Natural child: friendliness, creativity
- Adapted child: politeness, courtesy
- Nurturing parent: nurturing, caring
- Controlling parent: firmness, control
- Adult: problem solving, identifying compromises

Problems

- Controlling parent: being righteous, their way is best
- Nurturing parent: desire to take care of everyone
- Adult: clinically dismissing every idea
- Natural child: being silly, horseplay
- Adapted child: not participating, waiting to be asked

be successful. If the responding team member is also speaking from the adult mode, so much the better. However, communication problems arise when one is speaking as an adult and is responded to in the child or parent mode. This is called a *crossed transaction*. An example of an uncrossed (adult-to-adult) transaction is

CHEF SUPERVISOR   "Tomorrow will be a busy day for the kitchen." *(adult)*
KITCHEN TEAM MEMBER   "Good, we'll be prepared." *(adult)*

An example of a crossed transaction is

CHEF SUPERVISOR   "Tomorrow will be a busy day for the kitchen." *(adult)*
KITCHEN TEAM MEMBER   "Not again, I don't know how we are going to cope."
(child to parent)

Uncrossed transactions occur when the ego state addressed is the ego state that responds. If, for example, the controlling parent is used to address the adapted child and the reply is from the adapted child, we have an uncrossed transaction. The rule for an uncrossed transaction is that communication can continue indefinitely. However, crossed transactions usually mean that a break in real communication will occur. This does not necessarily mean that all crossed transactions are bad and that all uncrossed transactions are good. If, for example, a team member is shouting at the chef supervisor from a controlling parent ego state about a mistake made and the responding supervisor is in an adapted child ego state, he or she may respond with an uncrossed transaction by apologizing. If the apology is ignored, it is appropriate to break the communication and for the chef supervisor to shift to adult-to-adult communication for some problem-solving discussion.

Know your ego states. Use the adult to stimulate healthy discussion on the kitchen training sessions. Use the controlling parent to tell team members what the rules are concerning the sessions. Use the nurturing parent to reassure team members regarding their ability to assimilate the training methods to be used. Use the natural child to bring fun and excitement into the training sessions. Use the adapted child to be polite and courteous to team participants. At the end of each training session, review what happened. Select some areas of the training session that require work. Analyze the transactional ego state used and consider what other ego states might have worked better. Determine what the likely effects might have been, decide which offers the best ego state for future training sessions, and resolve to handle these areas more skillfully next time.

PSYCHOLOGICAL GAMES

In *Games People Play,* Eric Berne outlined a series of psychological games that people engage in. These repetitive and unsatisfactory interactions usually have negative effects.

People play psychological games, often unaware, and tend to choose as spouse and business associates those people who will play the role opposite to their own. This also holds true for foodservice organizations. Although there are many different games, in each one there are three basic elements:

1. A series of complementary transactions that on the surface seem plausible
2. An ulterior transaction that is the hidden agenda
3. A negative payoff that concludes the game and is the real purpose for playing

Games tend to be repetitious. People find themselves saying the same words in the same way—only the time and place may change. Perhaps the replay contributes to what is often described as "I feel as if I've done this before."

Just as some people have favorite ego states, they also have a favorite game role. Games may involve two or three of the dramatic roles of *victim, persecutor,* and *rescuer*—the manipulative roles learned in childhood. Games played from the persecutor or rescuer role serve to reinforce a negative position about others.

Games prevent honest, intimate, open relationships between the players, yet people play them because they fill up time and provoke attention.[4] (4).

THE GAME OF YES, BUT!

The game is likely to be Yes, But if the chef supervisor in a meeting presents a problem and then shoots down all suggestions. A person who plays Yes, But does so to maintain positions such as "Nobody's going to tell me what to do" or "People are stupid." In childhood they had parents who either tried to give them all the answers or didn't give any answers, so they took a stand against them.

To initiate this game, one player presents a problem in the guise of soliciting advice from one or more other players. If hooked, the other player advises, "Why don't you. . . ?" The initiator discounts all suggestions with "Yes, but. . .," followed by reasons the advice won't work. Eventually the "why don't you" advice givers give up and fall silent. This is the payoff of the game to prove the position, "Parents can't tell me anything" or "Parents are stupid."

In this game the child ego state "hooks" the nurturing parent in the other player. Although the transactions may appear to be adult to adult on the surface ("I've got a problem. Tell me the answer."), the ulterior transaction is child to parent ("I've got a problem. Just try to tell me the answer. I won't let you.").

THE GAME OF KICK ME

In the game of Kick Me, the player does something to provoke another player to put him or her down. Team member states, "I stayed out late last night and didn't prepare the *mise en place* for this morning." Chef supervisor responds, "Sorry about that. This is the last day I can give you extra time off." (Ulterior: Yes you are a bad boy and here is your kick.)

Though he or she may deny it, a person who is used to the game of Kick Me tends to attract others who can play the complementary hand and are willing to "kick."

THE GAME OF HARRIED

Harried is a common game acted out to justify an eventual collapse or depression. Chef supervisors who play Harried say "yes" to everything, volunteer to come early and work late, take on additional assignments, and bring work home. For a period of time they are able to act like Superman, but eventually appearances begin to reflect this harried state. They are unable to finish work, and their physical and mental health deteriorates. They collect and save so many feelings of depression that they finally collapse, so depressed they are unable to function. Other variations of this game are Harried Chef, Harried Manager, Harried Purveyor, Harried Waitperson, Harried Supervisor, etc.

THE GAME OF SEE WHAT YOU MADE ME DO

This game is played in the kitchen when a team member makes a mistake while the chef supervisor is watching from behind. Rather than taking responsibility for the error, the team member turns to the supervisor and angrily says, "See what you made me do!" thus blaming someone else for the mistake. If this happens often enough, the supervisor may feel guilty and leave the team member alone. In this way the purpose of the game is fulfilled—isolation. Another See What You Made Me Do player may be collecting feelings of purity instead of anger: "After all, it's not *my* fault. It's *your* fault I made my mistake. I'm pure."

THE GAME OF STUPID

Stupid is a game played when a secretary "accidentally" puts a letter in a bottom drawer and then, later, when it's rediscovered, makes a fuss, complaining, "How could I have done such a stupid thing! This was that letter that you wanted in Washington, D.C., last month."

OTHER POPULAR GAMES

Themes of other games that can often be easily recognized are the following:

- *I'm Only Trying to Help You:* "My advice is so good. Why do you want to think for yourself and reject my ideas, when I'm only trying to help you?"
- *Wooden Leg:* "Surely you can't expect much from me when I have such a handicap"—wrong race, wrong background, etc.
- *See How Hard I Tried:* "Don't blame me if things turn out wrong. After all, see how hard I tried."
- *Uproar:* "I'm stronger than you are. You stupid fool; you never do anything right."
- *Now I've Got You:* "I've caught you making a mistake and will now make you suffer."

Games may be foiled by refusing to play the expected hand or refusing to provide a payoff. For example, refusing to give advice or suggestions to a Yes, But player usually stops the game. Some of the ways to stop a game are show in Figure 12-3.

FIGURE 12-3 Game stoppers.

- Give an unexpected response.
- Stop exaggerating your own weaknesses or strengths.
- Stop exaggerating the weaknesses and strengths of others.
- Structure more of their time with activities, intimacy, and fun.
- Stop playing the rescuer, helping those who don't need help.
- Stop playing the persecutor, criticizing those who don't need it.
- Stop playing the victim, acting helpless or dependent when really able to stand on your own two feet

Why do we play psychological games? One of the major problems is that most people are unaware that they are playing these games. There are, according to Julie Hay, writing in *Transactional Analysis for Trainers,* "apparent advantages that accrue from playing psychological games, we find it hard to stop the repetitive sequences, even when we become aware of them."[5] When the game preferences of different team members have been identified, it is possible to determine how these interactions affect the culture of the training session or activity in the kitchen. Having spotted a game, it is then possible for the chef supervisor to work out how to behave differently so as to avoid it in the future. Thomas Quick says, "Transactional Analysis doesn't provide a universal explanation for every aspect of human behavior, but it provides some realistic bases. In a very short time using the transactional model you could train employees, especially those who deal with the public, so as to effectively deal with the various kinds of behavior they encounter."[6]

Summary

Transactional analysis is a tool that can help to improve interpersonal relations. It is a method of analysis by which one person can determine the basis from which another individual is communicating or interacting. Understanding transactional analysis contributes to successful training and supervision.

Developed by Eric Berne—who noted that if an individual's behavior is observed over a period of time, it becomes clear that that individual's disposition changes—it assumes three aspects: the ego states of parent, adult, and child, and they determine the way in which each communicates.

These different ego states may be subdivided again into the natural child, adapted child, nurturing parent, and controlling parent. Ego states are also referred to as the "tape recorder in your head." Generally, parent and child ego states are replays from our past. Each is indicative of a particular set of values, attitudes, thoughts, and behaviors from the past. The adult ego state deals with the "here and now." Knowing and understanding crossed and uncrossed transactions from different ego states facilitate successful communication, supervision, and training.

People play psychological games, often in an unconscious way. Although there are many different games, each has three basic elements:

1. A series of complementary transactions that on the surface appear plausible.
2. An ulterior transaction that is the hidden agenda.
3. A negative payoff that concludes the game and is the real purpose for playing.

Chef supervisors can assess the climate and culture that exist in the kitchen for training by spotting the various games that team members play.

Discussion Questions

1. How can transactional analysis assist the training effort?
2. What are the three ego states?
3. Why is the adult ego state conducive to learning?
4. What are the subdivisions of the parent and child ego states?
5. What are crossed transactions and uncrossed transactions?
6. Why do most psychological games have hidden agendas?
7. How can transactional analysis improve interpersonal relations within the kitchen?

Notes

1. Eric Berne, *Games People Play* (London: Grove Press/Penguin, 1968).
2. Brian Thomas, *Total Quality Training: The Quality Culture and Quality Trainer* (Berkshire, England: McGraw-Hill, 1992), 122.
3. Julie Hay, *Transactional Analysis for Trainers* (Berkshire, England: McGraw-Hill, 1992), 83.
4. Adapted from Berne, *Games People Play*.
5. Hay, *Transactional Analysis for Trainers,* 136.
6. Thomas Quick, "Simple Is Hard, Complex Is Easy, Simplistic Is Impossible," *Training & Development Journal*, May 1990, 96.

CHAPTER 13

MANAGING AND UTILIZING TIME

OUTLINE

- ❖ Introduction
- ❖ Time management misconceptions
- ❖ Choosing priorities
- ❖ Time leaks
- ❖ Time management skills
- ❖ Personal time management
- ❖ Summary
- ❖ Discussion questions
- ❖ Notes

OBJECTIVES

When you complete this chapter, you should be able to:

1. Identify issues associated with unproductive time use
2. Develop a plan for effective use of time
3. Recognize the pitfalls of procrastination
4. List the steps that cause time leaks
5. Distinguish between being busy and productive

Case Study: MS. BEE'S RESTAURANT

Ms. Bee's Restaurant has become a landmark in a city known around the world for its food and hospitality. As executive chef of Ms. Bee's, Lee Derby is expected to ensure that the restaurant retains its stature and profitability in a fiercely competitive restaurant market and to represent the restaurant as a shining example of culinary knowledge and professionalism. Chef Derby has found the balancing of these two roles to be increasingly difficult. The economy as a whole has taken a downturn in the past three years. The restaurant is still pulling its share of the city's restaurant traffic, both local and tourist, but the number of overall guests, particularly tourists, has decreased. Additionally, the guests who do dine at Ms. Bee's are spending less. They are ordering less expensive dishes and fewer add-ons such as appetizers and deserts.

Chef Derby is concerned about his ability to "get the job done." Maintaining the profit levels of the restaurant is requiring intense management of all profit and cost centers. Maintaining the restaurant's visibility to local guests and tourists requires that Chef Derby respond to numerous requests for interviews and guest chef appearances. He is working more hours every week and yet feels that he is accomplishing less each week. Chef Derby knows that he has a great kitchen team, but he also realizes that he is spending less and less time interacting with them. He is giving less attention to the preparation of the food and day-to-day operation of the kitchen. He is feeling more and more like an absentee chef and supervisor. Chef Derby considers an incident that occurred at the restaurant last night as evidence that he needs to be giving more attention to the operation of the kitchen.

Yesterday, Saturday, the restaurant was fully booked for dinner. Between 6 P.M. and 9 P.M. they would completely turn the dining room. Ms. Bee's has a reputation for its constantly changing menu and regional specialty dishes. One of the restaurant's very popular items is its Ribeye au Poivre. At 8 P.M. a large group of guests was seated. They were trade-show attendees from out of town and had made their reservations two months in advance. The host of the group, which was an appreciation dinner for his clients, had called on Friday to find out what kind of beef would be on the menu on Saturday evening. One of his clients, who only ate beef and particularly liked ribeye steak, could be an extremely difficult customer. The host was extremely pleased when he heard that Ms. Bee's would be offering their Ribeye au Poivre, an item he had greatly enjoyed on previous visits. Before they arrived at the restaurant, the host told his guest about the Ribeye au Poivre and how great it was.

The waiter came to take the group's order and immediately told them that he regretted they were out of the Ribeye au Poivre. The group's beef lover began to make a scene about the restaurant being out of the item at 8 P.M. on a Saturday night. He asked to speak to the chef and was told that the chef was unavailable. After thirty minutes of intense, unpleasant dialogue between the guest and various service staff and kitchen staff, the manager-on-duty and the sous chef resolved the situation when they sent a staff member to a neighboring restaurant to get a ribeye. They told the guest they had found one last ribeye and were preparing it for him. The incident left both the restaurant staff and all the guests in the restaurant with bad feelings.

Chef Derby was told about the incident on Sunday and was very disturbed by the failure of his staff to have sufficient product on hand when they knew a major trade show and conference was in town. He was also disturbed that it took thirty minutes before the manager-on-duty and sous chef thought to go across the street to the steakhouse owned by the owner's brother to get a steak. The general manager spoke to Chef Derby about the incident on Monday and told him that he felt Chef Derby had to get

better control of his kitchen staff and ensure that the restaurant's reputation was protected from this kind of incident.

Chef Derby resolved that even if he had to work 100 hours per week, he would get things under control.

Based on what you have learned from previous chapters and the content of this chapter, answer the following questions.

- Do you believe that the action planned by Chef Derby will allow him to achieve his goal and meet his commitment to Ms. Bee's Restaurant? Explain your answer, including the following:
  - Overall reason
  - Primary causal agents
  - Role of leadership and supervision/management
  - Specific steps that could have been taken to avoid the current challenges
  - Specific steps that should be taken in the future

INTRODUCTION

Lack of time is perhaps the most often used excuse in kitchens for not doing certain things: "It's a great idea, but we don't have time to do that here." How often have chef supervisors been overheard to say, "If we only had more time" or "We don't have time to get too heavily involved with fancy dishes or presentations here." Therefore, often things that affect overall quality and customer satisfaction, such as quality culinary practices and motivating the kitchen team, are not done because of "lack of time." The fact is that failure to implement agreed-on quality standards of cooking and presentation of menu items is not a question of time, but rather a question of poor planning, supervision, and leadership, and a failure to execute good *mise en place.*

Timing is a fundamental element of all chef training, and it is ingrained in every aspect of cooking, preparation, and presentation of food items.

Lack of sufficient time to implement quality foodservice often results from the selection of complex recipes inappropriate for the skill level of those preparing them. Failure to use a team approach to menu development and failure to anticipate the constraints of busy meal service periods, along with the absence of training plans, all contribute to a sense of lack of time. Therefore, lack of time is not the culprit in shoddy culinary practice; rather, it is the result of poor supervision, training, and management.

Time management means better organization to get as much as possible from the time available. Its aim is not to fill up life with activity, but to help identify what is wanted out of life and plan how to go about getting it.

> If you had a bank that credited your account each morning with $86,400, that carried over no balance from day to day, allowed you to keep no cash in account, and every evening cancelled whatever part of the amount you failed to use during the day, just what would you do? Draw out every cent, of course!
>
> Well, you have such a bank and its name is *Time*. Every morning it credits you with 86,400 seconds. Every night it rules off as lost, whatever part of this sum you failed to invest in good purposes. It allows no overdrafts. Each day it opens a new account for you, each night it burns the record of the day. If you fail to use the day's deposits, the loss is yours. There's no going back; there's no drawing against tomorrow.
>
> You must live in the present . . . on today's deposits. Invest it so as to get from it the utmost in health, happiness, and success.[1]

In agreeing with this message, a logical question each chef supervisor should ask himself or herself is: How am I using my time in relation to personal goals and the goals of my foodservice organization?

When the chef supervisor manages work time effectively, it can be prioritized so as to organize all of the elements crucial to the quality operation of the kitchen operation. The fact is, most people waste time, but productive chef supervisors waste less of it. There is no secret to the principles and techniques of time management. However, they can only work if they are adhered to.

Time management on an individual level is not concerned solely with the amount of time spent on certain issues in terms of minutes, hours, days, or months. It is of course wise and prudent to track how time is spent every day. This helps to determine where it might be wasted. The real goal is to free up time to get more done. The first step is to examine often-held assumptions about time and how these assumptions may prevent time from being used productively in the kitchen.

BOX 13-1

WHAT IS THIS BUSINESS?
CHEF AS ENTREPRENEUR

I thank God for Food Fetish, Inc. It was truly divine intervention that helped bring my business into a reality.

To become a business owner was never something that I consciously went after. At least not at first. I did not go into my culinary apprenticeship thinking that one day, I want to own a distributing company. I was raised with the idea and spirit of making things happen for yourself. If it is to be, it is up to me.

I remember telling my Chef once during my evaluation, that I would rather have more time off than the raise. He didn't understand then my preference. For me, it was always about my personal time. The freedom to do what I wanted, when I needed to do it was more important than the additional tax burden from the raise.

For years a group of us would get together to brainstorm on business opportunities that best utilized our individual expertise. We had great concepts, but no real intent. Eventually, we would see our ideas become someone else's reality.

I took additional classes and seminars on writing business plans, how to become a business owner, and other related topics. I accepted adjunct teaching positions at the two local culinary schools, and became a regular chef on a local television cooking show. Those opportunities gave me great insights on different career paths. I did not want to be the chef who stayed too long in the kitchen. The dinosaur who couldn't keep up or be on that ever-changing cutting edge. Working in a hot kitchen 5 or 6 days a week, 8 to 12 or more hours a day, on a concrete floor, will take its toll on anyone. Working weekends, nights, holidays was not how I wanted to spend the rest of my career. So owning a restaurant, bakery, catering business was not an option for me. My health and my family had already sacrificed enough. Our daughter was raised with me working the long days, and holidays that didn't really start until I got home. Her brother, 11 years younger, has a much different reality.

A serious conversation over wine and dinner with my specialty foods sales rep shifted my focus, and changed my course. We decided to combine our expertise and form our own distribution company. Focusing primarily on baking and pastry items because that was our strength, and there was a void locally for such a business, is what became our niche. Over the next 7 months, Charlton Douglas and I wrote and rewrote our business plan, secured financing, signed a lease on a warehouse facility, and started to buy supplies and equipment needed to run operations. We also quit our jobs!

As Co-Owner and Corporate Pastry Chef of Food Fetish, Inc. I get to utilize my 20+ years as a culinarian. I get to teach and train our customers on product usage, and to keep them aware of our ever-changing inventory because new ideas and techniques are always evolving. I do cooking demonstrations and competitions to keep my skills sharp, and to gain first-hand knowledge of new products and equipment that is now more readily available. I feel that I have gained many invaluable lessons and honed in on some strengths and weakness I didn't necessarily know that I possessed. I was technologically challenged and ignorant of accounting procedures needed to run a business. I never wanted to sell anything. I always ran the other way whenever I was approached to sell wares. I did not and really still don't like rejection or the word "no."

Amazing what you will do when you have to. When it's your bottom line, there is not an acceptable excuse. The word "no" becomes another opportunity. You learn to hire someone who is trained and capable to either help or do what it is that you cannot.

I believe that my past executive pastry chef experiences have helped shape my Food Fetish experience. The training of personnel, ordering supplies and equipment, scheduling, handling and storage of inventory, dealing with chefs and suppliers, are the same just on different scales. I now get the opportunity to see and talk to the chefs instead of just hearing about "Chef Mary Jane" up the street. There are no blinders on; I am not pigeon-holed in my own little pastry world, unaware of and too busy to see what is happening in my own backyard.

I love working for the Fetish. I have always been a hard worker, so why not work hard for something that I helped create and own? For me, starting my company was a great culmination of my skills, time and energy. Who could ask for anything more?

Kimberly Brock Brown,
CEPC, CCA, AAC,
Co-owner, Food Fetish,
Charleston, South Carolina

TIME MANAGEMENT MISCONCEPTIONS

There is never enough time to accomplish what is important in the kitchen—wrong. There is always enough time to accomplish what is important, and what can be postponed should be. It is this decision that determines whether time is being used wisely.

Some chefs use the following as an excuse for poor time management practices: "Other people make too many demands on my time." Others do not control how a chef supervisor spends his or her time. If other people have that much control over a supervisor's time, the supervisor is letting himself or herself be intimidated and is not behaving as a leader. Learning to say no can be one of the most effective time savers. When saying no, be courteous; give a brief explanation of why a request cannot be granted, and avoid a prolonged discussion about the reasons.

Busy schedules are used as reasons for not being able to prioritize work: "To control your time and your life, it is not only possible to prioritize, it is essential. Set priorities and stick to them."[2] Learn to delegate. This frees up time to tackle more creative projects that require attention. Other erroneous misconceptions of time management frequently cited by chef supervisors are:

- "I'm much too busy to plan any activities."
- "If only there were more hours in the day."
- "I can't devote that much time every day to one project."
- "I've so much to do I don't know where to start."
- "I prefer to do the simple tasks first and save the big ones for later in the day."

These statements usually are reasons to cover lack of self-discipline and poor individual planning ability. Working more hours every day produces mental and physical fatigue and devours personal time. Work smarter, not longer. The busier the chef supervisor, the more important it is to take time out to plan. Planning is key to effective time management. Without a plan, chef supervisors are unlikely to be in control of their workday. They will react to events as they happen rather than being the ones who set the agenda.

Procrastination is the thief of time. Sometimes procrastination kicks in as a way to avoid tasks that are unpleasant or uninteresting. Determine to deal with these areas head-on; steady progress is a great motivator. The most misleading of all assumptions about time is that "later" seldom arrives. Time cannot be lengthened or shortened, only used, and it cannot be saved and used later. A chef supervisor cannot choose not to use it. Either use the moment or lose it forever.

"Never put off until tomorrow what you can do today."[3] This familiar adage was written by the Earl of Chesterfield in 1749 and is clearly a warning against procrastination. However, just because a job can be done now does not necessarily mean that it should be done now. Sometimes priorities need to be chosen.

CHOOSING PRIORITIES

Obviously, all tasks and projects do not have the same importance. Chefs often feel as if they are under pressure to respond to situations or to persons exerting the greatest pressure. This causes some chefs to solve problems in the order in which they arise, do easy work first, or take care of the hard work first, on the assumption that doing so is the fastest way to get rid of it. Dealing with matters in this way should be avoided at all costs. "Lining up your ducks . . . its origins are obscure, but its meaning is transparent: if you're dealing with things in a logical, orderly sequence, you're sure to bring efficiency and results to your efforts."[4] This is also called "firefighting." Dealing with matters in the order they occur in the kitchen is fine in some circumstances, for example, expediting

FIGURE 13-1   Flow for quality time management and response to challenges.

table orders, but in most other situations, it is an unproductive use of time: "Important does not necessarily mean urgent, nor does urgent necessarily mean important."[5] The goal should be long-term solutions not just firefighting. The flow for both quality time management and effective response to challenges is shown in Figure 13-1.

Tasks should be analyzed based on urgency and importance. The priority matrix shown in Figure 13-2 can be used to conduct a quick task.

The simplest and most effective way to prioritize time is to analyze how time is spent in an average day and week. Because everyone has the same amount of time, the key question is whether chef supervisors are using the time effectively. Are they doing things that are unnecessary? If they are satisfied that they are doing necessary work only they can do, the next step is to set priorities: "Make a list of things to do. Compare what you want to do with what you are already doing or planning to do. The result will be a priority list that tells you what to do first, what to do next, and what to do last."[6] It is also helpful to keep a time log of a typical week to see how you actually spend your time. Disorganized priorities are common ground for procrastination. Of all management procedures, none is more relevant to time management than choosing to prioritize issues of quality.

FIGURE 13-2   Priority matrix.

High Urgency	High Importance
Low Urgency	Low Importance

- High Urgency + High Importance = High Priority
- High Importance + Low Urgency = Priority
- High Urgency + Low Importance = Low Priority
- Low Urgency + Low Importance = Low Priority

TIME LEAKS

Time "leaks" are working habits and practices that eat up time unproductively. Review the following list of potential time leaks and see if any apply to you.

- Spending too much time on problems brought by a team member
- Oversupervising the kitchen team
- Undersupervising, with consequent crises
- Scheduling less important work before more important work
- Starting a job before thinking it through
- Leaving jobs before they are completed
- Doing things that can be delegated to a team member
- Doing things that can be done by modern equipment
- Doing things that aren't part of the job
- Spending too much time on previous areas of interest or competence
- Doing unproductive things from sheer habit
- Keeping too many, too complicated, or overlapping records
- Pursuing projects that are probably unachievable
- Paying too much attention to low-yield projects
- Failing to anticipate crises
- Handling too wide a variety of duties
- Shrinking from unfamiliar duties
- Failing to build barriers against interruptions
- Allowing conferences and discussions to wander
- Allowing conferences and discussions to continue after their purpose is fulfilled
- Conducting unnecessary meetings, visits, and phone calls
- Chasing trivial data after the main facts are in
- Engaging in personal work or conversations before starting business work
- Socializing at great length between tasks

Do you leak time? If you do, then pay close attention to the time management skills discussed next.

TIME MANAGEMENT SKILLS

A chef supervisor can make the most effective use of his or her time by planning and getting organized. The reason for managing time is to be sure that the chef supervisor has enough of it to meet specific goals at some point in the future. Most people are familiar with personal planners or calendars. They can provide a convenient place to keep daily lists, plus extra space to keep records and charts that are essential for planning and are simple, yet powerful time management aids. It is important to remember that calendars and personal planner diaries are useful only if they are used. Reserve blocks of time to get the job done and develop the habit of planning time effectively. Planning activities that can assist you in managing your time better include:

- Make weekly and daily to-do lists in order of priority. Check off each task as it is completed. This will provide a feeling of accomplishment at the end of the day.

- Plan what needs to be done at least one day in advance. If a chef supervisor knows what tasks await tomorrow, he or she can organize tomorrow's to-do list today. Schedules serve as a disciplining tool, helping to do what is planned.
- Plan telephone calls in advance to ensure that an agenda is covered and reduce time spent on the phone.
- Plan meetings (one on one or with the entire kitchen team) in advance. If you called the meeting, take control of the agenda and stay on the subject.
- Evaluate your time management several times during the day. Take a look at the schedule about one-third of the way through the workday and again two-thirds of the way through. Are the objectives for the day being met? If not, what got in the way? Should it take priority over what was planned?

Planning is critical, but planning alone will not make the chef supervisor the "time manager" instead of the one being "managed by time." The chef supervisor must learn to handle common distractions, because they are part of the reality of life. Controlling the time taken by drop-in visitors requires both the chef supervisor's courtesy and good judgment. Limiting the number of people invited to the kitchen will reduce commotion and distractions for both the chef supervisor and the culinary team. If a chef supervisor needs to be with someone, go to his or her work area. It is much more difficult to get people to leave the chef supervisor's work area than it is for the supervisor to leave theirs.

Communicate efficiently. In today's technological world, communication takes place in so many forms that the communication itself can become a barrier to good communication. The chef supervisor must be a model of the efficient us of communication. Keep emails, phone conversations, and memos short. It will save time thinking, speaking, and writing and team members' time listening, reading, and understanding. Sorting and unsolicited email and regular business mail is time-intensive. The chef supervisor may need to have someone sort both email and regular mail, giving guidelines on what needs to be seen and what should be routed to other team members.

Time management also includes making timely decisions. The chef supervisor who fails to make a decision because of unwillingness to face unpleasant decisions and being overcautious hampers the performance of the total team. The chef supervisor should also complete one job at a time. Important tasks need plenty of uninterrupted time and cannot be completed between other activities. This wastes time. Each time a project is restarted, it is necessary to get familiar with the project again. The chef supervisor should delegate tasks to other team members. To delegate (not dump) tasks is a key time management skill. Sometimes a chef supervisor does not have time to delegate—the unexpected happens, and he or she must deal with it. There is only one protection here, and that is anticipating the unexpected before it occurs. Chef supervisors should allow flexibility in their schedule, because emergencies do occur and meetings do run overtime.

Two of the simplest but most valuable time management skills that chef supervisors can exercise are learning to say no and organizing their work area. In some cases, the demands placed on a chef supervisor's time will exceed his or her ability to accommodate all of them. When taking on more than can be handled, quality begins to suffer. Saying no does not have to offend someone. When offering an alternative, things can be worked out to everyone's satisfaction. Is valuable time spent looking for things? Consider how often each item is needed in the kitchen. The kitchen should be organized so it is easy to complete normal tasks.

> ⬡ **BOX 13-2** ⬡
>
> ## CHEF TALK:
> ## PLAN THE WORK AND WORK THE PLAN
>
> It has been said that time can't be managed. But what can be managed are activities and how we "spend" time! And all the experts agree. Managing our activities begins with good planning. So, by knowing what's important for us—planning our work and working our plan—we become wise chef managers.
>
> We have to make time for getting big tasks done every day. Plan your daily workload in advance, single out relatively small tasks that must be done immediately, then tackle the large tasks to completeness. In all, planning is the power tool for achievement!
>
> In the foodservice industry today there are greater demands and challenges than ever before. Especially as chefs we don't always believe we have enough time to meet our responsibilities to our company, our employees, and our families. That's a negative belief, not a positive belief.
>
> My day starts with an exercise program at 6:30 A.M.! After this is completed, I am ready to face number 2 on my list of priorities, networking with my staff regarding their needs for the day. So, as each item on the list is completed, I move to the next task.
>
> In addition, there are other ventures or affiliations that I am involved with, and thus, I need to balance my time, concentrating on accomplishing the greatest results with the least effort expended. Thus, making decisions and acting on these decisions will reflect leadership and a positive image to my staff.
>
> Through dedication, planning, and goal-oriented thinking, I believe any chef can achieve great success in his or her future endeavors.
>
> Bert Cutino, CEC, AAC, HOF,
> Co-owner, The Sardine Factory
> Restaurant on Cannery Row,
> Monterey, California

Bruce Tepper states: "Being busy has nothing to do with productivity. Maximizing how [to] use your time means a great deal more. It will open either more free time, or more time for creating new ideas."[7] Get an accurate indication of how time is actually used and decide where improvements can be made. Work the chef supervisor doesn't have to do is work the supervisor doesn't need time to do. This does not mean shrinking responsibilities or "passing the buck." An important part of being a good chef supervisor is knowing what tasks can be best done by themselves and those that can be delegated to other team members. A supervisor's job is not just to do things, it is also to organize and coordinate the kitchen team. Following are some ways to save time:

- Use waiting time. When waiting for an appointment, don't think of it as a waste of time, but as a gift of time. Use it constructively: to relax, to ponder a decision, to review the daily checklist, to read a food book or foodservice industry magazine article. Always carry a pen and notebook to write down ideas.
- Combine activities, such as discussing related matters over lunch.
- Have a place for everything and keep everything in its place. If something is worth having, it's worth knowing where it is when it is needed.
- Learn to master computer programs relative to kitchen operations. Maintain all menus and recipes in computers. Learn to type. Reduce the amount of paperwork in the kitchen.
- Schedule some "togetherness time." Time management should not segregate the chef supervisor from the rest of the kitchen team.

- Spend time as if you had to buy it. Before spending an hour reading a report or going to a meeting, ask, "Would I spend my own money to do this?" If time is looked at as a financial investment and how it is spent is monitored, less will be wasted.
- Maintain a regular physical exercise program. Exercising can help reduce stress. It also helps to maintain a sense of balance, discipline, order, and control in life. An exercise program results in feeling better, looking better, and greater self-confidence. Personal time is not a luxury or something to postpone until it can be fitted into the schedule. It is a requirement for maintaining a proper sense of balance and control in life.
- Constantly ask, "Is this the best use of my time right now?" Time management aims for relaxation and gives more time to relax in.

PERSONAL TIME MANAGEMENT

Life balance is one of the greatest challenges faced by chef supervisors. Life balance refers to the need to balance work and personal life such as family. Of course, no ones likes to think they have to "schedule" time for their family and for themselves, but the reality of today's fast-paced business world is that may well be the case. Scheduling time does not necessarily mean that chef supervisors schedule appointments for their children to see them. It does mean that planning must include time off. The fact that time to recharge batteries is needed by everyone is all too often forgot in the rush.

Chef supervisors must remember that they work smarter and more productively when they are rested and don't feel guilty about not being at work or not being at home. It also needs to be remembered that the same is true for all team members. Work may be the total focus of some team members, but it cannot be expected to be the total focus of all team members. Chef supervisors who manage their own time and the team's time in a manner that allows everyone to enjoy the fruits of their labor are chef supervisors who will have a loyal and highly productive team.

Summary

Everyone can use their time better, particularly busy chef supervisors. Look at how time is presently being used. Schedule necessary work and work that only the chef supervisor can do, rather than busy work. Do not confuse lack of time to complete tasks with lack of self-discipline or poor supervisory skills. Maintain a balance between controlling time and other people controlling it. Learn to prioritize tasks and say no to demands of low priority that may overload. In particular, trade off low-priority commitments for high-priority ones that come up unexpectedly in the kitchen. Learn to plan time. The busier a chef supervisor is, the more important it is to take time out to plan. Planning is key to effective time management.

Time leaks are working practices that eat up time unproductively. The reason for managing time is to ensure that there is enough of it to meet specific goals at some point in the future. Develop time management skills and become disciplined in their application using personal planners, diaries, and calendars. Provide time in schedules for the unexpected. A chef supervisor cannot anticipate everything that will happen, so time must be left in each day to handle crises. Consider investment time. This is the careful investment of time that is not only useful but also has the benefit of further payoff in terms of new skills. Time management is not a matter of dealing only with isolated activities. It is a process that goes on and on over a lifetime, involving thousands of activities.

Discussion Questions

1. Why is effective use of time critical to the success of overall quality management?
2. Why is the real goal of time management to free up time?
3. What are the elementary techniques that may be used to free up time?
4. How can the use of a time log assist a chef supervisor in prioritizing work?
5. What are time leaks?
6. How does the use of a calendar or personal planner aid in time management?
7. What is the meaning of the statement, "Being busy has nothing to do with productivity"?
8. What is investment time, and how might chef supervisors use it?

Notes

1. Barrie Hobson and Mike Scally, *Time Management: Conquering the Clock* (San Diego: Pfeiffer, 1993), 84.
2. Thomas J. Quick, "The Art of Time Management," *Training,* January 1989, 60.
3. Robert Hochheiser, *Time Management* (New York: Barron's, 1992).
4. Marc Mancini, *Time Management* (New York: Irwin, 1994), 73.
5. Alfred W. Travers, *Supervision Techniques and New Dimensions* (Englewood Cliffs, NJ: Regents/Prentice-Hall, 1993), 111.
6. Hochheiser, *Time Management,* 15.
7. Bruce B. Tepper, *The New Supervisor Skills for Success* (New York: Irwin, 1994), 43.

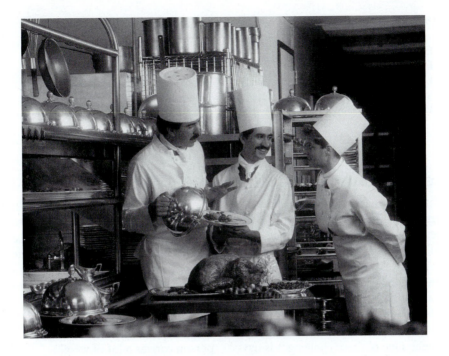

CHAPTER 14
RECRUITING AND SELECTING KITCHEN TEAM MEMBERS

OBJECTIVES

When you complete this chapter, you should be able to:

1. Identify the uses of job descriptions
2. Define various recruitment techniques employed to attract a pool of qualified job candidates
3. Describe the legal issues associated with recruiting and selecting job applicants

4. Understand the steps in screening potential new team members
5. Describe different types of interviews used to screen applicants
6. List the steps to be considered when interviewing potential team members
7. State appropriate and inappropriate questioning techniques
8. Understand elements associated with the hiring decision-making process

Case Study: ADAIR CATERING

Adair Catering provides service at all levels, from party-tray drop service to white-glove dinner service, within a 100-mile radius of its facility. It is not unusual for the company to have as many as six different full-service events and multiple drop events in a single day. The variety of types of service and food and the distance to many of the locations create many challenges for the Adair Catering management. One of these challenges is having the staff needed to provide quality service and food. The volume of business fluctuates greatly, so maintaining a full-time staff capable of handling all of the functions is not sound business practice. The company maintains a skeleton full-time staff and relies on on-call staff for all other needs. Adair Catering maintains a list of sixty on-call staff that includes everything from dishwashers and drivers to wait staff and cooks. Many of the on-call staff have full-time jobs elsewhere and moonlight with Adair for extra money.

Adair Catering has a number of large, full-service functions scheduled plus an increased load of drop events this week. Many of the on-call staff are unavailable because their full-time employers are also experiencing extremely high volume. The greatest challenge at the moment is finding dishwashing staff and drivers.

Today has been a very bad day among the full-time staff: Two dishwashers and one driver did not show-up for work, and one lead cook came to work drunk and had to be sent home. Mr. Adair has pots and pans stacking up, drops that need to be made, and three full-service lunches that he needs to check on because he is short on-call leads

and servers—and that is just this morning. The only bright spot in the morning has been the assurance from the dishwasher who did show up that he has a friend who can both wash dishes and has a chauffeur's license, so he can drive the company trucks. Ray has worked for Mr. Adair for about six months and has been a very dependable worker. His recommendation of this new person carries a lot of weight.

Ray calls Joe, who arrives thirty minutes later to meet with Mr. Adair. Joe is clean and neat—in fact, his shirt and pants are pressed—and he assures Mr. Adair that he would really like a chance to work for him. Mr. Adair checks his driver's license, which is a current chauffeur's license. When asked when he can start, Joe says "Immediately." Mr. Adair hires him and gives him the keys to the delivery truck along with instructions for the drops. He tells Joe that when he gets back, he is to help Ray do pots and pans and other scullery work, and they will discuss his potential status as a full-time staff member tomorrow.

The next day Mr. Adair tells Joe that he is very pleased with his work and he would like to take him on as a full-time employee as a combination driver/scullery worker. Joe accepts, and he is added to the payroll. Joe's work is exemplary, and he is able to handle the deliveries without any problem.

Two weeks later, however, Joe does not show up for work, and Mr. Adair asks Ray where Joe is. Ray says that Joe is in jail. Mr. Adair asks why he is in jail, and Ray says for driving without a license and forgery. Mr. Adair says, "Driving without a license! But he had a chauffeur's license. I saw it." Ray says, "That's why they are also charging him with forgery. Apparently the license was a fake."

Based on what you have learned from previous chapters and the content of this chapter, answer the following questions.

- What is the overall reason for the challenges at Adair Catering?

- What are the primary causal agents for the challenges at Adair Catering?
- What role did leadership and supervision/management play in the challenges at Adair Catering?
- What specific steps could have been taken to avoid the challenges at Adair Catering?
- What, specifically, can be done to avoid repetition of the challenges at Adair Catering?

INTRODUCTION

Finding and hiring the best people for the kitchen team is an important element of the chef supervisor's job. All recruiting and hiring decisions should be consistent with the vision and values of the foodservice organization. Good chef supervisors recognize that the main contributor to the success of an organization is the quality of its team members. People do make the difference. When the right people are chosen as the kitchen team, a quality culinary operation develops.

The process of recruiting and staffing is governed by many laws and procedural safeguards, and the chef supervisor has an important role to play in this process. Clearly, what is required is shared responsibility in this area. All involved management and team leaders should be allowed to contribute, but the final word should be left with the chef supervisor and not management. Making the chef supervisor responsible for final selection will result in a more cohesive and productive kitchen team. After all, the chef understands best what qualities are required to make a winning kitchen team and can usually better determine who is qualified. Involving chef supervisors in the selection process will also ensure that those selected for the kitchen team will have a greater sense of commitment to the team, because it was the team leader, the chef supervisor, who hired them. Conversely, the supervisor will have a greater stake in the new team member's success.

JOB DESCRIPTIONS

Job descriptions are used to format what the essential and desirable skills of a team member should be. They are similar to a good recipe. Just as a recipe helps the chef assemble the ingredients and states the time and temperature required to complete the dish, so does the job description help in choosing the right person. However, to make a great dish, the chef also needs intuitive skills based on experience. A well-developed job description is the foundation of the recruiting, selection, and performance appraisal sequence, as is shown in Figure 14-1. A job description can be considered a legal document in disputes between the employee and the employer pertaining to the performance of job duties. The job description for a position should be reviewed and updated regularly to ensure that it correctly reflects the requirements for the position.

FIGURE 14-1 Recruiting/training/performance sequence.

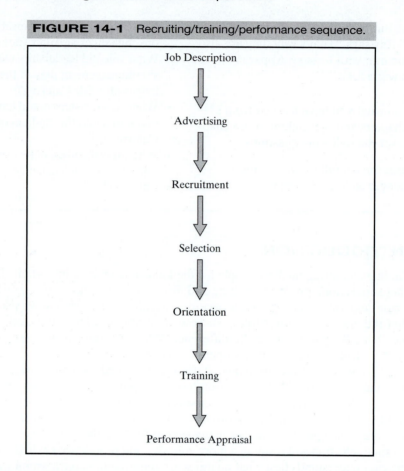

Job Description

Advertising

Recruitment

Selection

Orientation

Training

Performance Appraisal

RECRUITING

Recruiting involves seeking and attracting a pool of people from which qualified candidates for a kitchen team position can be chosen. The more applicants there are for a position on the team, the better chance the chef supervisor has of selecting the right person. The key to successful recruiting is to begin the process well in advance of any openings occurring in the team.

It has often been said that a foodservice organization's reputation precedes it. Therefore, the level of perception of a quality work environment can determine the quality level of a job applicant.

There are many ways to begin searching for new team members. Recruiting can be formal or informal, and it can be done internally or externally. The most reliable methods include:

- Advertising in newspapers and trade publications
- Asking friends, customers, or suppliers
- Seeking candidates at culinary colleges and local chefs' associations
- Reviewing past applicants
- Attending job fairs
- Networking with other foodservice organizations

In some areas of the United States, the public employment service is also a good source for recruiting. Private employment agencies provide another route. When using this type of service, the new team member sometimes pays the agency, but in most cases it is the employer who pays. Charges can range from 10 to 50 percent of the employee's first month's or first year's salary.

Networking is mostly a positive recruiting source. It can yield good results but can also cause problems. If a team member is recommended by a colleague but turns out to be unsatisfactory and must be "let go," the colleague who made the recommendation may be unhappy or angry about the outcome. Whatever method is used, it must always be in compliance with civil rights legislation.

Obviously, the best recruiting philosophy is to seek out quality people rather than accept what comes through various routes. This is the essence of recruiting. Active recruiting is the basis on which good chef supervisors acquire the best team members. They work on attracting talented chefs rather than hoping that qualified people will appear. This process of recruiting says to a potential team member, "You are someone special and I want you on my team."

Recruiting people who respond to quality operational goals is the basis for culinary success. Without the right *esprit de corps*, it will be almost impossible to effect quality at each step. When the best possible "neatness of fit" between people and organization occurs, the chef supervisor will have recruited an asset to the organization, not just a "warm body."

Seeking out qualified people through recruiting helps to reduce training costs and contributes to retaining that team member for a greater length of time. One of the disadvantages of active recruiting is that other foodservice operators see this practice as "poaching"—stealing another organization's employees. In the final analysis, however, it is the recruit who decides whether to take a job offer.

LEGAL IMPLICATIONS

It is important that chef supervisors and management consider the potential for discrimination in employment advertisements or notices. Title VII of the 1964 Civil Rights Act prohibits the use of phraseology that may be discriminatory. Care should be taken with regard to gender as part of the job title. The descriptions of team openings should be gender-neutral. Other potential descriptions or requirements that contravene the act are the requirement of a photograph; any reference to disability, religion, age, health, height, weight, marital status, citizenship, or ethnicity; or disbarring in some way any applicant who may be qualified. However, if there is a *bona-fide occupational qualification* (BFOQ) related to the advertised team position, then it is reasonable to include certain elements and requirements. According to Vincent Eade, in his book, *Human Resource Management in the Hospitality Industry,* "If a hotel wanted to staff its Asiatic restaurant only with Asiatics in order to create an authentic atmosphere, pre-employment inquiries aimed at determining national origin would be considered a BFOQ inquiry and not designed to discriminate."[1]

Additionally, the Equal Employment Opportunity Commission (EEOC) encourages all organizations to avoid recruiting primarily by employee referral, because this practice can perpetuate the current composition of the foodservice organization. If, for example, minorities and females are not well represented at all levels, then relying on employee referrals can also be considered discriminatory.

Legislation covering equal employment opportunities sets out strict legal criteria. Its purpose is to acquaint employers with the legal framework for recruiting and selecting new team members. Numerous laws influence recruiting and selection, and most are concerned with providing equal employment opportunity for all potential team members.

Civil rights laws state that employers may not discriminate in employment on the basis of an individual's race, religion, color, sex, national origin, marital status, age, "family" relationship, mental or physical handicaps, or juvenile record that has been expunged.[2] Foodservice employers may not retaliate against in any way or discharge employees who report, complain about, or oppose discriminatory practices or who file or participate in the complaint process. A number of the major pieces of employment legislation were previously discussed in Chapter 5 with regard to discrimination. These laws are discussed again here because of their importance. The following list summarizes the major federal employment legislation.

Equal Pay Act of 1963. Prohibits sex-based discrimination in rates of pay for men and women working in the same or similar jobs.

Civil Rights Act of 1964 (as amended in 1972). Prohibits discrimination based on race, sex, color, religion, or national origin. Title VII of the Civil Rights Act of 1964 applies to private-sector employers with fifteen or more employees.

Executive Orders 11246 (1965) and 11375 (1967). Prohibit discrimination on the basis of race, sex, color, religion, or national origin; require affirmative action. Applies to federal contractors and subcontractors with contracts in excess of $10,000; employers with fifty or more employees and contracts in excess of $50,000.

Age Discrimination in Employment Act (ADEA) (1967). Prohibits discrimination against individuals who are at least 40 years of age but less than 70. An amendment eliminated mandatory retirement at age 70 for employees of companies with twenty or more employees.

Pregnancy Discrimination Act (1978). Prohibits the exclusion of a pregnant woman from an employment opportunity based on pregnancy. This act was an amendment to Title VII of the 1964 Civil Rights Act.

Immigration Reform and Control Act (1986) Prohibits the hiring of illegal aliens. The act also prohibits employers from discrimination against job applicants on the basis of their citizenship status or national origin.

Americans with Disabilities Act (ADA) (1990). Prohibits employers from discrimination in employment decisions against qualified individuals with disabilities. Employment activities covered under this law include job application procedures, hiring, firing, advancement, compensation, training, recruitment, tenure, layoffs, fringe benefits, and all other employment-related activities.

Equal Employment Opportunities Commission (EEOC). This agency was created under the Civil Rights Act of 1964 to administer Title VII of the act and to ensure equal employment opportunity. Its powers were expanded in 1979. Originally, the EEOC was responsible for investigating discrimination based on race, color, religion, sex, or national origin. Now, however, it is also responsible for investigating equal-pay violations and handicapped and age discrimination. Preemployment guidelines have been developed by the EEOC to help employers phrase application forms and interview questions in a nondiscriminatory manner. The EEOC ensures that all applicants are afforded the same employment opportunities. Chef supervisors and managers must be aware that discrimination practices, even if they unintentionally violate individual civil rights, are against the law. Discrimination is not only unfair, it is illegal, and ignorance of the law is no defense.

See Appendix A for an extended listing of federal regulations relative to the workplace.

SCREENING

The recruiting process yields applicants whose qualifications must be assessed against the requirements of the job and the vision of the foodservice organization. The selection of new team members has long-term impact on team performance. Today, greater attention is being given to the selection process than ever before. Those potential team members who are thoroughly screened against developed criteria, specifications, and the company and team culture learn their tasks readily, are productive, adapt to the team philosophy, and generally adjust to their new jobs with the minimum of difficulty. As a result, the team member, the kitchen team, the foodservice organization, and customers benefit from a careful selection process. It is in the final selection of new team members that chef supervisors play a vital role. Therefore, they should fully understand the objectives and policies relative to evaluating and selecting these new team members.

What skills are required? Are there people available with these skills, or will they have to be trained? Careful screening may reduce the amount of training needed. Screening should produce a slate of potential team members who are best able to meet the job requirements and fit the rate of pay available. Screening and selection in some instances may also be affected by union contracts.

In matching people and kitchen team positions, research has demonstrated that complete, clear, and unambiguous job criteria and specifications reduce the influence of ethnic and gender stereotypes and help the chef supervisor differentiate between qualified and unqualified potential team members.

Most organizations require application forms to be completed, because they can provide a fairly quick and systematic means of obtaining a variety of information about the potential team member. As with interviews, the EEOC and the courts have found that many questions asked on application forms disproportionately reject females and minorities and often are not job-related. To keep in line with this legal requirement, application forms should be developed with great care and revised as necessary.

The information on the application form is generally used as a basis for further exploration of the applicant's background. It should be designed to provide as much information as possible that is predictive of job success. Even if potential team members come armed with elaborate and impressively designed résumés, it is still important that application forms are completed early in the application process.

Essentially, applicants' résumés state what *they* want the chef supervisor to know, not necessarily what the chef supervisor needs to know. Some applicants engage the services of so-called employment consultants to assist them in designing attractive and elaborate résumés that exaggerate their abilities. These résumés are often works of literary art and are simply examples of the writing skills of the consultant. One technique used to check the actual skills of these applicants is to ask them to reproduce specific résumé information on an application form. The applicant can then be asked to sign a statement that the information included in the application form is correct and that he or she accepts the employer's right to terminate employment if any of the information is subsequently found to be false.

Studies have shown that a high proportion of people lie on some aspect of their résumés. Therefore, background investigations are necessary. Inadequate reference checking can be a major cause of high employee turnover. If sources in addition to former employers are used, it is possible to obtain valuable information about the applicant's character and habits. Other points to remember are that the information should be job-related and that written documentation exists outlining that the employment decision was based on relevant information.[3] It is generally advisable to ask the applicant to fill out forms permitting information to be solicited from reference sources. Even then, many organizations are reluctant to put in writing an evaluation of former employees. One reason for this trend is that former employees who discovered that they had been given poor recommendations have sued several firms. Individuals have a legal right to examine letters of reference about themselves (unless they have waived the right to do so or were protected by the Privacy Act of 1974 or by state laws).

INTERVIEWING

The most crucial step in selecting potential team members is the face-to-face interview. An interview is a conversation or verbal interaction between two people (in this case, the chef supervisor and the applicant) to evaluate compatibility for a particular reason. It is a process for choosing the applicant who is most suited for the team position to be filled. The interview has three main purposes:

1. To validate previously submitted information
2. To discover those skills and attitudes necessary to achieve "neatness of fit" within the kitchen team
3. To predict the successful integration of the applicant into the foodservice organization's environment

When meeting somebody for the first time, it is natural to react to him or her in some way. Sometimes this is taken further and some definite judgments are made based only on the first impression. If this is done, the interviewer will usually tend, often without realizing it, to listen to the person selectively and observe him or her selectively. In other words, the interviewer will see and hear only those things that confirm the first impression and will filter out anything that contradicts it.

Research indicates that first impressions are based to a large extent on nonverbal cues: 55 percent on what is seen, 9 percent on what is said, and 36 percent on how it is said. Nonverbal cues are based almost entirely on reliving old memories. They are therefore based not on the person, but on others in the past.

There is no best way to interview. Interviews can be structured or unstructured, or they may be conducted in groups. Three interview types are most commonly used in the foodservice industry.

- *Structured interviews* consist of a series of carefully designed and structured questions that are asked by the interviewer of each job applicant. This type of interview is based on a clear set of job specifications. Through this type of interview, the interviewer maintains control of the interview by systematically asking prepared questions. An advantage of using a structured interview is that it provides the same criteria for all interviews.

FIGURE 14-2 Additional interview types.

- Board interviews
- Stress interviews
- Counseling interviews
- Evaluation or job appraisal interviews
- Exit interviews

- *Unstructured interviews,* as the name implies, require very little preparation on the part of the interviewer. These types of interviews are conducted without a predetermined checklist of questions. Open-ended questions are used. This type of interview may pose problems of subjectivity and bias on the part of the interviewer. However, unstructured interviews can provide a more relaxed atmosphere for interviewees.
- *Group interviews* are interviews in which several applicants are questioned together in a group discussion. They typically involve a structured and unstructured question format.

Other types of interviews are shown in Figure 14-2.

BOX 14-1

CHEF TALK: TEAM PLAYERS

One of my most difficult tasks as an executive chef is hiring the right players for my kitchen team. Because we have a strong team philosophy at our hotel, we go to great lengths to get the best possible people. I therefore look for individuals who can fit our high standards.

Among the qualities I consider important in a potential new kitchen employee are of course experience and how employment candidates present themselves for interview, but more important, I look for that special "hospitality attitude." For me that's a critical quality. People who possess hospitality attitudes are usually those who will also make good team players. These attitudes are not hard to tease out. I simply ask who the most important person is in the hotel. When the answer indicates that it is the guest, chances are they understand the concept of hospitality.

Previous work experience in similar establishments is not the only deciding factor in the hiring process. If the person's disposition is positive, then that can be a good basis to invest in developing and training that person.

Key to putting a great team together is "keeping them together." Therefore, investing in the existing team ensures that there is as little turnover as possible.

We employ a variety of screening processes before we get to the interview stage. Even then, not everyone who comes for an interview will be determined to be suitable. For the interview, I involve my existing team members. I seek their opinions and encourage them to participate in the interviewing of new members; after all, they will have to embrace them if they are selected. We share our opinions on the candidates, and collectively we evaluate their suitability.

Experience has taught me that some employment candidates can "talk a great game," but when it comes to actually cooking, they are left wanting. Administering a cooking test can tell you a lot, not only about their cooking skills but also about vital approaches to safety and sanitation.

Michael Ty, CEC, AAC,
MT Cuisine, LLC,
Las Vegas, Nevada

Although interviews are the most widely used method to select team members, they can create a host of problems. One of the most significant is that interviews are subject to the same legal requirements of validity and reliability as other steps in the recruitment and selection process. The interview should also follow EEOC guidelines. Interview questions should be tied to job descriptions, and these should detail only the characteristics of the employment position. The basic thrust of equal employment legislation is straightforward: Do not discriminate against people on the basis of their race, color, sex, religion, or national origin. However, subtle interpretations of the laws make this area one of the most actively pursued in the courts. If the interview questions stick to job-related items and are objective, and are applied consistently to all applicants—men, women, persons of all racial and all national groups—then the interviewer will most certainly stay within the law.

INTERVIEWING GUIDELINES

By putting the potential team member at ease, the interviewer is more likely to get a true picture of the applicant's skills, abilities, and attitudes.

The interview should take place in a pleasant and nonthreatening environment. Begin the interview by welcoming the applicant warmly. An applicant who is at ease will be more likely to answer questions spontaneously. Introduce yourself by name and title. Ask the applicant his or her preferred name and use it throughout the interview. Prepare the atmosphere by initiating a brief conversation on issues unrelated to the interview. Establish and maintain rapport with applicants by displaying sincere interest in them and by listening carefully. Indicate the intention to take notes or complete an evaluation form; be sure to extend this opportunity to the applicant. Strive to understand what is only suggested or implied. A good listener's mind is alert, and his or her face and posture reflect this.

Some interviewers tend to talk too much. According to Bill Marvin, in his book, *The Foolproof Foodservice Selection System,* "Most interviewers talk half of the time or more during an interview, but it is the candidate who should be talking 80 or 90 percent of the time. After all, how can you learn about an applicant if you do all the talking?"[4]

Focus attention fully on the applicant's responses to questions, and the questions, observations, and body language of the applicant, as these often provide clues to that person's attitude and feelings. Answer fully and frankly the applicant's questions. Use questions effectively to elicit truthful answers. Questions should be phrased as objectively as possible, without an indication of the desired response. During the interview, separate facts from inferences. Use open-ended questions that give the applicant an opportunity to talk and share information about past work experiences, training, or lifestyle. A number of the things to avoid doing in an interview are shown in Figure 14-3.

When an interviewer is not getting honest answers to carefully prepared questions, it is possible to hire the wrong person. To become an effective interviewer, the dynamics of verbal and nonverbal communication must be mastered so that dishonest applicants can be easily spotted. It has been reported that 80 percent of communication is nonverbal rather than verbal, and that 80 percent of that communication is manifest in a person's face, particularly in the eyes. An interviewer should be able to recognize the subtle nonverbal cues that indicate an attempt to deceive. Few applicants can lie without feeling tightness in the stomach, along with some involuntary change in facial expression or diverting of the eyes from the interviewer.[5] Verbal clues that sometimes

FIGURE 14-3 Things to avoid during an interview.

- Avoid biases and traps. This includes favoring people who have interests, backgrounds, or experiences similar to the interviewer.
- Avoid allowing an impressive attitude to overshadow the need to ask essential questions about skills and knowledge.
- Avoid the influence of "beautyism." Discrimination against unattractive persons is a persistent and pervasive form of employment discrimination.
- Avoid the "halo effect," judging an individual favorably or unfavorably on the basis of one strong point (or weak point) on which high (or low) value has been placed.
- Avoid allowing first impressions (good or bad) to overrule the information gathered from the interview.
- Avoid making a judgment on the basis of preinterview material and either spending the entire time trying to verify the material or simply rendering the interview pointless.
- Avoid making a decision too soon.
- Avoid the temptation of talking too much.

can indicate deception include remarks such as "to tell the truth," "to be perfectly honest," or "I wouldn't tell most people this." Sometimes verbal and nonverbal cues are combined, for example, an "honest to God" remark accompanied by a major break in eye contact, a shift in body orientation, or a movement of a hand to the face.

Be sure all of the information needed is obtained before ending the interview. Keep in mind the qualities needed for the job. Cover all major skills that are needed on the job. As a final step in the interview process, ask the applicant if there are further questions or more information to be discussed before closing the interview.

INTERVIEW QUESTIONS

To evaluate the qualifications of potential team members, the chef supervisor must ask a series of questions. However, certain types of questions violate EEOC guidelines. Other types of questions are inappropriate, but inexperienced interviewers may ask them unwittingly. Following are some examples of appropriate and inappropriate questions.

Name

Inappropriate: Inquiries about name that would indicate applicant's lineage, ancestry, national origin, or descent. Inquiry of previous name of applicant where it has been changed by court order or otherwise. Inquiries about preferred courtesy title: Mr., Mrs., and Ms.

Permissible inquiries: "Have you worked for this organization under a different name?" "Is any additional information relative to change of name, use of an assumed name, or nickname necessary to enable a check on your work and educational record? If yes, please explain."

Marital Status

Inappropriate: "Are you married, divorced, or separated?"

Permissible inquiries: Whether applicant can meet specific work schedules or has activities, commitments, or responsibilities that may hinder the meeting or work attendance requirements.

Age

Inappropriate: "How old are you?"

Permissible inquiries: Requiring proof of age in the form of a work permit or a certificate of age if a minor. If it is necessary to know that someone is over a certain age for legal reasons, this question could better be stated, "Are you 21 or over?"

National Origin

Inappropriate: "Are you native born or naturalized?" "Have you proof of your citizenship?" "What was your birthplace?" "Where were your parents born?"

Permissible inquiries: If it is necessary to know if someone is a U.S. citizen for a job, this question could be asked directly, without asking anything that might reveal national origin. If it is necessary to require proof of citizenship or immigrant status, employment can be offered on the condition that proof is supplied.

Mental or Physical Handicap

Inappropriate: "Do you have or have you ever had a life-threatening disease?" Questions regarding treatment for alcohol or drug abuse or an on-the-job injury. "Have you ever been treated for a mental condition?"

Permissible inquiries: For employers subject to the provisions of the Rehabilitation Act of 1973 and the Americans with Disabilities Act of 1990, applicants may be invited to indicate how and to what extent they are handicapped. All applicants can be asked if they are able to carry out all necessary job assignments and perform them in a safe manner. The employer must indicate that compliance with the invitation is voluntary or that the information is being sought only to remedy discrimination or provide opportunities for the handicapped.

Religion

Inappropriate: "What is your religious affiliation?" "What clubs/associations are you a member of?" "Can you work Saturdays or Sundays?"

Permissible inquiries: None. However, an applicant may be advised concerning normal hours and days of work required by the job, to avoid possible conflict with religious or other personal convictions.

Conviction, Arrest, and Court Records

Inappropriate: Any inquiries relating to arrests. Any inquiry into or a request for a person's arrest, court, or conviction record if not substantially related to functions and responsibilities of the particular job in question.

Permissible inquiries: Inquiry into actual *convictions* that relate reasonably to fitness to perform an actual job.

Military Record

Inappropriate: The type of discharge.

Permissible inquiries: Type of education and experience in the service as it relates to a particular job.

Credit Rating

Inappropriate: Any questions concerning credit rating, charge accounts, ownership of car, etc.
Permissible inquiries: None.

The following questions can provoke responses that help determine a person's motivation, initiative, insight, and planning abilities.

On Motivation

"How will this job help you get what you want?"
"What have you done to prepare yourself for a better job?"

The underlying intent of these types of questions is to determine the applicant's priorities and how motivated he or she may be.

On Initiative

"How did you get into this line of work?"
"When have you felt like giving up on a task? Tell me about it."

The intention here is to determine if the person is a self-starter or can complete an unpleasant assignment.

On Insight

"What is the most useful criticism you have received?"
"From whom? Tell me about it."
"What is the most useless?"

From answers to these questions, it is possible to develop an understanding of the applicant's ability to take constructive action on weakness and determine how the applicant can take criticism.

On Planning

"Tell me how you spend a typical day."
"If you were the boss, how would you run your present job?"

Reactions to these questions may tell how easily the applicant will fit into your corporate culture and team. They will also help elicit if they have a vision or can get bogged down by details.

General Questions

"Tell me about yourself."
"What practical experience have you had in this area?"
"What is your major strength? Weakness?"
"What types of people annoy you?"
"What have you done that shows initiative and action?"
"How do you spend your spare time?"
"What personal characteristics do you feel are necessary for success in the foodservice industry?"
"Where would you like to be in one year?"
"Why do you want to work for us?"
"Why do you want to leave your present job?"

Questions About the Foodservice Organization

"What do you know about our organization?"

"Why do you want to work for us?"

"Why would you like this particular job?"

"How can you benefit our organization?"

"What experience(s) have you had that suit you for our organization?"

"What position would you like to hold with us in five years? In ten years?"

"What interests you about our organization?"

"What kind of chef supervisor do you prefer?"

"What do you feel determines a person's progress in a good organization?"

"What are your ideas about how the foodservice industry operates today?"

In addition to verbal and nonverbal responses during the interview, much can be learned from the actions and appearance of the applicant. These positive actions include:

- Arriving early for the interview
- Being alert and responsive
- Being dressed appropriately
- Being well groomed, with clean hair and nails
- Making good eye contact
- Listening carefully
- Speaking well of other people
- Sticking to the point

Obviously, the person who arrives late for an interview, is inappropriately dressed and unclean, looks away, complains about other people, or exhibits inappropriate responses presents a negative image. The interview session provides the chef supervisor with an opportunity to form an impression about the applicant's abilities and general disposition and to make a reasoned judgment as to his or her suitability for the kitchen team.

MAKING THE DECISION

In reviewing all the pertinent data elicited from the screening step and the interview, the chef supervisor must ask: Is this the person I want for my team, and is he or she qualified and suitable? References have been checked to indicate accuracy of presented resume materials. It must be remembered that reference checking assumes that the past will indicate the future and that performance in one job has some continuity with the next. This is not always the case. What interviewers see is what they will get, and leopards don't change their spots. These applicants will never look or behave better than they have throughout the evaluation process.

Determine the applicant's temperament. How well will this person fit into the kitchen team? Can this person be trained and developed? What is his or her energy level? The foodservice industry has demanding, busy service periods. Is the applicant a team player? If all of the applicant's hobbies or interests center around individual activities such as reading or listening to music or other solitary activities, this might be an applicant who prefers being alone. Applicants who have a background that includes team activities will in many cases have a grasp of the imperatives of teamwork. In a kitchen team, ideal members are those who are "people-oriented."

FIGURE 14-4   Other factors in the hiring decision.

- *Compensation:* The rate of pay available affects the degree of selectivity.
- *Labor relations:* Unions may influence who is selected.
- *Training and development:* Training costs in terms of time and expense may be reduced or increased.

Remember also that the foodservice organization can only hire what it can afford. If the team vacancy that exists pays less than the potential team member is worth, and if there are no immediate promotional opportunities for this person to advance into, then this person will most certainly soon be looking for a better-paid position elsewhere.

Obviously, most of the team positions that chef supervisors are called on to fill are for cooks. Therefore a simple cooking test may be appropriate. Much can be learned of an applicant by asking him or her to cook a simple and inexpensive dish. This test can quantify the applicant's skill level much more than an impressive résumé containing a list of awards won at food shows ever will. It will also demonstrate the applicant's energy level, organizational abilities, application of safety and sanitation procedures, use of correct equipment, and attitude toward customer service. All of this information can be gathered from making a dish as simple as an omelet.

As is usual with many aspects of decision making regarding hiring new team members, not all of them will fit into each component of the job specification: A chef supervisor may like everything about them, but in one or two areas they fail to match the specifications. Sometimes it is necessary to evaluate the risk of hiring against what is generally known as "can do" and "will do" factors. "Can do" concerns the individual's knowledge, skills, and attitudes. "Will do" concerns the person's motivation, interests, and personality characteristics. Some element of risk is involved when the elements of "can do" are not entirely fulfilled. Experienced chef supervisors can calculate the risk by determining that training and development will fix the "can do" part, because the "will do" elements outweigh other factors. Therefore, the availability of training and development may permit the hiring of potential team members who can be made qualified. Other factors in the hiring decision are shown in Figure 14-4.

Summary

Recruiting and selection procedures that are effectively and carefully pursued and that are then applied correctly will combine to facilitate hiring the best possible candidates for the kitchen team. Recruiting and hiring decisions should be based on two questions: Will this person fit into our team, and does he or she have the skills and knowledge needed?

The chef supervisor has an important role to play and should be the final decision maker in the process of selecting new team members.

Legal issues relative to the recruitment and selection process should be scrupulously followed.

Chef supervisors should be aware of the legislation pertaining in this area.

Finding the "neatness of fit" between the foodservice organization and the potential new team member should be planned to reduce turnover and decrease training costs. Knowing the sources and methods of recruiting facilitates this process.

Job descriptions should be used to format the essential and desirable skills of new team members. The EEOC criteria with regard to employment applicants must be followed strictly so that all applicants are afforded the same employment opportunities. Discrimination in

---

FIGURE 14-5 Guidelines for effective interviewing.

- Put the applicant at ease.
- Focus attention on the applicant's responses to questions.
- Use open-ended questions.
- Avoid biases that may affect judgment.
- Avoid the halo effect.
- Don't allow first impressions to overrule information gathered from the interview.
- Know what questions are inappropriate and those that are permissible.

---

employment opportunity is illegal, and ignorance of the various laws is no defense.

Careful and effective screening of applicants will reduce the risk of selecting unsuitable team members. Screening requires the chef supervisor to actively check references.

Interviewing permits face-to-face evaluation of potential new team members. Therefore, interviewing skills are necessary, along with an understanding of the various types of interview processes. Guidelines for effective interviewing are shown in Figure 14-5.

Making the decision to hire an applicant is based on an evaluation of the data gathered through the application form, the screening stage, and the face-to-face interview. Additionally, a cooking test may be appropriate to determine skill levels. Elements of the decision to hire are based on this information, recognizing that past performance is not totally predictive of the future. Chef supervisors can only hire what the organization can afford.

Discussion Questions

1. Why are job descriptions used?
2. What methods are most commonly used in the foodservice industry to recruit new team members?
3. What is active recruiting?
4. How can seeking out "qualified" persons contribute to reducing costs?
5. What are the guidelines of the Equal Employment Opportunity Commission as they apply to recruitment and selection of employees?
6. Why should great care be taken in designing job application forms?
7. Why can inadequate reference checking lead to high employee turnover?
8. Why is the face-to-face interview the most crucial step in selecting potential team members?
9. What are the primary differences between a structured and an unstructured interview?
10. Why are open-ended questions used during a job interview?
11. What are five questioning areas an interviewer should not engage in during a job interview?
12. How might a chef supervisor ascertain the skill level of a cook applicant?

Notes

1. Vincent H. Eade, *Human Resources Management in the Hospitality Industry* (Scottsdale, AZ: Garsuch Sciarisbrick, 1993), 103.
2. Lloyd L. Byars and Leslie W. Rue, *Human Resource Management,* 4th ed. (Boston: Irwin, 1994), 183.
3. E. R. Worthington and Anita E. Worthington, *People Investment* (Grant's Pass, OR: Oasis Press, 1993), 108.
4. Bill Marvin, *The Foolproof Foodservice Selection System* (New York: John Wiley, 1993), 5.
5. Robert F. Wilson, *Conducting Better Job Interviews* (New York: Barron's, 1991), 25.

CHAPTER 15
INDUCTION AND ORIENTATION TRAINING

OUTLINE

- ❖ Introduction
- ❖ Induction training
- ❖ Orientation training
- ❖ Duration of orientation training
- ❖ Conducting induction and orientation training
- ❖ Follow-up and evaluation
- ❖ Summary
- ❖ Discussion questions
- ❖ Notes

OBJECTIVES

When you complete this chapter, you should be able to:

1. Differentiate between induction and orientation training programs
2. Identify the elements and essential information that form part of induction and orientation training

3. Describe methods of conducting induction and orientation programs and outline how they can benefit the foodservice organization and new team member
4. Describe topics for inclusion in kitchen orientation training programs.
5. Explain the value of follow-up and evaluation of induction and orientation training.

Case Study: ROCK HILL INN

Lisa was extremely glad that she had been hired as an apprentice at the prestigious Rock Hill Inn. She felt that her successful completion of the three-year apprenticeship would lead to opportunities in the finest restaurants around the country. Lisa had wanted to be a chef ever since she first began to help her mother in the kitchen. Starting at the age of 12, one of her greatest treats was to prepare food for her family and friends. She was eager to learn the "right way" to prepare food.

On Lisa's first day, she reported to Executive Chef Lang at 8 A.M., and Chef Lang immediately sent her to the Human Resource office to complete paperwork. After she completed the necessary paperwork, one of the Human Resource officers quickly reviewed the benefits package. Lisa was also given an employee handbook and instructed to read it carefully so that she would be familiar with the various company policies. After signing a form acknowledging that she had received a copy of the handbook, Lisa was told to report to Chef Lang. It was now 9:30 A.M.

Chef Lang met with Lisa and explained to her that as an apprentice she would be rotated through various areas of the kitchen and would receive training from virtually all the cooks and chefs. He gave her a training manual and a training journal. Chef Lang instructed her to familiarize herself with the manual and to ask her first supervising chef to show her how to keep a record of her training in the journal. He said that he reviewed the journal of each apprentice on a weekly basis. Chef Lang explained that her first assignment would be the banquet kitchen, because it was an excellent place to learn and refine her basic skills. He said she could expect to be in the banquet kitchen for six to eight weeks. He also told Lisa that generally on Mondays he brought all the apprentices (there were a total of twelve) together to discuss how their training was progressing and to discuss any concerns they might have.

Chef Lang escorted Lisa to the banquet kitchen, where he introduced her to the banquet chef, Hank. It was now 10:15 A.M. When Chef Lang left, Hank told Lisa that he was extremely busy and would meet with her later. He introduced her to two other apprentices, Jim and Gale, who were prepping for that evening's banquet. Hank told the apprentices to give Lisa some work to do and told her he would speak to her when things slowed down. Lisa noticed that Jim and Gale gave each other a "Yeah, right!" look as Hank walked away.

Gale told Lisa that she could start by peeling and fine-dicing 50 pounds of onion. She showed Lisa where the cutting boards were located and where to work. As she walked away, she said to Lisa, "Welcome to the grunt squad." Later, when Lisa was about half-finished with the onions, Jim told her that it had been decided that the onions needed to be thin-sliced rather than diced and that she would need to start over.

Jim told Lisa to put the diced onions in a container, label it, and place it in the walk-in refrigerator, "because someone would use it for something." It was now 11:30 A.M. Jim also told her that before she started cutting onions again, they would go get some lunch in the employee dining room. During lunch, Gale and Jim told Lisa all about being an apprentice or, as they called it, a "grunt" at the Rock Hill Inn. She asked how long they had been at the Inn, and they each said four months. She asked why they were still in the banquet kitchen, because Chef Lang had told her she would be there only six to eight weeks. Jim and Gale said that the training schedule in the manual was rarely followed and that Chef Lang had never reviewed their training journals. Lisa asked if the schedule and journals were discussed in the Monday meetings, and they said there had not been a Monday meeting in three months. Jim and Gale made it clear to Lisa that they were both looking to leave the Inn as soon as they could get another position, because they did not feel they were learning anything. They said all they ever did was cut and chop things, and sweep and mop floors.

After lunch, Lisa started peeling and slicing onions. It was 12:15 P.M. Lisa finished peeling and slicing the onions and then cleaned the area where she had been working. Jim then told her to sweep out the store rooms and walk-in refrigerators associated with the banquet kitchen. At 5:30 P.M. Hank came by and told her that she could leave for the day, and that he would meet with her at 7:30 A.M. the next day to give her a work schedule and discuss her duties with her. He asked her what she thought of being part of the team at the Rock Hill Inn, and she said, "It's ok, I guess." Hank told Lisa that she'd better get a more enthusiastic and positive attitude or she would not last long at the Inn.

Based on what you have learned from previous chapters and the content of this chapter, answer the following questions.

- What is the overall reason for Lisa's perceived lack of enthusiasm and positive attitude?
- What are the primary causal agents for Lisa's perceived lack of enthusiasm and positive attitude?
- What role did leadership and supervision/management play in Lisa's perceived lack of enthusiasm and positive attitude?
- What specific steps could have been taken to avoid Lisa's perceived lack of enthusiasm and positive attitude?
- What, specifically, can be done by the Rock Hill Inn to avoid similar perceived lack of enthusiasm and positive attitude by future apprentices?

INTRODUCTION

A new team member's first impressions about his or her job can make all the difference. The foundation for attitudes that may stay in place as long as that team member remains in the foodservice organization is established during orientation and induction. Orientation and induction training describe the types of training given to a new kitchen team member. They provide information about the total quality culture, mission, philosophy, job, and working conditions and cover the main activities and duties in which the new team member will be involved. They state the area of training in which the new team member will be instructed and the quality levels of performance expected. They also provide a systematic plan to accomplish these goals. By providing an orientation program, the chef supervisor communicates to new employees what is expected of them and how their jobs fit into the overall operation. It also helps employees fit into their jobs faster, to be more productive and satisfied, and to realize that the supervisor cares. Also, remember that how employees treat customers is often a reflection of how they are treated by management.[1]

INDUCTION TRAINING

Induction implies absorbing a new team member into the culture of the foodservice organization. It is deliberately separated from orientation as a training method. It is different from orientation insofar as it is not process-oriented. Typically, induction covers issues such as customer focus, philosophy, team focus, mission statement, corporate culture, commitment to goals, concepts of empowerment, and individual attitudes toward these goals. Induction does not need to cover specific job details, because its purpose is to evoke feelings and generate commitment. The chef supervisor conducting the induction should sell the organization's philosophy along with security, caring, and peace of mind by talking in general terms about benefits, recognition programs, and salary policies. New team members want to be part of a successful organization. Induction is introduced on the first day the team member begins the new job.

Although written policies concerning these issues are usually included in an orientation kit, most induction training is conducted by the team. Induction training is not just a series of slogans but a calculated rationale that is lived by each member of the team daily. It is shared rather than lectured. When an employee leaves an organization, needless staffing expenses are incurred, and service to customers is likely to decline. Potentially good employees may be "turned off" by improper orientation and poor training.[2]

When it is tactfully and correctly implemented, induction will result in a committed team member armed with the expectations of the mission of the organization.

ORIENTATION TRAINING

Orientation is the umbrella under which induction is carried out. However, orientation training is more of a systematic method to acquaint the new team member with all aspects of the new job. Orientation can be defined as a two-way informational and introductory session conducted by the employer to educate and excite all participants.[3] Its purpose is to make the new team member an effective contributor to the kitchen team in the shortest time possible.

New team members receive orientation from their fellow team members and from the organization. The orientation received from fellow team members is usually unplanned and unofficial, and it often provides the new team member with misleading and inaccurate information. This is one of the reasons why the official orientation provided by the foodservice organization is so important. An effective orientation program has an immediate and lasting impact on the new team member and can make the difference between a new team member's success or failure. Studies have identified a strong correlation between customer satisfaction and the employee's view of service quality. When employees view an organization's human resources policies favorably, customers tend to view the quality of service they receive favorably.[4]

It is ultimately the responsibility of the chef supervisor to carry out induction and orientation training. Each new team member brings to the workplace his or her own set of values. The new employee's values and attitudes may be quite different from those of the supervisor and other employees. The background of the new employee will have some effect on the way this person relates to the supervisor and to the new job.[5] In view of this, orientation training should be prepared with the same attention to detail as any other training program. It can be one of the best and most complete training investments made by the foodservice organization.

FIGURE 15-1   Planned orientation ROI.

- All new team members will receive information to allow them to fit into the kitchen as quickly as possible.
- The new team member is working productively from the first day.
- The new team member is assigned duties and is informed of the quality standards required.
- The new team member will be more inclined to have a sense of belonging and will consequently be motivated.
- The new team member will be more inclined to be confident and loyal.
- The scene is set for further training.
- Job expectations are fulfilled.

The highest proportion of employee turnover occurs within the first thirty days. This is largely a result of poor or nonexistent orientation training. The return on investment (ROI) from a planned approach to orientation is high, as shown in Figure 15-1. The type of operation in which the kitchen is located can affect how the orientation is conducted and who conducts. In all cases, however, orientation training should take place.

In a large restaurant or hotel, the training may take place in a formal setting and be highly structured. There are usually a large number of team members to be oriented to the company, the property, and their specific department. The consistency of the program is based on materials developed strictly for that purpose, particularly at the company and property levels. The initial part of the program may be conducted by the human resource department and cover information about the company and property for all new team members. The orientation of the new team members of the various departments is usually conducted in those departments, including the kitchen. The orientation of the new kitchen team members is conducted by the chef supervisor after the general orientation. In a chain property, there are generally standardized orientation materials for each department. If such materials are not available, they should be developed by the chef supervisor in conjunction with the human resource department. In larger properties the total orientation will generally take a half- to a full day.

The first three days at work is a critical time for the new team member and will have a definite effect on his or her future performance. The first day is an opportunity to set a positive tone and thereby avoid problems that might occur later.[6]

In smaller properties where there is no human resource person in house, the orientation is generally conducted by the chef supervisor with possible input from the general manager. Development of materials is done by the chef supervisors with input from the general manager. Conduct of the orientation becomes more of a challenge in a smaller property, because often the need for the new team member in production is immediate. The need must be recognized as a reality of the operation, but the chef supervisor who is quality-focused will not allow the orientation to be sidelined because of the need. The ROI on orientation training is too great and its effect on future quality too certain to dismiss it because of time challenges. In a small operation the mark of an excellent chef supervisor will be the scheduling of time for and conduct of orientation training for all new team members. Suggestions for conducting orientation training in smaller, time-challenged operations are shown in Figure 15-2.

FIGURE 15-2 Orientation and the smaller property.

- Schedule orientation time as part of the new team members' first day and first week.
- Prioritize orientation information into three or four levels and spread the information over shorter orientation sessions throughout the new team member's first week.
- Create orientation materials that can be used repeatedly.
- Develop a handbook for the basic information that a kitchen team member needs to know, and require the new team member to read the handbook before reporting for duty the first day.

The topics presented in the training plan should be based on the needs of the organization and the new team member. Generally, the foodservice organization is concerned with meeting the needs of its customers, making a profit, satisfying team member needs, and being socially responsible. New team members, on the other hand, are generally more interested in pay, benefits, and specific terms and conditions of

BOX 15-1

CHEF TALK:
MY FIRST DAY

It will remain with me forever, my first day in the kitchen. As an innocent young apprentice chef filled with expectations of my future in the culinary profession, armed with my new chef uniforms and my meager set of chef's knives, I began my "orientation" to the chef's profession, which I still love to this day. However, my first day on the job as an apprentice chef in Jury's Hotel in Dublin, Ireland, was anything but a pleasant experience. Induction and orientation training sessions were unheard of back then. In fact, the only information I was provided with was a duty roster in which I was listed as the "new body." Nobody had bothered to even find out what my name was. The roster as I remember was an 11-day cycle spread over 2 weeks. It was broken down into 7 late days, 6 early days, with every second Sunday off and a day off each week. Late days began at 9 A.M., off at 3 P.M., return at 6 P.M., until 10:30 P.M. Early days were 9 A.M. to 6 P.M.

On my first day I reported to the "back office" for a time card. I was directed to the male changing room. After considerable effort, I eventually found this room. When I got there, there was no available locker to store my street clothes after I had changed into my chef uniform. I re-ported to the head chef and introduced myself to him. He barely acknowledged my presence, and with a grunt waved me toward the sous chef, who assigned me to the garde manger department. The chef garde manger's method of induction and orientation was to give nicknames and engage constantly in ridicule. At the end of my first period that day I returned to the locker room to discover that my street clothes had disappeared. I had to cycle home that afternoon in my chef uniform. My parents were furious. They wanted me to remain at home and to consider some other profession. In any event, I did go back to the hotel that evening. Orientation was by the sink-or-swim method by the other chef apprentices. This was probably the worst type of orientation anyone could receive. As a result of that first day I formed attitudes about the organization that took many years to undo. If I had been inducted and orientated in a planned and sequential way, I know I would have been a much more productive worker. I have often wondered since then how many potential "Escoffiers" were turned off simply because of poor initial orientation or no orientation training at all.

Noel Cullen, Ed.D., CMC, AAC
(1948–2002)

FIGURE 15-3   Orientation kit content.

- Map of the foodservice organization's facilities
- Organizational chart
- Organization's policies and procedures handbook, which typically features information and guidance on the following topics:
  - Safety and sanitation procedures
  - Uniforms, dress code, and grooming policies
  - Union policies (if applicable)
  - Payroll procedures
  - Vacation, public and religious holiday policies
  - Group health insurance
  - Meals and break policies
  - Pension/savings plan
  - Attendance, hours of work
  - Incentive programs
  - Performance evaluations
  - Emergency procedures
  - Promotion policy
  - Harassment policy
  - Employee assistance programs
  - Security department's authority
  - Disciplinary rules and actions
  - Key telephone numbers
  - Training programs

---

employment. A good balance between the foodservice organization and the new team member needs is essential if the orientation program is to be successful.

Arrangements should be made to tour the foodservice facilities. In addition, comprehensive orientation kits should be prepared for all new team members and should include the type of information shown in Figure 15-3.

The chef supervisor may want to conclude the explanation of the orientation handbook policies and procedures by reviewing the most important points. Additionally, the forms that the new team member will need to complete should be highlighted during the orientation. *Reassure new employees. Let them know you are confident they can do the job and that they will get all the support they need from the team.*

Many foodservice organizations require team members to complete a questionnaire on the policy notebook or manual. The questionnaire is not graded, but it is checked. Other organizations require new team members to pass a test on safety and sanitation, emergencies, hazardous materials handling, and harassment policies. This will show whether there are areas of the notebook or manual that are unclear and need further explanation. The policy notebook or manual will contain policies on topics such as vacations, holidays, sick leave, absenteeism, tardiness, health examinations, accidents, safety, parking regulations, disciplinary actions, grievance procedures, health and group insurance, and other policies and benefits.

DURATION OF ORIENTATION TRAINING

It is impossible for a new team member to absorb in one long session all of the information in the foodservice organization's orientation program. Brief sessions should be used. These may last up to two hours, spread over several days. This increases the likelihood that the new team member will understand and retain the information presented. Frequently, when new team members arrive in the kitchen they are handed a departmental procedures handbook and are told to read the material and to ask any questions they may have. Task and station orientation should be well planned and conducted by the chef supervisor using appropriate menu and recipe guidance.

It is important to introduce the new team member to the other kitchen team members on the first day. During these introductions each team member's function and position in the team should be indicated, and an explanation of how each one fits into the department should be given. Ensure that employees are told about company goals and visions and their role in the dream.[7]

As with any training, time is involved: the new team member's and the chef supervisor's. However, induction and orientation training are truly a quality investment of time, one that can contribute to effective integration of the new team member and set the foundation for a long association with the organization.

CONDUCTING INDUCTION AND ORIENTATION TRAINING

If the chef supervisor does not communicate and deliver the induction/orientation program, other team members will. This may not be the type of orientation you wish the new person to receive. Unplanned orientation can be harmful. Existing team members can paint an unfavorable and untrue picture of the kitchen operation. Most people will have a tendency to relate and listen to those they feel are their peers, rather than the supervisor. Therefore, it is very important that the first impressions of the organization be created by the chef supervisor and that they be in the framework of real work situations.

New team members arrive with a certain amount of anxiety. They will have feelings of insecurity regarding confidence in their abilities to do the job and fit into the team. The type of positive work environment the chef supervisor creates can reduce these anxieties and facilitate a feeling of worth and belonging in new team members. It is much better to invest in training at this stage, because they will become productive in a shorter period of time.

In communication, an open style should be adopted. Speak to the team member in a bilateral way, as if to say, "We picked each other." Speak clearly and directly as one human being to another. Provide any background information he or she will need. Explain any technical terms and avoid using kitchen jargon. Too much information at one time is as bad as too little; break it into parts. Without making it obvious, repeat anything that is important for the team member to remember. Use open questions as much as possible. Listening to the new member during the orientation is important, not just because of what might be learned, but because it means a lot to the new team member. The intention is to communicate, not to intimidate, during this phase. Avoid "talking down" from a position of power. Show respect for the individual. A little awareness and genuine kindness go a long way. Develop an orientation program that not only goes over the rules but also stresses a "spirit of hospitality."[8]

◁ **BOX 15-2** ▷

CHEF TALK:
INDUCTION BY FIRE

Being a country boy with little exposure to the European culinary scene, I was a prime candidate for induction ceremonies that I later found out took place in almost every kitchen. The first night on the hot line, while setting up garnishes for the self-professed "king of the broiler," I ran out of oval platters, which were the only appropriate frame for the masterpieces coming hot and sizzling from the "master."

After being duly reprimanded for allowing the platters to run out, I was told to hastily retrieve platters from the dish room. Upon entering the dish room, I discovered there were no oval platters. With the screams of the broiler chef getting louder, I ran back to inform him of the situation. He glared at me and told me to go to the storeroom and get a "plate stretcher." Not thinking, I ran to the storeroom. I was directed to a cabinet, opened it, and rifled through not even knowing what I was looking for. Suddenly it dawned on me. Plate stretcher! I turned and walked out of the storeroom to the laughs and howls of those who witnessed what I had just done. From that moment on I was adopted into the kitchen brigade and no longer felt an outsider. Rightly or wrongly, this method of passing through the gate to the inner circle of acceptance still goes on today. In the pressured, highly technical world of culinary art, humor and acceptance go hand in hand. It is a necessity to laugh together, to perform together, to depend on each other. That's a team. And it's always apparent (from the food served) if there is a team in the kitchen.

Keith Keogh, CEC, AAC,
Corporate Chef, Levy Restaurants
Chicago, Illinois

Perception plays an important role in communication during an orientation or induction session. It can help immensely, but it can also devastate the most sincere effort to communicate effectively. The fact is that people often hear only what they want to hear. Knowing this, the chef supervisor should keep trying until the correct feedback is received. The negative aspect of this is that it can cause the new team member to become defensive, which will hinder the communication process. Problems in perception are often caused by differences in ethnic or cultural backgrounds, differences in educational levels, and difficulties with the particular language used. The cultural background of people has a strong influence on the communication process, which includes nonverbal and verbal communication. Investing time to start the new team member on the correct path will make things easier for the chef supervisor. Induction and orientation training assist in developing the quality management philosophy in the new person.

FOLLOW-UP AND EVALUATION

Formal and systematic evaluation of the induction and orientation training program is essential. New team members should receive a set of contingency plans and contacts in the event they need further clarification or assistance to ensure their careful induction and orientation into the foodservice organization. The chef supervisor should check regularly on how well new team members are doing and answer any questions that may have arisen after their initial induction and orientation. A formal scheduled follow-up should take place within one month after the team member becomes part of the kitchen team. The actual induction and orientation training plan should be reviewed at least once a year. The purpose of this evaluation is to determine if the plan is meeting the foodservice organization's and new team members' needs and to ascertain ways of improving the current program.

Feedback from new team members is one method of evaluating the induction and orientation program. This can be achieved by asking new team members to complete unsigned questionnaires or through in-depth interviews. Feedback of this type enables the chef supervisor and the foodservice organization to adapt and modify the program. Induction and orientation training programs for new team members take priority in development and implementation; once they are completed, work on other training aspects can begin. The first day on the job is an opportunity for the chef supervisor and the organization to set a positive tone and thereby avoid problems that might occur later. The way a new kitchen team member is treated during the induction and orientation period conveys an impression of the chef supervisor and the organization as having a well-planned, well-executed induction and orientation program.

Summary

Induction and orientation training programs are vital to assimilating new team members into the foodservice organization's philosophy. They also provide for clear understanding of what team members' jobs are and the level and standards of quality performance expected.

Induction is different from orientation in that it covers issues of corporate culture, philosophy, mission, total quality, customer focus, concepts of individual empowerment, and expected team member attitudes. Induction training is eventually conducted by the entire team. Orientation training is the umbrella under which induction takes place. The purpose of the orientation training plan is to systematically and sequentially orient the new team member to the job, the kitchen, and the other team members so as to enable him or her to contribute effectively to the organization in the shortest possible time. The first thirty days of the new team member's tenure in the job are vital. It is during this period that most employee turnover occurs, largely because of poor orientation training.

Orientation training should include an information kit that will enable the new team member to fit smoothly into the foodservice organization. It is the chef supervisor's duty to ensure that the new member is armed with the necessary information to understand rules and procedures. Induction and orientation training should take place over a period of time in a planned way, rather than as one long session. Formal and systematic follow-up should be planned. If the chef supervisor does not conduct the induction and orientation of the new team member, others will. Unplanned induction and orientation usually result in a negative view of the new job, the organization, and the chef supervisor by the new person.

The communication style of the chef supervisor during induction and orientation should be open and concentrate on removing anxiety and building feelings of security in the new team member. Topics for the induction/orientation training sessions should include the kitchen department functions, team members' duties and responsibilities, pay and benefits, rules and procedures of the organization, and a tour of the entire organization.

Formal evaluation of the induction and orientation training program should take place annually to ensure it meets with the needs and requirements of the organization and its future employees. A systematic follow-up to the initial induction and orientation should take place within at least one month to check on new team members' comfort with their new position.

Discussion Questions

1. What are the major differences between induction and orientation?
2. Why conduct induction training programs?
3. Why does the highest proportion of team member turnover in the kitchen occur within the first thirty days?
4. What critical items should form part of an orientation packet for new kitchen team members?
5. What are the advantages of receiving feedback on induction and orientation training programs?
6. What are the effects of unplanned induction and orientation with regard to new kitchen team members?
7. How long after the initial induction and orientation should systematic follow-up take place?

Notes

1. Karen Eich Drummond, *The Restaurant Training Program* (New York: John Wiley, 1992), 1.
2. Herman Zaccarelli, *Training Managers to Train* (Los Altos, CA: Crisp, 1988), 56.
3. Vincent H. Eade, *Human Resources Management in the Hospitality Industry* (Scottsdale, AZ: Garsuch Sciarisbrick, 1993), 173.
4. Cliff Barbee and Valerie Bott, "Customer Treatment as a Mirror of Employee Treatment," *Advanced Management Journal,* Spring 1991, 31.
5. Anna Katherine Jernigan, *The Effective Food Service Supervisor* (Rockville, MD: Aspen, 1989).
6. Marion E. Haynes, *Stepping up to Supervisor* (Los Altos, CA: Crisp, 1990), 76.
7. Jeff Weinstein, "Personnel Success," *Restaurants & Institutions,* December 1992, 113.
8. John J. Hogan, "Turnover and What to Do About It," *Cornell HRA Quarterly,* February 1992, 41.

CHAPTER 16
TEAM PERFORMANCE APPRAISAL

OBJECTIVES

When you complete this chapter, you should be able to:

1. State the elements on which chef supervisors evaluate team member performance in the kitchen
2. Describe the benefits and the effects of performance appraisals on the development of the kitchen team
3. Outline important methods of team member evaluation
4. Describe the preparation steps for appraisal interviews and outline the steps in conducting these interviews
5. Outline the procedures for evaluating weak team member performance

✿

Case Study: CANYON BLUFF RESORT

Canyon Bluff Resort's personnel policies require that all personnel be given a formal performance evaluation each year. Executive Chef Mike Harris feels it is best to do all performance evaluations at the same time, so February 1 of each year he begins doing employee evaluation. To complete the evaluations, he meets with two employees each day for three weeks. This year he has scheduled a full fifteen minutes for each meeting.

Chef Harris completes the evaluation form provided by Human Resources for each employee before the meeting. Occasionally he refers to the employee's personnel file if he remembers that there has been an incident involving the employee. Generally, he depends on his excellent memory to complete the form. Because the form has a graphic rating scale, he rarely makes written comments about the employee's performance unless he remembers something exceptional about the staff member.

Chef Harris feels strongly that if employees succeed in retaining their position at Canyon Bluff, their work has to be satisfactory, so most employees receive a satisfactory rating in each category every year. Chef Harris also feels that the evaluations really have little purpose other than to comply with company policy. He has been doing performance evaluations for the kitchen staff every year for the six years he has been at Canyon Bluff, and he has not seen any changes result from the evaluations. He does not expect the results to be any different this year. Chef Harris does consider the annual meetings with employees to be an opportunity to ask how their family is doing and to give them a pat on the back.

Based on what you have learned from previous chapters and the content of this chapter, answer the following question.

- Do you believe that the annual performance evaluation of kitchen staff at the Canyon Bluff Resort contributes to growth and improvement of the individual or the operation? Explain your answer, including the following:
- Overall reason
- Primary causal agents
- Role of leadership and supervision/management
- Specific steps that have been taken to ensure a positive result of the process or that should be taken to achieve a positive result of the process

INTRODUCTION

Performance appraisal is the systematic process of developing criteria for job performance. This involves outlining criteria to team members along with assessing team members' job performance relative to the criteria and communicating the results to the team members.[1]

Many chef supervisors look on performance appraisals as an unpleasant task. However, performance appraisals present the chef supervisor with opportunities to make valuable contributions not only to the team, but also to each individual member, thus improving the culinary operation. It is not unusual for those chef supervisors who rise from the ranks to find it uncomfortable to evaluate another team member's performance.

Performance appraisal and evaluation is the ongoing responsibility of all chef supervisors. They are required to consider how well members of the kitchen team are doing their jobs. Through appraisal it may be decided who should be recommended for promotion, transfer, reassignment, further training, salary increases, or even termination. One of the most important aspects, however, is encouraging team member performance improvement. In this regard, performance appraisals are used to communicate to team members how they are doing and to suggest needed changes in behavior, attitude, skills, or knowledge. This type of feedback clarifies for each team member the job task and overall quality expectations held by the chef supervisor. Additionally, appraisals often serve to validate the selection procedures used during the recruitment stage. (These were described in Chapter 14.)

Performance appraisals should be conducted periodically to let team members know how they are doing and to outline to them whether their performance is satisfactory or unsatisfactory. This typically is done through an appraisal interview.

EVALUATING PERFORMANCE

Performance evaluation is never an end in itself. It is the necessary preliminary step to conducting meaningful feedback discussions, making appropriate administrative recommendations, and determining where performance improvement is required. Evaluation of team members includes the following aspects of performance: work productivity and quality, dependability, team interactions, initiative, and leadership. Example areas of performance evaluation are shown in Figure 16-1.

Nearly all personnel are interested in how they are viewed by the chef supervisor. In the absence of specific feedback, team members often form their own conclusions by comparing their experiences with those of others around them. This can sometimes lead to wrong conclusions. Clearing up doubt or uncertainty is a major purpose of the performance appraisal:

A productive appraisal, along with providing a review of the employee's work, serves as a work session between supervisor and employee in which you take the time and effort to meet with an individual employee and set new

FIGURE 16-1 Areas of performance evaluation.

- Quality and amount of work performed
- Adherence to sanitation or safety procedures
- Adherence to food cost control procedures
- Quality of culinary skill
- Personal grooming or appearance
- Attendance
- Cooperation
- Ability to work unsupervised
- Initiative
- Knowledge of rules and company procedures
- Involvement as a team player
- Leadership potential

FIGURE 16-2 Benefits of performance appraisal.

- Team members learn what their strengths and weaknesses are within the team.
- New goals and objectives are agreed on between the chef supervisor and the team member.
- The relationship between the chef supervisor and the team member is brought to a new level.
- The team member becomes an active participant in the team objectives.
- The team may be restructured for maximum efficiency.
- The team member's commitment to the team is renewed.
- New training needs are identified.
- Time is set aside for discussing issues other than money.
- Team members feel they are taken seriously as individuals.

---

goals and objectives for the coming year. A productive appraisal recognizes that *people* are the most valuable resource of any organization.[2]

The benefits of a good performance appraisal are shown in Figure 16-2.

Performance appraisals also provide written records to substantiate actions. Therefore, they can serve as an information and team member feedback system. More and more administrative decisions taken by management are being subjected to review by outside parties. To verify the appropriateness of decisions made, it is necessary to document all meetings for review purposes. Performance appraisals serve as excellent records. Such documentation can also serve to confirm understandings between the chef supervisor and the team member.

METHODS OF EVALUATION

An evaluation decision is made by comparison. Whatever is being evaluated is compared to something else, and it exceeds or equals or falls short in comparison.[3] There are many methods of evaluation. Each has its merits. Indeed, many foodservice organizations use more than one. The following four methods are commonly used in the evaluation of kitchen team members in both small and large operations.

1. The *essay appraisal*, in its simplest form, requires the chef supervisor to write a paragraph or more covering a team member's individual strengths and weaknesses and his or her potential for further development. A major weakness of this method is its variability in length and content. Essay evaluations are difficult to combine or compare.
2. The *graphic rating scale* typically assesses a team member on the quality and quantity of work—outstanding, above average, or unsatisfactory—and on a variety of other factors that vary but usually include traits such as reliability and cooperation.
3. The *critical-incident appraisal* requires the chef supervisor to maintain a log of critical incidents of positive or negative behavior. So, for appraisal purposes the discussion with the team member is based on actual behavior. One of the challenges to this method is that it requires the chef supervisor to write down incidents on a regular basis. The benefit of this method is the avoidance of appraising on only the most recent performance, which is always top-of-mind.

4. *Behaviorally anchored rating scales* (commonly referred to as BARS) require that a job analysis has been conducted that identified performance behavior appropriate for different levels. The BARS method is objective. Each team member is rated against a predetermined specific set of behaviors identified on a job-by-job basis. The downside to this evaluation method is that it can be costly to initiate and time-consuming for the chef supervisor.

Even though there are a variety of performance appraisal methods to choose from, it is still possible to end up with inaccurate information on the kitchen team. To avoid this, chef supervisors should be trained in the techniques of performance appraisals. A common error in the performance appraisal process is the halo effect (discussed in Chapter 14). This occurs when the evaluator allows a single prominent characteristic of a team member to influence his or her judgment. Personal preferences, prejudices, and biases can also cause errors in performance appraisals. Chef supervisors with biases or prejudices tend to look for team member behaviors that conform to their biases. Figure 16-3 is a simple generic example of a graphic rating scale.

FIGURE 16-3   Graphic rating scale performance evaluation.

Team member:	John Smith				
Job Title:	Kitchen Team Member				
Department:	Kitchen				

Check all items relevant to team member's position. Rate each item on a scale of 1–5. Circle number at right:

1 = Needs much improvement
2 = Needs some improvement
3 = Satisfactory
4 = Very good
5 = Excellent

Part I: General Work Habits and Attitude

Sanitation and safety	1	2	3	4	5
Attendance and punctuality	1	2	3	4	5
Meets deadlines	1	2	3	4	5
Cooperates with team members	1	2	3	4	5
Accepts suggestions	1	2	3	4	5
Uses equipment properly	1	2	3	4	5
Prioritizes work well	1	2	3	4	5

Part II: Job Performance

Quality of work	1	2	3	4	5
Ability to solve problems	1	2	3	4	5
Uses original ideas	1	2	3	4	5
Communications ability	1	2	3	4	5
Time management	1	2	3	4	5
Hands-on skills	1	2	3	4	5
Interpersonal skills	1	2	3	4	5
Ability to work on a team	1	2	3	4	5

APPRAISAL INTERVIEWS

The performance appraisal process is not complete until there is a conference between the team member and the chef supervisor. These interviews allow discussion about the period since the last appraisal. They typically review the previous year and set a course for the coming year. These discussions help answer such questions as: "How am I doing?" "Where can I go from here?" and "How do I get there?" The first step in beginning an appraisal interview is to give the team member a few days' notice of the interview date so that he or she may prepare for it. Chef supervisors should preview relevant data for the interview during this time period. Select a time and a place for the interview that will be private and free from interruptions. The spirit that should permeate this interview is one of teamwork, a collaborative problem-solving approach. Traditionally, team members view a performance appraisal as an ordeal they must go through before they can find out whether they will receive a negative or a positive evaluation.

Start the interview by creating the impression that the interview is considered very important. Next, help the team member to feel that the interview is a valuable, constructive, cooperative process by placing emphasis on his or her development. Avoid any impression that the interview was arranged only for the purposes of warning or reprimanding. Assure the team member that its purpose is to give constructive and objective feedback.

The interview portion of the performance appraisal should consist of a thorough review of the team member's goals for the appraisal period, the degree to which these goals were accomplished, and setting new goals for the subsequent period. The discussion should be based on observed behavior and performance, not on the team member's personal characteristics. Team members will accept criticism when it is based on fact rather than vague remarks. This is where the actual appraisal evaluation method is used. This may be by the BARS method, a graphic rating scale, or a critical-incident appraisal method. Try to keep the interview friendly, natural, and informal. Remember, the interview is also used to give positive feedback.

The conduct of an effective appraisal requires attention to five areas: *mise en place,* environment, focus and engagement, closure, and documentation. Before the interview, the chef supervisor must do a *mise en place.* As a culinarian you know that *mise en place* means "everything in its place." In the kitchen this is the gathering of ingredients and supplies and doing preprep to ensure that preparation and service will go smoothly and last-minute scrambling for needed items can be avoided. Preparing for an appraisal interview differs only in what is being gathered. The chef supervisor must:

- Ensure that all relevant data concerning the team member is available.
- Select for the interview only those accomplishments and problems that are relevant to the discussion.

The success of the interview is directly affected by the *environment* established by the chef supervisor.

- Arrange the meeting area so the evaluator and the team member can sit face to face, without a desk between them, or with both sitting at the same side of the desk.
- Make the area comfortable, with the right temperature and comfortable chairs.
- Create a nonthreatening environment and display a supportive attitude.

The *focus* established by the chef supervisor must be on the behavior rather than the individual. Additionally, the greater the *engagement* of the team member in the interview, the more likely it is that the outcome of the interview will lead to improved performance.

- Focus feedback on the behavior rather than on the individual.
- Get the team member to commit to future goals and set benchmarks for accomplishment.
- Ask the team member for his or her opinions on work-related issues. Interviews are two-way streets. Encourage continued conversation.
- Allow for individual differences in the ratings. Don't compare an average but competent team member with a superstar.
- Evaluate honestly and carefully. Don't say, "I don't like your attitude." It is more appropriate to say, "Your behavior shows that you seem to resent doing the work that is asked of you. If that is true, you need to change your behavior." Give specific examples.
- Some questions encourage while others limit. State questions so that the team member will think and give detailed responses. Generally, avoid closed-ended questions that require yes-or-no answers. Listen actively and avoid forming conclusions on too little data.
- An interview cannot be conducted only as a series of questions. It is appropriate for the chef supervisor to add thoughts on various topics discussed. This will be either confirmation or clarification of the team member's understanding of the points discussed. Always allow the team member ample time to respond to any questions posed.

Closure is a critical step in the interview. It should be viewed as solidifying what the expectations are for future performance. When all the points have been covered that were planned, close the discussion. Three important issues need to be addressed at this stage:

1. Summarize the key points and check for team members' understanding. Invite them also to summarize.
2. Compare the points agreed on.
3. Team members should have a chance to review their problems and outline any concerns or work-related problems that they may have.

Following the interview closing, *document* the interview by writing a brief summary of the discussion. This should include action plans or action points (in some instances it is appropriate to have the team member sign this). If it was agreed to do anything during the course of the interview, follow through. If something that was agreed to is not acted on, it can have a serious effect on the team member's morale. It sends a message that the chef supervisor doesn't care. Follow-up is important with all team members, but it is crucial when dealing with weak team members. They need continued guidance and support from the chef supervisor.

Documenting appraisal interviews serves a secondary purpose. It can also be used to protect the chef supervisor and the foodservice organization if they are accused of bias or improper behavior by an individual or by another manager and a lawsuit is brought: "Any incidents that are out of the ordinary or that involve a significant clash of tempers or personalities should be included in the documenta-tion."[4] The documentation of the interview should be finalized by allowing the team member to review and sign the report on the interview. The team member's signature line should have the statement next to it that the signature is solely ac-knowledgement of having seen the document, not agreement with the content of the document.

Appraising a poorly performing team member can be particularly challenging. Per-formance appraisals do not always bring good news to a team member. Good and bad employees must be told how they are doing. Handling the bad news requires some special techniques:

- Have the relevant documentation available to demonstrate previous discussion of poor performance.
- Give specific examples of when work failed to match set quality standards. Show where work failed to match the work of other team members.
- Prepare a list of changes the team member is to make in his or her performance.
- Be positive about each team member's ability to improve. Arrange for further training sessions.
- Set short-term goals that are within the ability of the individual. Build progressively on successes.
- Be honest with team members. Spell out clearly what they have to do and outline the consequences if they do not improve.
- Make a short-term agreement with the team member on measurable performance improvements set against a specific time period. Agree to meet again after the short time period to assess progress.[5]

End the meeting on a positive note. Point out the team member's accomplish-ments. Reaffirm a willingness to continue to work with the team member until he or she reaches a satisfactory performance level. It is vital to get the team member's atten-tion if the performance is unsatisfactory. Chef supervisors should not gloss over prior performances and go easy on the team member. The team member may see what the chef supervisor may view as a tough review as an acceptable appraisal unless the un-satisfactory behavior is clearly stated.

COMPENSATION

Hourly wages or salaries are usually established collaboratively between upper management and the chef supervisor (unions may be involved if there is an agreed-on procedure in this area). Productive performance appraisals focus en-tirely on issues of strengths and weaknesses and the development of new goals and objectives. Once money becomes part of the discussion, interest in improvement tends to dissipate. If the team member does bring up the question of money during the appraisal interview, state that this will be discussed later and that now the in-terview will concentrate on performance only. If the issue of money persists, ex-plain that the interview is bound by company guidelines and that the chef supervisor does not make the final decision about salary increases. However, indi-cate clearly that a recommendation in this area will in large part be based on the outcome of this current appraisal interview.

Summary

A sound performance appraisal system draws on both the chef supervisor and the team member. Together they negotiate performance expectations for the future. Through appraisal it may be decided who should be recommended for promotion, transfer, reassignment, further training, a salary increase, or termination. Performance appraisals are used to communicate to team members their strengths and weaknesses on the job, and together with the chef supervisor, plans for future development can be made. Performance appraisals should be conducted periodically. They usually include aspects of work quality, attitude, and cooperation.

When used correctly and appropriately, performance evaluations may be an asset in identifying gaps in the training stage and act as information-gathering systems and morale boosters for the kitchen team.

Performance evaluation methods vary: supervisor-produced essays, graphic rating scales, critical incident appraisal, and BARSs. Every effort should be made to eliminate areas of bias and prejudice when evaluating team members.

Appraisal interviews are used to apprise the team member of acceptable or unacceptable behavior. They should contain a thorough review of the team member's performance outlined during a matter-of-fact, friendly interview. When the interview is concluded, both parties "sign off" on agreed goals. Issues discussed and agreed on should be documented.

Discussion Questions

1. What are the positive outcomes of team member performance appraisal?
2. How can performance appraisals be used to validate selection procedures?
3. What elements of team member performance are usually evaluated?
4. What are the benefits of performance appraisals relative to working relations between the chef supervisor, the foodservice organization, and the individual team member?
5. Why is it appropriate to maintain a written record of performance appraisal interviews?
6. Describe the procedures commonly used for conducting appraisal interviews.
7. What is the halo effect?
8. What important factors should be considered for conducting appraisal interviews?
9. What are the three important issues to be addressed at the conclusion of the interview?
10. How should the question of compensation be treated by the chef supervisor during the interview?
11. What is the methodology used to appraise weaker team members?

Notes

1. Donald W. Myers, Wallace R. Johnson, and Glenn Pearce, "The Role of Interaction Theory in Approval Feedback," *SAM Advanced Management Journal,* Summer 1991, 28.
2. Marion E. Haynes, *Stepping up to Supervisor* (Los Altos, CA: Crisp, 1990), 84.
3. Randi Toler Sachs, *Productive Performance Appraisals* (New York: AMACOM, 1992), 5.
4. Ibid., 43.
5. Alfred W. Travers, *Supervision, Techniques and New Dimensions* (Englewood Cliffs, NJ: Prentice-Hall, 1993), 181.

CHAPTER 17
WORK ENVIRONMENT

OUTLINE

- ❖ Introduction
- ❖ Job satisfaction
- ❖ Frustration
- ❖ Complaints
- ❖ Safe work environment
- ❖ Health and wellness
- ❖ Conclusions
- ❖ Summary
- ❖ Discussion questions
- ❖ Notes

OBJECTIVES

When you complete this chapter, you should be able to:

1. Identify the issues that contribute to team member frustration
2. Describe steps to deal effectively with team member complaints
3. Define the connections between motivation and job satisfaction
4. Outline the basic steps in health, safety, and accident prevention in the kitchen

5. State the advantages and disadvantages of counseling and know when to intervene or refer team members for outside help
6. Identify the benefits of employee assistance programs and their effects on team member wellness

Case Study: TEXAS MOON RESTAURANT

The Texas Moon Restaurant is considered by most employees to be an excellent place to work. Competition for open positions at the restaurant is fierce. The Texas Moon has extremely stringent selection criteria for all positions, but its reputation as one of the best places to work ensures that it always has a large pool of applicants for any opening. It is considered to be the finest restaurant in the state.

The Texas Moon has sixty-five staff members and ten managers, including the executive chef and two sous chefs. All Texas Moon employees are full-time. The Texas Moon is open 365 days per year, seven days per week. Staff works a five- or six-day week for a total of forty hours, and managers work a six-day week for a total of forty-eight hours. Employees receive health benefits after six months with the restaurant. The health benefits are subsidized by the restaurant at the rate of 50 percent for both single and family policies. Staff members receive one week of paid vacation per year after one year of service and two weeks of paid vacation per year after five years of service. Managers receive a two-week paid vacation per year after one year of service and a three-week paid vacation per year after five years of service. Additionally, managers receive two personal holidays per year. Employees also earn sick leave at the rate of one-half day per month after one year of service.

The Texas Moon management believes that outstanding performance should be recognized and rewarded. Employees earn performance recognition points toward in-volvement in an annual cuisine and culture trip and for other performance recognition rewards such as tickets to local attractions and movie tickets that are awarded annually. Last year's trip was to Mexico, and the six staff members and five managers who went on the trip became a developmental team for new menu items for the next year. Performance recognition points are awarded by managers and department heads for outstanding performance based on criteria developed by each department head. Managers are automatically included in a trip every other year. Managers do not participate in the other performance recognition awards. Managers receive a cash bonus if financial targets are achieved.

The Texas Moon has an established method for the scheduling of vacation days. The minimum vacation time that can be used at one time is one week, and the maximum is two weeks. Vacation scheduling is managed within each department. The calendar clearly shows the number of employees who may be on vacation at the same time during each week of the year. Texas Moon treats holidays such as Christmas, Thanksgiving, Rosh Hashanah, and July 4 the same as any other day in the year.

The Culinary Department has always based vacation scheduling on seniority. Beginning the first week in September, a vacation calendar is circulated in each department according to seniority. The Texas Moon Restaurant has fourteen full-time line and prep cooks. Three of the line cooks and two of the prep cooks have been with the restaurant for more than seven years each. For the past three years, the three line cooks and two prep cooks with the most seniority have selected vacation dates that included the major holidays. The other line and prep cooks have no opportunity to select holiday dates as part of their vacation dates, and resentment has steadily grown in the past few years over the scheduling of vacations.

John, a line cook, has been with Texas Moon for eighteen months. John was recognized for his outstanding performance and was one of the six staff members selected to travel to Costa Rica this year.

John mentioned the vacation scheduling to Tracey, one of the five managers, during the trip to Costa Rica. He stated that he was thinking about leaving the Texas Moon because he considered the scheduling of vacations in the Culinary Department to be unfair and inequitable. He also indicated that there were other team members in the Culinary Department looking for positions with other restaurants because of the vacation scheduling for the department.

Tracey asked each of the other five staff members on the trip, one from the Culinary Department, two from the Guest Service Department, and two from the Sales Department, how they felt about the scheduling of vacations in their department. All of the staff members indicated that seniority was the basis for scheduling, and they felt it created inequities and discontent. All of the staff members stated that they felt the system was designed to reward longevity, not performance.

Tracey organized an open discussion of the issue with the other four managers and all of the staff members during the trip. The five managers returned from the trip convinced that the general manager (who was not present on the trip) needed to address the issue of vacation scheduling to avoid the loss of valuable staff members.

Based on what you have learned from previous chapters and the content of this chapter, answer the following questions.

- What is the overall reason for the challenges at the Texas Moon Restaurant?
- What are the primary causal agents for the challenges at the Texas Moon Restaurant?
- What specific steps could have been taken to avoid the current situation at the Texas Moon Restaurant?
- What, specifically, can be done to overcome the challenges and generate motion in a positive direction for the Texas Moon Restaurant?

INTRODUCTION

The performance of team members is affected by many factors, and some of the most important and most often abused of those that relate to the work environment. The nature of the work environment, positive versus negative, has a major impact on team member performance. A positive work environment generates a more positive attitude among team members and leads to higher levels of quality.

An atmosphere of positivism can only be achieved when the foundation has been established to support that type of atmosphere. A foundation for team member positivism includes preparation by the chef supervisor for conflict resolution. The goal in a positive work environment is to not have conflict between team members or team members and management. The reality is that there will always be some conflict, and the maintenance of the positive environment requires quick and effective conflict resolution. Also key to a positive environment is the physical work environment. Employers are mandated to by the Occupational Safety and Health Act (OSHA) to provide a safe work environment. The company, and the chef supervisor as the representative of the company, are responsible for meeting the requirements of the law, and this does contribute to a positive work environment. However, the greatest contribution to a positive work environment will come not from just doing what the law requires, but from sincerely caring about the safety of team members. The other foundational piece for a positive work environment is employee wellness. *Safety* addresses the physical safety of the team member. *Employee wellness* addresses both the psychological and the physical well-being of the team member.

A well-laid foundation combined with a clearly delivered message of concern for the well-being of the employee will help to minimize team member frustration and achieve higher levels of team member job satisfaction. The goal of the chef supervisor should be to create and maintain a positive work environment. The result of pursuing this goal will be quality team member performance and high levels of guest satisfaction.

JOB SATISFACTION

Like motivation, job satisfaction means different things to different people. At its highest level, it is the kitchen team member who derives happiness from the knowledge that the foodservice customer had an outstanding dining experience. Generally, the satisfaction that individuals receive depends on the extent to which the job and everything associated with it meets their needs and wants.

- "Wants" are items that individuals feel will deliver satisfaction. Wants are perceived differently within the team, based on differences in age, educational level, sex, health, family relationships, personality, and other factors. They are very often of an intrinsic nature.
- Typically, "needs" represent tangible rewards such as pay and benefits.

Job satisfaction has been shown to be closely linked to turnover and absenteeism. The higher an individual's satisfaction, the less likely it is that he or she will leave the organization. According to *People Report* in November 2006, the average annual turnover rate for hourly employees in the restaurant industry was 107 percent.[1] This represents an unacceptable level by any measurements. The link between turnover and satisfaction in the foodservice industry indicates that many employees are unhappy. Is it pay or working conditions? Maintaining quality in all aspects in the kitchen requires a team that is stable and satisfied. Replacing a kitchen team member is time-consuming and expensive. Replacement has a direct effect on product quality delivered to the guest because of the ramp-up time required for a new team member to achieve 100 percent mastery of processes and procedures. It is far better and more cost-effective to invest in current team members rather than constantly hiring and training new people.

Replacement costs cover three areas: separation costs for the departing employee, recruiting and hiring a replacement, and the time and training costs of the new hire. Total replacement costs are two to three times the monthly salary of the departing team member.

The intangibles of a dissatisfied kitchen team member are potentially more costly. This includes the effect on morale within the team and its impact on customer satisfaction, and the missed opportunities to utilize the team member's talent and potential to grow.

Job satisfaction is affected by all of the elements discussed in this chapter. Chef supervisors should invest in the kitchen team through excellent supervisory skills and by providing conditions in the kitchen that provide the basis for job satisfaction. Mentally challenging work with which each individual can cope successfully is of primary importance. Ideally, each member should love food and have a strong sense of culinary professionalism. The atmosphere in the kitchen should be open and nonthreatening, led by a firm but friendly supervisor who seeks input and support from the team and in which each team member is valued. Satisfaction is not about winning popularity contests; rather, it is about creating a team and an environment in which the individual is respected. Most studies of job satisfaction conclude that a link exists between satisfaction and performance. The role the chef supervisor plays in this link is crucial.

FRUSTRATION

If the working day of a kitchen team member is examined, it will usually be obvious that all needs are *not* being satisfied fully. Team members may be prevented from reaching a particular goal or objective, or there may be conflicting goals. Either condition will produce a state of dissatisfaction and tension that may prevent a harmonious team spirit in the kitchen. Chef supervisors should understand the forces and factors that contribute to tension and dissatisfaction. Barriers to achieving individual goals produce a frustrating condition. Some typical sources of frustration are listed in Figure 17-1.

A frustrated individual may respond by engaging in disruptive behavior. The distance between frustration and aggression is a short one. Aggression typically involves verbal or physical attacks against the person or persons perceived to be the cause of the frustration. Chef supervisors have a responsibility to be sensitive to warning signs in this area. Not all sources of frustration are under the direct control of the supervisor. However, an awareness of potential areas of frustration and a sincere effort to handle them effectively through better organization, planning, and communication can help to remove many of the conditions that cause frustration.

When individuals sense that they are in danger, they may experience a feeling of anxiety. In contrast to fear, anxiety results when the source of danger cannot be identified. The physical symptoms of anxiety are similar to those associated with

FIGURE 17-1 Typical sources of frustration.

- Hostile chef supervisors
- Monotonous tasks
- Unpleasant working conditions
- Economic insecurity
- Unfair work assignments
- Abuse of established working procedures
- Lack of orientation training
- Being ignored

fear: nausea, trembling, a pounding heart, and dryness in the throat. This anxiety is a form of stress that is emotionally and physically harmful. Anxiety may account for various kitchen team members' behaviors that are often misunderstood or misinterpreted, particularly in individuals of different backgrounds and cultures. Anxiety is also frequently caused by the prospect of change. This activity can often be misinterpreted by supervisors as team members being difficult rather than simply anxious or frightened.

COMPLAINTS

Complaints are an indication of discontent among the kitchen team. The chef supervisor is the key to addressing complaints before they develop into something they are not and become even more difficult to resolve. Speedy resolution of grievances and complaints is part of a positive, well-led kitchen work environment. Wise handling of complaints affords the greatest opportunity to win kitchen team members' respect and to gain their confidence.

Most interpersonal conflicts in the foodservice industry have been between dining room and kitchen team members. A traditional animosity has always existed between these two groups. Chefs view themselves as the skills-oriented aristocrats of the foodservice organization. Service personnel are viewed by chefs as the lesser participants in the big scheme of things. Ironically, and this may come as a big surprise to many chefs, dining room team members also view themselves as aristocrats and the most important people in the organization. They have similarly low opinions of chefs. Of course, although both positions are ridiculous, they are a great source of conflict. Departments that conflict or fail to focus on the objective of customer satisfaction will doom the entire foodservice organization to failure. Every member of the organization must be a committed team player totally focused on continuous improvements that facilitate the provision of high-quality food and service; the two are inextricably intertwined.

Complaints from team members concerning other team members come to the forefront very quickly. Most people don't hesitate to complain about each other. It is a normal human phenomenon. Complaints about other people can be presented in a highly emotional way or in a cool, calculating manner. But usually this is done with a great deal of emotion, which colors the facts involved. This can make it difficult to determine the real problem as opposed to the symptoms.

In every case, the issue should be dealt with as soon as possible. The longer the complaint remains unresolved, the more other people get involved and the more the quality of the work will be affected. The quality of work has an immediate impact on customer satisfaction. If the chef supervisor has difficulty resolving the complaint, then it is appropriate to seek further help from senior management. The main point is that there should be some avenue by which the complaining kitchen team member can obtain a full and fair hearing, particularly if he or she is dissatisfied with the decision of the chef supervisor.

The "ideal" resolution of complaints avoids a "one loses and one wins" scenario and leads to a "win–win" scenario. A win–win scenario is achieved through participation by the team member with the chef supervisor in resolving the issue. One of the most useful approaches is the application of a systematic approach to resolving complaints as shown in Figure 17-2.

FIGURE 17-2 Systematic approach to resolving complaints.

The following steps can lead to a satisfactory investigation and resolution of the complaint:

1. Check the team member's record in detail. Look for evidence of tardiness or absenteeism. Get the facts. Perhaps there are hidden reasons for seeking attention by complaining.
2. Attempt to understand why the team member has made the complaint and what his or her feelings are. Allow the individual to "vent." Let him or her communicate freely and without interruption. Watch for body language and observe facial expressions.
3. When other persons are involved, check for accuracy of information.
4. Avoid an argumentative disposition when hearing the complaint.
5. Keep senior management informed.
6. Admit a supervisory mistake. Do not try to conceal it if you have caused the complaint.
7. Record the formal complaint; do not depend on memory. Be specific; include day, date, time, place, those involved, the type of complaint, and any other relevant facts.
8. Prepare a written statement that includes the resulting decision and the rationale for this decision.
9. Establish facts and a definition of the complaint with the team member. Seek solutions, exhausting all avenues. Finally, bring the resolution to a mutually agreeable set of terms that includes steps for avoiding future problems in the area of the complaint.

Complaints are sometimes used by kitchen team members to gain attention and to send messages regarding unfair wage scales, poor working conditions, and discriminatory actions against team members based on ethnic origin, gender, or sexual preference. The individual making the complaint is entitled to a fair hearing. Complaints that are not handled promptly and decisively can lead to problems of arbitration with labor unions. By bringing the complaint or problem to a win–win resolution, the chef supervisor is dealing with the immediate problem. However, win–win solutions can involve a promise to resolve the complaint through higher authority. What is important in dealing with complaints is that the chef supervisor recognizes that the old-style Theory X-type supervisor is replaced with a Theory Y type, which in some instances represents a major shift in attitude for the chef supervisor. It replaces the notion that complaining kitchen team members are adversaries and instead focuses on solutions, assuming that both parties are aiming for the same goals. The win–win approach is consistent with an environment that encourages continuous improvement of product and service. In the foodservice industry, positive, motivated, happy team members are critical to success.

SAFE WORK ENVIRONMENT

Foodservice employers are required by law to provide working conditions that do not impair the safety or health of kitchen employees or indeed any other unit or department member. Therefore, employers must provide an environment that protects employees from physical hazards, unhealthy conditions, and unsafe or dangerous practices by other kitchen team members. Effective health and safety practices promote a positive work climate in the kitchen by providing for the physical and emotional well-being of all team members as well as enhancing their economic security.

Safety hazards in the foodservice industry range from the use of knives and power-driven equipment to slippery floors and chemical cleaning materials. These hazards can produce accidents resulting in individuals falling, cutting themselves, burning themselves, receiving an electric shock, scalding themselves, or worse. These accidents occur because of ignorance of safety procedures and carelessness.

In the late 1960s, Congress became increasingly concerned that each year job-related accidents accounted for more than 14,000 deaths and nearly 2.5 million disabilities.[2] Eventually, these concerns led to the passage of the Occupational Safety and Health Act (OSHA) in 1970. The act was designed to "assure so far as possible every working man and woman in the nation safe and healthful working conditions and to preserve our human resources." It established the Occupational Safety and Health Administration (also called OSHA) to carry out its mandate. One of the responsibilities of OSHA is to develop and enforce mandatory job safety and health standards. These standards cover workplace issues of machinery and equipment, materials, power sources, processing, protective clothing, first aid, and administrative requirements. OSHA also requires that supervisors train and inform employees of any known safety hazard in the kitchen. The Hazard Communication Standard (HCS) requires employers to inform employees as to what chemicals they are working with and to detail their risks and what can be done to limit these risks. The HCS is achieved through training programs and detailed labeling on or near chemical containers. Material Safety Data Sheets (MSDS) are part of this standard. A system of priorities for workplace inspections (which includes kitchens) has been established by OSHA:

- Inspection of imminent danger situations
- Investigation of catastrophes, fatalities, and accidents resulting in hospitalization of five or more employees
- Investigation of valid employee complaints of alleged violation of standards or of unsafe or unhealthful working conditions
- Follow-up inspections to determine if previously cited violations have been corrected[3]

OSHA provides a free on-site consultation service that helps employers identify hazardous conditions and corrective measures. A minimum fine of $5000 is mandatory for intentional violations, with a maximum fine of $70,000 for intentional or repeat violations. A maximum fine of $7000 applies for all other violations, including failure by an employer to post the required OSHA notice.[4]

One of the best methods for identifying potential hazards in the kitchen is simply to consult the team. Have them develop a list of accident-prevention measures. They see hazards in and around the kitchen every day.

Chef supervisors may unintentionally reinforce unsafe acts by not correcting them when they are first observed. Through mandatory and proper supervision, unsafe work practices can be corrected. The nature of food production requires that many items of equipment be sharp or hot. The most common types of kitchen accident injuries are related directly to these two areas, as well as to the presence of wet or greasy floors and the element of human error. The most common types of injuries and their causes in the kitchen include the following.

- *Lacerations.* These are caused by improper use of chef's knives, slicers, choppers, broken ware, or glass.

- *Power-driven equipment.* When used improperly, blenders, mixers, slicers, grinders, or buffalo choppers can cause accidents. The chef supervisor is responsible for ensuring that each kitchen team member is fully trained in the safe use of all power-driven equipment.
- *Glass and dishware.* Glasses, bowls, cups, and plates are sources of injury. Broken glass in dishwashers or sinks causes accidents. Glasses and dishes should be stored separately to avoid crushing.
- *Burns.* Common injuries in the kitchen, burns and scalds of varying degree can result from contact with the hot surfaces of grills, ovens, stove burners, steam tables, fryers, and any other heating equipment that might be in use.[5]
- *Slips and falls.* Falls in the kitchen are typically caused by wet or greasy floors left unattended. The danger from greasy or wet floors is compounded by team members rushing about during busy periods. The kitchen team should be made aware by the supervisor of the necessity to keep floor surfaces safe. Kitchen team members should wear shoes with rubber soles or ones made from Neoprene to prevent slipping. Leather-soled shoes should never be worn in the kitchen. Safety shoes that have strong uppers without openings should be worn, as these help prevent cuts or crushing injuries.
- *Fires.* Because most kitchens usually have open flames of some type, potential fire hazards are obvious. More fires occur in foodservice establishments than in any other type of business operation. Chef supervisors should check these potential fire hazards regularly. Special fire-protection equipment should be provided in all areas where fires are likely to occur. These include hoods, grills, deep fryers, ovens, and stove tops. Direction in the use of fire extinguishers and evacuation procedures for guests and employees should be part of every new kitchen member's induction and orientation training.

Because training alone will not assure continual adherence to safety, chef supervisors should observe team members at work and show approval for safe work practices. When unsafe actions are observed, immediate corrective action should be taken.

Make work interesting. Fatigue and stress can contribute to the cause of accidents. Simple changes can often be made in the kitchen to make tasks more meaningful.

Establish a safety committee composed of kitchen team members and other dependent department supervisors and managers. The safety committee provides a means of getting team members involved directly in the operation of the safety program. The duties of the committee include inspecting, observing work practices, investigating accidents, and making recommendations. The committee should meet regularly, at least once a month, and attendance should be mandatory. Additional ways to promote safety are shown in Figure 17-3.

FIGURE 17-3 Methods for promoting safety.

- Publish safety statistics. Monthly accident reports should be posted. Ideas and suggestions should be solicited as to how these accidents can be avoided.
- Use bulletin boards and menu wall display areas throughout the kitchen to display posters, pictures, sketches, and cartoons depicting safety situations.
- Set high expectations for safety. Encourage the kitchen team to recognize positive safety actions and acknowledge those who contribute to safety improvements.

HEALTH AND WELLNESS

PHYSICAL HEALTH

Until the last two decades, safety and accident prevention received far more attention than did employee health. However, this has changed. Statistics show that occupational diseases may cost industry as much as or more than occupational accidents.[6] Many foodservice organizations now not only have attempted to remove health hazards from the workplace, but also have initiated programs to improve employee health. Some employers offer preventive health programs. These programs provide routine medical services such as flu vaccinations at a reduced charge or no charge.

STRESS

Stress comes from two basic sources: physical activity and mental or emotional activity. The physical reaction of the body to both is the same. The kitchen can be a stressful environment, particularly during busy service periods. However, not all stress is harmful. Positive stress is a feeling of exhilaration and achievement. This can be associated with a successful busy service period during which everything went well in the kitchen. Team members performed well as a group, record numbers were served, and 100 percent customer satisfaction was achieved. On the other hand, negative stress may cause people to become ill. Some of the causes of negative stress are shown in Figure 17-4.

Arguments with supervisors or fellow team members are a common cause of stress. Feeling trapped in a job to which a person is ill-suited can be equally painful. Other strains include lack of communication on the job and lack of recognition for a job well done. Stress has been linked to many things. It manifests itself in several ways: increased absenteeism, job turnover, lower productivity, and mistakes on the job. Stress-related disorders include tension, high blood pressure, muscle tightness

FIGURE 17-4 Causes of negative stress.

- Conflicting expectations between chef supervisor and team member
- Uncertainty over team member's expected contribution to the team effort
- An unpleasant kitchen environment
- Poor preparation for the job
- Threats and hostility
- Performance evaluations
- Lack of social interaction
- High noise levels in the work environment
- Tasks that do not fully utilize team members' skills
- High temperature levels
- Long and irregular hours
- Personality conflicts
- Working during public holidays
- Group pressures
- Insensitive supervision

in the chest, ulcers, and others requiring medical attention. Burnout is considered to be the most severe form of stress. Career burnout usually occurs when work is no longer meaningful to the individual team member. The factors that cause burnout are those that cause stress; in fact, burnout and stress have been viewed as intercon-nected issues.

COUNSELING

Counseling is used by kitchen team builders to ensure good relations and to generate a team spirit. Team members may have problems of a personal nature that demand the chef supervisor's attention. These problems may or may not be job-related. Changes in an individual's behavior, such as excessive absenteeism, tardiness, hostility, moodiness, withdrawal, and a decline in job performance, should be monitored. Good coaches in-teract with their team on a constant basis and are usually in the best position to iden-tify and observe these changes.

There are advantages and disadvantages to the chef supervisor assuming the role of counselor. The primary advantage is that the chef supervisior has the opportunity to become well acquainted with the individual. He or she can learn the team member's pattern of judging, valuing, thinking, and understanding and can predict an individual team member's behavior. However, the disadvantage to assuming the role of coun-selor within the team is that the chef supervisor may not be adequately trained to deal with complex human problems. It is then advisable to refer the team member to a spe-cialist. Needless to say, the act of referring a team member for assistance requires con-siderable tact and skill.

Among emotional and personal crises, alcoholism and drug abuse are considered to be personal matters. They also become the chef supervisor's problem when they af-fect the team member's ability to perform satisfactorily in the workplace.

Typically in large organizations, employee assistance programs (EAPs) exist. These programs are in place to help employees overcome problems, and they provide guidance and referrals to outside professional help.

The most prevalent problems among individuals are personal crisis situations in-volving mental, family, financial, or legal matters. These are problems that may be brought to a chef supervisor's attention. Depending on the type or difficulty of the problem, in-house counseling or referral to an outside agency may be necessary.

Chef supervisors should be aware that the behavior of some team members might be adversely affected by some elements of the "physical" kitchen environment, which may necessitate reassigning, or rotating individuals to different sections of the kitchen.

It is estimated that one of every sixteen workers in the United States is affected by alcohol.[7] The result is lost work time, declining productivity, and increased absen-teeism. Alcohol abuse has been a problem for the hospitality industry in general and for kitchen employees in particular. Many theories for its prevalence have been put forward, from the notion that the accessibility of alcohol contributes to the problem to the idea that the hot kitchen environment encourages the use of alcohol.

The approach to handling alcoholism is to monitor all kitchen team members reg-ularly and systematically. Evidence of declining performance on the job should be carefully documented, so that the individual can be confronted with unequivocal proof that his or her work is suffering. Offers of help should be made available without any penalty to the individual. Mention of alcoholism should be avoided. The team member should be allowed to seek aid as for any other health problem.

Drug abuse among employees is one of the wider societal issues confronting industry. Although alcohol is the most commonly abused substance, marijuana, cocaine, heroin, crack, and varieties of abused prescription drugs are found in the foodservice industry. Various approaches are used to assist individuals with a dependency. They range from outpatient treatment for an extended period to inpatient treatment. A recent survey by the federal government estimated that one in every four Americans uses drugs, and that between 10 and 23 percent of Americans use drugs while on the job.

It has been estimated that substance abuse costs U.S. employers over $100 million annually. At any given time, approximately 25 percent of all employees in the workforce are troubled by a personal problem serious enough to affect job performance. Related accidents cost industry over $32 billion annually in disability programs, workers' compensation, lost productivity, and poor morale. Employees who use drugs claim disability five times more often, have four times as many accidents, and are sixteen times more likely to be absent from work.[8]

In recent years few workplace issues have received as much attention as acquired immune deficiency syndrome (AIDS). This is particularly important for the foodservice industry from the standpoint of transmission of the virus. There is no evidence that AIDS can be transmitted through casual contact or through food preparation. However, one of the major problems employers face is educating team members and customers on this issue. Because no cure or vaccine for AIDS presently exists, many foodservice organizations are turning to education as the most viable means of combating both the medical and social dilemmas posed by AIDS. Figure 17-5 shows the potential benefits of an AIDS education program for kitchen team members.

Employees who test HIV-positive are protected under the Americans with Disabilities Act (ADA). This act provides comprehensive civil rights protection to individuals with AIDS. It bans discrimination against people on the basis of their disability. Employers are prohibited from dismissing or transferring infected team members from food-handling duties simply because they have AIDS or have tested HIV-positive. In a 2001 lawsuit, *EEOC v. Marsh's Sun Fresh,* the court awarded $80,000 to the plaintiff. This suit was based on the unlawful termination of an HIV-positive employee.[9] Management has a responsibility to maintain the confidentiality of any employees who report they have AIDS or any other illness.

FIGURE 17-5   Benefits of an AIDS education program.

- Prevention of new infections among individuals by helping everyone understand how human immunodeficiency virus (HIV) is and is not transmitted (HIV is the first stage of AIDS).
- Alerting managers and chef supervisors to the legal issues raised by HIV infection in the workplace.
- Helping to prevent discrimination by fearful or misinformed employees, which can decimate productivity. Through education, the same employees are equally capable of creating a humane, supportive, and therefore healthy working environment.
- Raising morale through AIDS education training

Unfortunately, all indicators are that the AIDS epidemic will continue to spread. It is important for chef supervisors to understand that these issues are present among the kitchen team. It is also important for chef supervisors to recognize their limitations as counselors. However, through their roles as coaches and educators, much can be done to make it known that help is available.

WELLNESS PROGRAMS

Wellness programs are becoming a common feature in foodservice organizations. Although these types of programs have long existed in other industries, they are relatively new to the foodservice sector. Essentially, wellness programs are designed to prevent illness and enhance the well-being of each individual. They include periodic medical exams, stop-smoking clinics, improved dietary practices, weight control, exercise and fitness, stress management, immunizations, and cardiopulmonary resuscitation (CPR) training. Documented results from these types of programs have shown a reduction in employee sick days and lower major medical costs. It is expected that as health care costs continue to increase, wellness programs will grow.

CONCLUSIONS

Supervising people in what can at times be an unpleasant environment at a busy service time (hot, noisy, steamy, and stressful) requires a great deal of skill. In addition to knowing how to cook and understanding the principles of heat transfer, the chef who can also build a team and tap into their collective culinary resources will succeed. There are no good reasons why kitchens should be unpleasant places, even during busy service. Poor physical working conditions can be overcome.

BOX 17-1

CHEF TALK:
HOSTILE ENVIRONMENT

There was a time when chefs believed it necessary to act out the often-portrayed image of the crazy, unreasonable, temperamental chef. This disposition often manifested itself in undesirable traits such as shouting, throwing things around the kitchen, and arguing loudly with waiters, other chefs, and managers. The kitchen area was a hostile domain. These old-style chefs were not approachable; they were aloof and generally indifferent to employees. I particularly remember, as an apprentice chef, that I "knew my place." As a lowly trainee I was not expected to converse with those higher than me. In fact, open communication was not the order of the day. The pecking order was through the supervisory layers: chef, chef de partie, sous chef, and finally, the head chef. Heaven forbid if you had to ask for time off within your scheduled time. I came to work scared and left scared for the first year of my apprenticeship. Back then, the head chef practically had the power of life or death over each member of the kitchen staff. I believe that if the work climate in the kitchen had been different then, more conducive to communication, I would have learned a lot more and probably could have contributed a lot more to the operational goals. That head chef was eventually dismissed, and the day he left the kitchen staff had a party.

Noel C. Cullen,
Ed.D., CMC, AAC

Considering the team member in a holistic way, with all that entails, is now considered to be a worthwhile investment. Needless to say, when frustration on the job is dealt with effectively and a safe and healthy work environment exists in the kitchen, job satisfaction is possible. What is more difficult to overcome is the breaking of the stereotypical animated image of temperamental chefs. The modern chef, as the literal translation of the word means, is a leader as well as a first-class culinarian.

Summary

Most conflicts in the foodservice industry are interpersonal, between kitchen team members and other departments.

Frustration is a common contributor to conflicts, complaints, and grievances. Most frustration is caused by hostility, unpleasant working conditions, lack of training, insecurity, and being ignored on the job.

Complaints in the kitchen should be dealt with as soon as possible after they are made. The longer the complaint remains unresolved, the more other people get involved. Work quality suffers immediately, which impacts on customer satisfaction. The ideal resolution of complaints is a situation in which all feel they have "won."

Job satisfaction has been shown to be linked to turnover and absenteeism. The greater the individual's job satisfaction level, the more productive he or she becomes. Job satisfaction revolves around the creation of a team environment in which each person is valued and respected.

Chef supervisors have a responsibility to ensure that a safe work environment exists, a place free from physical hazards, unhealthy conditions, and unsafe or dangerous practices. Effective health and safety practices promote a positive work climate.

Chef supervisors should be aware of the counseling role they may be asked to play with regard to team members' personal problems. They should know their limitations in this area and know how and when to seek professional help.

As with all other considerations for a safe kitchen environment, stress and stressful situations must be recognized and avoided.

Discussion Questions

1. How does team member frustration affect total quality management? How can these elements of frustration be removed from the kitchen?
2. What are the steps a chef supervisor should follow in dealing with team member complaints?
3. What does the term *win–win* mean?
4. What are the differences between "needs" and "wants" in terms of job satisfaction?
5. What, if any, are the links between job satisfaction and team member turnover?
6. What propelled the passing of the Occupational Safety and Health Act in 1970?
7. What are the advantages and disadvantages of chef supervisors engaging in counseling?
8. What elements contribute to stress in the kitchen?
9. Wellness programs in the kitchen can contribute to reducing costs. How?
10. What can be done to reduce interpersonal conflicts in the kitchen?

Notes

1. Dina Berta, *Nation's Restaurant News—HR & Services,* "People Report: Worker Turnover Rate Continues to Climb," November 2006, www.peoplereport.com/newsclippings/200611_NRN_PostConferenceCoverage.pdf.

2. Arthur Sherman, George Bohlander, and Herbert Crudden, *Managing Human Resources,* 8th ed. (Cincinnati: South-Western, 1988), 576.

3. Jack E. Miller, Mary Porter, and Karen Eich Drummond, *Supervision in the Hospitality Industry,* 2nd ed. (New York: John Wiley, 1992), 98.

4. *Applied Foodservice Sanitation,* 4th ed. (East Lansing, MI: Educational Foundation of the National Restaurant Association, 1992), 258.

5. Ibid., 259.

6. Lloyd L. Bryars and Leslie W. Rue, *Human Resources Management,* 4th ed. (Boston: Irwin, 1994), 499.

7. Sherman et al., *Managing Human Resources,* 592.

8. Joseph L. Picogna, *Total Quality Leadership: A Training Approach,* (Morrissville, PA: International Information Associates Inc., 1993), 312.

9. National Restaurant Association, *Legal Monitor: Grocer Settles HIV-Discrimination Lawsuit with EEOC for $80,000,* www.restaurant.org/legal/lm/lm2001_06.cfm, 2001.

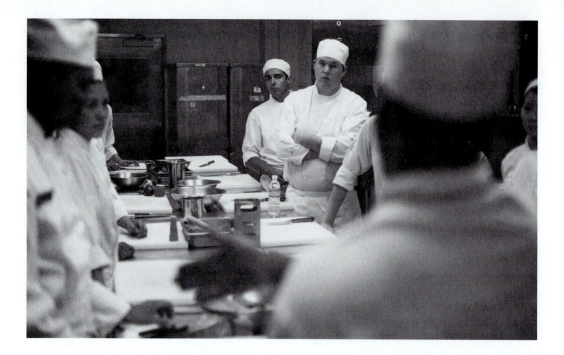

CHAPTER 18
DISCIPLINE AND THE KITCHEN TEAM

OUTLINE

- ❖ Introduction
- ❖ The chef supervisor's role
- ❖ Approaches to discipline
- ❖ Administering discipline
- ❖ Approaches to positive discipline
- ❖ Exit interviews
- ❖ Summary
- ❖ Discussion questions
- ❖ Notes

OBJECTIVES

When you complete this chapter, you should be able to:

1. Define discipline in its broader sense as it applies to the role of the chef supervisor
2. Describe the discipline parameters in which the chef supervisor operates relative to unions and the Equal Employment Opportunities Commission
3. Outline the steps in the progressive approach to discipline

4. State the guidelines for administering discipline in a fair and equitable way
5. Distinguish between positive and negative approaches to discipline
6. Define the strategies and rationale for conducting exit interviews.

✍

Case Study: STONE LION HOTEL AND CONFERENCE CENTER

Bruce Connors joined the management team at the Stone Lion Hotel and Conference Center three months ago as executive chef. Jesse Atwood is the executive sous chef. Jesse has been working at Stone Lion for six years, working his way up from dishwasher. Chef Connors believes in empowering his staff. He believes in delegating duties and authority. He does not believe in micromanaging his staff once he has delegated responsibilities to them. One of Chef Connors first actions as executive chef was to delegate the authority to hire and fire personnel to the executive sous chef, Jesse. His belief was that as executive sous chef, Jesse had a better understanding of the performance of the staff and could make more considered judgments regarding their performance.

Today the Stone Lion human resource officer (HRO) informed Chef Connors that the number of dismissals and new hires in the kitchen has been consistently increasing over the past two months. Additionally, one of the employees recently dismissed has filed a wrongful dismissal charge with the Labor Board. In preparation for responding to the charge the HRO met with Jesse. The HRO asked Jesse why he had fired the individual in question. Jesse stated, "The guy's work was sloppy and he was slow." The HRO asked to see the documentation of the employee's performance and Jesse stated, "The guy was not in the new position long enough to document anything. I needed to get rid of him, so I got rid of him."

The HRO informed Chef Connors that the employee had been with the Stone Lion for three years with a previous history of performance problems. The employee had been placed in the new position by the executive sous chef two weeks before he was dismissed. The HRO stated that it was clear that the Stone Lion could not defend the dismissal. Either the former employee would be reinstated or a settlement amount would be negotiated to avoid further "fallout." The HRO also indicated that after speaking with the executive sous chef, it was clear this was not the only incidence of improper dismissal. Chef Connors assured the HRO that he would meet immediately with Jesse and "straighten things out."

Based on what you have learned from previous chapters and the content of this chapter, answer the following questions.

- What is the overall reason for the situation that has arisen at the Stone Lion Hotel and Conference Center?
- What are the primary causal agents for the situation that has arisen at the Stone Lion Hotel and Conference Center?
- What role did leadership and supervision/management play in the situation that has arisen at the Stone Lion Hotel and Conference Center?
- What specific steps could have been taken to avoid the situation that has arisen at the Stone Lion Hotel and Conference Center?
- What, specifically, can be done to avoid a repetition of the situation that has arisen at the Stone Lion Hotel and Conference Center?

INTRODUCTION

Occasionally, a team member will do something that requires disciplinary action by the chef supervisor. It may be an issue of job performance; too many absences; outright violation of an order, rule, or procedure; or some illegal act such as stealing, fighting, gambling, or involvement with illegal drugs.

The words *discipline* and *disciple* share the same root, which means to "mold" or "teach." True discipline should teach a correct action. Yet many chef supervisors think of discipline merely as punishment or reprimanding a team member for a mistake. The word *disciple* literally means follower. Therefore, good discipline is based on leadership, which includes the ability to guide, coach, correct, and affirm the actions of others. Discipline is an inner force that develops within each team member and causes him or her to want to follow high standards in life and the workplace. Effective discipline is not just about reprimanding or inflicting penalties. True discipline involves an entire program that teaches and guides individuals to become loyal, motivated, responsible team players.

Discipline in a broader sense concerns the process of socialization. Team members are given the quality values and rules necessary for survival and growth of the foodservice organization. This process is complete when the team member comes to accept those values and rules as legitimate. Within the kitchen team, the rules serve a purpose, and each member benefits by obeying.

Application of discipline has come to be split into two distinct areas. On the one hand is the traditional notion of discipline as punishment and on the other hand is the positive discipline approach. *Positive discipline* is about exploring other ways to obtain compliance with the rules. It is about reversing the concept of discipline as punishment only and placing emphasis on development along with encouraging responsibility and self-directed behavior. It is an extension of the training and coaching process.

THE CHEF SUPERVISOR'S ROLE

No chef supervisor enjoys the act of disciplining a team member, but this is an unavoidable part of the job. The kitchen may be running smoothly, with each team member doing his or her job well. Then a team member is careless, an accident occurs, and the chef supervisor must take corrective action. Good leadership ability minimizes the need to be punitive. If the team members respect the chef supervisor, then it is likely that there will be a good team atmosphere and it will be easier to head off problems. Kitchen team members who feel their chef supervisor is interested in their welfare will not be disruptive.

The vast majority of team members accept rules and directions as a condition of employment and generally do not set out to break rules. These same team members will observe how the chef supervisor reacts with members who get out of line. Each individual is concerned with getting fair treatment. Morale within the team is lowered when it is observed that some individuals get away with violating rules or if team members witness unduly harsh discipline.

Before any discipline actions are contemplated, the ground rules for performance and conduct should be clearly communicated to the team. This set of policies and procedures is part of the induction and orientation programs. (These were detailed in Chapter 15 on induction and orientation training.) However, just because they were included, it is unwise to assume they have been read and are understood. Some rules need constant reiteration. These rules concern issues of safety and sanitation and should be policed constantly. Team members must know from the outset what the penalties are for any rule infraction in this area. This information should not be in the form of threats and warnings. They should be stated clearly and succinctly: "Knowing the consequences has its own security: people know where the boss stands, and they know what will happen if they go beyond the limits."[1] The reasons for a particular rule should always be explained. Acceptance of a rule is heightened when team members understand the reason for it. Rules and procedures should always be written, and the language used should be clear and unambiguous. If there has been lax enforcement of a rule, then the rule must be restated along with the consequences of its violation before disciplinary action can begin. Although an individual must be advised in advance of all rules and their violation, some conduct can be reasonably expected to be generally known as unacceptable.

APPROACHES TO DISCIPLINE

Discipline should not only be fair and consistent but also conform to legal requirements. Despite worker protection laws, the Equal Employment Opportunity Commission (EEOC) reports that a high percentage of all charges filed are for discriminatory dismissals.[2]

Chef supervisors who operate in a union environment have to take extra care when disciplining team members. Binding labor contracts set forth rules and procedures that must be followed, and they set penalties on management and workers for failing to abide by the rules. Even minor deviations from labor contract procedure can overturn an otherwise justified disciplinary action. With these contracts there is usually a provision for impartial review or an arbitration process. Additionally, in union-organized establishments, workers often have an increased awareness of their rights that may cause individuals to challenge the chef supervisor's disciplinary decisions. This does not mean that any form of discipline is impossible under union contracts. On the contrary, it may be easier. The nature of collective bargaining requires both union and management to be rigid and specific regarding rules and procedures.

DISCIPLINE AND THE HOT STOVE RULE

A hot stove with its radiating heat gives a *warning* that it should not be touched. Team members who ignore the warning and touch the hot stove, like those who violate a rule, are assured of being burned. The hot stove burns immediately, and it burns each person who touches it in the same manner. Therefore, disciplinary policies should be administered quickly and impartially. Team members should be disciplined for what they have done, not because of who they are. The four principles of the hot stove rule are shown in Figure 18-1.

Generally, discipline is imposed in a progressive manner. By definition, *progressive discipline* is the application of corrective measures in increasing degrees. It should motivate team members to take corrective action on misconduct voluntarily. This progressive approach is aimed at nipping the problem in the bud by utilizing only enough corrective action to remedy the problem. The sequence and

FIGURE 18-1 The hot stove rule.

Principles
- An unpleasant experience
- Immediate action
- Consistent punishment
- Impartiality

severity of the disciplinary action varies with the type of offense and the circumstances surrounding the misconduct. Following is a typical sequence of progressive discipline.

Step 1 *Oral reprimand.* When a team member makes an immediate change in the way something is done or breaks a minor rule, an oral reprimand may be appropriate. In general, these reprimands should be made in private, away from other team members. The rule is to "discipline in private, praise in public." The chef supervisor should ensure that he or she makes clear and specific what should be stopped (or started). Remember, most people fear public embarrassment more than the discipline action itself. In the course of the reprimand, be firm and fair. Do not argue or debate side issues, but treat the individual with respect. There are times, however, when it is necessary to reprimand instantly, without first considering an individual team member's sensitivity. This concerns misconduct in the critical area of food sanitation and safety. Because of potential risks to public health, the chef supervisor should react immediately. When this happens, it is best to soften the reprimand as much as possible. The important point is to stop the team member from continuing the harmful action. As with all elements of discipline, actions requiring reprimands should always be documented.

Step 2 *Written reprimand.* For the second offense the team member receives a written reprimand. This typically informs the team member that his or her conduct is in violation of rules or procedures and that further violations will result in suspension or loss of pay. Additionally, this reprimand is placed in the team member's personnel file. Copies of this reprimand are also given to the union steward if this action is applicable. If the team member is probationary, the letter will usually indicate that improved performance is necessary. Probation is usually handled in writing so that a written record exists in the event that termination is necessary if the required improvement does not occur.

Step 3 *Suspension.* Violations of rules and minor illegal acts often are treated with a temporary layoff or suspension. This suspension is without pay and consistent with the seriousness of the offense. The details are written and given to the individual. This written communication indicates also that another violation will call for discharge.

Step 4 *Termination.* If after a third offense it appears that there is little chance of bringing the individual's performance up to an acceptable level, termination may be the best course of action. It is presumed that the team member has been given every opportunity to conform.

BOX 18-1

CHEF TALK:
USING THE CORRECT LANGUAGE

Working as an executive chef in a highly unionized hotel requires careful disciplinary strategies. Not least among them is knowing all the elements of the union/hotel contract and using appropriate language in the disciplinary process. I learned an important lesson on this subject when I dismissed a dishwasher.

Following a late-night banquet, I was summoned to the pot-wash area in the kitchen. There I met "Joe," a dishwasher who was employed as a night porter. His job was to wash and sanitize the kitchen pots, pans, and utensils and prepare the kitchen for the breakfast chef. When I came upon Joe he was staggering around the dish room, dripping wet. (He had fallen into the large pot sink and had been rescued by the manager, who had summoned me.) There was a strong smell of alcohol from him. I asked him what had happened. How had he fallen into the sink? In his response he was barely coherent, his eyes rolling; he could hardly stand upright. He was clearly in no condition to work. I informed him that the best thing was for him to go home and come to see me the following day. Joe arrived the next day, and I informed him that I was recommending his discharge. I felt comfortable with my decision. He had exhausted all previous disciplinary steps and had been warned verbally and in writing, with each warning appropriately documented.

However, I was not prepared for what was to follow. Within a week I was summoned to the general manager's office. There I found not only the manager but also Joe and his union representative. Following preliminary discussion to establish the sequence of events leading up to the disciplinary action, I was asked by the union official why I had dismissed Joe. At this stage I was feeling rather agitated by what I considered to be a waste of time, going over what I felt was an obvious open-and-shut termination action. I responded, "because Joe was drunk on duty."

The union official turned to me and asked me what credentials I possessed that enabled me to make such a judgment. "Was I a qualified medical doctor?" I was taken aback. Looking at the union official, I said, "You know what my credentials are!"

The end result of that meeting was that Joe had to be reinstated with full pay because I had accused him of being "drunk." What I should have said was, "his condition would lead any reasonable person to believe he was under the influence of alcohol." Joe's excuse to the union was that on that particular night he had taken medication for an ear infection, which gave him the appearance of being under the influence of alcohol.

Within six weeks Joe was again discovered on duty in a similar condition. This time I made sure I had a colleague with me to witness the situation. Joe was dismissed, but this time I used the correct language.

Noel Cullen, Ed.D., CMC, AAC
(1948–2002)

Some infractions are so serious that discharge is permitted with the first violation. Cases involving instant dismissal are rare. They usually involve illegal acts or serious conduct that threatens the safety and security of other individuals or the foodservice organization. Team members must be given an opportunity to improve, and specific reasons for discharge must be documented. This category also includes requested resignations. When it appears that a team member's interests are not being met by the foodservice organization, it may be appropriate to request him or her to seek employment elsewhere: "The decision to discharge an employee must be based on quality and quantity of evidence, not hearsay, personal prejudices, speculation, or rumors."[3] Some

FIGURE 18-2 Major violations justifying immediate dismissal.

- Possession of, drinking, smoking, or being under the influence of intoxicants or narcotics on the foodservice establishment's property
- False statements or misrepresentation of facts on employment application forms
- Sleeping on the job
- Stealing company or personal property
- Fighting on company property
- Issues that threaten the well-being of team members or guests
- Gross discourtesy to guests
- Gross negligence involving sanitation/safety
- Excessive absenteeism without prior notification
- Sexual harassment
- Refusing to follow reasonable job-related directives from the chef supervisor

of the major violations that frequently require dismissal are shown in Figure 18-2. Some of the violations requiring progressive discipline are shown in Figure 18-3. These violations are basic and are not intended to be all-inclusive or to cover every situation that may arise.

ADMINISTERING DISCIPLINE

Discipline should be administered as soon as possible after the infraction has taken place or has been noticed. For the discipline to be most effective, it must be taken immediately without involving emotional or irrational decisions. Notation of rule infractions in a team member's record does not constitute advance warning and is not sufficient to support disciplinary action. A team member must be advised of the infraction for it to be considered a warning. Noting that the team member was warned about the infraction and having him or her sign a form acknowledging the warning are both good practices. Failure to warn a team member of the consequences of continuous rule violation is one reason often cited for overturning a disciplinary action.

It must be recognized by the chef supervisor that each act of discipline is different and that each team member must be handled differently. The better the chef supervisor knows all team members and how they react, the better he or she can handle disciplinary actions. Sometimes other reactions are experienced. For example, rather than

FIGURE 18-3 Violations that may lead to progressive discipline.

- Tardiness
- Absence for one day without notifying supervisor
- Leaving the kitchen without permission
- Use of abusive language
- Not performing to set quality standards
- Disorderly conduct during working time
- Racial slurs
- Obscene or immoral conduct

being motivated to improve performance, a team member may be motivated to retaliate or "get even." The following guidelines will help ensure a positive reaction.

DISCIPLINE AND THE OFFENSE

Match the discipline to the offense. A trivial rule infraction does not require harsh or unreasonable discipline. A team member's previous record must be considered. Determining the appropriateness of the discipline action involves serious consideration of:

- The circumstances surrounding the incident
- The seriousness of the incident
- The previous record of the team member
- The disciplinary action taken in similar situations
- The existing rules and disciplinary policies
- The provisions in the labor contract (if applicable)

The chef supervisor must take the correct steps and stay calm to match the discipline and offense effectively.

Know the facts: Investigate thoroughly. Determine who was involved in the incident, what happened, where it happened, and what the team member's involvement was.

Interview: Discuss the discipline problem with the team member in private. Keep it as informal as possible in order to allow discussion to proceed calmly.

Listen: First ask the team member to tell his or her side of the story. Ask questions to get further details; try not to interrupt until the individual has finished. Listen with an open mind. Do not prejudge the situation.

Stay calm: Control feelings and emotions. Do not argue. Do not engage in any type of name calling. The chef supervisor may win the argument, but will lose the loyalty and contribution of an important team member.

Avoid entrapment: Do not set out to "get" a team member. Do not get involved unless something is wrong.

Be firm but fair: Being firm does not suggest getting tough. Being firm but fair involves explaining to a team member why behavior is unacceptable. Do not humiliate the team member in any way.

Document: Make notes on what happened and what the resulting action was. Records of disciplinary action are important for the purpose of demonstrating later that there was a fair and equitable resolution of the incident.

Inform others: Be sure to inform the team member of the intended course of action. Remember, the chef supervisor is not the final voice in matters of discipline. The foodservice organization and the union (if applicable) should be informed. Matters of serious discipline are much too important for one person.

It is always a good idea for the chef supervisor to discuss intended disciplinary actions with the foodservice establishment's management or with members of the human resources department. These are the people who have to support the chef supervisor's actions. It is also wise and prudent to discuss intended disciplinary action with a trusted colleague. This will help to establish a better perspective for the action.

FIGURE 18-4 Guidelines for reducing trauma associated with dismissal.

- Make the discussion private, brief, and businesslike.
- Be tactful, honest, and straightforward.
- Give any information regarding severance pay or other benefits.
- Outline the period the team member has before he or she must leave the organization.
- Avoid any personality differences between the chef supervisor and the team member.

TERMINATING A TEAM MEMBER

Before a decision is reached to terminate a team member, the following questions should be answered:

- Was the team member forewarned of the possible disciplinary consequences of his or her actions?
- Were the work requirements required of the individual reasonable in relation to the safe, orderly, and efficient conduct of the foodservice organization?
- Were all reasonable efforts expended to fully and fairly determine the facts?
- Was the team member given ample opportunity for improvement?
- Were all other options of disciplinary action considered?
- Was the team member afforded "due process" and a fair hearing?
- Are there any unusual or mitigating circumstances surrounding the case?
- Is this action discriminatory?

For most supervisors, dismissing a team member can be a painful experience. Often it gives supervisors a feeling that they have failed the individual in some way. The best way to think of termination of a team member is to consider it as an act of "unhiring." Regardless of the reasons for dismissal, it should be accomplished with consideration of the individual. Every effort should be made to ease the trauma a dismissal can create. Figure 18-4 provides guidelines that can help to reduced the trauma associated with dismissal. Being dismissed can be a terrific blow to a team member. It is important to allow the team member to leave with self-esteem intact.

APPROACHES TO POSITIVE DISCIPLINE

One approach to disciplinary action is *positive discipline,* or discipline without punishment, an idea originally developed by John Huberman, a Canadian psychologist. Punitive and positive disciplines differ in both attitude and procedure.[4] Most of the time, individuals are unaware that they are doing something they are not supposed to do. Despite the fact that they receive good induction and orientation training and that rules and procedures are clearly posted or contained in employee manuals, there are still things they don't know. They may observe some other team member doing something and believe it's all right for them to do it. A positive approach to discipline therefore is continuous education. When discipline is applied positively, it is used to teach and mold. Team members will see that it is for their welfare. Positive discipline shows the team member that obeying the rules and safety or sanitation regulations benefits them as well as the organization.

What, then, is positive discipline? The philosophy behind positive discipline is that most people come to work wishing to do a good job. They appreciate being treated as adults. They want to learn, welcome responsibility, can be self-directed, and are capable of self-discipline. The dynamics of positive discipline is a team effort whereby the team members and the chef supervisor engage in joint discussion and problem solving to resolve incidents of rule infractions.

Positive discipline focuses on the early correction of team member misconduct. Positive discipline may seem to be similar to progressive discipline, but its emphasis is on giving team members reminders rather than reprimands.

STEPS IN POSITIVE DISCIPLINE

Step 1   This is an oral reminder. In a private discussion with the chef supervisor, the team member is encouraged to explain the reason for the misconduct. In a friendly way, the rules and procedures are restated along with the reasons for having them. The chef supervisor refrains from reprimanding or threatening the team member with further disciplinary action. This meeting may be documented, but a written record is not placed in the team member's file unless the misconduct occurs again. During this meeting the team member agrees not to repeat the misconduct.

Step 2   If improvement is not made following step 1, a second meeting takes place with the offending team member. During this private meeting the chef supervisor adopts the role of counselor. At this stage, however, a written reminder is given to the team member that summarizes the discussion and the concluding agreement. Both the team member and the chef supervisor then sign it.

Step 3   When steps 1 and 2 fail to produce the desired results, the team member is placed on "decision-making" leave with pay. The purpose of this paid leave is to allow the offending team member time to decide whether to remain part of the team, whether to return and abide by the rules and conditions, or to leave. If the team member returns, it is on the basis of an agreement to conform to the organization's rules and that further infractions will be followed by termination. The foodservice organization pays for this specified leave in order to demonstrate its desire to retain the team member. Paying for the leave eliminates any negative effects that suspension without pay has on individuals.

Step 4   If the agreed improvements do not take place, then the team member has broken the agreement. There is then a clear reason for termination.

Positive discipline works. Organizations that have used it report success:

> Many people who use it report that about 75 percent of the time employees decide to come back and follow the rules. They may not maintain their turnaround indefinitely but three months or even three weeks of productive behavior is preferable to finding and breaking in somebody new. And it is infinitely better than the hostile employee you are likely to end up with after an un-paid layoff.[5]

EXIT INTERVIEWS

Team members who leave voluntarily often provide feedback on their experience with the organization that can be useful in averting further employee turnover. Exit interviews enable chef supervisors to compile data about the kitchen work environment, along with establishing the effectiveness of induction and orientation training programs. They are used to establish the primary reasons people leave.[6]

Exit interview data can help in determining if there is a trend in voluntary departures. To get the most accurate data from departing employees, the interview is best conducted by a supervisor other than the chef. Another approach is to turn the whole procedure over to the human resources department. Some of the questions appropriate for this interview are

- "What did you like most about working here? What did you like least?"
- "If you were a consultant to our organization, what changes/improvement would you recommend?"
- "What was it like working for Chef . . . ?" If the answer is vague or answered weakly, "on the grounds that nobody is perfect," the interviewer may want to ask: "What would have made Chef . . . a better supervisor, in your opinion?"
- "Where are you going to be working?" This question attempts to gather information about competitors and find out if professional recruiters are poaching from the kitchen.

To get as much information as possible from the interview, probe for specific details from each answer. It is important that no team member should leave the foodservice organization without being interviewed. Those team members who leave voluntarily have to be replaced. This process is expensive not only in terms of dollars and time but often also in terms of team morale.

Summary

Discipline should not be interpreted only as punishment. It is also about molding and teaching team members to become loyal, motivated, responsible workers.

Discipline is an inner force that develops within team members and causes them to want to follow high standards in life and the workplace. Effective discipline is not just reprimanding or inflicting penalties. Discipline is split into two distinct areas: discipline as punishment and the positive discipline approach. The leadership abilities of the chef supervisor may minimize the need to be punitive.

Chef supervisors should ensure that each member of the kitchen team understands the policies and procedures of the foodservice organization. Disciplinary actions must be in accordance with EEOC legislation and other discriminatory laws. Chef supervisors should know and understand all union labor contract procedures and agreements relative to employee discipline.

Discipline should be administered in a consistent, fair, and equitable way. Progressive discipline involves the steps of oral reprimand, written reprimand, suspension, and termination. Administering discipline requires the chef supervisor to gather the facts and treat the offender with all "due process," and to know the advance steps before termination.

Positive discipline approaches require the chef supervisor to act in a way that invests in the team member by shifting responsibility to the individual. Its philosophy is that most people are self-disciplined and that, with counseling and guidance, team members who break rules can become productive. An important element of the process is the third step, which provides offending team members with a paid period in which to decide their future with the organization, thus placing the responsibility on them for the next steps.

Exit interviews with team members who leave voluntarily provide the organization with information that can assist in profiling the kitchen as a workplace and the chef as a supervisor.

Discussion Questions

1. Why does true discipline involve more than punishing or reprimanding?
2. What are the two distinct application areas of discipline?
3. What is the effect on the kitchen team morale with regard to selective application of discipline?
4. What are the rules within the kitchen that require constant reiteration?
5. Why do minor deviations from labor contract procedures overturn otherwise justified disciplinary actions?
6. What is meant by the hot stove rule as it pertains to discipline?
7. What are the steps of progressive discipline?
8. List five major rule violations that frequently require team member dismissal?
9. What are the consequences of failing to warn a team member of continued rule violations?
10. What are the guidelines for administering discipline in a fair and equitable way?
11. What are the fundamental differences between positive and negative discipline?
12. What benefits can accrue to the chef supervisor and the foodservice organization as a result of exit interviews?

Notes

1. Jack E. Miller, Mary Porter, and Karen E. Drummond, *Supervision in the Hospitality Industry,* 2nd ed. (New York: John Wiley, 1992), 257.
2. E. R. Worthington and Anita E. Worthington, *People Investment* (Grant's Pass, OR: Oasis Press, 1993), 56.
3. Vincent H. Eade, *Human Resources Management in the Hospitality Industry* (Scottsdale, AZ: Garsuch Sciarisbrick, 1993), 204.
4. George L. Frunzi and Jack Halloran, *Supervision: The Art of Management,* 3rd ed. (Englewood Cliffs, NJ: Prentice-Hall, 1991), 380.
5. Miller et al., *Supervision in the Hospitality Industry,* 259.
6. Barbara A. Pope, *Workforce Management* (Chicago: Business One Review, 1992), 89.

CHAPTER 19
PROBLEM SOLVING AND
DECISION MAKING

OUTLINE

- ❖ Introduction
- ❖ The decision-making process
- ❖ Empowerment and decision making
- ❖ Problems
- ❖ The Pareto principle
- ❖ Rules for problem solving and decision making
- ❖ Summary
- ❖ Discussion questions
- ❖ Notes

OBJECTIVES

When you complete this chapter, you should be able to:

1. Describe the primary elements of sound decision making and problem solving
2. Outline the elements in the decision-making process
3. Evaluate the links between decision making, empowerment, and quality management
4. State reasons why problems recur within the kitchen
5. Define the steps used to identify problems relating to issues of quality and customer satisfaction

6. Use the strategies of the Pareto principle to chart causes and effects of problems
7. Describe elements of open and closed problems

Case Study: JL BEACH CLUB

July 4th was always an extremely busy day at the JL Beach Club. The sunrise breakfast, pool- and beachside lunch buffet, and the extravagant evening BBQ for all club members, combined with the private parties in the JL's private beach cabanas, pushed the limits of the JL's kitchen staff. Jed Murray, general manager of the JL, was beginning to think that this year the kitchen staff would not be able to meet the challenge. There is only one week left before the big day, and the menu and staffing plans had not been finalized for any of the events except the private parties—and the guests booking the events determined the menus for these parties.

Jed had begun meeting with Chef Loman in May to plan the menus, staffing needs, and logistics. Chef Loman had joined the JL in April. Jed discussed with Chef Loman at the first meeting how important the July 4th events were to the JL members. Chef Loman assured him that he would create appropriate menus and plan for sufficient staff to meet the challenges of the day.

Jed and Chef Loman met again in late May to review the chef's menus and staffing plan. Jed told Chef Loman that the menus were too ambitious and that his staffing plan grossly exceeded what they normally spent on staff. Chef Loman met with Jed again in early June to review his revised menus and staffing plan. Jed was very disappointed with what the chef presented. He told Chef Loman that the menus and staffing he proposed were not up to "JL standards." Jed told Chef Loman to again revise his menus and staffing plans, and that they would meet two weeks before the 4th for a final review.

Jed met with Chef Loman again two weeks before the 4th and reviewed the menus and staffing plan. Jed still did not feel that the menu and staffing plan were acceptable. Chef Loman pointed out that they were quickly running out of time to arrange for supplies and staff. Jed suggested that they just use the original menu and staffing plan the Chef had presented in May. The Chef agreed but pointed out that the cost would be higher. Jed told Chef Loman to revise the menus and staffing plan one more time to get the cost down.

Jed asked Chef Loman today, one week before the 4th, to see the revised menu and staffing plan. Chef Loman told Jed, "I will get them to you when I can. Currently I am arranging for staff, ordering supplies, and developing the work orders to ensure that we are ready for the 4th."

Based on what you have learned from previous chapters and the content of this chapter, answer the following questions.

*   Summarize what has taken place at the JL Beach Club.
*   What is the overall reason for the situation that has arisen at the JL Beach Club?
*   What are the primary causal agents for the situation that has arisen at the JL Beach Club?
*   What role did leadership and supervision/management play in the situation that has arisen at the JL Beach Club?
*   What specific steps could have been taken to avoid the situation that has arisen at the JL Beach Club?
*   What, specifically, can be done to avoid a repetition of the situation that has arisen at the JL Beach Club?

INTRODUCTION

To succeed and become a more effective supervisor, the chef must learn to make sound decisions and solve problems. This is much easier said than done. There is an old business adage that says, "A manager has only challenges, not problems." There is a more recent adage that says, "Four hundred challenges in one day are a lot of problems!" The potential for challenges in the kitchen is endless. Nothing is concrete, and new challenges confront the chef supervisor every day. The only constant is change. The problem may be customer satisfaction, motivating the kitchen team, time usage, competition, money, personal relationships, or health. These problems recur periodically, and their solutions involve decisions. How well and how creatively those problems are solved, and what the basis of the decision-making process is, determine the effectiveness of the chef supervisor.

Problem solving does not come from divine inspiration (although that might be helpful); it is a skill that can be learned. Making decisions is a part of everyday life. Some decisions are made by default: A decision is delayed to the point that some other event removes the opportunity for decision making. Others are made on the basis of feelings or emotions and are often made in haste. Good decisions, however, are made on the basis of careful thought using facts and logic. There is no substitute for good decision making. Decisions are choices between two or more options. Before a choice can be made, the exact nature of the problem must be understood. The chef supervisor must know exactly what the problem is before attempting to correct the situation.

Chef supervisors need to be decisive. When the time for action arrives, action must be taken. Decisions are not made in a vacuum. Each decision affects the team and future decisions.

THE DECISION-MAKING PROCESS

To avoid jumping to conclusions, a rational procedure should be followed when making decisions. This procedure will enable the chef supervisor to make decisions based on facts and logic, not on emotion. For any decision there are three basic options:

1. To proceed
2. To oppose
3. To take no action (let the problem solve itself)

The starting point in the process is to analyze the situation. Ensure that the real problem has been analyzed. Break up the problem into small parts. The six-step model is an effective model for problem solving and decision making. The steps in the model are as follows.

1. *Objective:* What is the desired result of the decision? This refers to the desired end result. It should not contain the method by which the chef supervisor arrives at the decision.
2. *Examine:* Determine the problem through careful investigation. This is the "why" portion of the decision. Once all potential causes of the problem have been located, the cause can be determined.
3. *Evaluate:* Gather the facts. Make a list of possible solutions to the problem. Narrow this list to a handful of best solutions. The initial step in the process is to make a broad list that can later be narrowed.

4. *Determine:* What are the alternatives and other options? What are the best alternatives: Evaluate the potential best solutions. The greater the number of alternatives, the more likely it is that the best choice will be among them.

5. *Choose:* What is the best option? Making a choice does not complete the decision-making process. Choosing involves writing a detailed plan outlining the action steps. This typically requires who is responsible, the start dates and end dates, what is involved, what changes will take place, and how these changes will take place.

6. *Implement:* What is the best choice? Implement the solution and evaluate its progress. Follow up using the plan developed in step 5. Monitor it at every stage. Evaluation provides the decision maker with information to judge the quality of the decision.

Using this six-step model is the starting point: "Often defining the problem is the important step. If the problem is not clearly defined, all the good intentions and committed efforts that follow will not guarantee that you will find the right solutions, let alone implement them."[1]

EMPOWERMENT AND DECISION MAKING

Empowerment is a concept represented by many elements: personal, team, and organizational. Foodservice organizations today are searching for quality and continuous improvement—doing more with less. An empowered kitchen team will recognize that the necessary changes and solutions will not come from top management alone. The chef supervisor and the kitchen team need to initiate decisions that solve problems in their own area: "To ensure high levels of employee commitment, organizations of the twenty-first century will involve key employees in the decision-making process when determining organizational design."[2] This is done when the team adopts its own process of empowerment.

Today's chef supervisors must be prepared to be directive when needed and to facilitate when needed. The chef supervisor making the decision and "telling" the team what the decision is does not draw on the power derived from a collaborative decision-making process. This approach is one that is not easy to adopt. It takes time, patience, and leadership to implement. The leader of an empowered team focuses on development of the team members, creating an environment for performance, learning, and development more than or giving orders. The facilitative chef supervisor recognizes how critical the direct relationship between the kitchen team and the chef supervisor is in team empowerment.

Decision making is the core process of working with empowered teams. There are different levels of participation in decision making. The lowest level is telling people what to do. One of the highest levels is when the kitchen team makes decisions together. The next critical step in team decision making is to take the chef supervisor out of the process altogether. Some of the outcomes of empowered problem solving are shown in Figure 19-1.

The more the team is consulted, the more time it takes. However, there is a trade-off: The more people are involved in making a decision, the more committed they will be to implementing it.[3] Empowered decision making solves problems. Allowing individuals to make decisions from the bottom up is by far a better approach to improving

FIGURE 19-1 Empowered problem-solving outcomes.

- Improvement of the foodservice organization's performance by dealing successfully with sources of dissatisfaction of internal or external customers (the dining room team members are an example of the kitchen's internal customers)
- Development of problem solvers who do not jump to solutions before the causes of the problem have been analyzed
- Establishment of a problem-solving process that maximizes each kitchen team member's contribution
- Implementation of solutions to problems that effectively eliminate the problems through prevention

---

BOX 19-1

CHEF TALK: FINDING GILMAN

Why are there so many challenges in the course of a business day? Many are small, some are big, some are with clients, and others are with employees. For some unknown reason, the restaurant industry seems to be a "hotbed" for such challenges, day in and day out. The solutions to problems often surprise even the experienced manager.

Faced with heavy bookings during the holiday season, I was disappointed to learn that two of our key apprentices were leaving to join our competition. Disappointment turned to anger when I learned that they had left without giving formal notice. After a quick assessment of the situation, a frantic search began to fill these positions with at least one good cook and to "make do" for the rest of the season. We began the task of advertising and interviewing hopeful candidates in a hurried fashion.

I was in the midst of negotiating the terms of purchase on a new manufacturing facility for our soup and sauce production. A building had been located and architects had been summoned for the initial design work. Though the facility seemed perfect for our needs, the architects informed us that possibly a firm with food knowledge would be more appropriate for the design work. Yes, just one more challenge was added to my stack.

Upon returning to the restaurant, I learned that we still had not located a replacement for the apprentices. Entering the kitchen, I noticed a new face at the pot sink. Before I could even say good morning, he extended his hand and introduced himself. "Gilman" thanked me for giving him the opportunity to be a part of our company. Seeing how excited he was about the pot-washing position, I opted to discuss his choice of our company. He stated without a thought, "Opportunity is why I'm here. I will begin a kitchen career in any position, pot sink, dishwasher, it doesn't matter. I won't stop, however, until I become a chef!" I discovered that he had come from a rich Cajun and Creole heritage and a long line of good cooks. But the shocker was that this was a career change for Gilman. He had graduated five years earlier from Louisiana State University in architecture. After working in his field at one of the most respected firms in Baton Rouge, he came to realize that his true love was cooking. A quick glance at the pot sink that morning turned out to be a golden opportunity, not only for Gilman, but for our company as well. Gilman realized his dream of becoming a chef. As an added bonus, we discovered our own resident architect on staff. With Gilman's architectural background and our knowledge of food and food production, imagine the team. I will never walk past the pot sink again without stopping and shaking a hand or two. Who knows what gem lies in that stack of dirty pots?

John Folse, CEC, AAC,
Executive Chef/Owner
Chef John Folse & Co.,
Donaldsonville, Louisiana

FIGURE 19-2   Empowered decision making.

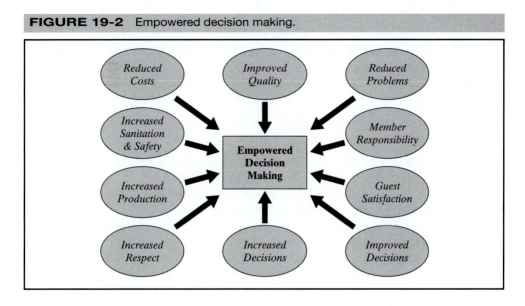

the culinary operation and satisfying customers' needs. Empowered decision making has many positive outcomes, as shown in Figure 19-2.

PROBLEMS

What is a problem? A problem is a situation that a person judges to be bad or something that needs to be corrected. A problem can be experienced in a number of ways but usually is looked on as a shortfall, a deficit, a lack, a disharmony, a puzzlement, an inconvenience, a discomfort, or a pain of some sort. A problem implies that a state of wholeness does not exist and "should" exist.[4]

The causes of many problems in the kitchen are generally linked to the quality of the food served. Associated with this are problems of timely service and production. Obviously, no two establishments have the same level or number of individual problems in these two areas. However, almost certainly, when all of these problems are analyzed, they will be "people issues," such as level of training, attitudes, or skills. Very often the easiest problems to solve are ones that concern products or equipment. Problems arise in spite of the best planning efforts. Problems arise because circumstances change or the unexpected happens. Some problems might have been foreseen and prevented; others are largely outside the control of the chef supervisor. When problems are handled improperly, they can contribute to increased costs and can lower the morale of the kitchen team.

The reasons that problems occur in the kitchen are generally centered on the following:

- ***Team members may fail to do certain things.*** They may forget to inform the chef supervisor that food materials have run out or that they have failed to arrive.
- ***Team members may do some things but fail to complete the job.*** They listen to complaints concerning food items from wait staff or customers but fail to follow through by solving the problem.

- ***Team members may do the wrong things.*** They get confused during service, prepare the wrong order, or overcook or undercook dishes.
- ***Team members may do tasks poorly.*** Food quality is reduced or there is indifference to quality and/or customer service.
- ***Team members may be poorly motivated.*** Lack of leadership of the team affects motivational levels.

The following questions may be used to identify some problems related to issues of quality and customer service:

- Has the quality level of each menu item been established with each team member?
- Has the customer profile for the menu items been clearly identified?
- Has the foodservice establishment confirmed its menu acceptance by customers?
- Were the customers involved in determining the menu?
- Is there a clear relationship between customer expectations and the kitchen team?
- Are the customer satisfaction levels measurable? If not, can they be made measurable?
- Have all team members been trained to fulfill their roles?
- Has team responsibility been identified in each quality step?
- Has the menu been evaluated to ensure consistent quality levels during busy periods?
- Is there a shortfall between "actual" and "target" quality levels?
- Is there an opportunity to achieve better-than-target at no additional cost?
- Does the target level reflect competitive best practices?
- Can everyone on the kitchen team contribute to solving the problem?

In the empowered kitchen team, each member has the responsibility that was traditionally given to the executive chef. If any member sees a problem or has an idea, he or she is responsible for bringing it to the team. Each member should be looking for ways to grow and develop, and to contribute to solving problems.

THE PARETO PRINCIPLE

Many aids and mechanical methods and procedures exist to assist in problem analysis. These range from what is known as "mind mapping" to mathematical probability ratings. Perhaps the best-known problem analysis method is the Pareto principle. Using the Pareto principle allows for collecting data, charting it, and grouping problems to determine causes and effects.

Vilfredo Pareto, an Italian economist who conducted extensive research on income distribution, discovered that in his native country 80 percent of the wealth was held by only 20 percent of the population. In international comparative research, he established the same ratio. He eventually realized that he had discovered a universal law: 80 percent of anything is attributed to 20 percent of its cause. For example, 80 percent of the important decisions are accomplished in 20 percent of the time. This 80–20 rule has come to be called the *Pareto principle.*

In problem solving, this can also be determined as 80 percent of the effect can usually be attributed to 20 percent of the cause. Therefore, the Pareto principle may be used to chart those 20 percent of key problem causes that lead to 80 percent of the problems. An analysis of customer complaints, for example, can identify areas of concern that are related directly to the bulk of complaints. Diagrams and charts are used

TABLE 19-1: Complaints in a Restaurant

Summary of Data	Number of Complaints	Rank	Percentage of Complaints
Food cold	13	3	17
Service unfriendly	2		
Food undercooked	1		
Food overcooked	4	4	—
Flatware dirty	1		
Dining room cold	3		
Long wait to be seated	27	1	36
Room crowded	2		
Portions too small	1		
Decor	1		
Service slow	19	2	25
Noise level high	1		
Total	75		78

to present the frequency of occurrences of complaints to determine where the bulk of problems with customer service lie. Over a period of time, data can be accumulated from customer comment cards. Table 19-1 and Figure 19-3 show examples of using the Pareto principle.

From the data in Table 19-1 and Figure 19-3, it is possible to establish what areas are receiving the most complaints.[5] From the total number of 75 complaints, 59 are divided among three areas. This represents 78 percent of all the complaints. Therefore, corrective action can be taken to reduce almost 80 percent of the total complaints. Solutions to the three areas can be determined: (1) ways to speed up seating; (2) ways to speed up service; and (3) ways to ensure that the customer receives hot food.

FIGURE 19.3 Percentage of total complaints.

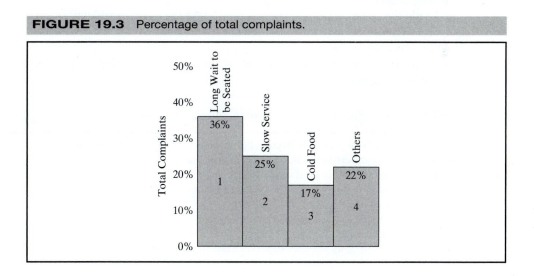

RULES FOR PROBLEM SOLVING AND DECISION MAKING

Solving problems is a part of regular daily activities in the kitchen and our personal lives. Problem solving can be both challenging and frustrating. It has often been said that problems are opportunities to be creative. On the other hand, problem solving can be so difficult that it is often necessary to use a sequential process. Knowledge gained from experience is a valuable asset, and its importance should not be underestimated. Fear of failure can also be a powerful force in decision making. There is no such thing as a decision without risk or a set of personal traits that guarantee correct decision making. Most people make decisions on the basis of "risk avoidance." Sometimes risk avoidance blocks a person from applying innovative solutions and ideas. Other elements that contribute to poor decision making in solving problems are shown in Figure 19-4.

What is the ideal best solution for a problem? The ideal "best" solution probably doesn't exist. There are many possible solutions for each problem, and some are better than others. The best solution is nothing more than the best compromise under the circumstances.

The essential elements of problem solving are

1. Recognizing the problem
2. Specifying the problem:
   - What is the problem and what is *not* the problem?
   - Where is it and where is it *not?*
   - Where did it happen?
   - How big is the problem?
   - Does it change with time, and if so, how?
3. Identifying possible causes:
   - What aspects stand out from the answers to the previous questions?
   - What aspects can be eliminated?
   - Using the experience of the chef supervisor and that of the team, what could have caused the problem?
4. Testing causes:
   - Could the cause or causes have accounted for the entire problem?
   - Are they within the control of the chef supervisor?
5. Alternative solutions:
   - What could the chef supervisor or the kitchen team do that would remove or reduce the cause?

FIGURE 19-4 Factors that may lead to poor decision making.

- Getting involved with problems beyond the scope or ability of the kitchen team
- Failing to involve others in the solution of the problem
- Relying only on previously used solutions
- Failing to investigate the cause of the problem adequately
- Failing to seek advice
- Not suspending judgment to generate solutions
- Not being open-minded
- Allowing people to think the chef supervisor has the best answers

- What would the consequences of each action be?
- Which is the best solution?

6. Implementing a plan:
- What must the chef supervisor do to implement the solution?

7. Reviewing effects:
- Is the problem solved?
- Were there any unforeseen consequences to the actions?

OPEN AND CLOSED PROBLEMS

Closed-ended problems are those in which the boundaries and constraints are fixed. They usually have one solution.

Examples

- "Where should we locate?"
- "What supplier should we use?"
- "How do we handle accounting problems?"

Open-ended problems are those where boundaries and constraints can be questioned and may change during the solution.

Examples

- "What dishes should we feature on our new menu?"
- "How do we solve our quality problems?"
- "What are tangible rewards for outstanding performances?"

POTENTIAL PROBLEMS

The chef supervisor must also recognize and deal with "potential problems." The chef supervisor who deals with issues only when they become "problems" becomes a fire-fighter rather than a problem solver. The following guidelines can assist in dealing with potential problems before they become problems.

1. Recognize the potential problem:
- What could go wrong?

2. Specify the potential problems:
- What is likely to go wrong?
- Where is it likely to go wrong?
- When is it likely to go wrong?
- How big a problem will it become?
- How is it likely to happen?

3. Decide the action:
- Can it be prevented from happening?
- If so, what action can be taken to prevent it?
- If not, what action can the chef supervisor take to reduce its effects if and when it happens?

4. Plan the action:
- What steps can the chef supervisor take now to prevent it and reduce its effects?
- What steps can be taken later to reduce its effects and prevent it from happening again?

5. Implement the action:
   - Defining the problem is often the key to successful problem solving skills.
   - If the problem is not clearly defined, all the other steps and efforts will be rendered useless.

Summary

One of the most important duties of the chef supervisor is to make decisions and solve problems. Good decisions help the foodservice organization, whereas poor ones weaken it.

Decisions should be made on the basis of careful thought using facts and logic. Decisions are choices between two or more options. The decision-making process includes three basic options:

1. Proceed.
2. Oppose.
3. Take no action (let the problem solve itself).

Decision making follows six steps:

1. Set the objective for the decision.
2. Examine the problem.
3. Evaluate the facts.
4. Determine alternatives.
5. Choose the best option.
6. Implement the choice.

Empowerment is about giving decision making to the kitchen team. Decision making is given to the team in order to solve problems at the root source. The chef supervisor facilitates this process. Common outcomes of team-empowered decision making include reduction of problems, greater responsibility, reduced costs, and better decisions.

The causes of many problems in the kitchen are generally linked to food quality, and most of these problems are "people" issues. These include:

- Failing to do things
- Failing to complete the job
- Doing the wrong things
- Doing tasks poorly
- Poor motivation

By taking a proactive stand to solving potential problems, the kitchen team may avoid many problems of quality.

The Pareto principle is an effective method for determining where problems lie. The Pareto principle is also known as the 80–20 rule. Using this system can help discover where most of the problems can be found in the kitchen program.

Using a structured and sequential set of steps allows for a more thorough decision-making and problem-solving procedure. These steps include:

- Recognizing problems
- Specifying problems
- Identifying possible causes
- Open and closed problems
- Potential problems

Discussion Questions

1. What are the three basic options in decision making?
2. What are the elements of the six-step model used to define problems?
3. How does the role of the chef supervisor change within the concept of team empowerment?
4. What are the links between decision making and team empowerment?
5. Why do most problems in the kitchen center around people issues?
6. What are the steps used to identify problems of quality and customer service?
7. What are the elements of the Pareto principle?
8. What are the uses of the Pareto principle relative to identifying and solving problems?
9. Why do most people make decisions on the basis of risk avoidance?
10. What is the difference between an open and a closed problem?

Notes

1. Richard N. Chang and P. Keith Kelly, *Step by Step Problem Solving* (Irvine, CA: Richard Chang Associates, 1993), 83.

2. Florence Berger, Mark D. Fulford, and Michelle Krazmien, "Human Resources Management in the 21st Century: Predicting Partnerships for Profit," *Hospitality Research Journal* 17, no. 1 (1993), 94.

3. Cynthia D. Scott and Dennis T. Jaffe, *Empowerment* (London: Crisp, 1991), 80.

4. Donald J. Noone, *Creative Problem Solving* (Hauppauge, NY: Barron's, 1993), 22.

5. Adapted from Brian Thomas, *Total Quality Training* (London: McGraw-Hill, 1992), 121.

APPENDIX A

FEDERAL REGULATIONS AND EXECUTIVE ORDERS

EMPLOYMENT REGULATIONS

National Labor Relations Act (Wagner Act) (1935)

Purpose   To establish a national policy of encouraging collective bargaining, guaranteeing certain employee rights, and detailing specific employer unfair labor practices and to establish the National Labor Relations Board (NLRB) to enforce these provisions.

This act was further amended by the Labor-Management Relations (Taft-Hartley) Act of 1947 and the Labor-Management Reporting and Disclosure (Landrum-Griffin) Act of 1959, which establishes a balance between management and union power to protect the public interest and provides detailed regulations for internal union affairs.

Applies to   Private employers and unions.

Penalties   The NLRB has the power to investigate, dismiss charges or hold hearings, issue cease-and-desist orders, or pursue cases via Circuit Courts of Appeals or U.S. Supreme Court.

Regulatory Agency   National Labor Relations Board.

Title VII of the Civil Rights Act (1964)

Purpose   The principal federal law relating to most types of employment discrimination; its purpose is to give everyone an equal chance to obtain employment. The law has a number of objectives, specifically:

- Outlaws certain discriminatory employment practices
- Creates a federal agency to enforce the law and give it regulatory powers
- Sets penalties for violators of the law
- Requires state laws to uphold Title VII
- Requires that certain records be maintained by designated persons or agencies
- Does not alter state or federal veterans' preference laws

Title VII prohibits employment discrimination based on race, religion, sex, color, or national origin. Employers are also prohibited from discriminatory practices regarding:

- Recruiting and hiring
- Job advertising
- Ability and experience
- Occupational qualification
- Testing
- Prehire inquiries
- Employment status
- Compensation
- Merit, incentive, or seniority plans
- Insurance, retirement, and welfare plans
- Promotion and seniority
- Dress and appearance
- Leave-of-absence benefits
- Discharge
- Retirement
- Union membership
- Persons opposed to discriminatory practices or exercising their rights under Title VII

Applies to   Private or public employers who have 15 or more employees, private and public employment agencies, hiring halls, or labor unions with 15 or more members.

Penalties   Court-decreed affirmative action programs and back pay.

Regulatory Agency   Equal Employment Opportunity Commission.

Freedom of Information Act (FOIA) (1966)

Purpose   To reduce privacy protection by authorizing the release of private information under certain conditions. This act could apply to employee access to personal records, employee information provided to other businesses, and disclosure of personnel information to third parties. This act was created to allow access to records held by federal agencies. Many states have laws that affect both privacy protection and freedom-of-information protection.

Applies to Federal agencies and federal records, but the FOIA may be used by anyone as a means of accessing federally maintained information used for decision making.

Age Discrimination in Employment Act (1967, 1978, 1986)

Purpose The act promotes the employment of older persons based on ability rather than age; it prohibits arbitrary age discrimination in employment of workers 40 years or older; it helps employers and workers resolve age-related employment problems.

Applies to Private employers with 20 or more workers; all governments, regardless of number of employees. Federal employment has no upper age limit. Applies also to employment agencies and unions with 25 or more members.

Penalties Court-decreed affirmative action programs, back pay, fines up to $10,000, and possible imprisonment.

Regulatory Agency Equal Employment Opportunity Commission.

Immigration Reform and Control Act of 1986

Purpose The act requires employers to hire only citizens and aliens who are authorized to work in the United States.

Applies to All employers who hire someone to perform labor or services for wages or other pay.

Penalties Fines range from $100 for record-keeping violations to $10,000 per unauthorized employee for hiring unauthorized persons.

Regulatory Agency U.S. Immigration and Naturalization Service.

Drug-Free Workplace Act (1988)

Purpose Requires each employer-holder of government contracts to certify to the federal contracting agency that it will provide a drug-free workplace by publishing a company policy statement describing unlawful behaviors, required

employment conditions, violation penalties, by publicizing the program within the company, and by taking appropriate disciplinary or rehabilitation steps for violators. This does not mandate drug testing.

Applies to Employers with employees that hold or seek federal contracts of $25,000 or more and on federal grants.

Penalties Suspension or termination of grants and/or debarment from federal procurement process for up to 5 years.

Regulatory Agency The Federal Contracting Agency.

Americans with Disabilities Act (1990)

Purpose Provides broad nondiscrimination protection for individuals in employment, public services, public accommodations, and services operated by private entities, transportation, and telecommunications. Title I states that no entity covered by this act shall discriminate against a qualified individual because of a disability with regard to a job application procedure or in the hiring, advancement, or discharge of employees, employee compensation, job training, and other terms, conditions, and privileges of employment.

Applies to As of July 1992, all businesses with 25 or more employees, and as of July 1994, all businesses with 15 or more employees.

Penalties Administrative enforcement and/or individual suits to include injunctive relief and back pay but not compensatory and punitive damages. These latter remedies may be pursued under the Civil Rights Act of 1991.

Regulatory Agency Equal Employment Opportunity Commission.

Civil Rights Act (1991)

Purpose Extends punitive damages and jury trials to victims of employment discrimination based on the employee's sex, religion, disability, as well as race. Under previous acts, employees could only seek back pay.

Applies to All businesses with 15 or more employees.

Penalties Punitive damages caps as follows: $50,000 for businesses with 100 or fewer employees; $100,000 for firms with 101 to 500 workers; and a maximum limit of $300,000 for businesses with over 500 employees.

Regulatory Agency Equal Employment Opportunity Commission.

Family and Medical Leave Act of 1993

Purpose Permits employees to take up to 12 weeks of unpaid leave per year from work for the birth or adoption of a child; for the case of a seriously ill child, spouse, or parent; or for a serious illness afflicting the worker. Employers must guarantee the worker can return to the same or a comparable job. Employers must also continue health care coverage during the leave period. During the leave time, workers are not eligible for unemployment or other government compensation.

Applies to Employers that have 50 or more employees within a 75-mile radius. Employees who have not worked at least one year and have not worked 1,250 hours or 25 hours a week in the previous 12 months are not covered by the law. This law took effect in August 1993.

Regulatory Agency Equal Employment Opportunity Commission.

COMPENSATION REGULATIONS

Most compensation benefits are based on the provision of the Old Age, Survivors, Disability and Health Insurance Program (OASDHI). More that 90 percent of the U.S. labor force is covered by these programs, which include Social Security, unemployment insurance, Medicare, and Medicaid benefits. The OASDHI also covers welfare services such as Aid to Families with Dependent Children (AFDC).

Workers' Compensation (each state has its own laws)

Purpose It financially compensates workers or their dependents for work-related injuries, diseases, or death. Because the employer is responsible for any job-related damage a worker may sustain, laws have been enacted at the state level to institute insurance programs to cover employees.

Applies to Most employees except farm workers, home workers, and federal employees.

Regulatory Agency A state industrial commission.

Unemployment Compensation— Title IX of the Social Security Act (1935)

Purpose The act provides for financial assistance to workers who have been laid off through no fault of their own. Funds are raised through state employment compensation taxes. Each state maintains its own program. The program provides benefits only to employees whose employers are paying the tax. States may establish certain eligibility requirements, such as a minimum length of time worked or having earned a minimum set wage.

Applies to Any employer with one or more employees who worked some part of 20 or more weeks must pay federal or state unemployment tax. Also covered are employers paying wages of $1,500 or more in any calendar quarter. Some states may have more rigid requirements than the federal minimum.

Regulatory Agency The state unemployment commission.

Social Security Act (1935)

Purpose The act was originally created to provide a minimum income for retired workers. Amendments have increased coverage to compensate dependents of a deceased worker and totally disabled workers; and hospital and medical insurance to include Medicare for people over age 65. Funding is through taxes collected from both employers and employees based on income earned. These taxes are authorized by the Federal Insurance Contributions Act (FICA).

Applies to Most workers in the United States. Some civilian federal employees are covered instead by a federal retirement system.

Regulatory Agency Social Security Administration in the U.S. Department of Health and Human Services.

Minimum Wage Act (1938)— Amendment to the Fair Labor Standards Act (1938)

Purpose This federal law specifies a minimum hourly wage and standard work week. Additionally, the law establishes overtime pay, equal pay, required records, and child labor standards.

Applies to All enterprises affecting interstate commerce. It includes laundries and dry cleaners, construction firms, hospitals, public and private schools, and a retail or service establishment with annual gross sales of not less than $362,500 and any other business with annual gross sales of at least $250,000.

Penalties Back pay, fines up to $10,000, and possible imprisonment.

Regulatory Agency The U.S. Department of Labor's Wage and Hour Division.

Equal Pay Act (1963)— Amendment to the Fair Labor Standards Act (1938)

Purpose The Equal Pay Act is part of the Fair Labor Standards Act. It prohibits differential wages paid to men and women doing substantially the same work. If both sexes are doing the same work with similar skills, responsibility, working conditions, and effort, then the pay must be equal.

Applies to All businesses affecting interstate commerce, including local, state, and federal agencies.

Penalties Back pay, fines up to $10,000, and possible imprisonment.

Regulatory Agency The U.S. Department of Labor's Wage and Hour Division.

Occupational Safety and Health Act (1970) (OSHA)

Purpose The act created regulations and enforcement practices to render the work environment safe and healthy for workers.

Applies to Any firm affecting interstate commerce having one or more employees.

Penalties Violation citations and fines up to $10,000 for each violation.

Regulatory Agency The Occupational Safety and Health Administration in the U.S. Department of Labor.

Employment Retirement Income Security Act (ERISA) (1974)

Purpose The act was enacted to ensure that private employee pension plans will actually provide something when the recipients retire and become eligible for the benefits. ERISA is a complex regulation requiring retirement-plan managers to adhere to specific fiduciary duties, maintain records and reports, and remain within specified investment restrictions.

Applies to Employees with pension plans. ERISA requires companies with pension plans to subscribe to specific regulations regarding the administration of the plans, but it does not require employers to have any pension plans.

Regulatory Agency The Pension Benefit Guaranty Corporation, a federal agency, administers the plan-termination insurance program (which ensures that employees obtain vested retirement rights if the plan fails). The Internal Revenue Service Office of Employee Plans and Exempt Organizations handles tax implications, and the U.S. Department of Labor's Labor-Management Services Administration handles other aspects of managing ERISA. Congress has considered creating a single entity to be in charge, the Employee Benefits Administration.

Individual Retirement Accounts (IRA) (Revenue Act of 1978)

Purpose The original purpose of the act was to enable small businesses to have employee retirement plans without the administrative burden of ERISA. The IRA allowed a business to pay $7500 or up to 15 percent of an employee's gross salary (whichever is smaller) to a bank, savings and loan, mutual fund, or insurance company for investment for the employee. In 1981 it was expanded to allow employees to contribute an additional $2000 to their company retirement fund or to their own IRA.

Applies to Any employer or employee. For an individual to be eligible, he or she must have compensation included in his or her income during the year.

Regulatory Agency Internal Revenue Service.

GLOSSARY OF TERMS

Active listening Encouraging the speaker to continue talking by giving interested responses that show that the listener understands the speaker's meaning and feelings.

Affirmative action Actions or programs designed to improve employment opportunities for members of protected groups, such as minorities, the aged, and the handicapped.

Androgogy Concept of adult education.

Apprentice A worker serving a special training period that combines formal schooling with job experience in preparation for entry into a skilled job.

Authority The rights and powers to make the necessary decisions and to take the necessary action to get the job done.

Autocratic leadership A leadership style characterized by a high concern for task (getting the job done) and a relatively low concern for people.

Body language Expression of attitudes and feelings through body movements and positions.

Brainstorming Generating ideas within a group without considering their drawbacks, limitations, or consequences.

Budget As a planning tool, it commits organizational resources to projects, programs, or activities, and results are measured in quantifiable terms over predetermined time periods. As a control device, it compares actual performance against expectations.

Case study A form of training that provides trainees with materials that describe particular situations for which the trainees are to analyze the case and make recommendations.

Closed-end questions Interview questions that require specific and usually restricted responses.

Coaching Individual, corrective on-the-job training for improving performance.

Collective bargaining The process of negotiating and administering a union contract.

Communication The process of passing along information and understanding from one person to another person or group.

Critical incident technique A form of performance appraisal in which supervisors observe and record outstanding employee behavior, good or bad.

Culinarian Person who works in a kitchen preparing food.

Cultural empathy Being sensitive to cultural differences and similarities by seeking to understand others' approach to life and their ways of thinking and living.

Decision Conscious choice among alternatives.

Delegation The process of distributing work to others and providing them with the appropriate resources and authority to do the task.

Democratic leadership A leadership style characterized by a high concern for both people and task accomplishment.

Demotivator An emotion, environmental factor, or incident that reduces motivation to perform well.

Discipline Punishment of employees for violating the rules or performance requirements of the organization. The process of socializing employees to accept and follow the rules and values of the organization.

Dissatisfiers Factors in the job environment that produce dissatisfaction, usually reducing motivation.

Diversity Physical and cultural dimensions that separate and distinguish individuals and groups: age, gender, physical abilities and qualities, ethnicity, race, and sexual preference.

Downward communication The process of passing along information and understanding from the higher levels of the organization to the lower levels.

Due process The means by which employees are given a chance for fair treatment by their employers. The process includes such protective measures as having reasonable work rules, a chance to defend against any accusations, and review by higher levels of management.

Employee rights The concept that employees are to be treated fairly and with dignity by their employers; and if there are violations of those rights, employees should have recourse against the employers.

Empowerment Giving employees permission to make decisions. In the foodservice industry, empowering employees to satisfy the customer.

Ethnocentrism A belief that one's own culture or ways of doing things is best.

Exempt employee An employee who, under the provisions of the Fair Labor Standards Act, is exempt from the overtime pay requirements of the act; generally considered to be persons employed in a bona-fide executive, administrative, or professional capacity.

Exit interview An interview of a terminating employee to learn the employee's honest reactions or his or her reasons for leaving the organization, usually conducted on the last day of employment.

Expectancy theory A motivation theory that holds that individuals are motivated to act when they believe their actions will bring about desirable results for themselves.

Facilitator A new dimension to the supervisor's job that gives emphasis to the supervisor taking appropriate measures to make it easier for workers to do their jobs, as well as removing obstacles that hinder performance.

Foodservice organization Any establishment that prepares and serves food utilizing professionals.

Grievance procedure A procedure set up either by management or by management and the union to resolve employee complaints fairly.

Grievances Real or imagined complaints of workers against management or working conditions, often related to union–management relations.

Halo effect The tendency to assume that because one or a few things are done well by a person, all things about that person are good.

Hazard Analysis Critical Control Point (HACCP) A food preparation safety system that targets high-risk foods and preparation at critical points and seeks to maximize safe food handling.

Hierarchy of needs theory Abraham Maslow's motivation theory that identifies and arranges in order of dominance the five levels of human needs.

Hot stove rule A disciplinary technique designed to ensure fair treatment to all employees by comparing the taking of disciplinary action to what happens when one touches a hot stove.

Human relations movement A belief that the workplace is a social setting, and as such, more attention has to be given to human needs, motivation, and interpersonal relations.

Hygiene factors Frederick Herzberg's concept that the job-related factors of working conditions, interpersonal relations, organizational policies and procedures, quality of supervision, and pay can cause worker dissatisfaction.

Induction training The absorbing of new team members into the culture and philosophy of the organization.

Insubordination Refusal by an employee to follow a direct order from a supervisor.

Job description A written statement that sets forth in general terms the duties of the position and related responsibilities so people can understand what is done by the person holding that particular job.

Job interview A purposeful conversation between an employer and a job applicant that deals with the exchange of relevant information about job-related matters.

Job rotation Periodically moving team members to different jobs for such purposes as cross-training and relieving worker boredom.

Job satisfiers Frederick Herzberg's concept that the job-related factors of achievement, recognition, responsibility, advancement, and opportunity for growth give employees satisfaction on the job and thus serve as motivators.

Job specifications A written listing of the specific requirements to perform the job.

Job talk   A training technique of imparting information from the supervisor to the team member. Relies on an illustrated lecture.

Leadership   The ability to influence others to do something voluntarily rather than because it is required or because there is fear of the consequences of not doing it or expectation of reward for doing it.

Learning objective   A training goal stated in measurable or observable terms.

Management by objectives (MBO)   A results-oriented management technique that seeks employee involvement, leading to supervisor and employee mutually setting goals and evaluation criteria and that will serve as the basis for evaluating that person's contribution to the overall organizational goals.

Management by walking around (MBWA)   An active management technique in which the supervisor visits each workstation for hands-on management and supervision.

Mise en place   Preparation, everything ready; in kitchens, refers to preparation prior to food service. A collection of items necessary to prepare menu items.

Morale   Group spirit with respect to getting the job done.

Motivation   The stimulating or causing of purposeful activity that is directed to satisfying needs or wants.

Negative discipline   Maintaining discipline through fear and punishment.

Nonexempt employee   An employee who, under the provisions of the Fair Labor Standards Act, is entitled to overtime pay for hours worked in excess of the statutory requirements.

Nonverbal communication   Communication without words. Use of gestures, facial expressions, or body language.

On-the-job training   Training that is done at the workplace under regular working conditions.

Open-end questions   Interview questions that allow for a range of responses.

Organization   A collection of individuals who are working together to reach common goals.

Organizing   The prelude to action and the process of mentally and physically preparing and arranging for the necessary resources to accomplish results.

Orientation   The programmed introduction of new employees into the organization, during which they learn what is important to the organization, to the supervisor, and to fellow employees.

Participative management   A style of management that seeks to give employees meaningful involvement in their job and conditions of employment.

Performance appraisal   Systematic evaluation of the employee's work performance and potential with the organization.

Personal space   The area within 2 to 3 feet of a person.

Persons with disabilities   People who have or are considered to have a physical or mental impairment that substantially limits one or more major life activities.

Planning   The process by which management determines expected outcomes and coordinates resources, personnel, and activities to reach these objectives.

Policies   Written statements of the goals and intentions of the top management of the organization.

Positive discipline   A punishment-free formula for disciplinary action that replaces punishment with reminders and features a decision-making leave of absence with pay.

Procedures   Written statements that spell out the details of what is to be done and how.

Productivity   A measure of the relationship that exists between outputs, such as so many pieces per hour, to inputs, such as hours worked to produce the items.

Pygmalion effect   J. Sterling Livingston's concept that the performance level of subordinates is affected by the supervisor's expectations and abilities.

Quality   The concept that the product or service meets the stated and implied specifications.

Rating scale   A form of performance appraisal that requires the evaluator to make a selection from several predetermined choices.

Reengineering   Redesign of work processes and implementation of the new design.

Role model   One who serves as an example for the behavior of others.

Role playing   A form of training that attempts to create common and realistic learning situations (such as performance reviews or disciplinary actions) by having employees act out assigned roles.

Rules   A form of control that spells out the code of conduct that is required by the organization, and, in many cases, states the penalties for violation.

Scientific management   The concept developed by Frederick Taylor that holds that work is most efficiently performed when management studies each job scientifically, determines the basic elements of each, standardizes the methods and tools used, selects workers suited to the specific jobs, provides for job specialization, and sees to strong supervisory support.

Sexual harassment   Unwelcome advances, requests for sexual favors, and other verbal or physical conduct of a sexual nature when compliance with any of these acts is a condition of employment, or when comments or physical contact create an intimidating, hostile, or offensive working environment.

Situational leadership   Adaptation of leadership style to the needs of the situation.

Socialization   The process by which people learn and come to accept the appropriate values and behaviors for various situations.

Supervisor   An employee who is in a management position and has authority to perform such management duties as assigning work, hiring, firing, and making promotions and transfers, or who can effectively recommend such actions.

Supportive leadership   A leadership style characterized by a high concern for people and a relatively low concern for task accomplishment.

Theory X   Douglas McGregor's concept that some supervisors assume a generally negative view of workers, believing that the typical employee is lazy, dislikes work, and must be closely supervised.

Theory Y   Douglas McGregor's concept that some supervisors assume a generally positive view of workers, believing that the typical employee is willing, personally responsible, and responds best to a minimum of supervision.

Total quality management (TQM)   A business and management philosophy/process in which all efforts are expended through concerted effort directed at servicing customers by continuous improvements, utilizing and maximizing human resources.

Training   Planned and organized activity that seeks to provide employees with the necessary skills and attitudes to function effectively on the job.

Transactional analysis   Theories and techniques that can be used by individuals and groups to determine the basis from which another individual is communicating or interacting.

Unstructured interview   A form of interview in which the questions and sequence are accommodated to the applicant's unique background and responses to prior questions.

Upward communication   The process of passing along information and understanding from the lower levels of the organization to the higher levels.

Values   Strongly held beliefs that either define right or wrong or indicate preferences.

Win–win problem solving   A method of solving problems in the kitchen in which the chef supervisor and team member discuss the problem together and arrive at a mutually acceptable situation.

Work standards   The established time that a normally capable worker should take to do a specified task.

Workers' compensation   A form of no-fault insurance that entitles workers who are injured or who become ill because of job-related conditions to compensation in the form of money, medical treatment, and vocational rehabilitation, if necessary.

APPENDIX C

❧

BIBLIOGRAPHY

Aguayo, Rafeal. *Dr. Deming.* New York: Carol, 1991.

Anderson, Peggy, ed. *Great Quotes from Great Leaders.* Lombard, IL: Lombard, 1989.

Barbee, Cliff, and Valerie Bott. "Customer Treatment as a Mirror of Employee Treatment," *Advanced Management Journal,* Spring 1991.

Barker, Joel Arthur. *Paradigms: The Business of Discovering the Future.* New York: HarperCollins, 1993.

Becker, Dennis, and Paula Borkum Becker. *Powerful Presentation Skills.* Boston: Mirror Press, 1994.

Belasco, James A. *Teaching the Elephant to Dance.* New York: Crown, 1990.

Bennus, Warren, and Burt Nanus. *Leaders: The Strategies for Taking Charge.* New York: HarperCollins, 1985.

Berne, Eric. *Games People Play.* London: Penguin, 1964.

Bernstein, Charles, and William P. Fisher. *Lessons in Leadership: Perspectives for Hospitality Industry Success.* New York: Van Nostrand Reinhold, 1991.

Blanchard, Ken, John Carlos, and Alan Randolph. *Empowerment Takes More Than a Minute.* San Francisco: Berrett-Koehler, 1996.

Blanchard, Ken, and Michael O'Connor. *Managing By Values*: San Francisco: Berret-Koehler Publishers, 1997.

Blanchard, Kenneth, Patricia Zigarni, and Drea Zigarni. *Leadership and the One Minute Manager.* New York: Morrow, 1985.

Byars, Lloyd L., and Leslie W. Rue. *Human Resource Management,* 4th ed. Boston: Irwin, 1994.

Cain, Herman. *Leadership Is Common Sense.* New York: Van Nostrand Reinhold, 1996.

Carlzon, Jan. *Moments of Truth.* Cambridge, MA: Ballinger, Harper & Row, 1987.

Casio, Wayne F. *Applied Psychology in Human Resources Management,* 5th ed. Upper Saddle River, NJ: Prentice Hall, 1998.

C.E.R.T. *Customer Relations.* Dublin, Ireland: CERT, 1990.

Cherrington, David J. *The Management of Human Resources,* 4th ed. Englewood Cliffs, NJ: Prentice Hall, 1995.

Christensen, Julia. "The Diversity Dynamics: Implications for Organizations in 2005." *Hospitality Research Journal* 17, no. 1 (1993).

Cichy, Ronald, Martin P. Sciarini, and Mark E. Patton. "Food-Service Leadership: Could Attila Run a Restaurant?" *The Cornell Hotel and Restaurant Administration Quarterly* 33, no. 1 (1992).

Clonz, Angela, and Neil H. Snyder. *The Will to Lead: Managing with Courage and Conviction in the Age of Uncertainty.* New York: Irwin, 1997.

Cohen, William A. *The Art of the Leader.* Englewood Cliffs, NJ: Prentice Hall, 1990.

Crosby, Philip. *Quality Is Free.* New York: McGraw-Hill, 1978.

Crosby, Philip. *Quality Is Free: The Art of Making Quality Certain.* New York: John Wiley, 1989.

Cullen, Noel C. "Reengineering the Executive Chef." *Chef Magazine,* October 1993.

Cullen, Noel C. "Total Quality Management for the Modern Chef." *National Culinary Review,* August 1996.

Dale, Barrie G., Cary L. Cooper, and Adrian Wilkinson, *Managing Quality & Human Resources: A Guide to Continuous Improvement.* Oxford, England: Blackwell, 1997.

Davidow, William H., and Bro Utall. *Total Customer Service: The Ultimate Weapon.* New York: Harper Perennial, 1990.

Deming, W. Edwards. *Out of Crisis.* Cambridge, MA: MIT Center for Advanced Engineering Study, 1989.

DePree, Max. *Leadership Is an Art.* New York: Dell, 1989.

Dessler, Gary. *Human Resources Management,* 7th ed. Upper Saddle River, NJ: Prentice Hall, 1997.

Drucker Foundation. *Leader of the Future.* San Francisco: Jossey-Bass, 1996.

Drummond, Karen Eich. *Human Resources Management for the Hospitality Industry.* New York: Van Nostrand Reinhold, 1990.

Drummond, Karen Eich. *The Restaurant Training Program.* New York: John Wiley, 1992.

Dumont, Raymond, and John M. Lannon. *Business Communications,* 2nd ed. Boston: Brown, 1987.

Eade, Vincent H. *Human Resources Management in the Hospitality Industry.* Scottsdale, AZ: Garsuch Sciarisbrick, 1993.

Equal Employment Opportunity Commission. *Sexual Harassment Charges EEOC & FEPAs Combined: FY 1992–FY 2002.* www.eeoc.gov/stats/harass.html.

Fernandez, John P. *Managing a Diverse Work Force: Regaining the Competitive Edge.* Lexington, MA: Heath, 1991.

Ferris, Gerald R., and M. Ronald Buckley. *Human Resources Management: Perspectives, Context, Functions and Outcomes,* 3rd ed. Englewood Cliffs, NJ: Prentice Hall, 1995.

Fisher, Cynthia D., Lyle F. Schoenfeldt, and James B. Shaw. *Human Resources Management,* 3rd ed. Boston: Houghton Mifflin, 1996.

Francis, Dave, and Don Young. *Improving Work Groups: A Practical Manual for Team Building.* San Diego: Pfeiffer, 1993.

Gallos, Joan V., Jean Ramsey, and Associates. *Teaching Diversity.* San Francisco: Jossey-Bass, 1997.

Gatewood, Robert D., and Hubert S. Field. *Human Resource Selection,* 4th ed. Fort Worth, TX: Dryden Press, 1998.

Go, Frank M., Mary L. Monachello, and Tom Baum. *Human Resources Management in the Hospitality Industry.* New York: John Wiley, 1996.

Goad, Tom W. *Delivering Effective Training.* San Diego: Pfeiffer, 1982.

Gomez-Mejia, Luis R., David Balkin, and Robert L. Cardy. *Managing Human Resources,* 2nd ed. Upper Saddle River, NJ: Prentice Hall, 1998.

Hammer, Michael, and James Champy. *Reengineering the Corporation: A Manifesto for Business Revolution.* New York: HarperCollins, 1993.

Hargrove, Robert. *Masterful Coaching.* San Francisco: Pfeiffer, 1995.

Harris, Thomas. *I'm OK, You're OK.* London: Pan, 1978.

Hart, Lois B. *Training Methods That Work.* London: Crisp, 1991.

Hay, Julie. *Transactional Analysis for Trainers.* Berkshire, England: McGraw-Hill, 1992.

Heneman, Herbert G., Robert L. Heneman, and Timothy A. Judge. *Staffing Organizations,* 2nd ed. Boston: Irwin, 1997.

Herzberg, Frederick. "One More Time: How Do You Motivate Employees?" *Harvard Business Review* 46, no. 1 (1968).

Herzberg, Frederick. *Work and the Nature of Man.* Cleveland: World, 1966.

Hilgert, Raymond L., and Cyril C. Ling. *Cases and Experiential Exercises in Human Resources Management.* Upper Saddle River, NJ: Prentice Hall, 1996.

Hobson, Barrie, and Mike Scally. *Time Management: Conquering the Clock.* San Diego: Pfeiffer, 1993.

Keiser, James R. *Principles and Practices of Management in the Hospitality Industry,* 2nd ed. New York: Van Nostrand Reinhold, 1989.

Kets de Vries, Manfred F. R. *Leaders, Fools and Imposters.* San Francisco: Jossey-Bass, 1993.

Kinlaw, Dennis C. *Coaching for Commitment.* San Diego: Pfeiffer, 1993.

Kleiman, Lawrence S. *Human Resources Management: A Tool for Competitive Advantage.* San Francisco: West, 1997.

Klein, Allen. *Quotations to Cheer You Up.* New York: Wings Books, 1991.

Koonce, Richard. "Redefining Diversity: It's Not Just the Right Thing to Do. It also Makes Good Business Sense." *Training & Development,*

December 2001, www.findarticles.com/cf_ntrstnws/m4467/12_55/83045836/print.jhtml, 1.

Kotschevar, Lendal H. *Management by Menu.* Dubuque, IA: Brown, 1987.

Kouzes, James M., and Barry Z. Posner. *Credibility: How Leaders Gain and Lose It, Why People Demand It.* San Francisco: Jossey-Bass, 1993.

Leeds, Dorothy. *Marketing Yourself: The Ultimate Job-Seekers Guide.* New York: HarperCollins, 1991.

Levinson, Charles. *Food and Beverage Operation Cost Control and Systems Management.* Englewood Cliffs, NJ: Prentice Hall, 1989.

Lewis, Pamela S., Stephen H. Goodman, and Patricia M. Fandt. *Management: Challenges in the 21st Century.* San Francisco: West, 1995.

Maddux, Robert B. *Team Building: An Exercise in Leadership.*, Menlo Park, CA: Crisp, 1992.

Mager, Robert F. *Preparing Instructional Objectives,* 2nd ed. Belmont, CA: Fearon, 1971.

Marvin, Bill. *The Foolproof Foodservice Selection System.* New York: John Wiley, 1993.

Maslow, Abraham. *Motivation and Personality,* 2nd ed. New York: Harper & Row, 1970.

Maxwell, John C. *Developing the Leader Within You.* Nashville, TN: Nelson, 1993.

McGregor, Douglas. *The Human Side of Enterprise.* New York: McGraw-Hill, 1960.

Milkovich, George T., and John W. Boudreau. *Human Resources Management,* 8th ed. Boston: Irwin, 1997.

Milkovich, Michael E. *Improving Service Quality.* Delray Beach, FL: St. Lucie Press, 1995.

Miller, Jack E., Mary Porter, and Karen E. Drummond. *Supervision in the Hospitality Industry*, 2nd ed. New York: John Wiley, 1992.

Mondy, Wayne R., and Robert M Noe. *Human Resource Management.* Upper Saddle River, NJ: Prentice Hall, 1996.

Morgan, William J., Jr. *Food and Beverage Management and Service.* Lansing, MI: Educational Institute of the American Hotel and Motel Association, 1981.

Morgan, William J., Jr. *Supervision and Management of Quality Food Production: Principles and Procedures,* 4th ed. Berkeley, CA: McCutchan, 1995.

Morris, Daniel, and Joel Brandon. *Re-engineering Your Business.* New York: McGraw-Hill, 1993.

National Restaurant Association. *Industry at a Glance.* www.restaurant.org/research/ind_glance.cfm, 2003.

National Restaurant Association. *Legal Monitor: Grocer Settles HIV-Discrimination Lawsuit with EEOC for $80,000.* www.restaurant.org/legal/lm/lm2001_06.cfm, 2001.

Noe, Raymond A., John R. Hollenbeck, Barry Gerhart, and Patrick M. Wright. *Human Resources Management: Gaining a Competitive Advantage.* Boston: Irwin, 1997.

Peters, Thomas, and Nancy Austin. *A Passion for Excellence: The Leadership Difference.* New York: Random House, 1985.

Peters, Tom. *Thriving on Chaos: Handbook for a Management Revolution.* New York: Harper & Row, 1988.

Peterson, Jim L. "Self-Esteem Is Essential to Building a Team." In *Lessons in Leadership.* New York: Van Nostrand Reinhold, 1991.

Picogna, Joseph L. *Total Quality Leadership: A Training Approach.* Morrisville, PA: International Information Associates, 1993.

Quick, Thomas J. "The Art of Time Management." *Training,* January 1989.

Riley, Michael. *Human Resources Management.* London: Butterworth-Heinemann, 1992.

Rinke, Wolf J. *The Winning Foodservice Manager: Strategies for Doing More with Less,* 2nd ed. Rockville, MD: Achievement, 1992.

Roberts, Wess. *Leadership Secrets of Attila the Hun.* New York: Warner Books, 1987.

Roosevelt, Thomas R., Jr. *Beyond Race and Gender.* New York: AMACOM, 1991.

Ryan, Kathleen, and Daniel K. Oestreich. *Driving Fear out of the Workplace.* San Francisco: Jossey-Bass, 1991.

Schwartz, Andrew E. *Delegating Authority.* New York: Barron's, 1992.

Scott, Cynthia D., and Dennis T. Jaffe. *Empowerment.* London: Crisp, 1991.

Sherman, Arthur, George Bohlander, and Herbert Crudden. *Managing Human Resources,* 9th ed. Cincinnati, OH: South-Western, 1997.

Shiba, Shoji, Alan Graham, and David Walden. *A New American TQM, Four Practical Revolutions in Management.* Portland, OR: Productivity Press, 1993.

Shriver, Stephen, J. *Managing Quality Services.* East Lansing, MI: The Educational Institute of the American Hotel & Motel Association, 1998.

Smith, Steve. *Build That Team.* London: Kogan Page, 1997.

Stamatis, D. H. *Total Quality Services: Principles, Practices, and Implementation.* Delray Beach, FL: St. Lucie Press, 1996.

Sullivan, Richard. *The H.I.T. Man (Humor in Teaching).* Edmund, OK: Central State University, 1990.

Swift, Jill A., Joel E. Ross, and Vincent K. Omachonu. *Principles of Total Quality Management,* 2nd ed. Boca Raton, FL: St. Lucie Press, 1998.

Tanke, Mary L. *Human Resources Management for the Hospitality Industry.* Albany, NY: Delmar, 1990.

Tepper, Bruce B. *The New Supervisor: Skills for Success.* New York: Irwin, 1994.

Thomas, Brain. *Total Quality Training: The Quality Culture and Quality Trainer.* Berkshire, England: McGraw-Hill, 1992.

Toler Sachs, Randi. *Productive Performance Appraisals.* New York: AMACOM, 1992.

Travers, Alfred W. *Supervision, Techniques and New Dimensions.* Englewood Cliffs, NJ: Prentice Hall, 1993.

Van Hoof, Hubert B., Marilyn E. McDonald, Lawrence Yu, and Gary K. Vallen. *A Host of Opportunities: An Introduction to Hospitality.* New York: Irwin, 1996.

Vroom, Victor H. *Work and Motivation.* New York: John Wiley, 1964.

Walker, John R. *Introduction to Hospitality.* Upper Saddle River, NJ: Prentice Hall, 1996.

Walton, Mary. *The Deming Management Method.* New York: Putnum, 1986.

Walton, Sally J. *Cultural Diversity in the Workplace.* New York: Irwin, 1994.

Werther, William B., and Keith Davis. *Human Resources and Personnel Management,* 5th ed. New York: McGraw-Hill, 1996.

Wilson, Robert F. *Conducting Better Job Interviews.* New York: Barron's, 1991.

Woods, John A. *Teams and Teamwork.* New York: Macmillan, 1998.

Woods, Robert H., and Judy Z. King. *Quality Leadership and Management in the Hospitality Industry.* East Lansing, MI: The Educational Institute of the American Hotel & Motel Association, 1996.

Worthington, E. R., and Anita E. Worthington. *People Investment.* Central Point, OR: Oasis Press, 1993.

INDEX